Such A Great Salvation

The Collected Essays of Alan Stibbs

'Alan Stibbs was a voice crying in the wilderness, a lonely evangelical scholar in a sea of liberalism. We owe him much.'

John Stott, rector emeritus of All Souls, Langham Place

'Alan Stibbs wrote wonderfully incisively and wonderfully simply. His writings are of enduring value to any who wish to understand key topics in a biblical and godly way. To have his writings collected in this way is a great gift to God's people.'

Mike Ovey, principal of Oak Hill Theological College

'A godly humility combined with razor sharp mind and a passion for God's Truth worked out for day to day Christian living – these are the hallmarks of Alan Stibbs. It is hoped that this book will introduce the works of a great, yet generally forgotten evangelical to a whole new generation.'

Melvin Tinker, vicar of St John Newland, Hull

'Alan Stibbs' lucid and constructive writings are extraordinarily relevant to today's theological scene. At the time they were a very important help to many embattled evangelicals. Today little has changed in the essential theological debates and their very welcome republication can again be just as useful.'

Oliver Barclay, former general secretary of the University and Colleges Christian Fellowship

'Alan Stibbs was insufficiently appreciated in his lifetime and has been almost forgotten since, but he was for many years the best theological mind serving British evangelicals, and his unobtrusive influence shaped many ministries decisively. This collection of his occasional writings, of which all are outstanding and some have landmark status, will reintroduce him to the discerning and will surely draw forth the admiration that is truly his due.'

J.I. Packer, professor of theology, Regent College, Vancouver

Such A Great Salvation

The Collected Essays of Alan Stibbs

Edited by
Andrew Atherstone

MENTOR

Andrew Atherstone is tutor in history and doctrine, and Latimer research fellow, at Wycliffe Hall, Oxford. His publications include *Oxford's Protestant Spy: The Controversial Career of Charles Golightly* (2007), *The Martyrs of Mary Tudor* (second edition, 2007) and *Oxford: City of Saints, Scholars and Dreaming Spires* (2008). He is also editor of *The Heart of Faith: Following Christ in the Church of England* (2008).

Scripture quotations in chapters 1 and 3 are taken, unless otherwise stated, from the Revised Standard Version (rsv), copyright 1952 by the Division of Christian Education of the National Council of the Churches of Christ in the United States of America. Used by permission. All rights reserved.

Scripture quotations in all other chapters are taken, unless otherwise stated, from the Authorised Version (av). Other quotations are from the Revised Version (rv) and the New English Bible (neb).

ISBN: 978-1-84550-423-6

Introduction and Bibliography © Andrew Atherstone 2008

10 9 8 7 6 5 4 3 2 1

Published in 2008
in the
Mentor Imprint
by
Christian Focus Publications, Ltd.,
Geanies House, Fearn, Ross-shire,
IV20 1TW, Great Britain.

www.christianfocus.com

Cover design by Daniel Van Straaten
Printed by CPD, Wales

Contents

ACKNOWLEDGEMENTS

In this volume, eighteen of Alan Stibbs' best and most enduring shorter writings are brought together. They cover themes such as the cross of Christ, justification by faith, the inspiration of Scripture, the priority of preaching, the nature of the church, and the role of the sacraments. For permission to republish these works, thanks are due to Mr John L. Stibbs, the Church Pastoral Aid Society, Church Society, Inter-Varsity Press, Paternoster Press, the Religious and Theological Studies Fellowship, and Westminster Chapel.

Alan Stibbs (1901-1971)

ALAN STIBBS (1901-1971):
MISSIONARY, PREACHER, THEOLOGIAN

BY ANDREW ATHERSTONE

> No-one in his generation did more to help people, and especially
> students, to understand the Bible, to love the Bible and to obey it.
> ... His memorial is in many lives and in many pulpits throughout
> the world.[1]

So declared one evangelical commentator on the death in July 1971
of Alan Stibbs, who for more than thirty years exercised an influential
ministry as a Bible expositor and cogent teacher of Christian doctrine.
After returning from the mission field in China in the mid-1930s, he
played a significant part in the resurgence of conservative evangelicalism
in Britain after World War Two, alongside other leaders like Martyn
Lloyd-Jones and John Stott. From Oak Hill College in north London,
Stibbs aimed to revive biblical preaching and biblical thinking across the
country. His powerful sermons made a profound impact upon countless
congregations and his pithy writings helped to stimulate the rebirth of a
robust evangelical theology.

Here Am I, Send Me!

Alan Marshall Stibbs was born in Plymouth on 14 August 1901, the
first child and only son of James R.W. Stibbs and his wife Amy née
Marshall, who were both Christian believers.[2] His father was a nautical
pilot, guiding shipping through the bustling port, and a paymaster in

---

For comments on this introductory chapter I am especially grateful to Oliver Barclay, Michael
Griffiths, James Packer and David Wheaton.

[1] *Inter-Varsity Fellowship Annual Report 1971*, p. 21.

[2] For details of Stibbs' early life, see especially *China's Millions* vol. 54 (November 1928),
p. 173 and *Crusade* vol. 17 (May 1971), p. 22.

the Royal Navy Reserve. As a young boy, aged ten, Stibbs responded personally to the call of Christ at an open-air meeting in the centre of Plymouth one Sunday evening in 1912. A friend of his father preached on the text 'Choose ye this day whom ye will serve' (Josh. 24:15) and there and then he responded, 'Lord, I am going to serve Thee'. The following summer at a Children's Special Service Mission (CSSM) in Newquay – a forerunner of Scripture Union beach missions – he came to a fuller grasp of what his earlier decision involved and 'trusted Christ as my Saviour'. Although he soon began to sense a call to overseas missionary work, his main field of ministry for the time being was amongst his school fellows at Plymouth College, where he started a Scripture Union group which grew to eighty members within five years.

At the age of sixteen, Stibbs began to give his first Bible expositions to his peers. Members from his local class of the Crusaders Union (a nationwide evangelical initiative amongst young people, established in 1906) met together before school on three mornings each week to read the Scripture Union Bible passage for the day and it was usually left to him to comment upon it. He explained to the school magazine: 'By so doing, we try with God's help and blessing to encourage one another in His service and we would, at all times, seek to lead boys to recognize Jesus Christ as their own personal Saviour.'[3] This was the first exercise of a Bible teaching gift which he used to great effect throughout his life. It was a formative experience, and he reflected: 'Doing this for two years I came to see that preachers and speakers shouldn't just choose passages they like, they should believe that God has a message from every part of his Word.' In his final year at school, Stibbs' call to the mission field became clearer. In the autumn of 1918 he came into contact with John B. Martin and W.H. Aldis, both of China Inland Mission, who encouraged him in that direction.[4] A friend also lent him a book which happened to be about China. Soon afterwards he inscribed on the front page of his Bible the word 'CHINA', with a large 'I' in the centre because he was convinced that was where God wanted him to serve. Next to it he wrote, 'Here am I, send me' (Isa. 6:8).

It was to be another decade before Stibbs reached the mission field. After Plymouth College, (where he rose to become 'head of school'), he went up in 1919 to Christ's College, Cambridge on a Tancred Divinity Studentship to read classics. He managed only a third class in Part I of the tripos, so transferred to theology at which he proved more

---

[3] *Plymothian* vol. 34 (April 1918), p. 35. I am grateful to Heather Chapman for this reference. See also A.M. Stibbs, *Expounding God's Word: Some Principles and Methods* (London, 1960), pp. 7-10.

[4] On Aldis, see Andrew MacBeath, *W.H. Aldis* (London, 1949).

successful, graduating with a first-class degree in 1923 and carrying off a number of scholarships and prizes.[5] The shift to theology proved a good way to prepare for Christian ministry, even though the Cambridge faculty in the 1920s was dominated by Anglican modernists and other liberal academics, who were hostile towards evangelicalism and especially disdainful of the Cambridge Inter-Collegiate Christian Union (CICCU).[6] Influential divinity professors such as J.F. Bethune-Baker, Alexander Nairne and F.C. Burkitt taught radical new theories about the authorship and origins of the Bible, and pushed at the boundaries of traditional Christian orthodoxy. Yet Stibbs was persuaded by an old CSSM friend, Edmund Clark, that the best way to answer the liberal critics was to tackle the subject from the inside. It was a valuable testing ground, as he later explained:

> At Cambridge God allowed me to prove that His Word is trustworthy. I was led, quite unexpectedly, to read modern theology, only to be told by some that there was no place in the ranks of theological scholarship for those who would not accept modern critical theories with regard to the Bible. But I was told by God of the three men, to whom Nebuchadnezzar said that there was no place in his kingdom for any who would not bow down to his image. And the same God, who kept them in Babylon, kept me in Cambridge. I learnt, from experience in the place of trial, that God's Word is to be trusted rather than men's. I know Whom I have believed.[7]

After graduation, Stibbs stayed on in Cambridge for an extra year to train for Anglican ordination at Ridley Hall.[8] Rees Howells tried urgently to recruit him to teach at his new Bible College in Swansea (opened in June 1924),[9] but Stibbs was already committed to serving a curacy at Holy Trinity, Hull. He found Howells' proposal more attractive, but believed he must go to Yorkshire out of obedience to God's call.[10]

---

[5] *Cambridge University Reporter*, 18 June 1921, p. 1164; 16 June 1923, p. 1151. *List of Past and Present Members of Christ's College, Cambridge with Annual Report to 31 December 1923*, pp. 76, 89-90. I am grateful to Carolyn Keim for these references.

[6] On the CICCU, see Oliver Barclay and Robert Horn, *From Cambridge to the World: 125 Years of Student Witness* (Leicester, 2002).

[7] *China's Millions* vol. 54 (November 1928), p. 173.

[8] On Ridley Hall, see F.W.B. Bullock, *The History of Ridley Hall, Cambridge* (2 vols, Cambridge, 1941-53); Michael H. Botting, *Fanning the Flame: The Story of Ridley Hall, Cambridge: Volume 3, 1951-2001* (Cambridge, 2006).

[9] Information from Michael Griffiths, July 2007. On Howells, see Norman Grubb, *Rees Howells: Intercessor* (London, 1952).

[10] *China's Millions* vol. 54 (November 1928), p. 173.

China Inland Mission

Alan Stibbs' teenage passion for China was eventually fulfilled when he signed up with China Inland Mission (CIM), the largest mission agency working in east Asia. CIM was an interdenominational movement founded by Hudson Taylor in 1865 systematically to evangelize the region, which remained largely unreached by the Christian gospel.[11] Taylor's manifesto, *China: Its Spiritual Need and Claims*, had motivated many to offer themselves for this adventure, including the 'Cambridge Seven' (C.T. Studd and his friends) who sailed for China in 1885.[12] The work was dangerous and numerous missionaries lost their lives, especially during the horrors of the 1900 Boxer Rebellion,[13] yet during the early twentieth century there were far more applicants than CIM could take. Amongst the many young women who applied in the late 1920s, Isobel Kuhn was accepted by CIM while Gladys Aylward was turned down – though both went on to have famous ministries in China.[14] Eric Liddell, the Scottish Olympic sprinter portrayed in the film, *Chariots of Fire*, was already a national hero when he went out to China, aged 23, with the London Missionary Society in 1925.[15] Stibbs was part of this missionary movement. He sailed for western China in October 1928 on-board the P&O steamship *SS Malwa*, and was stationed by CIM in the city of Shunking (Nanchong) in the province of Szechwan (Sichuan).[16] The field of work was immense. In the 1920s Szechwan was the most populous province in China with 60 million inhabitants, at a time when the total population of England and Wales was less than 40 million. China itself in 1928 was home to over 450 million people.

---

[11] On Hudson Taylor and CIM, see Leslie T. Lyall, *A Passion for the Impossible: The China Inland Mission, 1865-1965* (London, 1965); Alvyn Austin, *China's Millions: The China Inland Mission and Late Qing Society, 1832-1905* (Grand Rapids, 2007); Howard Taylor, *Hudson Taylor and the China Inland Mission: The Growth of a Work of God* (London, 1918); Marshall Broomhall, *Hudson Taylor: The Man Who Believed God* (London, 1929).

[12] See Norman P. Grubb, *C.T. Studd: Cricketer and Pioneer* (London, 1933); John C. Pollock, *The Cambridge Seven: A Call to Christian Service* (London, 1955).

[13] See Marshall Broomhall, *Martyred Missionaries of the China Inland Mission: With a Record of the Perils and Sufferings of Some Who Escaped* (London, 1901).

[14] See Carolyn Canfield, *One Vision Only: A Biography of Isobel Kuhn* (London, 1959); John Tallach, *God Made Them Great* (Edinburgh, 1974); Alan Burgess, *The Small Woman* (London, 1957); Carol Purves, *Chinese Whispers: The Gladys Aylward Story* (Leominster, 2004).

[15] See D.P. Thomson, *Scotland's Greatest Athlete: The Eric Liddell Story* (Crieff, 1970); Sally Magnusson, *The Flying Scotsman* (New York, 1981).

[16] *China's Millions* vol. 54 (October 1928), p. 156; *China's Millions* vol. 55 (June 1929), p. 96.

One of the distinctive principles of CIM was that missionaries should build an indigenous church which was authentically Chinese, rather than importing Western customs, music and clothing. Therefore Stibbs' first task was to learn the Chinese languages and immerse himself in the local culture. One of the lessons which the experience impressed upon him was the need to communicate the Christian faith in ideas which hearers could understand, for which 'you must begin where people are'. His model was the Apostle Paul preaching at the Areopagus in Athens (Acts 17), as he later explained:

> ... when I was preaching on the streets of China, I didn't quote from the Scripture because in their eyes it had no authority. Instead, I sometimes quoted the common Chinese proverb which says virtue has virtue's reward and evil has evil's recompense. And from there I proclaimed the fact of God's Day of Judgment and his offer of mercy through faith in Christ.[17]

He preached and taught in local congregations in and around Shunking, began a Bible Training School in the city,[18] and sometimes gave theological lectures to conferences of Chinese believers and missionaries.[19] Yet much of Stibbs' work was in evangelism and discipleship 'one-to-one', through personal conversation and Bible study. For example, he helped to disciple an ex-Taoist priest who had been converted to Christ, spending an hour each day reading the Books of Joshua and Romans with him. In turn, the new convert helped the missionaries by teaching them about Chinese religions.[20] Stibbs also acted as examining chaplain to the Bishop of West China, former CICCU president Howard Mowll (later Archbishop of Sydney).[21] The bishop suggested that two Chinese workers, Hsiao Tung-fan and Chao Teh-sheng, spend three months with Stibbs in the spring of 1932 preparing for ordination, on which Stibbs commented:

> If this idea materializes I shall be concerned that they may grow in more than intellectual knowledge. I shall hope also myself to profit from the experience, and to learn more how to reach, understand and help the Chinese man of the heart, hidden as he is behind the difficulties of a strange language and the closely guarded covering

---

[17] *Crusade* vol. 17 (May 1971), p. 22.

[18] *China's Millions* vol. 60 (September 1934), p. 175.

[19] *Inter-Varsity Magazine* vol. 5 (Lent Term 1933), CICCU Supplement.

[20] *China's Millions* vol. 57 (November 1931), p. 216; *China's Millions* vol. 58 (April 1932), p. 72.

[21] On Mowll, see Marcus Loane, *Archbishop Mowll: The Biography of Howard West Kilvinton Mowll, Archbishop of Sydney and Primate of Australia* (London, 1960).

of surface politeness and coveted reputation. The Chinese loves to save his face and hide his heart. It is only in the warm intimacies of realized friendship that he welcomes another inside the surface pretence. But that is where we need to get to help them most. Please pray that by the love of Christ constraining us we may be given the sympathy and patience that are the conditions of growth into such effectiveness of ministry.[22]

The work was slow, and evident fruit was rare, yet Stibbs remained committed to the task. He wrote home:

In some ways the last six months have often seemed disappointing as far as any immediate results are concerned. One day recently Pastor Wang told me that he had dreamt that he and I were climbing a very steep ascent, and began to wonder whether we should ever reach the top. Then I said to him: 'The promises of God are sure. There must be a way up.' This is our confidence, that God is going to bring us through into the satisfaction of a ministry that one feels has got there and achieved something for His glory. To this it is only fair to add that increasingly during the last month or two we have become conscious of small but definite signs that God is beginning to answer prayer – the cloud like a man's hand that holds promise of abundance of rain.[23]

Stibbs never witnessed the Chinese revival for which he earnestly prayed. It was only in the second half of the twentieth century, after the Western missionaries had been expelled, that the gospel began to spread at a phenomenal rate.

There was not much opportunity for romance on the mission field, since CIM usually kept single men and single women apart. Nevertheless Stibbs met and married a missionary nurse, Olive Lacey, who had arrived in China two years before him. The couple were well matched spiritually. Shortly before her departure from England, at a conference at Swanwick, she had publicly testified to God's call upon her life:

Miracles do happen in these days – unfortunately, we are so often blind to them. The greatest, it seems to me, is that of a life transformed by the process of the New Birth and sanctification of the Spirit. Conversion to me meant revolution; an upsetting of all previous ideas, and a new view of life and its meaning. Two years after my conversion I knew that the Lord wanted me in the foreign mission field – but how and where? For the last ten years the urge

---

[22] *China's Millions* vol. 58 (April 1932), p. 72.
[23] *China's Millions* vol. 58 (April 1932), p. 71.

within has grown stronger, and all my work, first as a bookkeeper, and then as a nurse, has been with the mission field in view, recently narrowing down to China. That I must offer for service in China became a fact in my inner consciousness which would not be ignored. When I look out on the field, and see its vast scope, its almost unlimited opportunities, and tremendous possibilities, and see the task set before me, I want to say with St Paul, 'Who is sufficient for these things?' Thank God that he gave us the answer as well as the question, in assuring us of the sufficiency of our God: 'I can do all things through Christ which strengtheneth me.'[24]

Alan and Olive's son, John Lacey Stibbs, was born in Shunking in November 1932.[25] A daughter, Beryl, followed four years later, after their return to England.

Missionary work in China was dangerous and stressful, and Stibbs' health began to suffer. In July 1933, for instance, he was struck down by an attack of dysentery.[26] The constant strain was heightened by the intermittent civil war between nationalists and communists. Violence swept across the country as the nationalist Kuomintang, led by Generalissimo Chiang Kai-shek, attempted to annihilate the communist insurgents. The Red Armies survived the onslaught, but only after their massive retreat, or 'Long March', into north-west China from October 1934, which consolidated the rise to power of Mao Zedong amongst the communists. Guerrilla warfare frequently broke out in Szechwan Province. At one point Stibbs with his wife and young son were forced to flee from their mission station in Shunking for safety, as the fighting drew close.[27] Other Christian workers did not escape. For example, John and Betty Stam, a young CIM couple serving in Jiangxi Province, were brutally beheaded by communist soldiers in December 1934, leaving an orphaned baby daughter.[28] For Stibbs and his family there was welcome respite from these troubles when they arrived back home in England on furlough in March 1935.[29] They intended to return to China, but on medical advice Stibbs was compelled to retire from the mission field, lest his health buckle under the stress.[30] Instead he took up a short curacy at St John's Church, Penge in south London. In the providence

---

[24] *China's Millions* vol. 52 (August 1926), p. 119.

[25] *China's Millions* vol. 59 (February 1933), p. 31.

[26] *Inter-Varsity Magazine* vol. 5 (Lent Term 1933), CICCU Supplement.

[27] *Inter-Varsity Magazine* vol. 6 (Lent Term 1934), CICCU Supplement.

[28] See Mary Geraldine Taylor, *The Triumph of John and Betty Stam* (London, 1935).

[29] *China's Millions* vol. 61 (May 1935), p. 82.

[30] *Inter-Varsity Magazine* vol. 8 (Lent Term 1936), CICCU Supplement.

of God, the Stibbs family was thus preserved from being caught up in the devastation and atrocities of the Second Sino-Japanese War, which erupted in July 1937 and led to millions of civilian deaths throughout China. Many missionaries were killed or confined to concentration camps until the end of World War Two.

Evangelicalism Resurgent

In October 1937 Stibbs was recruited for the staff at Oak Hill theological college in north London, as tutor in New Testament and doctrine. A year later he was promoted to vice-principal and remained at the college (living in 'The Farm House') for the rest of his life. Oak Hill was one of the youngest Anglican theological colleges, opened in 1932, part of the legacy of Charles Baring Young, scion of a wealthy evangelical dynasty.[31] Unlike Stibbs' own college, Ridley Hall in Cambridge, Oak Hill was intended primarily to train non-graduates for Anglican ministry. In the early years most of the students were young men who had left school at fourteen or sixteen and had been employed in family firms or as junior clerks.[32] More significantly, unlike Ridley Hall which was dominated in the 1930s by the 'liberal evangelical' movement, Oak Hill was explicitly intended as a 'conservative evangelical' college. By its trust deed it was to be 'distinctly and definitely Protestant and Evangelical in the strictest sense of those terms'. Its first principal, Prebendary H.W. Hinde (formerly vicar of St Mary's, Islington) announced that the college would be 'unashamedly Protestant' and would 'fearlessly proclaim the Gospel and base all its teaching on Holy Scripture.'[33] Hinde recruited Stibbs to the small staff team (principal and four tutors) of this exciting new initiative, and from this base at Oak Hill the vice-principal went on to play a leading role in the resurgence of conservative evangelicalism across Britain.[34]

Stibbs quickly became known as a preacher and Bible expositor, and was often in demand for evangelical conferences and conventions. A contemporary, writing in 1971, called him 'One of the truly great expository preachers of the last twenty years.'[35] Another proclaimed:

[31] See Rudolph Heinze and David Wheaton, *Witness to the Word: A History of Oak Hill College 1932-2000* (Carlisle, 2002); Alfred F. Jarvis, *Charles Baring Young of Daylesford, 1850-1928: His Life and Work* (London, 1950).

[32] Heinze and Wheaton, *Witness to the Word*, p. 52.

[33] *Record*, 15 January 1932, quoted in Heinze and Wheaton, *Witness to the Word*, p. 43.

[34] For Stibbs' tribute to his first principal, see A.M. Stibbs, 'Herbert William Hinde 1877-1955: An Appreciation', *Oak Leaf* no. 20 (1956), pp. 7-8. On Hinde, see further Marcus Loane, *These Happy Warriors: Friends and Contemporaries* (Adelaide, 1988).

[35] *Crusade* vol. 17 (May 1971), p. 5.

What stands out over everything is Alan Stibbs' fidelity when expounding the Christian Faith as recorded in the New Testament, or for that matter, the Bible as a whole. Trained in the Cambridge Exegetical School of Lightfoot, Westcott and Hort he was never happier than when unfolding the text and interpreting the Bible according to the Canon of Scripture itself. Whether in the pulpit of a parish church, the lecture room of a theological college, in conference or meeting, or on the shores at a children's seaside service, he was always quite consistent. He was not interested in reporting the message through the insights of a Barth, a Dodd or even a Bonhoeffer! He was quietly wedded to the primary sources. ... He will be remembered as one of the most courteous and selfless exemplars of the New Testament doctrines and ethics which he taught.[36]

Stibbs' distinctive method of preaching was driven by his theological conviction that the Bible is 'the infallible Word of God', authored by God Himself. In an article on 'The Revival of Biblical Theology', he explained:

Nothing is more needed in our day than a full re-discovery of the teaching of Holy Scripture, together with the practical application of its guiding principles to the pressing problems of life in the world. While there may be a widespread recognition of this need, its fulfilment is slow to materialize. Nor is the underlying reason far to seek. The prevalence of Biblical criticism and the devotion of so much attention to knowledge and theories about the Bible and its human origins rather than to the direct understanding and exegesis of the actual text of Holy Scripture have inevitably weakened in Christian preachers and teachers their concern to expound the Bible itself, and their practical readiness to submit to its witness as authoritative. ... Clearly what we need is a revival of reverence for the divine authority of the Scriptures, and of regard for the didactic significance of their actual statements. We need, as ministers of the Word of God, to give ourselves to the exegesis and exposition of the actual Biblical text.[37]

Oliver Barclay suggests that Stibbs' lack of interest in the latest theories of the liberal critics was heightened by his years as a pioneer on the mission field in China, where modern Western scholarship had little impact and it was essential to rely instead upon the revelation of the Bible.[38]

---

[36] *Christian Graduate* vol. 24 (December 1971), p. 128.

[37] A.M. Stibbs, 'The Revival of Biblical Theology', *Christian Graduate* vol. 2 (September 1949), p. 91.

[38] Oliver Barclay, *Evangelicalism in Britain 1935-1995: A Personal Sketch* (Leicester, 1997), p. 34.

According to one recent historian, although Stibbs was 'shy and self-effacing', he was 'a sharp thinker and superb speaker, whose addresses at student conferences (especially at communion services) were memorable and moving.'[39] He threw himself energetically into the work of the Inter-Varsity Fellowship (IVF), founded in 1928, and was frequently heard expounding the Bible at events like the Inter-Varsity Conference, the Theological Students' Conference, the IVF Ministers' Conference, and conferences of the Graduates' Fellowship, the Christian Medical Fellowship and the Training Colleges Christian Union (TCCU). Because of his passion and ability in working with students, Stibbs was elected as a vice-president of IVF in 1954.[40] In this ministry he often joined forces with his friend Martyn Lloyd-Jones (minister of Westminster Chapel in central London), with whom he had much in common, both in gifts as a Bible teacher and in leadership style. Barclay recalls that Stibbs and Lloyd-Jones were

> basically shy men who did not seek the limelight. Lloyd-Jones used to say that when he and Stibbs were together at a conference, they both found it difficult to mix in, and were soon to be found quietly drinking coffee together in a corner. None of the leaders of what proved to be a major renewal of evangelical strength were examples of the strong leadership frequently advocated in business or management today. If they were expounding the Bible, it was a different matter, as they spoke with the authority of the Bible message. ... These men were not naturally forceful leaders, but their leadership was mightily effective.[41]

J.I. Packer concurs in this verdict:

> Throughout the Bible what makes a leader of God's people is not some magic of personality or temperament, but the word which God gives him, first to obey Himself and then to speak to others. Alan was a quiet and gentle person; he was not, in the ordinary sense a 'platform man', being essentially a teacher with an intimate style who preferred small classes; nonetheless he brought the word of God to us and in so doing became our leader and guide.[42]

---

[39] T.A. Noble, *Research for the Academy and the Church: Tyndale House and Fellowship: The First Sixty Years* (Leicester, 2006), p. 31.

[40] *Inter-Varsity* (Summer Term 1954), p. 23. On IVF see Douglas Johnson, *Contending for the Faith: A History of the Evangelical Movement in the Universities and Colleges* (Leicester, 1979); Geraint Fielder, *Lord of the Years: Sixty Years of Student Witness* (Leicester, 1988).

[41] Barclay, *Evangelicalism in Britain*, p. 53.

[42] *Oak Leaf* (1972), p. 13.

Stibbs was concerned not only to teach the Bible, but to train the next generation of Bible teachers. He warned that Christian congregations were placed in 'spiritual peril' when their ministers focused upon social work or administration to the neglect of 'the Word of God, faithfully preached and thoroughly taught'.[43] Throughout his decades at Oak Hill, he gave a weekly exposition or 'Bible Analysis' of a New Testament text at one of the early-morning chapel services, a model for the ordinands.[44] Under the auspices of the IVF Graduates' Fellowship he ran two expository preaching study groups in central London from 1951 – one group for ministers (held at All Souls, Langham Place) and one group for laymen (held at St Andrew's, Holborn).[45] Stibbs explained that the intention was to help redress

the widespread deficiency of the preaching ministry in the pulpits and congregations of our land. For many who appear in public to minister the Word no longer speak as those who are persuaded that God is the author of Holy Scripture. In their training their handling of Scripture has been diverted from its proper use, and attention has often been directed to unprofitable questions. In their handling of the Bible in the pulpit they pick and choose too freely according to their own fancy. The Old Testament is either largely neglected, or, when introduced, too often treated as of questionable authority. More respect is paid to the qualifications of the human writers of Scripture than to the divine authority of the inspiring Spirit. In consequence, the profit and salvation which God sought, when it pleased Him to teach us by the Holy Scripture, are not offered as they ought to be from our pulpits, least of all in the preaching of the Old Testament.

Ought it not, therefore, to be a particular challenge to our Graduates' Fellowship constituency to seek by prayer, and, as God may guide and enable, by active effort, to remedy this deficiency? If we desire the kind of ministry God intended in our local congregations, obviously those who are to minister His Word from our pulpits need training very differently and much more adequately for this high and holy task. Perhaps those of us who are ministers ought to begin by earnestly seeking from God grace and equipment the more properly to use Holy Scripture when we ourselves stand to preach the Word of God in the congregation. It is with such a practical goal in view that a monthly 'Expository

---

[43] *Times*, 30 January 1954, p. 7.

[44] Heinze and Wheaton, *Witness to the Word*, p. 61.

[45] *Christian Graduate* vol. 4 (1951), pp. 69, 102, 138; *Christian Graduate* vol. 5 (1952), pp. 38, 77, 117, 153.

Preaching Study Group' is being started in central London; and it would be pleasing if similar groups could be started in other localities.[46]

Stibbs was also involved in other networks of preachers. For example, he and Lloyd-Jones, along with a number of other evangelical ministers in London, began the 'Westminster Fellowship' in 1942, a quarterly fraternal at Westminster Chapel for mutual encouragement. This meeting, by invitation only, helped to strengthen interdenominational evangelical relationships over many years. Stibbs acted as secretary and Lloyd-Jones as chairman.[47]

The post-War resurgence of evangelicalism through preaching and student ministry went hand in hand with the recovery of biblical scholarship. Here again Stibbs played an influential part, as a strategist behind the scenes in some pioneering ventures. With Lloyd-Jones and others he was involved, for example, in the founding in 1944 of London Bible College, to provide theological education from an evangelical and interdenominational perspective. In fact, he was invited to join LBC's initial teaching faculty, but declined.[48] Stibbs also took a lead in a parallel initiative, the creation of Tyndale House in Cambridge.[49] He was a member of IVF's Biblical Research Committee and in July 1941 he hosted a seminal conference at Kingham Hill School in the Cotswolds near Oxford (where Oak Hill College had been evacuated during the war), when a residential library for biblical research was first proposed. The fifteen participants at the conference were leading evangelical scholars and ministers, drawn from a range of denominations (Anglican, Baptist, Brethren, Presbyterian, Welsh Calvinistic Methodist). Through their combined energies Tyndale House opened its doors in January 1945 and Stibbs contributed to its work until the end of his life – as a regular speaker at the Tyndale summer school, as chairman of the Biblical Theology study group, and as chairman of the Tyndale Fellowship Committee. His influential Tyndale Lectures for 1947 and 1952, *The Meaning of the Word 'Blood' in Scripture* and *The Finished Work of Christ* are both republished in this volume.

---

[46] A.M. Stibbs, 'The Proper Use of Scripture', *Christian Graduate* vol. 4 (June 1951), pp. 63-64.

[47] Iain H. Murray, *David Martyn Lloyd-Jones: The Fight of Faith 1939-1981* (Edinburgh, 1990), pp. 86-89.

[48] Harold H. Rowdon, *London Bible College: The First Twenty-Five Years* (Worthing, 1968), p. 27. See also, Ian Randall, *Educating Evangelicalism: The Origins, Development and Impact of London Bible College* (Carlisle, 2000).

[49] See further, Noble, *Research for the Academy and the Church*.

Another sign of the resurgence of British evangelicalism was the exponential rise in the publication of evangelical literature from the 1940s onwards. Barclay reflects that Stibbs was 'never so good on paper' as when heard in person powerfully expounding the Scriptures.[50] Preaching and training preachers were his key ministries, yet in the midst of these demands Stibbs' pen was often busy writing lectures, articles and short books (for details, see the select bibliography at the end of this volume). Amongst his book-length studies, he published commentaries on Genesis 12-25 (the life of Abraham), 1 Peter and Hebrews. He was editor or assistant editor to groundbreaking works from the IVF, such as *Search the Scriptures* (1937), *The New Bible Handbook* (1947) and *The New Bible Commentary* (1953), which helped to equip generations of Bible readers and Bible teachers. Stibbs also published a popular trilogy – *Understanding God's Word* (1950), *Obeying God's Word* (1955) and *Expounding God's Word* (1960) – with tools for interpreting the Bible correctly and exhortation to act upon its message. His reformed ecclesiology was laid out in *The Church: Universal and Local* (1948), expanded as *God's Church: A Study in the Biblical Doctrine of the People of God* (1959), very different from the institutional and hierarchical understandings of the church then widespread. Packer suggests that when Stibbs returned from China 'he came as a prophet ... prepared providentially by his experience in the young churches which he had been serving to revitalize English evangelical thinking about the church.'[51]

Although a lifelong Anglican, ordained as an Anglican minister and on the staff of an Anglican theological college, Stibbs 'crossed denominational barriers with frequency and enthusiasm.'[52] As has been seen, much of his ministry was exercised, and many of his friendships built, in interdenominational contexts such as CIM, IVF and the Tyndale Fellowship. Towards the end of his life, he explained why he loved to work in partnership with evangelicals of every description but why he had resisted calls to leave the Church of England:

> From my earliest experience of Christ I am thankful that I've enjoyed a deep fellowship with other Christians whatever their denomination. This fellowship is based fundamentally upon our common gospel and our common concern to preach Christ. As a result, I have often had more unity of spirit with somebody in another denomination who had these fundamental primary loyalties, than with somebody

---

[50] Barclay, *Evangelicalism in Britain*, p. 53.
[51] *Oak Leaf* (1972), p. 21.
[52] *Church of England Newspaper*, 30 July 1971, p. 1.

in my own denomination who didn't share them. On the other hand I don't feel that I should pull out with the thought that we could create a group that was 100% loyal to the truth. Seeing that we are all imperfect in this world, there can never be a perfect Church in this life. Besides, however gloomy the outlook on the surface, I believe that God would remind us like he did with Elijah 'I have still 7,000 in Israel who have not bowed the knee to Baal.'[53]

Therefore, Stibbs also threw his energies into some specifically Anglican concerns, seeking the revival of evangelicalism within the Church of England. He was involved, for instance, with the Church Pastoral Aid Society (as author of numerous pamphlets) and the annual Islington Clerical Conference (as a regular speaker). He was also a founder member in 1960 of the Church of England Evangelical Council (CEEC), which originated as an IVF Anglican policy group – though he was distressed by its increasing theological breadth and left his final CEEC meeting 'almost in tears at what he felt was its departure from his hopes for it.'[54] In his attempts to bring Anglicanism back to its evangelical and reformed roots, Stibbs protested at the intrusion of medieval catholicism and ritualism into the National Church. He spoke, for example, against the legalization of mass vestments and some of the other liturgical innovations of the 1960s, because of the unevangelical theology which underpinned them.[55] His exposition of the Lord's Supper and defence of the reformed theology of the *Book of Common Prayer* appeared in 1961 as *Sacrament, Sacrifice and Eucharist* (republished in this volume). Due to his well-known concern to promote biblical doctrine within the Church of England, Stibbs was considered in 1961 as a possible warden for Latimer House, a newly-established Anglican evangelical research institute in Oxford. Yet he was only a few years from retirement and the post went instead to his young friend, J.I. Packer.[56]

Hold Fast to Christ!

In 1965 Stibbs retired from his duties as vice-principal at Oak Hill, but remained on the staff part-time as senior New Testament lecturer

---

[53] *Crusade* vol. 17 (May 1971), p. 37.

[54] Barclay, *Evangelicalism in Britain*, p. 85.

[55] See, for example, *Times*, 14 January 1958, p. 10; 27 May 1958, p. 9; *Church of England Newspaper*, 7 February 1969, p. 10; A.M. Stibbs, *Why I Value the North Side Position* (London, 1963).

[56] Oxford Evangelical Research Trust, council minutes, 20 September 1961, Latimer Trust Archives, London.

– he suggested his new title should be 'Senior Tutor in Basic Biblical Studies', or STIBBS for short.[57] Having taught at the college for so long, he had become 'a legend in his own time'.[58] Principals came and went – H.W. Hinde, Leslie Wilkinson and Maurice Wood (Bishop of Norwich from 1971) – but Stibbs outlasted them all. A glittering array of young theological tutors passed through, like Stuart Babbage, J. Stafford Wright, J.I. Packer, Derek Kidner, Philip Crowe, George Carey and John Goldingay, yet Stibbs remained to the end.[59] Carey called him Oak Hill's '*éminence grise*'.[60] Just before Easter 1971 Stibbs stood up in the college prayer meeting and gave testimony to God's faithfulness – that in the course of one hundred terms of lecturing at Oak Hill, he had never had to cancel a single lecture through illness.[61]

Stibbs planned to go into full retirement in the summer of 1971, but in May he was suddenly struck down with a brain tumour. His series of expositions of the Letter to the Hebrews had to be cut short, but his last word to the college was on the theme of 'one sacrifice for sins for ever' (Heb. 10:12). It was an appropriate finale, friends observed, because the 'theme song' of his life had been 'the finished work of Christ on the Cross'.[62] As Stibbs lay in hospital, he exhorted David Wheaton (the newly appointed principal of Oak Hill), 'Hold fast to Christ, David! Hold fast to Christ! He is the only Foundation!' They were his last known words.[63] After only a few weeks' illness, he died at St Christopher's Hospice, Sydenham on 26 July 1971, one month short of his 'three score years and ten'.[64]

In tribute, John B. Taylor (vice-principal of Oak Hill and later Bishop of St Albans) declared:

> A.M.S. has gone home to the only retirement he would have really enjoyed – the Presence of his glorious Lord. Undoubtedly his greatest gift was the ability to expound the Scriptures and he did this with compelling clarity, intensest loyalty to the text and with the aptest illustrations and application. His aim was to persuade his

---

[57] *English Churchman*, 28 August 1970, p.8; Heinze and Wheaton, *Witness to the Word*, p. 145.

[58] Heinze and Wheaton, *Witness to the Word*, p. 144.

[59] Stibbs and Packer developed a close friendship from their time together at Oak Hill in 1948-49 and Stibbs preached a 'substantial sermon' at Packer's wedding in July 1954. See Alister McGrath, *To Know and Serve God: A Life of James I. Packer* (London, 1997), pp. 35, 69.

[60] George Carey, *Know the Truth: A Memoir* (London, 2004), p. 65.

[61] *Church of England Newspaper*, 30 July 1971, p. 1.

[62] *Church of England Newspaper*, 30 July 1971, p. 1.

[63] Heinze and Wheaton, *Witness to the Word*, p. 161.

[64] *Church Times*, 30 July 1971, p. 11.

hearers of the wonders of God's book, not of the cleverness of its expositor and in this he was outstandingly successful as hundreds of Old Oaks will testify. Perhaps it was because he was so self-effacing that he exercised so great an influence. He never aspired to be a principal, though many colleges would have liked him; he never had ambitions for the great public platforms though his preaching ministry appealed to thousands; at heart he was a teacher and he liked his classes small and manageable. This, he felt, was his gift and he stuck to it, with the result that every year men went out from Oak Hill into the Anglican ministry with his indelible mark upon their preaching and theology.[65]

A few years earlier, Maurice Wood had written that Stibbs would be gratefully and affectionately remembered for three key reasons:

First, as befits a Scholar and a Cambridge First, he has meticulously quarried and clearly presented the great nuggets of Biblical truth which came alive to us in his lectures, sermons, and Bible Analyses. Secondly, he has lived out in practical holiness and transparent humility, the lessons first taught him by the revelation of the Holy Spirit, and then shared with us. Thirdly, he has demonstrated in every word and gesture and attitude, his unshakeable conviction in the Divine authority and inspiration of Holy Scripture.[66]

At the Thanksgiving Service at All Souls, Langham Place, the Apostle Paul's farewell address to the Ephesian elders (Acts 20) was read to the congregation, with its passionate affirmation: 'I shrank not from declaring unto you the whole counsel of God.'[67] It was a fitting summation of Alan Stibbs' influential ministry – a life spent faithfully proclaiming the gospel of Jesus Christ, and in training others to do the same.

[65] *Church of England Newspaper*, 30 July 1971, p. 1.
[66] *Oak Leaf* no. 29 (1965), p. 2.
[67] *Church of England Newspaper*, 1 October 1971, p. 2.

24

1

THE GOSPEL WE PROCLAIM (1965)

> I went up again to Jerusalem ... and I laid before them ... the gospel which I preach among the Gentiles, lest somehow I should be running or had run in vain. (Gal. 2:1-2)

> And now, my brothers, I must remind you of the gospel that I preached to you; the gospel which you received, on which you have taken your stand, and which is now bringing you salvation. (1 Cor. 15:1-2 NEB)

In both of these statements St Paul refers to 'the gospel which I preach'. Paul thus emphasizes not only the distinctive message which he preached, but also the particular terms in which he preached it. The concern, therefore, of our present study is to be twofold; first, to seek afresh to appreciate the content and the wonder of the gospel of God; and, second, to submit ourselves to some personal self-examination concerning the gospel we preach and the terms in which we preach it.

The Message of the Gospel

Its essential content

> For I delivered to you as of first importance what I also received, that Christ died for our sins in accordance with the scriptures, that he was buried, that he was raised on the third day in accordance with the scriptures ... (1 Cor. 15:3-4).

Originally delivered as a Bible study at the Islington Clerical Conference in January 1965 and first published by the Church Pastoral Aid Society.

Here is the essential content of the gospel. It is, first, the truth concerning the person of Jesus, that He is God's Christ. Men must be made aware who He is. It is, second, the news concerning His accomplished work – His death and resurrection. Men must be told what He has done.

We have here the Christian faith in its briefest statement. Similarly, Paul says elsewhere, 'God was in Christ reconciling the world to himself' (2 Cor. 5:19). For our sake Christ 'died and was raised' (2 Cor. 5:15). And again, 'Jesus our Lord ... was put to death for our trespasses and raised for our justification' (Rom. 4:24-25). Or more fully, in writing to the Colossians, Paul declares first of Christ's person as God incarnate that 'He is the image of the invisible God', the lord of creation, and that in Him as man 'the whole fulness of deity dwells bodily' (Col. 1:15, 2:9). He also adds in the same context concerning Christ's work that 'God was pleased ... through him to reconcile to himself all things ... making peace by the blood of his cross' (Col. 1:19-20); and that as 'the first-born from the dead' He is 'the head of the body, the church', and so the lord of the new creation (Col. 1:18).

Its scriptural character

These fundamental gospel truths concerning the person and work of Christ are, as Paul twice reiterates in 1 Corinthians 15:3-4, 'in accordance with the scriptures'. For by 'the Spirit of Christ within them' the prophets of Old Testament times were enabled, as Peter declares, to predict both 'the sufferings of Christ and the subsequent glory' (1 Pet. 1:10-11). So we find that when Paul preaches in the synagogue at Thessalonica to Jews who know and reverence the Old Testament, he begins from these scriptures; and shows from them on the first sabbath that the promised Messiah must suffer, and on the second sabbath that the promised Messiah is to rise from the dead. Then, on the third sabbath, he is able to offer them Jesus as this kind of Messiah, as the obvious fulfilment of the prophecies of Scripture (see Acts 17:2-3).

Similarly, when Paul exhorts Timothy to 'preach the word' (2 Tim. 4:2), when he reminds him that 'the sacred writings' are able to make men 'wise unto salvation through faith which is in Christ Jesus' (2 Tim. 3:15 AV), it is the Old Testament which he has in mind. This means therefore (as our own Anglican Article VII implies) that we ought still to be using the Old Testament to preach the gospel of Christ. Yet few do in the way in which it used to be done.

The example of Jesus Himself

In His own teaching of His chosen disciples Jesus concentrated on two main subjects. His first concern was to make them aware of the truth concerning His person, to lead them to an informed and considered judgment concerning His identity as the promised Messiah. He spent considerable time doing this. Not until they had confessed that He was the Christ did He begin to indicate to them the character of the work which, in consequence, He must do.

But from this point on, this was His chief and frequently reiterated theme, that He 'must suffer many things, and be rejected ... and be killed, and after three days rise again' (see Mark 8:29-31; compare Mark 9:30-31, 10:32-34). After this work was accomplished He made plain that these truths were spoken of beforehand by the prophets, and that they provide the substance of the gospel which is now to be preached: 'Thus it is written, that the Christ should suffer and on the third day rise from the dead, and that repentance and forgiveness of sins should be preached in his name to all nations' (Luke 24:46-47). So this should be the substance of our gospel – the truths concerning the person and work of Christ, and in that order, first the person and then the work. It is only an awareness of who He is that gives its unique and far-reaching value to what He has done. Salvation is offered to men not through any cross or anybody's crucifixion, but solely through the death for sinners of the incarnate and sinless Son of God. So Paul reminds the Corinthians that he decided to know nothing among them 'except Jesus Christ and him crucified' (1 Cor. 2:2). Here the original phraseology emphasizes that Paul means Jesus recognized as God's Christ, and 'this one' (not 'anybody') crucified. And in our preaching we should follow Paul as he followed Jesus.

The Preaching of the Gospel

This gospel, so Paul's testimony indicates, is a gospel which needs to be preached. For it is a record of objective historical facts which men need to be told and to have explained. Its content cannot be discovered from within our own minds by human reasoning and reflection. The gospel has to be given to us, by divine action and by divine revelation. Men must be told it, if they are to embrace it. Such truth at once makes plain the great significance of the functions both of the Scriptures and of the preacher. It is the preacher's responsibility to confront men with the news of what God has done; and to explain to men from the God-given word why He has done it; and thus to offer to men the opportunity to embrace the divinely-intended benefits in the divinely-indicated way.

Let us, then, from the Scriptures seek to consider the gospel which we ought to be preaching, if we are fully to discharge our responsibility as preachers, particularly in relation to different types of hearer. Let us, that is, consider some essentials of the gospel, particularly in their relevance to the varied situations in which, as preachers, we find ourselves, both outside and inside the church. Let us ask in these connections what our preaching of the gospel ought to embrace or explicitly to include.

Preaching to the godless and the ignorant

Let us begin with the complete outsider – the person who has no reverence for God and no knowledge of the Bible. How should we introduce the gospel to him? What we know of Paul's preaching gives us two answers. First, at Lystra, when the people tried to worship Paul and Barnabas as gods come down in the likeness of men, they said:

> Men, why are you doing this? We also are men, of like nature with you, and bring you good news, that you should turn from these vain things to the living God who made the heaven and the earth and the sea and all that is in them ... he did not leave himself without witness, for he did good and gave you from heaven rains and fruitful seasons, satisfying your hearts with food and gladness (Acts 14:15-17).

Here we learn that it is part of the gospel, part of the good news to be proclaimed, to preach the one true God, and to do this from the witness afforded by God's bounty in creation. Such evidence affords sufficient ground to urge men to turn from their vanities to acknowledge Him – to give Him worship and thanks. It is in these very terms that Paul describes the conversion of many in Thessalonica. He says they 'turned to God from idols, to serve the living and true God' (1 Thess. 1:9). For some this is how conversion must begin. We need to preach 'repentance to God' (Acts 20:21). Second, St Paul wrote:

> When Gentiles who have not the law do by nature what the law requires ... They show that what the law requires is written on their hearts, while their conscience also bears witness and their conflicting thoughts accuse or perhaps excuse them on that day when, according to my gospel, God judges the secrets of men by Christ Jesus (Rom. 2:14-16).

Here there is significant reference to the witness of conscience. In relation to this very witness Paul says that it was part of his gospel to preach a coming day of judgment, and to announce the divine appointment of Jesus to be the Judge. He was then able to add that this same Jesus has already come into human history to do a work by means of which He can be the Saviour. God's resurrection of Him from the dead is evidence both of God's acceptance of Jesus' sacrifice and of Jesus' power to save us from the coming wrath (see Acts 17:31; 1 Thess. 1:10).

Such truths provide a taking-off ground for a personal moral challenge concerning both the hearer's present inner condition and his hope of any satisfying future beyond the grave. For every man has his own sense of guilt; every man has a measure of awareness or fear that the wrongdoer must expect the ultimate outworking of inevitable judgment. It is part of the full gospel, and sometimes its most effective introduction, to make this awareness more explicit and more compelling, by declaring from God's word that God Himself has made it plain that 'all have sinned' (Rom. 3:23), that the sinner deserves God's displeasure and condemnation (Rom. 1:18), that God has appointed Christ to deal with sinners, that He must act, and can act, only in one of two ways, either in salvation or in judgment.

These truths, indeed, explain the character and purpose of Christ's two advents into world history. He came the first time to save, to do a work by which men who will repent and believe in Him can find deliverance and be given new life. He will come the second time both to complete the salvation of all who have trusted Him and to execute judgment upon persistent evildoers (see 1 Thess. 5:9-10; 2 Thess. 1:7-8). Which happens in our case we decide. We can meet Christ now in grace as our Saviour; or else we can have Him meet us then in wrath as our Judge. What God commands all men everywhere to do is to repent – that is, to turn to God now, and to believe in the gospel. It is, indeed, with such a command that Jesus Himself began His public ministry (Mark 1:15).

Preaching to religious churchgoers

Next let us consider people who are religious but as yet unconverted, people like the Jews to whom Paul often preached. In our situation many of these are churchgoers and by men's reckoning insiders; but by God's reckoning they are unsaved. Such people have a reverence for the true God; and in some cases they also have a considerable knowledge of the Bible. But they have never, as sinners, personally acknowledged

Jesus as Saviour and Lord. They often have no real use for a message of life through Christ's death, of cleansing through His blood, of justification in God's sight through propitiation for sin by Christ's sacrifice. Indeed, the preaching of the cross in such terms is to them either absurd or offensive, either, as Paul says, 'folly' or 'a stumbling block' (see 1 Cor. 1:21-25).

How then should we preach the gospel to such people? One answer provided by the example of apostolic preaching is to preach the resurrection; and in declaring what happened to Jesus for our salvation to concentrate emphasis on the action in it of God Himself. For the raising of Christ from the dead was God's action; and it demonstrates God's acknowledgement of His person, God's acceptance of His work, and God's appointment of Him, because of it, to be the Saviour. This is how Peter preached on the day of Pentecost itself (see Acts 2:23-24; 36).

Men may thus be brought to change their attitude first towards the person and then towards the work of Jesus. By such preaching they may be given to see that Christ's shameful death happened by God's ordering and for their rescue. Those who reject it are shutting themselves out from the benefit of what God Himself has not only thought necessary, but has also actually achieved for their salvation. Far from the curse and shame of His crucifixion proving that Jesus cannot be God's Christ, the wonder is that these are the consequences of our wrongdoing which God ordained that His Christ should endure on our behalf.

This explains, the preacher can then say, both Christ's work and the preacher's task as alike divinely appointed and plainly complementary. For:

> God was in Christ reconciling the world to himself, not counting their trespasses against them, and entrusting to us the message of reconciliation. So we are ambassadors for Christ, God making his appeal through us. We beseech you on behalf of Christ, be reconciled to God. For our sake he made him to be sin who knew no sin, so that in him we might become the righteousness of God (2 Cor. 5:19-21).

This means, in other words, that what God has done for men by Christ's death makes present peace with God possible for sinners who are estranged from Him, and who would otherwise be the proper objects of His wrath and displeasure. And it is the preacher's responsibility to help men to see the character and the consequences of Christ's work and to urge men here and now to embrace the available benefit and 'be reconciled to God'. Otherwise, in a day when salvation can be at once enjoyed, some who by their presence in the congregation seem to be active participants, may actually 'accept the grace of God in vain' (see 2 Cor. 6:1).

Preaching to professed believers

In the third place, let us consider those who have professed faith in Christ – the confessed believers. How should we preach the gospel to them? Paul's words to the Corinthians from which we started (1 Cor. 15:1-2) show that people who have accepted the gospel may still need to be reminded of it and personally challenged with regard to it. For the full employment of salvation depends upon holding it fast; and there may be active pressures tempting some to abandon their faith in it, or subtly and fatally undermining their hold on it. So we find here that Paul asks, 'Do you still hold fast the gospel as I preached it to you? If not, your conversion was in vain' (1 Cor. 15:2 NEB).

Let us particularly note from the context that the sphere in which the faith of these Corinthian Christians was weak and in danger of being made useless, concerned the truth of the resurrection from the dead and particularly the bodily resurrection of Jesus Himself. So as a preacher of the gospel, what Paul explicitly indicates here in considerable detail is both the grounds for believing that Christ was raised – that is, the testimony of many eye-witnesses – and the serious consequences of denying it.

There is danger still in taking faith in Christ's resurrection for granted. Individuals who have begun to believe in Christ continually need to be assured of its certainty and made aware of its decisive significance. The very experience of salvation depends, so Paul teaches, upon believing in one's heart that God raised Christ from the dead (see Rom. 10:9-10). For if Christ has not been raised our faith is futile and we are still in our sins; and 'Then those also who have fallen asleep in Christ have perished' (see 1 Cor. 15:17-18). So this truth needs to be proclaimed and its certainty made plain.

In addition, since Christ has been raised, we have substantial ground for believing in our acceptance with God; we have a guarantee that new life from God and that realized victory over sin and death are ours to enjoy; and we have an explicit pledge and an objective proof and pattern of the hope set before us in Christ – that our bodies are to be similarly glorified. 'Thanks be to God', as Paul says at the end of his exposition, 'who gives us the victory through our Lord Jesus Christ' (1 Cor. 15:57).

These truths are all part of the full gospel of our salvation and they need to be so preached that men may embrace them and enjoy the benefits of believing in them. For a so-called gospel without hope beyond the grave is no gospel at all. So Paul speaks to the Colossian Christians of 'the hope laid up for you in heaven'. 'Of this', he adds, 'you have heard before in the word of the truth, the gospel' (Col. 1:5); and he goes on to emphasize the importance of 'not shifting from the hope of the gospel which you heard' (Col. 1:23). So if we are to follow Paul's example and to equip believers to endure to the end, and to triumph in the end, these truths ought to be given their proper place in the gospel we proclaim. We ought more frequently and more adequately to preach Christ's resurrection and to proclaim our hope in Him of the resurrection of the body and of the life of the world to come.

Preaching to Christians who live unworthily

In the fourth place, many who have a genuine experience of the forgiveness of sins and of new God-given life in Christ, nevertheless live unworthily as Christians. They need to be made aware that the full gospel is a gospel not only of past deliverance and future hope but also of present salvation.

Here the positive truth which demands explicit proclamation as a part of the gospel is the truth concerning the gift of the indwelling Spirit. When individuals believe in and confess the glorified Christ as Lord, He baptizes them with the Spirit. This gift is the birthright and birthmark of all who by faith become Christ's (see Eph. 1:13). For instance, on the day of Pentecost those who repented and were baptized in the name of Jesus Christ were promised the immediate enjoyment not only of forgiveness of sins but also of 'the gift of the Holy Spirit' (Acts 2:38). Baptism by water is clearly a symbolic witness to both of these benefits – to cleansing through the blood of Christ and quickening by the life-giving Spirit.

Later, when Paul found in Ephesus a group of disciples concerning whose full faith in Christ and the gospel he was in doubt, the question which he asked them was 'Did you receive the Holy Spirit when you believed?' When they said 'No', he rightly concluded that their faith was not faith in Christ. What he then preached to them was not some second blessing to be enjoyed as a subsequent experience after becoming Christians. Rather he treated them as unsaved and preached to them salvation through faith in Christ (see Acts 19:1-7).

Similarly, when people today hear the gospel preached and they believe in the Saviour, they need to be made fully aware that in consequence they receive not only forgiveness of sins but also the gift of the Spirit. In his epistles the apostle Paul repeatedly reminds believers in Christ of this truth. Writing to the Thessalonians he says: 'God has not called us for uncleanness, but in holiness. Therefore whoever disregards this, disregards not man but God, who gives his Holy Spirit to you' (1 Thess. 4:7-8). Again, writing to the Corinthians, whose spiritual condition was so unworthy, he does not say that what they need is the gift of the Spirit. Rather he reminds them that the Spirit already dwells in them both corporately and individually (see 1 Cor. 3:16; 6:19). Similarly, writing to the Romans and listing the benefits which are simultaneously to be enjoyed when we are 'justified by faith', he adds: 'God's love has been poured into our hearts through the Holy Spirit which has been given to us' (Rom. 5:5). Indeed, he adds later, 'Any one who does not have the Spirit of Christ does not belong to him' (Rom. 8:9).

Faithful preaching of the New Testament gospel ought, therefore, to make this truth unmistakably plain – and then to confront genuine believers with the consequent challenge to live differently, not as an achievement still beyond them, but as a way of life now made possible by nothing less than the power at work within us of God's indwelling Spirit. So we can and ought to work out our own salvation with fear and trembling, remembering that God Himself is now at work within us to give us both the desire and the energy to do what is pleasing to God (see Phil. 2:12-13).

Safeguarding the Truth of the Gospel

Let us consider the gospel we proclaim compared with the gospel as others preach it, and particularly as compared with the gospel as it ought to be preached.

As others preach it

First, in terms of self-examination let us learn from St Paul to be willing to submit our preaching to the judgment of others. We find that when a visit to Jerusalem gave him the opportunity, Paul laid before the leaders of the church in Jerusalem the gospel which he was preaching among the Gentiles, in order to make sure that his work would not prove ineffective through his leaving out from his preaching things which were essential

(Gal. 2:1-2). On this issue, he says, all was well. They 'added nothing to me'. They recognized 'that I had been entrusted with the gospel to the uncircumcised' and 'they perceived the grace that was given to me'. They 'gave to me ... the right hand of fellowship' (Gal. 2:6-9).

On the other hand, we find, in the second place, that such comparison of the gospel he preached with the teaching and practice of others involved Paul in the necessity, for the gospel's sake, of steadfast contention for the truth and of uncompromising denunciation of error. Also he found himself compelled to do this within the fellowship of the church and in direct relation to others who also claimed to be preaching the gospel. When, for instance, some strove to make circumcision a part of the gospel and essential to salvation, when they tried to insist that Paul's fellow-worker Titus must be circumcised, Paul absolutely refused to yield to such pressure. To the Christians in Galatia he reported: '... to them we did not yield submission even for a moment, that the truth of the gospel might be preserved for you' (Gal. 2:5). For if in the mother church of the homeland of the Christian faith Paul had failed thus to stand fast for the truth of the gospel, or if he had failed later at Antioch to oppose even Peter to his face (see Gal. 2:11-14), it is the Gentile Christians of the mission field who would have been either brought into bondage or deprived, because uncircumcised, of full fellowship at the Lord's table.

Is it not true in our day that a similar issue in relation to the gospel of our salvation is raised by the insistence of some on the necessity of so-called 'apostolic succession' and all that that implies? For instance, Archbishop Michael Ramsey in his book, *The Gospel and the Catholic Church*, puts the episcopate alongside the Canon of Scripture as an equally essential 'utterance of the Gospel of God':

> Both the Canon of Scripture and the Episcopate are 'developments', and it would seem highly arbitrary to select one of these and to call it essential, while rejecting or ignoring the other. It would be more reasonable to seek in both of them, through their close inner connexion and their place in the life of the one Body, the utterance of the Gospel of God.[1]

There is no adequate reason why we should add this necessity to our gospel. Rather there is every reason why, in the interests of the spiritual well-being, freedom and fellowship in Christ of many true Christians and churches, we should uncompromisingly resist such pressure, lest we all be brought into bondage and lest another gospel – which is not another – supplant the God-given truth.

---

[1] Michael Ramsey, *The Gospel and the Catholic Church* (second edition, London, 1956), p. 63.

There is, too, in our day all the more danger of this because loyalty to scriptural sanction and authority has been grievously weakened; and some are virtually suggesting – particularly for the furtherance of ecumenical unity – that we may expect to be given by the Spirit fresh light, which is supplementary to the witness of the Scriptures and may even supersede them. On such an issue the apostle Paul is unqualified in his denunciation; he writes: '... even if we, or an angel from heaven, should preach to you a gospel contrary to that which we preached to you, let him be accursed' (Gal. 1:8). The question is – do we not still need some of this evangelical intolerance?

As it should be preached

Finally, above all else, or, as Paul says, 'first of all', we need to preach that 'Christ died for our sins'. This means, as the Scripture indicates, that in His own person as the sinner's proxy He bore the penalty due to our sins, and bore it in its full extreme form by suffering the shame and the curse of public execution, of vile crucifixion, of hanging upon a tree. Consequently, the remission of sins, which we offer to men from God when we preach the gospel, is grounded not on the avoidance of justice, but on its full satisfaction.

In this gospel of God, mercy and truth meet together, righteousness and peace kiss each other. In dealing with sinners, God has found a way to be both just and the justifier – a just God and a Saviour. Also, the whole purpose of the redemption which the gospel provides is to ensure that there should be in our lives both a new practice of right living – that 'we might', as Peter puts it, 'die to sin and live to righteousness' (1 Pet. 2:24) – and a new prospect, 'the hope of glory', to keep us rejoicing and living soberly (see Rom. 5:2; 13:11-14).

This gospel is addressed to sinners who are unfit for God's presence, who are unable to live holy lives, and who deserve the death penalty. It tells us there is hope for men in such an awful plight because of what God Himself has done for us. 'For our sake he made him to be sin who knew no sin, so that in him we might become the righteousness of God' (2 Cor. 5:21). This means, in other words, penal substitution and acceptance by proxy, or through being married to God's proper Man. This is the gospel which by God's grace it is ours both to embrace and to proclaim. Here each reader must, before God, examine himself and ask: Is this the gospel through which I have myself found salvation? Is this the gospel whose amazing truth I delight to offer to others? May God help us fully to believe this gospel and to be found faithful in preaching it.

2

THE PLACE OF THEOLOGY (1947)

Christianity is essentially a way of life and not just a philosophy about life. To become a Christian is a matter not of theory but of practice and of transforming experience. Faith in Christ and loyalty to Him involve more than bare, and possibly barren, intellectual assent; they mean nothing less than personal committal and unfaltering daily obedience. This is unquestionably what glorifies God most obviously before men – not the orthodox declaration of the learned theologian, but the consecrated and sacrificial devotion of the martyr and the saints.

But Christian doctrine and theology are not, therefore, unimportant. If vital Christianity is an art and not a science, it nevertheless has a science, and only those who know and hold to it can ever excel in the art of Christian living. Mere pious aspiration and devout intention, however sincere and persistent, are not enough to make men free from the bondage of inherited prejudice and selfish misconception. Only the knowledge of the Truth will make us free. If we are to enter into life, if we are to avoid the ways which end in death, we need to know the Truth and to know it with increasing discernment. Otherwise how can we follow it and enjoy its benefits?

Further, full and detailed understanding of the Truth is the more necessary because the issues at stake in following or forsaking it are so momentous. Here we are confronted by nothing less than the choice between freedom and bondage, life and death. What is more, a careful study and an adequate comprehension of divinely revealed Truth are absolutely indispensable to faithful Christian devotion, because of ourselves – unless we allow ourselves to be instructed by the Spirit and informed by the word of God – we are bound to choose the wrong road.

First published in *The Churchman* vol. 61 (March 1947).

For 'the way of man is not in himself; it is not in man that walketh to direct his steps' (Jer. 10:23). 'There is a way that seemeth right unto a man, but the end thereof are the ways of death' (Prov. 14:12; 16:25).

The doctrines or dogma of Christianity are its governing principles – the truths which Christians hold, and by which they are held. As a necessary framework for the support of Christian living they may be compared to the bones of the human body. These bones are all necessary and must be preserved unimpaired. If a bone is broken or removed, particularly if it is an important bone, full healthy function and movement are thereby hindered or even made impossible. For instance, if a man breaks a main bone in his leg, for the time he cannot walk, even though all the other bones in his body are sound. If he has to be moved, he must be carried. There are Christians in a somewhat similar spiritual state. The man who can help to rectify such a physical condition is a doctor capable of setting the broken bone. In setting it the doctor does not heal it, but he puts it in the way of healing; and everything depends upon its being set properly. To be able to set bones a knowledge of anatomy is indispensable. Just as a would-be doctor studies the parts of the human skeleton, so a would-be Christian preacher ought to study with care and in close detail the constituent parts of the system of Christian doctrine. For without such knowledge we cannot hope to be able to put the spiritually needy in the way of healing.

St Paul calls true Christian doctrine sound or healthful. Knowledge of it by Christians, and its unbroken maintenance in the church, are absolutely essential to spiritual health. As the opening sentence of the so-called Athanasian Creed says, according to the probable meaning of the original Latin, 'If any man would be in a sound or healthy spiritual state, before all things it is necessary that he hold fast the Catholic faith.' If, like St Paul, we are to fight a good fight and to finish our course, to endure faithful to the end, we must keep the faith. Or again, if we are to fulfil a helpful Christian ministry, we need, by holding to the faithful word, to acquire an ability to exhort believers in the healthful doctrine and to convict the gainsayers (see Titus 1:9). The study of doctrine is therefore indispensable. To neglect it is to endanger our own spiritual health and to fail to acquire the knowledge necessary to help others to become and to keep spiritually fit.

Knowledge limits and determines use. Theory affects practice. The way to change a man's conduct is to change his beliefs. 'As a man thinketh in his heart, so is he' (Prov. 23:7). These truths are so obvious as scarcely to need illustration. The more a man knows of what a thing will do and how to use it, the more he will turn to that thing when in need. Electricity is an amazing force. It is capable of very many uses. But those who would use it to advantage need to know and to abide by its laws. Otherwise, instead of obtaining benefit, they may suffer damage from handling it. People of ancient days who thought matter was evil and man's physical body of no worth, were led by this belief either into reckless indulgence or rigorous asceticism. What they believed determined what they did.

Similarly, because of the fresh and fuller discovery at and after the Reformation of the supreme value in the sight of God of the individual soul, and of the free and equal right of access to God of all alike without distinction through Christ the one Mediator, many men in these last four centuries have laboured and suffered and died – and more have done so in our own day – to uphold the rights and to secure the liberty of the individual. Faith in the sanctity of human personality is something which Christianity has inspired. But this very belief in the rights and liberty of the individual, true and important as it is in its place, unless it is complemented by belief in the sovereignty of God and belief in man's continual and necessary dependence on Him, and in the ultimate unity of God's purpose for all men in Christ, only leads in practice, as modern history has shown, to unhealthy self-assertion, unsocial individualism, merciless economic competition and increasing international war.

Instead of worshipping God as a dependent creature, and delighting in trustful obedience, man has become his own end and a law unto himself. As some cynic has said, 'The Englishman is a self-made man, and worships his maker.' Still worse, we have seen Germany striving to be a self-made state, to establish a self-made empire, and to worship Hitler as its personified spirit. Or again, instead of joining fully with others in the corporate life and the mutual service of the larger family of God's purpose, men have tended to shut themselves off, each within his own preserve to do each as he liked, and to tell his inquisitive and impertinent neighbour to mind his own business. So the Englishman's home has been his castle, defended against the intruder, and consequently not altogether a place in which homeless evacuees may easily find a welcome! Protestantism has been a multiplicity of sects, unable to unite in the common cause of educating the rising generation in the fear of God and in the knowledge of Christian Truth. Social progress has been hindered by the unyielding tenacity of privileged minorities, who have in their own eyes done no more than claim their rights as individuals. There has arisen open friction and ill-feeling, both socially and internationally, between the 'haves' and the 'have-nots'.

A violent reaction in thought and practice has inevitably followed – first communism within the state, and then Hitlerism among the states, both seeking to override by forcible and revolutionary methods the right to possession of those who seem to have more than their fair share. In Germany, as we have seen, totalitarian Nazism swept aside all belief in the right of the individual man or state, and made Germany and Hitler the one end of all policy. There seems to be no limit to the devilish evils to which such reaction can lead. The human race, having failed in spite of its Christian enlightenment to acknowledge and trust in God, who gave man his potential dignity, and who alone can make possible its true realization, has come under the curse of trusting in itself. 'Cursed be the man that trusteth in man, and maketh flesh his arm, and whose heart departeth from the Lord' (Jer. 17:5).

All this unbalanced or one-sided practice of the past can only be properly rectified, and the obvious and awful excesses and evils of violent reaction restrained and avoided, by the rediscovery and fresh application to life of those other equally important Christian truths, which in their zeal for the truths which have given them individual freedom and importance, most men, even genuine professing Christians, have tended to overlook. In these days of tremendous upheaval and inevitable change, if we as Christians are rightly to appreciate and not foolishly to abandon what of Christian good we have inherited, and if we are to rectify the grievous deficiencies and obvious one-sidedness of some of our past ways of life by a new but not undue emphasis on other complementary Christian truths about life, it is Christian doctrine which we need to study and more fully to grasp. For the only adequate equipment with which to face and to seek to solve the vast problems of our day and generation is not simply faith, however zealous, in one or two truths of Christianity, but nothing less than a thorough knowledge and an obedient devotion to the whole Truth of the Christian gospel – the Truth as it is in Jesus.

This need to recognize the practical importance of a knowledge of Christian doctrine is the more urgent because for a generation or more doctrine has been disliked. In our modern universities students have been expected to be acquainted with every view and to be dogmatic about no view. The reading of so-called theology, far from establishing students in informed and unhesitating Christian conviction, has resulted in the majority of cases in the development of a spirit of tolerant and liberal uncertainty. In the supposed pursuit of Christian love men have neglected the study, and forsaken the observance, of divine law. Consequently, in spite of their genuinely good intentions, they have lost their way. For, as Jesus Himself said, 'If thou wouldst enter into life, keep the commandments' (Matt. 19:17). The only way to enter into life, the life of love, is by fulfilling the law – by observing to do all that is written therein. Justification before God and the sanctifying Spirit are given to the penitent believer in Christ in order that he may be put right and kept right with the law of God – 'that the righteousness of the law may be fulfilled in us who walk not after the flesh, but after the Spirit' (Rom. 8:4). Yet how few hold with conviction and can teach with authority a knowledge of the character and the precepts of God as revealed in His word.

Love is the fulfilling of the law; because to the stern, cold and exacting letter of command or prohibition love adds the spirit of warm, glad and willing obedience. The spirit of love delights in the law. But many in this modern age have been tempted into thinking that they can disregard the law and throw off restraint, supposing that in the fancied possession of a Christian spirit they have something better, and so need the law no longer. Such neglect of law and of its practical applications is nothing less than suicidal folly. It is a denial of the spirit of Christ who said, 'Till heaven and earth pass, one jot or tittle shall in no wise pass from the law till all be fulfilled' (Matt. 5:18). Consequently many have a zeal but not according to knowledge. They are on the wrong road; and yet they are trying in their pursuit of it to exhibit a Christian spirit.

Let some quotations show that many are now alive to these realities of the situation. In *The Ten Commandments in the Twentieth Century* John Drewett writes:

> It is possible to distinguish between the rules of a game and the spirit of a game. You may keep all the rules and yet have a very unhappy game, because, as we say, the spirit was lacking. The Commandments are rules of life, but the Gospel supplies the spirit. We may have the right spirit, but if we don't keep the rules we shall not be able to play the game at all. Love goes beyond justice but it can never tolerate injustice, and often Christian love, because it thinks justice is a hard thing, degenerates into a shallow sentimentality.[1]

> Amos ... had he lived today ... would have recognised that modern science had revealed to this generation the universality of natural laws. On this knowledge we have constructed our machine age. ... But, at the same time, as he was impressed with our conquest of nature, Amos would have been appalled at our utter disregard for moral laws ... Amos would see a scientific civilisation using its knowledge of the physical world for its destruction, because it has failed to observe those other laws, which God has laid down in the

---

[1] John Drewett, *The Ten Commandments in the Twentieth Century* (London, 1941), p. 12.

realm of human conduct, and which are as binding in their own sphere as the laws of physics are in engineering. The supreme irony of our civilisation is that it is based on the universality of natural law, but has as thoroughly rejected moral law as any of the former civilisations.[2]

In *Creed or Chaos?* Dorothy L. Sayers, writing at the beginning of the recent war, says:

> We are waging a war of religion. Not a civil war between adherents of the same religion, but a life-and-death struggle between Christian and pagan ... Even those who say it is a war to preserve freedom and justice and faith have gone only halfway to the truth ... At the bottom it is a violent and irreconcilable quarrel about the nature of God and the nature of man and the ultimate nature of the universe; it is a war of dogma ... It is our own distrust of dogma that is handicapping us in the struggle. The immense spiritual strength of our opponents lies precisely in the fact that they have fervently embraced, and hold with fanatical fervour, a dogma, which is none the less a dogma for being called an 'ideology'. We on our side have been trying for several centuries to uphold a particular standard of ethical values which derives from Christian dogma, while dispensing with the very dogma which is the sole rational foundation for these values.[3]

> It is worse than useless for Christians to talk about the importance of Christian morality unless they are prepared to take their stand upon the fundamentals of Christian theology. It is a lie to say dogma does not matter; it matters enormously.[4]

> Theologically, this country is at present in a state of utter chaos, established in the name of religious toleration, and rapidly degenerating into the flight from reason and the death of hope. We are not happy in this condition and there are signs of a very great eagerness, especially among the younger people, to find a creed to which they can give whole-hearted adherence.[5]

Speaking in Convocation in May 1940, Dr Michael Furse (then the Bishop of St Albans) said:

> The people of this country want to be Christian but they have largely been living on the heritage of the past, and unless it is ensured that the foundations of Christian character are securely

---

[2] Ibid., p. 21.
[3] Dorothy L. Sayers, *Creed or Chaos?* (London, 1940), pp. 7-8.
[4] Ibid., p. 12.
[5] Ibid., p. 14.

and permanently laid by the teaching of Christian doctrine within the fellowship of the Christian Church, there is no guarantee that this country will not revert to paganism.

Writing the Introduction to *The Cambridge Syllabus of Religious Teaching* (1937), Dr J.S. Whale said:

> Many discerning people now realise that unless a rediscovery of Biblical Christianity takes place in the near future, the new generation will lack even an emotional attachment to Christian faith and practice, and that in becoming unchristian it will soon be definitely anti-christian.

In April 1941, Karl Barth wrote *A Letter to Great Britain from Switzerland*. In this he pointed out that many of the reasons put forward by Englishmen for the necessity of resisting Hitler were thought to be Christian, when as a matter of fact they were not fully Christian at all. They were only humanitarian. He made bold to say quite bluntly that the conceptions put forward by many 'are concerned with principles which might also be those of a pious Hindu, Buddhist or Atheist; and that, however beautiful and fruitful they may be, they do not touch at all on the peculiarly Christian truths on which the Church is founded.'[6]

What many, therefore, have for some time been realizing is our desperate need of Christian theology – 'a rediscovery of Biblical Christianity', as Dr Whale puts it. We need to gain, to hold firmly and uncompromisingly, and then to be held and dominated by, scriptural conviction about God and His Truth. We need to be in a position to give as our reason for our chosen path of conduct not some humane consideration only, but the word and the will and the glory of God alone. We need in new and far deeper ways and with much more far-reaching application to daily life, to seek first the kingdom of God and His righteousness; to replace the ideals of humanism by the compelling theological convictions of Christian believers; to become genuine disciples of the Christ by seeking to understand and humbly to submit to and to abide by the meaning for us of His word of revelation (see John 8:31-2). Then we shall know the Truth and the Truth will set us free. Then we shall be able to answer men's moral questionings and religious hunger with the God-given authority of faithful stewards and able ministers of the word of God: 'Thus it is written, and thus it must be.'

For Christianity is essentially and undeniably doctrinal. Without doctrine, and right doctrine, we cannot have or practise Christianity.

---

[6] Karl Barth, *A Letter to Great Britain from Switzerland* (London, 1941), p. 16.

The Christian faith cannot be handed on without doctrine, clearly stated and effectively taught. From the first the early Christians continued stedfastly in the apostles' doctrine or teaching (Acts 2:42). This is the true apostolic succession – not to have an unbroken line of orders from St Peter, but to hold fully and unfalteringly to the faith once for all delivered to the saints. In Christianity it is the doctrine which is permanent and unchanging. Christians, by the inspiration of the Spirit, may continually discover in it fresh and fuller implications, and see new and more far-reaching applications, but no new Truth can be added to the God-given revelation. Only those who accept and hold to the deposit of doctrine, to the word written, can become or remain truly Christian.

Our present danger is lest, through the widespread lack of acquaintance with the fulness of Christian Truth, we fail as Christians to rely on and to use our resources of God-given revelation, and follow others in looking elsewhere for the much-needed light. For the age in which we find ourselves needs a comprehensive all-embracing view of life and history big enough to encompass the vast world problems of our day. Such a full-orbed view Christianity has; but very few Christians have it.

Dr Arthur Dakin (Principal of the Baptist College, Bristol) says:

> We tend to approach theology from the point of view of particular problems ... We thus deal with aspects; and to a large extent they remain aspects. We specialize on points – important points, no doubt; but we miss the compelling power of the whole. The truth is that we assume in our theological teaching that the student begins with this comprehensive view, take it for granted that he knows Christian theology in its main outlines, then proceed to make him wise at disputed points. I have learned that the assumption is unwarranted. The student of today simply does not know. And, moreover, one can be a student of modern theology for a very long time without ever feeling the compelling power of Christian dogma as a whole ... We have ideas, Christian ideas many of them; but we lack the co-ordination of them into a coherent and cogent system. Yet nothing less than a complete system, one would think, can match the confusion of our time.[7]

We need to regain the habit of God-centred thinking. We need to study, to take pleasure in, and to seek out, the greatness of the will and the ways

---

[7] Arthur Dakin, 'Calvin's Age and Ours', *Expository Times* vol. 52 (July 1941), p. 396.

and the works of God, to seek in reverent contemplation to appreciate more of His character, His majesty and His glory. We need to break away from our puny limited self-centred outlook, into which we only bring in the thought of God in relation to ourselves and our own immediate interests, to see the whole of life, creation, history, providence, judgment and redemption in their relationship to God. The thought which such contemplation produces is theology; the interpretation of the ways of God with men to which it leads is doctrine; and it is such theology and such doctrine for which men wait. The people who do know their God shall be strong and do exploits. Without such vision and such knowledge the people perish.

It is such all-embracing knowledge which Paul prayed might be given, not just to himself or to one or two learned theologians, but to all the Christians of the churches in Asia. He coveted for them by divine illumination and unveiling a comprehensive grasp of the greatness of God's purposes – purposes starting with His deliberate choice before the foundation of the world, and finding their consummation in a dispensation of the fulness of the times in which all things are to be summed up in Christ (Eph. 1:3-23 etc). For Christ is the source and the sustainer and the consummator of all things. By Him they exist. In Him they consist. Through Him and His cross and blood-shedding they have been reconciled to God. He fills and fulfils all things. He is far above all, in all things pre-eminent. It is this greatness of Christ which we need to grasp, if as Christians our thinking is to be big enough to see world problems in their true perspective, if we are to possess and to make known God's gospel for our times. In other words, we need to gain a new and much greater acquaintance with the fulness of the doctrine of God in Christ – that is, with scriptural Christology and biblical Christianity.

This task, according to the New Testament, is a task for all. If Paul's prayers are still to be answered, all Christians ought to be theologically-minded, all Christians ought to be well taught in doctrine. The task is, therefore, a task for us. Further, it is certain that the majority of Christians will not pursue this way of knowledge unless some set a lead and can by their teaching help others to follow. The Christian church needs more workers able to give sound scriptural teaching and solid doctrinal teaching, teaching set forth in a way suitable and intelligible to particular listeners. Who better can undertake this task than those who are fully persuaded of the deity of Christ, of the sole sufficiency of His redeeming work, and of the final authority of the Holy Scriptures as the rule of faith? Who better can undertake this task than those

45

who pray to and trust in God to endue them with the Spirit of wisdom and revelation in the knowledge of Him? Yea, more, without these things the task cannot be properly undertaken. This is why the failure of evangelicals both to study and to teach Christian doctrine has had such serious consequences. Let us, then, fail no longer. Let us without further delay, or excuse, or indolent presumption, set out to make ourselves masters of the doctrines which we profess so zealously to hold, that we may not be mere negative defenders or guardian watch-dogs of orthodoxy, frightening people away by our severity, but positive exponents of biblical theology, attracting hearers both by the life-giving truth which we proclaim and by our own obvious knowledge of our subject. Let us set ourselves, let us make it our ambition, ever more full to know whom we believe, and what we believe, to the full extent which divine revelation makes possible, that we may be able to give a reason of the hope that is in us, and to set forth more effectively, both to God's glory and to men's edification, the fulness of the Truth as it is in Jesus.

3

WITH ALL OF YOUR MIND (1961)

Man is a rational animal, a creature with a mind, capable of knowledge and understanding, of wisdom and discernment. The first and chief object of such knowledge should be God Himself. This is the very essence of eternal life – to know God, to acknowledge, to appreciate and to enjoy Him. The truly wise man's supreme ground for satisfaction is therefore to be found in his knowledge of God, particularly his knowledge of the love of God in Christ. This can but demand the exercise of all our powers. For such truth is unfathomable; it outreaches all man's powers of grasping it. The love of Christ simply surpasses knowledge. 'How unsearchable are his judgments, and his ways past tracing out!' (Rom. 11:33). The quest and satisfaction of eternity will still be getting to know God.

God makes Himself known through His word. By communicating His truth in this way God has treated man as a creature possessing a mind. Man's mind can engage in no higher exercise than that of seeking to learn more of God by studying and understanding His word, by which God's character, and the wealth of His purposes of blessing for those whom He makes His in Christ, are revealed.

God also makes Himself known through His actions. How better can man's mind be occupied than in seeking to understand God's ways? 'Great are the works of the Lord, studied by all who have pleasure in them' (Ps. 111:2). 'Whoever is wise, let him give heed to these things; let men consider the steadfast love of the Lord' (Ps. 107:43). Some scientific discoverers have spoken of 'thinking God's thoughts after him'.

First published in *The Christian Graduate* vol. 14 (September 1961).

We also need to use our minds in order to discern what is well-pleasing to God. We are meant in understanding to grow up and to become mature, and no longer to be like children liable to be easily misled. We are meant to have our powers of understanding exercised by use, not only to distinguish between right and wrong, so that we may refuse the evil and choose the good; but also to acquire insight and to practise discernment that we may 'approve what is excellent' (Phil. 1:10), or choose the best; and all in order that with delight, as those deliberately choosing it, we may do God's will.

Such use of the mind is impossible to the sinful and the unregenerate. 'The unspiritual man ... is not able to understand' (1 Cor. 2:14). The mind must first be renewed and illuminated by the Spirit of God Himself. Then it will function as God intended. Thus enabled by God's grace we can, and we ought to, find the highest use of the mind in our approach to God in worship and prayer, and in our testimony about God in preaching and teaching. Our powers of comprehension and communication should be worked to the full and find their crowning function in acknowledging God's worthiness and giving Him praise, in praying that He may be openly glorified and His will done, and in proclaiming the wealth and the wonder of His unfailing providence and His saving grace. Thus to love God worthily demands not only all our heart and soul and strength, but also all our mind.

4

THE BIBLE AS REVELATION:
THE SPIRITUAL ISSUE (1940)

Evangelicals are divided on the biblical issue. This issue has split our ranks. Nor is such a result anything but inevitable as long as our differences of attitude to the Bible are so radical. For to some the Bible is absolutely unique and from above – God-given; while to others it is only outstanding and from beneath – man-wrought. To some it is, and makes ours, an indispensable revelation without which men cannot see the truth about God; it provides a final standard or court of appeal by which all claims to have found the truth can and must be judged. To others it is rather the product of the spiritual discernment of men of old, a discernment which by the same Spirit men today may not only equal but even supersede; so that a man enlightened by the divine Spirit may so discern fresh or fuller truth as to be able rightly to criticize and even to discard parts of Scripture. To some the Bible is special God-given revelation. Its words are, like its Author, the same yesterday, today and for ever. It is the appointed medium through which all men of every age may hear the authentic voice of the divine Spirit. To others the Bible is, however greatly inspired, still a product of men, something historical, the work of a particular age, which like all human thoughts or deeds cannot in every part win the same credence or reverence from every subsequent generation. The Spirit of God may have to say to men now other, if not better, things than were written aforetime.

These different views cannot both be right. They are not merely complementary aspects of a larger whole just waiting to be united. Rather, as experience has proved, they will not mix. Nor is there hope of vital unity among us until we are afresh agreed in the conviction that

First published in *The Churchman* vol. 54 (October 1940).

the Bible, which is history, is like the Incarnation absolutely unique history, because it is also and first of all special God-given revelation. For just as sinful men have been reconciled to God by the one perfect God-given sacrifice, offered once for all for ever, so spiritually blind and misguided men have been enlightened by a written word, equally God-given and once for all delivered to the saints. It cannot therefore be anything less than unbelief and presumption to question or to try to add to the sufficiency of either. Consequently, those who would in effect take from or add to the canon and authority of Scripture are not simply exhibiting a spirit of praiseworthy enquiry; they are tampering with essential foundations. Such action cannot but be viewed by many with serious misgiving. With what result is all too obvious. Confidence is undermined. Men who ought to be leaders are no longer wholeheartedly trusted and followed. Financial support is withdrawn from evangelical societies. There are suspicion and division in the camp. Groups become occupied in self-defence against one another instead of in united advance against the common foe. Opportunities for aggressive evangelical witness are lost. It is surely time, therefore, that we faced the situation afresh, not for further mutual criticism, but in order to renew among us an all-absorbing loyalty which is both true to our Lord Himself and adequate to reunite us in active co-operation in His service.

Obviously the Bible is historical. It is both a product and a record of history, a book or collection of writings written like other books by men and about men. Its various authors were each and all of them men of their own particular age and environment. Much of its contents is a record of events, a description of things that have happened. Simply as a historical record the Bible is worthy of a place in any library. It is a history book.

But the Bible is no ordinary history. It has, again quite obviously, special and unique characteristics. Its writers suggest, and their record implies, that the history they report has been ordered by God to further ends beyond the immediate ones common to all happenings in time and circumstance. Further, the facts recorded have been specially selected and presented to fulfil a higher purpose than that of providing information and understanding concerning events and people of the past. The object of this record is rather to give the reader moral instruction and spiritual enlightenment. The record is history; but it is more, it is prophecy, it is revelation.

There is inevitably a fundamental difference between history viewed wholly as history and history viewed primarily as revelation. In the latter case, what matters most is not the facts themselves but their prophetic interpretation, the deeper meaning read into them by spiritual insight. This insight was the distinguishing characteristic of the prophet or seer. The words of the prophets of the Old Testament make it plain that they could not but speak because of what they had seen. They were aware that their understanding was the consequence of divine unveiling. They spake the word of the Lord that they saw. They were even aware at times that the word, which they could not but speak, contained more of truth and revelation than they themselves could penetrate and fathom. They were more sure of the truth and of the divine origin of the vision than they were of their own power to understand it; but proclaimed and written down it must be. Nor are there lacking in the New Testament confirming indications that in the light of the fuller revelation given through the coming of Christ, and by the outpouring of the Spirit, many words of the Old Testament were seen to have a significance beyond anything comprehended before. The words of the prophets mean more to believers in Christ than they did or could mean to the prophets themselves or to the men of their own age; not unto themselves but unto us did they minister (1 Pet. 1:10-12).

Perhaps the most remarkable illustration of the difference between words regarded as history and words interpreted as revelation is to be found in the utterance of Caiaphas – his only utterance recorded in the New Testament. To his fellows of the Sanhedrin he said, 'It is expedient for you that one man should die for the people, and that the whole nation perish not' (John 11:50). In their historical setting the meaning of these words is obvious enough. They were a counsel of political expediency. It was better, as Caiaphas saw it, to make Jesus a scapegoat and sacrifice one life, than risk a popular Messianic rising. That could only call forth drastic Roman intervention and then the priestly aristocracy, to which Caiaphas belonged, would be the first to suffer. But his words were thought worthy of a place in the Gospel record for an entirely different reason. The evangelist interpreted them prophetically. To him they were revelation – a revelation all the more remarkable because it was so completely hidden from the mind of the man who uttered the words. 'This he said not of himself: but being high priest that year, he prophesied that Jesus should die for the nation' (John 11:51). The high priest had a unique yearly office, which only he could fulfil. It was his responsibility on the Day of Atonement to enter alone into the most holy place, not without blood which he offered for himself and for the errors of the people (Heb. 9:7). And it was none other than he, who fulfilling his office in a way far beyond his knowing, gave counsel to the Jews that in this year, the year when all types were fulfilled, it was expedient that a man – not an animal victim – die for the people (John 18:14). He put his hand, as it were, on the Sacrifice which was to take away sin and procure salvation. And these words of his are in the holy Scriptures not because of their importance as history, but because of their significance as revelation.

Other illustrations are not far to seek. As a historical figure, a man of his age and environment, Melchizedek was possibly a person of little or no significance. No ordinary writer of world history would think him worthy of mention. His significance in Scripture is wholly due to features which are apparently arbitrary or incidental. His name happened to mean king of righteousness. He happened to be king of Salem; and Salem means peace. He also happened to combine in his person the offices of king and priest – a combination not found in Judaism. Also the very brevity of the mention made of him in Genesis left him without record of his birth or death. He simply appears as one living and in office. In all these features the inspired writers see revelation. The Messiah is a priest for ever after the order of Melchizedek. For Melchizedek in figure or as revelation is 'made like unto the Son of God' (Heb. 7:1-4). He has no beginning nor end; he follows none; he is superseded by none; he abideth a priest continually; he is a priest upon his throne; he is first king of righteousness and then king of peace. Melchizedek, therefore, has his place in the Old Testament story, and is still worthy of study by the Christian, not primarily as history but as revelation, not for his own sake but as illustrating the office and work of Jesus the Son of God.

Again, in writing to the Corinthians, Paul deals at length with the practical question of eating meat offered to idols. As history this was then a current issue in the Corinthian church. To many who now read the words, the problem as history is no longer a present one. It provides a study from which the reader is completely detached. It does not concern him personally. But as revelation the chapters (1 Cor. 8-10) in which Paul deals with this question illustrate the practical application of guiding principles, by which Christians ought always to determine their conduct. It is this use of the Scriptures as revelation, rather than the reading of them as mere history, which gives them their abiding value. An understanding of the historical setting of their first composition is not unimportant; but a prayerful desire to apprehend and a devout determination to apply the underlying spiritual principles are much more important. It is to enable us to learn not merely historical facts but spiritual and moral truth that, by divine ordering and grace, the Scriptures have been written and the illuminating Spirit given.

True devotional approach to the history of the Bible will therefore make more of its moral or spiritual significance than of its immediate historical features and circumstances. Not that an understanding of the latter can be disregarded; but it becomes subservient to the apprehension of the former, and not an end in itself. Further, such approach is impossible without due recognition of the place of analogy in giving instruction. The use of figure, type and parable is an effective because concrete method of making meaning plain; and it is certainly made more effective when the illustration chosen is itself fact and not fiction. The use of such a method of teaching was freely and widely adopted by our Lord Himself. The first reason justifying the method is the inherent correspondence between the governing principles of God's work in nature and God's doing in grace. And the second reason is that in realms outside man's direct knowledge the use of allegory or figure is the most effective way of conveying to men that limited measure of understanding which alone is possible to them. The ascended Lord seated at God's right hand is difficult to visualize as concrete history in time and space. But as revelation no better expression of the truth about Christ's present position and relationship to God is available to finite minds. We darken understanding when in fancied superiority of judgment we discard such figurative language as obsolete.

There is need, therefore, of a return to reverent appreciation and positive interpretation of scriptural 'figures of the true' and foreshadowings of the truth. For their function in giving insight into the fulness of truth is easily impaired by historical criticism, just as the reflection of the heavens seen in a pool disappears from view when the surface of the water is disturbed: or just as a telescope ceases to give men a vision of things far distant and otherwise out of sight, when people are turned aside to investigate when and how and by whom the telescope was made.

Allegorical interpretation and reasoning from analogy may, of course, all too easily be overdone. Alone they would prove nothing; therefore, justification for each particular case must be found elsewhere in Scripture and not in the allegory or analogy itself. But when their use is legitimate, they do help and illumine understanding as nothing else can. And more, there is a use of them which is consecrated and authorized by the New Testament writers. Our teaching, therefore, ceases to be apostolic and even becomes anti-apostolic if by criticism of Old Testament passages we undermine the force of New Testament references to them. By this we prevent present-day readers from seeing Christ's person and work illustrated in Old Testament figures and foreshadowed in Old Testament prophecies. For example, supposing we doubt and question the historicity or divine origin of Numbers 21.

According to this chapter people bitten by snakes were told by God's command to look at a serpent of brass; and those who looked lived. If we discredit the story, we have only made it the more difficult for ourselves and for those we teach to see any value or meaning in the words, 'As Moses lifted up the serpent in the wilderness, even so must the Son of Man be lifted up, that whosoever believeth in him should not perish, but have eternal life' (John 3:14). Yet these words are attributed to our Lord Himself; and were certainly accepted by the evangelist and by the early church as an explanation of the purpose of Christ's death. The story of Numbers 21 should still be of value to the Christian not so much as history, but rather as revelation, as a figure of the true. Yet how few preachers today ever proclaim from this analogy that 'there is life for a look at the Crucified One'.

Not that one wants to encourage excessive allegorical interpretation, but only to secure a full and balanced use of every portion and manner of the divine speaking in the prophets. Unquestionably, in our study of Bible stories the chief interest should be not in fanciful theoretical interpretation, but in practical moral application. This we see illustrated forcibly in Nathan's 'Thou art the man' (2 Sam. 12:7) or in our Lord's 'Go and do thou likewise' (Luke 10:37). Without the frequent reiteration of this moral emphasis there is danger lest some become so absorbed in and satisfied with interpreting the pictures of Scripture that they neglect to practise its precepts.

There is yet another common way in which modern critical approach to the Bible has largely detracted attention from the revelation and the helps to spiritual understanding to be found in the Scriptures. Students have become absorbed in a professed attempt to get nearer to the history by investigating origins and authenticity. Increase in historical understanding has been pursued to the neglect of spiritual apprehension. For example, the endless pursuit of a solution to the synoptic problem may be a fascinating task for academical research; spiritually it has proved itself virtually a blind alley. By going inside the focus registered by the inspired writers in an attempt to get nearer to the original history, spiritual vision of the revelation given in the Gospels has been blurred and distorted. Our supposed quest of the Jesus of history has impaired our ability to see in all its fulness in the Gospels the God-given revelation of the Christ, the Son of God. We have handled the first three Gospels with too much criticism and too little faith. We have studied them too much by the limited natural sight of the scholar, and too little by the indispensable spiritual insight of the believer. We have studied them with too much self-confidence and too little reverence.

This tendency and deficiency in modern biblical scholarship are shown still more outstandingly in the widespread failure to appreciate the fourth Gospel. For this Gospel is admittedly more revelation than history. It is still history; and yet it is history written by one who cannot but bring out and make plain the revelation which he has seen in the history. For example, he records words of Jesus spoken when He cleansed the temple, 'Destroy this temple, and in three days I will raise it up' (John 2:19). That is history; it is what was actually said at the time. The evangelist adds, 'He spake of the temple of his body. When therefore He was raised from the dead his disciples remembered that He spake this; and they believed the scripture and the word which Jesus had said' (John 2:21-22). That is revelation; it is what convinced disciples afterwards saw in the words by faith. Things recorded in this Gospel are written not just to give information about the historical facts but to promote faith in the revealed Person. Such is the climax of its own record. Doubting Thomas was offered the sight and touch of the historical facts – the print of the nails in the hands, the pierced side. He responded in worship as one who had received a revelation. Thomas answered and said, 'My Lord and my God' (John 20:28). From henceforth he was a believer. These things in the fourth Gospel are written that we may share his belief – that is, that we 'might believe that Jesus is the Christ, the Son of God, and that believing we might have life through His name' (John 20:31). The true reader of this Gospel, the reader who realizes the object of the writer, is the man who rises from its study not merely conscious that he has learnt history, but overwhelmingly aware that he has received revelation, and in awe and worship acknowledging it. This is the object for which all Scripture was written.

How then, do we approach and use the Bible? That is the spiritual issue on which so much depends. Christian believers down through the centuries have unquestionably regarded Scripture as primarily conveying revelation rather than as merely recording history. The Bible has been to them the sufficient and authoritative medium through which the Spirit gives knowledge of God in Christ and insight into the fulness of truth. But are we letting the Bible be the same to us? For such a conviction about the character and purpose of the Bible, once it is firmly established and given its proper place, cannot but affect one's whole approach to its study. The man with this conviction is prepared to find that parts of Scripture, which may by modern scholarship be judged of inferior value and of little import as history, may as revelation afford to the diligent seeker light and insight obtainable nowhere else.

He believes with Paul that the things written aforetime were written for our learning and that rightly used they can bring us comfort and hope. He therefore approaches them as a humble disciple expecting to be taught; not as a self-confident critic, ready to pass judgment.

It is here that the roads divide. For once a passage of Scripture has been depreciatingly criticized as history, it is not easy or even possible for most men sincerely to turn to it as something capable as revelation of proving itself profitable for instruction in righteousness. One interest inhibits the other. The inevitable law operates: 'For unto every one that hath shall be given, and he shall have abundance: but from him that hath not shall be taken away even that which he hath.' The Scriptures do not enlighten the critical, any more than our Lord's parables enlightened the unfriendly or the merely curious. They see, but they do not understand.

In our approach to Scripture, therefore, we have to decide which interest is to predominate and to direct the study we pursue. There are, for instance, many events of which there are more than one account in Scripture. How are we to approach these different narratives? The critical historian is easily induced to set one against the other, to make much of their differences and even to insist on their inconsistencies, thus forcing the conclusion that they are, at least in some particulars, mutually exclusive and that they cannot both be true. But if both narratives are equally accepted as inspired and written for our learning, surely the reverent disciple ought to adopt an entirely different attitude. It is for him to approach the narrative with a mind prepared to accept both, and expecting to obtain a fuller meaning from the two together and so to gain more understanding than can be obtained from either alone. Architects' drawings commonly give an elevation as well as a plan. As illustrated by a stereoscope, bifocal vision enables men to see things in perspective. In the same way, duplicate narratives in the Bible are meant to help understanding and increase insight; not to provide material for setting Scripture against itself. There are parts of the Bible which as a result of critical scholarship are now only heard by many as a discord: whereas rightly directed scholarship and teaching ought to help Christian believers to hear in such passages not only the dominant air, but also the richness and balance of a larger harmony. 'He that hath ears to hear, let him hear.' That is the crux – the spiritual issue.

It is this humble, reverent, believing attitude to Scripture, the attitude of the submissive disciple, of the expectant and willing learner, which has been so largely undermined in our day. As hearers and readers of the word we sit too much in the seat of the unresponsive if not of the critical. There is need for us all to practise in much fuller measure, and to encourage in others, a devout use of the Bible with a view to practical spiritual profit. It was the faith and experience of the Reformers that the Scriptures could be used by any and every seeking soul as a personal means of grace, as the God-appointed medium for realized fellowship with God in the Spirit. 'The Scriptures were for them a personal rather than a dogmatic revelation.' 'To them the chief function of Scripture was to bring Jesus Christ near us.' It is this use of the Scriptures that is not encouraged and practised as once it was; and in place of which the tendency is to reintroduce (supposedly to our help, but actually to our peril) the so-called altar and the priest. The quest for God cannot be suppressed. But it is a tragedy indeed, if, in this erstwhile land of the Book, men and women, and still more children, are no longer taught to find God and to learn His ways in and through that Book.

The attitude of the Church of England to the Bible is plainly expressed in the Thirty-Nine Articles, particularly of course in Article VI. The Holy Scriptures are there declared to be sufficient and to contain all things necessary to salvation. They set the limits as well as the norm of Christian doctrine. 'Whatsoever is not read therein, nor may be proved thereby, is not to be required of any man that it should be believed as an article of the Faith.' But it is not enough to give solemn formal assent to such a declaration. What is needed is a renewed positive loyalty to this conviction both in personal discipleship and in public ministry. It is not enough to be inspired by a vague inherited Christian sentiment. It is still less satisfactory to preach such sentimental idealism and to imagine that we are thereby propagating the gospel. What is needed is a renewed appeal to and exposition of scriptural truth and scriptural standards. The imagined leading of the Spirit may only result in departure from the highway of truth and life unless it comes through, or is plainly confirmed by, the teaching of Scripture. 'To the law and to the testimony: if they speak not according to this word it is because there is no light in them' (Isa. 8:20).

This is the established experience and traditional conviction of the church. The Bible is the sufficient and final authority in all matters of doctrine, the unquestioned rule of faith and of practice. But too many of us have ceased fully to regard it, or continually to use it, as such. We do not go as we ought to the Bible for our guidance. We do not let the voice of the Spirit through Scripture settle things in our hearts or in our assemblies. We pay more heed to what this committee 'finds', or that professor thinks, than to what the Bible says. We are not united as we ought to be because we have ceased to let the inspired word of divine revelation be the final arbiter of our differences and the practical guide book of our counsels. We hear little of what the Spirit saith to the churches, because we listen so little for His voice in the one place where it can most certainly be heard – in the Scriptures.

It is not that we are not often reading from the Bible. What is at fault is the spirit in which we approach its study or hear its message. The word, if it is to save our souls, needs to be received with meekness and responded to obediently. We have acquired too much of the detached mind of students whose satisfaction is found in knowing all about it. What we need is a revival of the devotion of wholehearted disciples who have left all to follow Christ; and for whom His word is law. In fact, we cannot be true disciples, nor can we know the truth and be freed from our misconceptions and our bondage, unless we abide in His word (John 8:31-32).

Further, we ought frankly to face up to the Bible's own claims for itself. These claims ought to be neither evaded nor exaggerated but humbly accepted. For such submissive acceptance of the Bible's own self-authentication is fundamental to its right use. It is the indispensable test and evidence of our sincere acceptance of Scripture as the rule of faith. There is surely no practical honesty in our professed readiness to accept the ruling of Scripture on other matters equally outside man's natural powers fully to investigate and decide, unless we are equally and indeed first of all ready to accept the testimony of Scripture concerning its own character. It is an inevitable characteristic of the supreme authority that it must be self-authenticating. Its word is the last word: the final and decisive word. Writings which make such claims for themselves as the Scriptures do must either themselves be a sufficient and final authority, or else their statements on other matters ought to be rejected as equally presumptuous. There is no middle ground for those faced, as we are, with the practical question whether as evangelicals we will once again let Scripture be our final court of appeal in all matters of faith and practice.

There is need, then, for us to set ourselves, and to encourage and help others, not merely or primarily to turn to the Bible with trained natural powers and intellectual equipment to discover its literary origins and to evaluate and criticize its history as history; but rather to go to it in a spirit of faith in God, believing that by His providence and through the activity of the inspiring Spirit, it has been written and preserved for our practical moral instruction; to go to it expecting that through it the ever-present Spirit will make known to the humble and diligent seeker the character and ways of God; to go to it praying that in and through the Book (though it is largely a book of past history) we may see and hear for ourselves the word of present revelation.

It is on such a basis, the constraining bond of a positive, practical, spiritual loyalty to the authority of Scripture (rather than by any fresh attempt to penetrate the unknowable in order to produce a more widely acceptable theory of inspiration) that there is hope of fresh union and corporate advance among evangelicals. We shall act together, with respect for each other's scruples and with confidence in each other's motives, when we are each and all persuaded that the one common rule of faith and practice, the rule by which according to the light given us now or hereafter we shall abide, is the word of God written. The relinquishing of one-sided prejudices, when it becomes necessary as indeed it must, will then no longer be a reluctant, unconvinced yielding to men of different mind, but instead a glad and humble surrender to the compulsion of revealed truth; that is, to the compulsion of God's Spirit; that is, to God Himself.

For there remaineth yet much more light to break forth from God's word. But if we are to enjoy and benefit from its illumination, we must be as those who look for the light. We must be wholeheartedly prepared to examine ourselves by it and then to walk in it; otherwise we shall be as the scribes of old, who having the key of knowledge entered not in themselves and hindered from entering the many who, granted a little guidance, would gladly have entered. For unquestionably with the open Book in our hands we have the key to the situation. The question is how are we using it? May God give us the grace so to use the key of knowledge, that we ourselves and leading multitudes after us may enter in and follow on to know the Lord through the Holy Scriptures! For they are still able to make us 'wise unto salvation'. But only 'through faith which is in Christ Jesus' (2 Tim. 3:15). We can only enter in by faith, not by sight. We need, therefore, to read and to preach the word in faith. For without faith the Bible ceases to be revelation; without faith it is impossible to please God.

5

THE AUTHORITY OF SCRIPTURE (1945)

Its Source

Authority, as the word itself reveals, is related to authorship. If the Scriptures were simply the product of its various human writers, then the authority of its different parts would vary accordingly; and far from being absolute, such authority would be more likely to become obsolete. But if, behind and above the human writers, there has been at work the special originating and inspiring activity of God, causing specific things to be written for our learning and revealing His mind and will through chosen men, then the authority of Scripture is in all its parts equal and supreme because it is the authority of God Himself.

This does not mean that the practical value and relevance of its various parts to its readers may not vary considerably. Also, it is obvious that special authority belongs to those words which are direct statements of God or of Christ, and are sometimes expressly indicated to be so by such phrases as, 'Thus saith the Lord' or 'Verily, verily, I say unto you.' Nevertheless, inasmuch as we believe that all the parts of Scripture are of God and have their content, form and place by divine revelation and appointment, they all equally share in God-given authority. So the Westminster Confession says, 'The authority of the Holy Scripture for which it ought to be believed and obeyed dependeth not upon the testimony of any man or church, but wholly upon God, the author thereof; and therefore it is to be received because it is the word of God.'

First published in *Inter-Varsity Magazine* (Summer Term 1945).

Its Characteristics

As an expression of personality words tend to possess and reflect the same character as their author. God is unchanging, the same yesterday and today and for ever. So His word abides for ever (1 Pet. 1:23); it never passes away, or becomes obsolete, or ceases to be true. Also, God is the living God. So His word is living – a present vital force, the medium of the present expression of His active will. Again, God is the great Doer. His doing is the sure complement of His speaking. So His word is always being fulfilled. It never becomes a dead letter. It 'effectually worketh' in those who believe (1 Thess. 2:13). Finally, because it is God's word its authority is supreme and final. It judges others. It criticizes its would-be critics. It fixes the standard by which all else is measured. When God thus speaks it is like the Time Signal: it must be right. So if all men think differently, they must all be wrong. For when He speaks, God cannot but be vindicated as right (see Rom. 3:4).

Its Confirmation

Everything that helps to show that the Bible is unique and supernatural and divine in origin, serves to confirm its supreme authority. The testimony of the saints individually and of the church of God corporately is very significant and strong. This does not, however, mean that the authority of the church is greater than that of the Bible, any more than the authority of John the Baptist, who bore witness to Christ, was greater than that of Christ. The supreme and decisive witness is that given in the heart of the believer by the Spirit of God. So the Westminster Confession says, 'We may be moved and induced by the testimony of the church to an high and reverend esteem of the Holy Scripture ... yet notwithstanding our full persuasion and assurance of the infallible truth and divine authority thereof is from the inward work of the Holy Spirit bearing witness by and with the word in our hearts.'

Further, we may rightly ground our confidence in the Bible's own claims for itself. If we are, as Christians must, to quote Scripture as our authority for beliefs which are quite beyond our powers to investigate and prove, then to be consistent we ought to accept the testimony of Scripture concerning its own character. It is an inevitable characteristic of the supreme authority that it must be self-authenticating. Because God could swear by no greater, He sware by Himself. Writings which make such claims for themselves as the Scriptures do, must either themselves be a sufficient and final authority, or else their statements on other matters ought to be rejected as equally presumptuous; there is no middle ground.

Also, though we cannot personally verify the authority of the whole of Scripture in all its parts, we may rightly make belief in it an article of faith for two reasons: first, our knowledge of Him whose word it is, and second, our experience of the compelling divine authority of those parts through which God has spoken direct to our own souls (see and study carefully the significance of John 8:31, Mark 11:27-33 and John 5:45-7).

Its Importance

The recognition of the divine authority of Scripture is of supreme importance, because as the expression of God's truth for men – truth fulfilled in Jesus Christ, and in the Scriptures permanently recorded for our learning – the Bible provides a definite objective standard and check, a court of appeal or rule of faith by which the orthodoxy of all opinions can rightly be tested. A Christian is one who by the Spirit confesses Jesus as Lord; but the Christ whom he thus acknowledges himself bound to follow cannot rightly be the Christ of his own fancy and feelings, but must be the Christ of the apostolic testimony, the Christ whose character is only to be fully discerned in all the Scriptures. It is not enough for truth to be 'Christian' and 'spiritual'. If it is to be truly these it must also be 'scriptural'. Supposed Christian sentiment or the imagined leading of the Spirit may only result in departure from the highway of truth and life unless it is based on and is plainly confirmed by the teaching of Scripture (see Isa. 8:20). Further, this scriptural test is all-sufficient. This is the confessed faith of the church as expressed, for instance, in Article VI of the Thirty-Nine Articles of the Church of England. The Holy Scriptures are there declared to be sufficient and to contain all things necessary to salvation. They set the limits as well as the norm of Christian doctrine. 'Whatsoever is not read therein, nor may be proved thereby, is not to be required of any man that it should be believed as an article of the Faith.' The practical application of this test is illustrated in the record of our Lord's temptation. There every attempt of the devil to mislead was countered by the quotation of a principle enunciated in Scripture. Similarly, on other occasions our Lord appealed to Scripture as authoritative and decisive: 'It is written' and 'Thus it must be'.

Its Practical Implications

It is not enough to give these things our assent. Only those really believe who act accordingly. The ultimate issue here is moral and not merely intellectual. We show the real authority we ascribe to Scripture by the daily use we make of it and the obedience we give to its teaching. Christians frequently need to be exhorted afresh to be doers of the word. We ought to go to the Bible more for guidance. We ought to let the voice of the Spirit through the Scriptures settle things in our hearts and our assemblies. We ought to let the inspired word of divine revelation be the final arbiter of our differences and the practical guide book of our counsels. We ought to be brought more to an agreed mind by yielding, not to one another's opinions, but to the compulsion of revealed truth. For we cannot believe in the divine authority of Scripture without being confronted with the solemn responsibility – to obey its Author, whose mind and will are therein made known. Let us pray for grace to show our assent by our obedience.

6

THE INFALLIBILITY OF THE
WORD OF GOD (1952)

Our words 'infallible' and 'infallibility' have in the course of the centuries been used in two different ways, which need to be carefully distinguished. They have been used of persons, particularly since 1870 of the Pope; and in this connection 'infallible' means 'incapable of erring', 'not liable to be deceived or mistaken'. They may also be used of things or statements, like the Bible and its words; and here 'infallible' means 'not liable to fail', 'sure', 'certain' (see *The Shorter Oxford English Dictionary*). The second of these two uses is historically the earlier. This is the sense in which the words were used in the sixteenth and seventeenth centuries, and it is because of their use in this sense then that the use still survives in the same sense with reference to the word of God in some of our evangelical confessions, such as the Inter-Varsity Fellowship Doctrinal Basis, which speaks of the 'infallibility of Holy Scripture'.

This assertion can be at once supported by illustrations. For instance, the word 'infallible' occurs once in the Authorised Version of 1611 in Acts 1:3, where we read that the risen Lord showed Himself alive to the apostles 'after His passion, by many infallible proofs'. In his treatise *On the Lord's Supper*, written in the middle of the previous century, Archbishop Cranmer wrote of Holy Scripture as that 'wherein whatsoever is found must be taken for a sure ground and an infallible truth' (ch. 1); he also referred to 'the true catholic faith grounded upon God's most infallible word' (ch. 17). Similarly, the famous Westminster Confession of the early middle of the seventeenth century speaks of 'the infallible truth and divine authority of Holy Scripture' (ch. 1). In

First published in *Inter-Varsity* (Summer Term 1952).

each of these contexts the word 'infallible' means 'incontrovertible' and 'unassailable', something 'sure' and 'certain', which will never fail, which cannot be brought to nought; something, therefore, absolutely and unchangeably trustworthy.

This fundamental sense of the word is confirmed etymologically by the correspondence of our Latin derivatives 'infallibility' and 'infallible' with the parallel Greek forms ἀσφάλεια and ἀσφαλής which are found in several places in the New Testament and are commonly translated 'certainty' or 'certain' (see Luke 1:4, Acts 21:34, 22:30, 25:26) or 'sure' (in Heb. 6:19, 'as an anchor'). For as our parallel English words make plain, the basic verbal root means 'to fall' or 'to fail'; or, even more originally, 'to cause to fall' or 'to overthrow'. And so with the addition of a negative prefix the compound form ἀσφαλής or 'infallible' describes something which is 'secure' or 'sure', because it cannot be overthrown or because it may be counted on not to fail. This is exactly what Luke wished Theophilus to know concerning the gospel facts in which he had been instructed (see Luke 1:4, and note the occurrence of the significant word ἀσφάλεια translated 'certainty', or, as we might say, 'infallibility').

The rightness of ascribing 'infallibility' in this sense to the words of God can also be confirmed theologically. For a person's words express his essential character. To say of anyone, 'You cannot trust his words', means 'You cannot trust him'. Since, therefore, God is absolutely unchanging and trustworthy these characteristics inevitably distinguish His words. By contrast, so said the prophet (see Isa. 40: 6-8), all flesh is as grass which withers and fades; men have their day and disappear. Similarly their words are authoritative for a time and then become obsolete. How different is God! He does not die and depart, He lives and abides; He is the same yesterday and today and for ever. Similarly His word does not and cannot become obsolete; it cannot lose its worth and become valueless; it lives and abides (see 1 Pet. 1:23-25), it is always true and trustworthy; or, as our forefathers said and we may endorse, it is 'infallible'. It cannot fall or fail through attack from without or through corruption from within. It is, as our Queen will be told at her coronation [in June 1953] when a Bible is given to her, 'The most precious thing which this world affords'. It is, indeed, the only sure and certain thing in the created order. For, as Christ Himself explicitly declared, 'Heaven and earth shall pass away, but My words shall not pass away' (Matt. 24:35).

Because it is in this sense the infallible God-given word, it may be asserted of the Bible that its statements will never deceive or disappoint those who trust in them; its testimony is wholly sure and certain, never false and misleading; so we believe. It is, however, important on the other hand to recognize that the same infallibility cannot be properly predicated of the Bible itself with reference to the way in which it may be used of God to help men to find and to follow the truth. In other words, there may easily be misunderstanding and possible danger in speaking in an unqualified way of the Bible as an infallible 'guide'. For full active 'guidance' is a function of a person, not of a book. Also, the Bible may be and has been misquoted to support error and misused to mislead men. For there is nothing in the Bible, taken by itself, to prevent men from using or understanding it wrongly. In this connection its inherent and essential worth as the infallible word of God only fully functions when it is the present means of communication between the illuminating Spirit and the responsive soul. Whether the understanding and the guidance actually gained by its use are true and trustworthy depends not on the Bible alone, but on the Holy Spirit as the promised infallible Guide into all truth, and on the believing and conscientious obedience of the hearer to what the Spirit thus says to him. This admission, however, does not alter the fundamental fact that rightly understood the written word of God has its own inherent and independent infallibility; and the concern of our evangelical forefathers of the sixteenth and seventeenth centuries in speaking of the infallible truth of Holy Scripture was to assert their conviction that these writings afford a sure and unassailable – because God-given – ground of confidence, a ground which will never become insecure or let the believer down.

Just as there are given facts of history in the incarnation, death and resurrection of Christ which are finished and incontrovertible, and to which we must look for salvation because they have an unfailing or infallible value which is present and eternal, so there are once-for-all given Scriptures similarly made ours by the special intervention and providence of God in history to which we must turn for the only sure and certain light and understanding, promise and hope. Surely, therefore, it is of no small importance for healthy Christian living that we should be able and willing to confess that our confidence in these Scriptures as unfailing or infallible is not misplaced. For this quality is present and eternal; the Scriptures, though written so long ago, are still and always will be infallible. 'For ever, O Lord, Thy word is settled in heaven. Thy faithfulness is unto all generations' (Ps. 119:89-90). The promises and commandments of God never become 'a dead letter'.

The final confirmation of the infallibility of the word of God is, therefore, to be found in its fulfilment. Not one word does or can fail of all that He has spoken (see Josh. 21:45, Matt. 5:18). Not only is God's word true in its testimony about the past, not only is it sure in its interpretation of the eternal significance of what God has done in Christ for our redemption, but it is also sure and certain in its witness to what God will do, in its promises and predictions of God's actions in grace and His intervention in judgment. God's word is 'infallible' as no other word is, because it tells us something sure about the otherwise unknown and uncertain future, something which assuredly will be fulfilled. It is therefore meant, as Paul so plainly asserted, to give us comfort and hope (see Rom. 15:4). It is, as Peter declared, that 'more sure word of prophecy' to which we do well to take heed 'as unto a light that shineth in a dark place' (2 Pet. 1:19).

Of this 'infallibility' we cannot be assured by scientific investigation or logical demonstration. Ultimate faith in the reliability of Scripture is entirely a matter of knowing whom we have believed and of resting on the faithfulness of God, whose word it is. It is entirely a matter of being assured by the witness of the Spirit of God that God has said it, and because He has said it, it is sure of fulfilment, it cannot fail, it is and always will be true; it is, in fact, 'infallible'. So the Westminster Confession declares of Holy Scripture (ch. 1) that 'our full persuasion and assurance of the infallible truth and divine authority thereof is from the inward work of the Holy Spirit, bearing witness by and with the word in our hearts'. Balaam declared long before that 'God is not a man, that He should lie; neither the Son of Man, that He should repent: hath He said, and shall He not do it? or hath He spoken, and shall He not make it good?' (Num. 23:19).

The Bible is, therefore, unique simply and solely because it is 'of God' and not merely 'of men'; and it is our wisdom as well as our high privilege not only thus to confess our faith in its unique character, but also to ground our confidence upon its witness as absolutely and always reliable, as unfailingly true and trustworthy, as sure of ultimate vindication by corresponding fulfilment; as, in a word, 'infallible'.

7

THE WITNESS OF SCRIPTURE
TO ITS INSPIRATION (1958)

The purpose of this essay is to consider the witness of Scripture itself to its own inspiration. To begin with there is a need to distinguish clearly between two different meanings or possible implications of the word 'inspiration' when it is thus used of Holy Scripture. The prevalent ideas associated with this term do not conform to that denotation of the word which has scriptural authority and justification, and which supplies the particular meaning which we have in view in a study of this kind.

Meaning of Inspiration

When the word 'inspiration' is used of the Bible it is often thought to describe a quality belonging primarily to the writers rather than to the writings; it indicates that the men who produced these documents were inspired men. In contrast to this idea, which indubitably has its place, we find that the Scripture employs the word bearing this meaning primarily to describe not the writers but the sacred writings. 2 Timothy 3:16 reads πασα γραφὴ θεόπνευστος. This the Revised Standard Version renders 'All scripture is inspired by God.' Let us here notice three points about this statement.

+ The Greek adjective θεόπνευστος (meaning literally 'God-breathed') is a compound which begins with an explicit recognition of God as the author; the inspiration is divine.

+ The human agents in the production of the Scripture are here not even mentioned.

First published in Carl F.H. Henry (ed.), *Revelation and the Bible: Contemporary Evangelical Thought* (Grand Rapids: Baker, 1958).

◆ The Scripture, or writing thus produced, is here described and is intended to be thought of as 'divinely inspired', or as the Authorised Version renders it, 'given by inspiration of God'.

What, therefore, we are in this essay to consider as inspired, or produced by divine inspiration, is not primarily the condition or activity of the biblical writers, but the biblical writings themselves, the actual written words of Scripture.

Place of Self-Authentication

Some will certainly raise the objection that Scripture ought not thus to be appealed to for its own vindication. To quote Scripture in support of Scripture seems, admittedly, from one standpoint, to be arguing in a circle and to be logically inconclusive. It is important, therefore, to see that in this particular case no occasion exists for such misgiving.

First, let us recognize that every man has surely a right to speak for himself; and that testimony to oneself ought not be ruled out as completely improper. Indeed, if men were not liars and deceivers, or not prejudiced and blind and lacking in full understanding, their own testimony about themselves would be sufficient. Consider the unique example of the perfect Man. Although Jesus recognized that the truth about Himself needed confirmation by independent witness to satisfy normal human standards, he nevertheless said 'Even if I bear witness of myself, my witness is true' (RV, compare John 5:31; 8:13-14).

Not only so, but some truths about people may never be known unless the individuals concerned themselves bear witness to them. If what they thus say is unreliable, no other means of discovering the truth may exist. Somewhat similarly, the Bible discloses from God Himself truths which cannot otherwise be discovered. For our knowledge of them we are wholly dependent upon divine revelation thus communicated through the Scriptures. Surely no justification exists for thus believing what the Bible teaches about other doctrines wholly beyond independent human confirmation, if we cannot equally rely completely on what the Bible teaches about itself. Moreover, if we are to accept Scripture as our supreme rule of faith and understanding in the one, we ought similarly to do so in the other. In other words, we cannot rightly turn to the Bible for testimony to the otherwise unknown unless we do accept also its testimony to itself.

In the third place, if we believe that the Bible not only claims to be, but is, a book from God, then behind and beyond all its human writers and contributing agents God Himself must be acknowledged as its author; and God cannot lie. His word is always true and always trustworthy. The Bible's witness to itself ought, therefore, to be treated as authoritative and decisive; in a very real sense we need none other.

When men wish to confirm witness given about themselves they appeal to one greater; they take an oath and swear by almighty God. Similarly, when God wished to make men doubly sure of His word of promise, He confirmed it by an oath. But when He came to swear, since there was none greater by whom He could swear, He swore by Himself (Heb. 6:13-18). He thus made Himself the guarantor of the truth and trustworthiness of His own word. This supremely illustrates the principle that in any realm of activity the supreme authority must be self-authenticating. It is impossible to get endorsement or confirmation of such utterances by appeal to some greater authority. Similarly, if the Bible is from God and therefore possesses supreme authority among men in what it says, it cannot be other than self-authenticating. Truth is settled by what it says rather than by what others may say about it or in criticism of it.

Finally, relief from the possible embarrassment of dependence upon a single witness – and that in this case the witness of Scripture to itself – is provided by the Trinity and the eternity of the Godhead. For God is Three in One; and God still speaks. So the truth and trustworthiness of Scripture, as the authoritative and unbreakable divine word, are confirmed to the Christian believer by the witness during his earthly life of the incarnate Son of God, and by the present continuing witness of the illuminating and indwelling Spirit of God.

What Scripture Declares About Itself

Let us now consider in detail some of the statements made in Scripture about itself and its production. Such statements, we shall note, inevitably bear witness also to Scripture's consequent distinctive character and authority.

All Scripture is 'God-breathed'

We have noted that in 2 Timothy 3:16, 'All scripture is inspired by God' (rsv), the Greek adjective θεόπνευστος means literally 'God-breathed', that is, 'inspired of God'. The word 'inspired', however, is not to be understood as indicating something 'extra' superimposed on the writer or writing, to make the writing different from what it would otherwise be. It indicates rather how the writing came into being. It asserts that the writing is a product of the creative activity of the divine breath. The word thus goes right back to the beginning or first cause of the emergence of Scripture, and indicates that Scripture has in its origin this distinctive hallmark, that it owes its very existence to the direct creative activity of God Himself. Although men wrote it, it is God who brought it into being. Its content and character have all been decisively determined by the originating and controlling activity of the creative Spirit. For this reason the context affirms that Scripture is profitable 'for teaching, for reproof, for correction, and for training for righteousness', since its character and quality, and indeed its very existence, are God-determined.

This idea of God 'breathing' and of the divine 'breath' is familiar to students of the Old Testament. It is a graphic metaphor applied to the activity of God, especially to the Holy Spirit, who is the executor of the Godhead. So we read in Psalm 33:6, 'By the word of the Lord were the heavens made; and all the host of them by the breath of his mouth.' The breath of God is thus almighty to create. By this breath not only the heavens but also man was created. 'And the Lord God formed man of the dust of the ground, and breathed into his nostrils the breath of life; and man became a living soul' (Gen. 2:7). Or again, we read in Job 33:4, 'The Spirit of God hath made me, and the breath of the Almighty hath given me life.' The breath or breathing of God speaks, therefore, of the activity of the One who is the first and final cause of all things. Scripture is said to be the product of His activity, the work of the Holy Spirit of God Himself. Nor should we overlook that what is thus said to be Spirit-produced is the actual written word. Its emergence and its enduring record were the consummation and intended goal of the Spirit's activity.

Men spake from God

The ascription to Scripture of this special divine origin and consequent unique character is either explicitly or implicitly confirmed as true by many statements made elsewhere in the Bible. For instance, in 2 Peter 1:19-21 the prophetic word given to us in Scripture is said to be the more sure, and a source of light in our darkness to which we ought to give heed, because of its extraordinary and divine origin. Let us note carefully the sequence of thought in Peter's reasoning. 'First of all', he writes, 'you must understand this, that no prophecy of scripture is a matter of one's own interpretation, because no prophecy ever came by the impulse of man, but men moved by the Holy Spirit spoke from God' (RSV).

So the primary truth about Scripture, the very first thing we need to recognize about it, is that no prophecy in it was produced or can be interpreted through any individual man acting independently and alone. Genuine prophecies and their true interpretation do not just break forth 'from man'. The Spirit of God brings such prophecies to expression to reveal the mind of God; and the same Spirit alone can make plain, to those who hear and study these prophecies, what that mind is.

This essential dependence of true prophecy upon God and not upon man is primarily shown in the way in which it came to exist at all. For it was not brought into being simply by any man's desire, decision and determination to give it utterance. It is not 'from man'. Man is not the prime mover in its production. Indeed, man acting independently and solely on his own will and initiative cannot produce it. For true prophecy has never emerged, except when men have been taken up into an activity of the Spirit of God, and borne along to the place or into the circumstances and the conditions where they gave utterance to words of which God was the primary originating cause. Clearly, therefore, what matters most for us is the actual words they were thus enabled to express. The enduring God-given witness to the truth is contained in, and conveyed by, the writing. These words, therefore, we ought to accept as brought into being by the Spirit of God for our instruction. They have supreme and final authority because they are from God Himself. He is their real author.

In any attempt to appreciate the method of inspiration, or the way in which men specially chosen and prepared were moved to speak divinely intended words, it becomes us, as finite creatures, to recognize in humility and with reverent awe that the ways of God are past finding out. Men still cannot fully tell how a human child is brought to birth and a new independent personality created. In a very real sense a baby has human parents and is 'born of woman'. Yet in a deeper sense it is 'of God'. If this is true of ordinary child-birth, how very much more was it true of the birth of him who was 'conceived of the Holy Ghost, born of the virgin Mary'. Also, it seems in harmony with the revealed truth of God to suggest that a similarity in principle prevails between the manner of the birth of the incarnate Word of God and the method of the composition of the written word of God. Scripture was, so to speak, 'conceived or inspired of the Holy Ghost, and thought and uttered by human prophets'. Scripture is obviously the work of human writers; and yet it is still more the product and result of a special and supernormal activity of the Spirit. So we may rightly believe it to possess a corresponding perfection.

In thus considering the divine inspiration of Scripture, the difficulty for the human mind is to reconcile the perfection of the divine determination of the finished product with the true freedom and inevitable imperfections of the human writers. How can these two characteristics both apply to the production of Scripture? In principle this problem is only a particular form of the general difficulty always involved in any attempt to reconcile divine predestination and human freewill.

A significant scriptural illustration of the joint working of human freedom and divine predetermination is provided by the one utterance of Caiaphas which is said to be prophecy. To his fellow-members of the Jewish Sanhedrin he said, 'It is expedient for us that one man should die for the people, and that the whole nation perish not' (John 11:50). In their immediate historical setting the meaning of these words is obvious enough. They were a counsel of political expediency. It was better, as Caiaphas saw it, to make Jesus a scapegoat and to sacrifice one life, than to risk a popular messianic uprising. For such an uprising could only call forth a drastic Roman intervention, and then the priestly aristocracy, to which Caiaphas belonged, would be the first to suffer. Such was the meaning intended by human freedom.

These words of Caiaphas were thought worthy of a place in the gospel record for an entirely different reason, however. The evangelist interpreted them prophetically, as words not from Caiaphas but from God. He saw the meaning intended by the controlling Spirit. To him the words were a revelation – a revelation all the more remarkable because it was so completely hidden from the mind of the man who uttered the words. 'And this spake he', writes John (11:51), 'not of himself [note the words] but being the high priest that year, he prophesied that Jesus should die for that nation.' For the high priest had a yearly office which only he could fulfill, that is, on the Day of Atonement to make a propitiation for the sin of the people with the blood of sacrifice. And none other than he, fulfilling his own priestly office in a way far beyond his knowing, gave counsel to the Jews that in this year, the year when all types were fulfilled, it was expedient that a man, not an animal victim, die for the people. He designated, as it were, the sacrifice which was to take away sin and procure salvation. And so his words about the death of Jesus appear in the Scriptures not as an expression of the natural mind of Caiaphas, though on the lower level they are expressive of this, but as an expression of the mind of the Spirit, revealing the purpose of

God thus to provide the sacrificial Lamb to take away the sin of God's people.

If, therefore, the inspiring Spirit can thus secure the utterance of divinely intended words from the mouth of an opponent of Christ, and words actually spoken by him in an entirely different sense from their divinely intended meaning, is it unreasonable to believe that all words of Scripture – many of them spoken and written by devout saints and uniquely illumined souls – are, all of them, to be received not chiefly nor exclusively as from man, but rather and primarily from God? It behoves us, therefore, submissively to receive them as an expression of the divine mind and as intended to contribute toward our better understanding of God's ways.

Words of prophets and apostles were God-given

If we are to do full justice to the witness of Scripture concerning its inspiration, another necessary and rewarding study pertains to the biblical use of the term 'prophet', and the biblical indication of how true prophets function.

What distinguishes and characterizes the prophets of Scripture is that they were men unto whom 'the word of God came'. As simply stated by a writer a century ago, the biblical term 'prophet' constantly designates 'a man whose mouth utters the words of God'.[1] 'A prophet in the Bible is a man in whose mouth God puts the words which he wishes to be heard upon earth.' To illustrate this meaning on the more human level, let us notice the description given in Scripture of Aaron's relation to Moses as his spokesman. It is recorded that God said to Moses, 'Thou shalt speak unto him, and put words in his mouth... And he shall be thy spokesman unto the people; and he shall be ... to thee instead of a mouth, and thou shalt be to him instead of God' (Exod. 4:15-16). Again later, God said, 'See, I have made thee a god to Pharaoh: and Aaron thy brother shall be thy prophet' (Exod. 7:1). Clearly, therefore, a prophet is one who speaks words which God puts into his mouth.

Next, let us observe from the record in 1 Samuel 3, how Samuel was 'established to be a prophet of the Lord', and how 'all Israel from Dan even to Beersheba knew'. The chapter dramatically records his first experience of the word of God coming to him. It was not a private message for his own soul, but a word about Eli that had to be publicly

---

[1] Louis Gaussen, *Theopneustia: The Plenary Inspiration of the Holy Scriptures* (London, 1841), p. 62 [reprinted in 2008 as *The Divine Inspiration of Scripture* by Christian Heritage, an imprint of Christian Focus Publications].

uttered. He was thereby called to become a prophet, and to speak forth the word which God had thus given to him. From then on this became his repeated experience. The Lord revealed himself to Samuel in Shiloh by the word of the Lord. And the word of Samuel came to all Israel.'

It was through the burden and constraint of such an experience of being given God's words to proclaim that prophets said with conviction, and unmistakable awareness, 'Thus saith the Lord.' It was clear that thereby they meant, 'These are not my ideas, but words from God himself, which I simply must declare.' Such was the irresistible urge, and at times the almost intolerable burden, of being compelled to become the Lord's mouthpiece. 'The Lord God hath spoken, who can but prophesy?' (Amos 3:8).

Here we cannot do better than let Scripture provide its own explicit and repeated witness through a selection of quotations. All indicate in different ways that the prophets' spoken and written words were God-given. When they had declared their message, it was characteristic of the prophets, for instance, to add 'For the mouth of the Lord hath spoken it' (Isa. 40:5, 58:14, Micah 4:4). Jeremiah looks for the man 'to whom the mouth of the Lord hath spoken, that he may declare it' (Jer. 9:12). Aaron is said to have spoken to the elders of the children of Israel 'all the words which the Lord hath spoken unto Moses' (Exod. 4:30). David declares, 'The Spirit of the Lord spake by me, and his word was in my tongue' (2 Sam. 23:2). The Lord is said to have 'put a word in Balaam's mouth' (Num. 23:5). Similarly 'the word of God came upon Shemaiah the man of God' (1 Kings 12:22). And God said unto Jeremiah, 'Behold, I have put my words in thy mouth' (Jer. 1:9); and to Ezekiel, 'Thou shalt speak my words unto them' (Ezek. 2:7).

The unmistakable scriptural testimony, therefore, is that in their inspired utterances David and the prophets functioned as the mouth of the Holy Spirit. The Apostle Peter explicitly acknowledged this in the very early days of the church. He appealed, for instance, to 'this scripture ... which the Holy Ghost by the mouth of David spake before concerning Judas' (Acts 1:16). He prayed to God as himself the author of Psalm 2, 'who by the mouth of thy servant David hast said, Why did the heathen rage?' (Acts 4:25). Similarly Zacharias recalled what God 'spake by the mouth of his holy prophets' (Luke 1:70). So according to the language and witness of the Scriptures its prophecies may be said to be the words of God put into, or expressed through, the mouth of man.

The evidence about prophetic utterance thus far adduced concerns primarily the period and the production of the Old Testament Scriptures. The New Testament also, however, contains some explicit witness to similar activity by the inspiring Spirit, giving to the apostles right utterance in the things of God for the edification of His church. When Christ Himself had warned his commissioned witnesses about the opposition they would meet, and about the ways in which they would need to answer charges brought against them, He had said, 'But when they deliver you up, take no thought how or what ye shall speak: for it shall be given you in that same hour what ye shall speak. For it is not ye that speak, but the Spirit of your Father which speaketh in you' (Matt. 10:19-20). Christ also promised His apostles similar divine cooperation in the recording of His own work and teaching when He said of the Spirit, 'He shall teach you all things, and bring all things to your remembrance, whatsoever I have said unto you' (John 14:26). He similarly promised that the Spirit would guide them into all truth by speaking to them words from God and from Christ. For as Christ said, even the Spirit speaks 'not of himself; but whatsoever he shall hear, that shall he speak ... for he shall receive of mine, and shall shew it unto you' (John 16:13-14).

We find, too, in confirmation of this that Paul later testifies that his apostolic insight and utterance are wholly Spirit-given. He says that the purposes of God in Christ toward men, and the things prepared for them, are wholly beyond the natural perception and imagination of men; but that God has revealed them to his apostles by his Spirit, and that they are by the same Spirit enabled to give right expression to them 'not in the words which man's wisdom teacheth, but which the Holy Ghost teacheth' (1 Cor. 2:9-13). So in New Testament and Old Testament alike, the very words of apostles and prophets were God-given.

In this connection it is also noteworthy that the men whom the Spirit of God thus used to utter his messages were conscious at times of the compulsion of both divine constraint and restraint. On the one hand, they had to declare all the God-given words; on the other, they could not add other words of their own choosing. This compulsion is particularly noticeable in the case of the prophets who would have chosen to speak differently if they could; but they could not. So Balaam said, and repeated, 'If Balak would give me his house full of silver and gold, I cannot go beyond the commandment of the Lord, to do either good or bad of mine own mind; but what the Lord saith, that will I speak' (Num. 22:18; 24:13). Similarly Micaiah, when urged to speak good unto King Ahab and not evil, answered, 'As the Lord liveth, what the Lord saith unto me, that will I speak' (1 Kings 22:13-14).

The prophets' sense of compulsion to speak their God-given words, and these only, is significantly complemented in Scripture by a solemn injunction and ultimately by a severe warning to all who read God-given words, not to add to or take away from what is written. So in Deuteronomy 4:2 we read, 'Ye shall not add unto the word which I command you, neither shall ye diminish ought from it'; and in Revelation 22:18-19, in the section which by God's providential overruling closes the whole Canon of Scripture, we read, 'For I testify unto every man that heareth the words of the prophecy of this book, If any man shall add unto these things, God shall add unto him the plagues that are written in this book: and if any man shall take away from the words of the book of this prophecy, God shall take away his part out of the book of life, and out of the holy city, and from the things which are written in this book.'

Scripture quoted in Scripture as the word of God Himself

When parts of Scripture already recorded are quoted in Scripture by later writers, it is noteworthy that the words thus quoted are sometimes introduced simply as words spoken by God, or as being the utterance of the Lord given through a human prophet. Significantly, too, this characteristic applies not only to those words which in the Old Testament are explicitly said to be utterances of God, but also to words from other parts of the Scripture as well.

So in the Gospel according to Matthew, for instance, Old Testament quotations are introduced which are said to have been 'spoken by the Lord through the prophet' (RV), or 'what the Lord had spoken by the prophet' (RSV) (see Matt. 1:22; 2:15). Also, our Lord Himself in His discussions with the Pharisees about divorce, according to Matthew 19:3-6, not only quoted Genesis 2:24 as an authoritative statement about marriage, but explicitly introduced it as a statement made by the Creator Himself at the time of man's creation. 'Have ye not read', said Jesus, 'that he which made them at the beginning made them male and female, and said, For this cause shall a man leave father and mother, and shall cleave to his wife: and they twain shall be one flesh?' Furthermore, our Lord treated this statement as a decisive authoritative expression of the divine mind and purpose about marriage, sufficient in itself to justify the deduction that for men to separate those joined in marriage by divine appointment is wholly improper. Here, therefore, because divine in origin, words from these ancient Jewish writings are appealed to as determining for all time what is proper in the marriage relationship.

Later in Hebrews 1:7-8, words about God, spoken in praise by the Psalmist, are quoted as spoken by God Himself and therefore as carrying decisive weight and authority. We read, 'And of the angels he saith, Who maketh his angels spirits, and his ministers a flame of fire' (a quotation from Ps. 104:4). 'But unto the Son he saith, Thy throne, O God, is for ever and ever' (a quotation from Ps. 45:6).

Not only are words from the Old Testament thus introduced as spoken by God himself, but sometimes in the New Testament they are used as words having present application, because the living unchanging God is speaking them now. They are his present words for today. So 2 Corinthians 6:16 quotes words from Leviticus 26:12, 'I will dwell in them and walk in them, and I will be their God, and they shall be my people', to indicate God's present purpose for his redeemed people, and to justify Paul's appeal to his readers that they separate themselves from idolatry and uncleanness. Similarly, in Hebrews 3:7 words from Psalm 95:7, 'Today if ye will hear his voice', are quoted not as words spoken by the Psalmist long ago, but as words being spoken in the present by God the Spirit – 'as the Holy Ghost saith'.

Scripture, therefore – so Scripture itself bears witness – may be used as a means of present living communion between God and the individual soul. For what God has once said he may be regarded as still saying (except, of course, where his own fuller revelation has superseded what was previously given only in part or in figure); and responsive words which believers of old have thus been stirred to utter, believers today may rightly still make their own. For example, in Hebrews 13.5-6, we read, 'Be content with such things as ye have: for he hath said, I will never leave thee, nor forsake thee [a quotation from Josh. 1:5]. So that we may boldly say, The Lord is my helper, and I will not fear what man shall do unto me [a quotation from Ps. 118:6].'

All this rich wealth of meaning and usage still to be found in Scripture is possible only because it can be treated and trusted as divinely provided for the permanent enrichment of God's people. It is, therefore, to be regarded and used as God-given, words issued on his authority and therefore words of supreme and unchanging worth. Such then is Scripture's own witness to the character and consequence of its divine inspiration.

Divinely-intended purpose of Scripture

Since the direction of too much attention to the details of the process of the production of Scripture by human writers may only perplex us with questions which we cannot answer, it is well that we should recognize that any workman's activity is to be properly understood and appreciated only in the light of his aim and ultimate achievement. This means that in seeking to estimate the full significance of the divine inspiration of the Bible, we should not primarily look at the materials, the men and the method used in its composition, but consider rather the finished product as a whole in the light of its divinely intended purpose. For the completed revelation of Scripture, taken as a whole, is meant to serve ends which cannot be served by its constituent parts or contributing human authors and sources taken independently.

Modern historical and literary criticism, with its excess of devotion to analysis and source criticism, has largely been a movement in the wrong direction which has often involved a real disregard both of the true source and of the proper purpose of the inspiration of Scripture. It is important, therefore, that we recognize the twofold end of Scripture as a divinely inspired whole. This is, in the first place, Christological and in the second, soteriological. The purpose of Scripture is, first, to testify of Christ, 'For the testimony of Jesus is the spirit of prophecy' (Rev. 19:10). In the volume of the book it is written of him (see Heb. 10:7). The purpose of Scripture is, second, to make men 'wise unto salvation through faith which is in Christ Jesus' (2 Tim. 3:15). Scripture has been inspired of God to promote the salvation of the world. The Scripture was written, and Christ died and rose again in fulfilment of its prophetic revelation, that repentance and remission of sins might be preached in Christ's name to all nations (see Luke 24:46-47). The New Testament was added to the Old Testament in fulfilment of the promise that the Holy Spirit would guide the apostles into all the truth about the Christ (see John 16:12-15). The full significance of the divine inspiration of Scripture can, therefore, be seen in its proper context only if it is seen as an essential part of the redeeming activity of God for the salvation of mankind.

Scripture serves this divine purpose by providing a true record of what God has done in history for man's salvation, and of those events which under God's providence have happened and been recorded for man's instruction. This record is by divine inspiration doubly true. On the one hand, it is historically reliable; it corresponds in its witness to what happened. On the other hand, it is sublime and perfect in its discernment and presentation of spiritual values. These two complementary senses in which the scriptural record is true are explicitly emphasized in John 19:35, 'And he that hath seen hath borne witness, and his witness is true: and he knoweth that he saith true, that ye also may believe' (RV). Here John means that what he says is true or factually accurate, for he speaks as an eyewitness; and that his form of presentation is 'ideal' (Greek ἀληθινὸς), in harmony with and an adequate expression of the true meaning and value of the events thus recorded, a presentation intended to lead the reader to faith in the person and work of Christ.

For its proper use Scripture, which bears such witness to its own divine inspiration demands, from those readers who are enlightened by God's Spirit to share in this conviction about it, the submission of unquestioning acceptance. For Scripture provides, not data to be critically sorted out for acceptance or rejection before we can know the truth, but data to be treated as true and trustworthy and of supreme worth, data within whose witness all pursuit of the truth must work, if such pursuit is to progress in proper understanding and enjoyment of all the truth which God has thus been pleased to reveal.

Final Practical Authentication

Scripture itself explicitly mentions two distinguishing characteristics by which words which claim to be divine in origin may be recognized as genuine, because corresponding in character to their author.

One test is the test of fulfilment (see Deut. 18:21-22, Matt. 5:18). For God does not move indecisively. He never speaks without completing his purpose (see Num. 23:19). Fulfilment of Scripture is, therefore, one of the proofs of its divine inspiration. So when Scripture witnesses to its own fulfilment, or declares that what it says must yet find fulfilment, it confirms its own witness that Scripture is divinely inspired.

The other test of the divine origin of words is the test of unchanging endurance, in contrast to the words of men which have their day and become obsolete. For in the last analysis all words are like their authors in character. Since men are like the grass that withers, their words similarly cease to carry weight and become a dead letter. But not so with God. He lives and abides. He never changes. He is the same yesterday and today and forever. So when he speaks His words correspond in character to their author. They too have enduring and abiding worth. Therefore Scripture's unfailing survival and strength as a fresh, living, undeniable word of truth in every generation confirm its divine origin. In a world of transient glory, in the midst of an insecure and impermanent created order, the scriptural word, and the scriptural word alone, not only continues to confront each generation anew, but increasingly vindicates its truth in fulfilment. 'Heaven and earth shall pass away', said Jesus, 'but my words shall not pass away' (Matt. 24:35). 'For all flesh is as grass, and all the glory of man as the flower of grass. The grass withereth, and the flower thereof falleth away: but the word of the Lord endureth for ever' (1 Pet. 1:24-25).

8

JUSTIFICATION BY FAITH:
THE REINSTATEMENT OF THE DOCTRINE TODAY
(1952)

The title of this paper virtually makes two assumptions, first that the doctrine of justification by faith ought to be reinstated because it is worthy, and second that it needs to be reinstated because it is neglected and does not hold the place that it should either in our praise to God or in our preaching to men. A proper sense of its full glory and wonder is weak, if not lacking, among many Christians. What is worse, there is no consciousness that truth of inestimable value is lying unappreciated; we are not aware that we are losing much by our failure to dwell upon it. Indeed, to many who occasionally try to think about it, it seems rather unreal, theoretical and abstract; it has even been disparagingly described as a legal fiction, a method of reasoning by which it is pretended that something is true which is not true. So thinkers and preachers pursue it no further; and it is certainly not preached from our pulpits as it ought to be.

Not only so, many Christians who personally rejoice before God in the blessings of justification by faith cannot worthily declare to others what they themselves enjoy. So the truth is not preached and taught as it ought to be even by them, because its theology is inadequately understood; and this unsatisfactory situation is made worse because able thinkers, with no evangelical experience of its truth, often misunderstand it themselves and then misrepresent it to others in their teaching. Also, the ancient historic creeds, which in our day many tend to regard as an adequate theological basis for Christian reunion, make no explicit mention of justification by faith, while the great Reformation confessions, which do recognize the importance and expound the truth of this doctrine, tend to be obscured and forgotten.

A paper read to the Tyndale Fellowship Summer School at Cambridge in July 1951, first published in the *Evangelical Quarterly* vol. 24 (July 1952).

Is it not time, therefore, to ask whether Luther was wrong when he asserted that justification by faith is the article by which the church stands or falls? Or was the discernment of the late Dr H.R. Mackintosh at fault when he wrote, 'The doctrine of justification by faith ... has a way of turning up again with new majesty and power in every period of revival'?[1] Or was Paul a fool when he chose to suffer the loss of all things that he might gain Christ and be found in Him, not having a righteousness of his own, which is of the law, but that which is through faith in Christ, the righteousness which is of God by faith? (see Phil. 3:7-9). Or ought we to wake up to our own error, our own lack of discernment, our own folly in choosing? Ought we to choose afresh and to set ourselves to reinstate the truth which is after all the indispensable secret of personal salvation, of spiritual revival, and of the very existence of the true church of God?

If we are thus to move towards worthy reinstatement we need first of all to realize that the very phrase 'justification by faith' tends to limit or misdirect us by its incompleteness. It would be theologically wiser, and in practice more profitable, always to state explicitly by whom and in relation to whom the believer is justified, in whom his faith rests and who is thus justified when he does believe. In other words, we ought to speak not merely of 'justification by faith', but rather of 'the justification of the sinner by God and in God's sight by faith in Christ, crucified and exalted'. This would then make plain that 'justification by faith' is no mere legal fiction or subjective fancy, no mere formal dogma or illusory experience, but an action of God wrought in the sphere of our personal and individual relation to Him.

In his book on *F.D. Maurice and the Conflicts of Modern Theology*, Professor A.M. Ramsey summarizes Maurice's exposure of the weakness of the protestant by saying, 'The Protestant, because he treats his principle of justification by faith as a shibboleth, slips from faith in Christ the justifier into belief in an experience of being justified, and great is the fall.'[2] However unfair this may be as a generalization, let us acknowledge its measure of truth, let us heed its implied warning, and let us fix our faith and urge others to place theirs not in a dogma nor in an experience of justification, but in the living God who justifies us freely by His grace through the redemption that is in Christ Jesus.

Similarly, in the second place, if the doctrine of justification by faith is to be properly appreciated and thus worthily reinstated, it ought not to

---

[1] H.R. Mackintosh, *The Christian Experience of Forgiveness* (London, 1938), p. 5.
[2] A.M. Ramsey, *F.D. Maurice and the Conflicts of Modern Theology* (Cambridge, 1951), p. 29.

be considered in isolation, but rather viewed from varied standpoints in explicit relation to every essential feature of the gospel. For instance, the apostle Paul has indicated that the meaning of 'to be justified' needs to be interpreted in the divine and eternal context of being foreknown, foreordained and called by God on the one hand, and being glorified by Him on the other (see Rom. 8:28-30). Let us then survey more in detail and one by one these complementary considerations which are indispensable to the full and worthy understanding of justification by faith.

The Sovereignty of God in Holiness and Grace

We need with fresh acknowledgement and full awareness to be recalled to the recognition that God is sovereign in the universe, the First and Final Cause of all things; and particularly we need to be recalled to the conscious confession that the only righteousness which ultimately matters is to be accepted as right in God's sight and to be acting in harmony with His will. In contrast to the godless or secular thought so widely and so subtly prevalent, we need deliberately to return to theocentric thinking, in which from first to last God is the supreme pole or rather Person of universal reference. Sin can, for instance, only be seen in its true character and full horror if it is seen not just as transgression of some impersonal law but rather as rebellion against God and His appointed ways.

What matters supremely is not just that right is right and wrong is wrong, but that God is God and that He loves righteousness and hates iniquity. Things sinful are the inevitable objects of His wrath. In relation to the sinner the God of holiness is a consuming fire. Yet in His sovereign freedom to do His own pleasure, this same God delights to show mercy to the unworthy and the undeserving, and to devise means by which the estranged should be reconciled and the banished reinstated. Nor are these two complementary activities of holiness and grace satisfactorily held together in outworked harmony anywhere else except in the propitiation of Christ's sacrifice, and in the consequent gospel which offers to the sinful God's own way of being Himself just and yet at the same time the justifier of him who has faith in Jesus (see Rom. 3:21-28).

The Primary and Final Authority of the Word of God

Nothing has perhaps undermined more our hold on and appreciation of the truth of justification by faith than modern criticism of the Bible;

for it has subtly deprived most of us of any adequate awareness of the supreme sanction belonging to the God-given word. We need to realize afresh and with compelling force that what settles things in the universe is God's will as it is declared by His word. Once God speaks, then, either it is or it shall be as He says. Of this there can be no final gainsaying, for every word will be vindicated by corresponding fulfilment. Therefore, there can be nothing more certain and secure than this. So our Lord Himself said, 'Heaven and earth shall pass away, but my words shall not pass away' (Mark 13:31).

Nothing, therefore, can be more important and more decisive for the individual man, and most of all for the convicted sinner, than to be declared righteous by God Himself. For if God says that in His sight I am righteous, then I am righteous. I may boldly ask, as did Paul, 'Who shall lay anything to the charge of God's elect? It is God that justifieth; who is he that shall condemn?' (Rom. 8:33-34). I now have no possible accuser or gainsayer to fear in earth, heaven or hell. Nor is this word of God an empty declaration or legal fiction, pretending that something is which is not. For His word is the decisive and creative word. What He declares is thereby constituted essential truth and infallible or incontrovertible fact.

For instance, if it is proper in this British Realm to regard a verdict of the High Court or an Act of Parliament to which the Royal Assent has been given as decisive, as indeed a word that can henceforth be acted on or proved operative, how much more is the solemnly declared word of the living God decisive in heaven itself. If the former borough of Cambridge, recently declared a city by Royal Charter [in March 1951], is now rightly able publicly to call itself a city, how much more may I who still know myself to be a sinner say with Luther – a sinner, yes, but 'simul iustus et peccator'. For by the double sanction of God's word and covenant I have incontestable right to confess that as a believer in Christ and His redeeming work I am justified with God. Is not this something to wonder at and to glory in – the gracious pleasure and the royal writ of the divine King, who has given me the standing of being righteous in His sight? For if God calls me 'righteous', who can call me otherwise? Is not this a boldness and a glorying which we need to see reinstated in our worship and our witness?

To this one may add that in the day in which we now live the fact that justification by faith is a revealed and scriptural doctrine, is in some quarters not only an original but also an up-to-date advantage. For in the book previously quoted, Professor A.M. Ramsey has written of our times:

The climate of thought has so changed that theologians commonly see it as their function not to demonstrate the validity of the Christian faith by the methods of contemporary secular thought so much as to study the Biblical revelation in its own categories and to draw from it some light to guide our steps in a dark world where diabolical forces are seeking whom they may devour.[3]

Man's Guilty, Helpless and Hopeless State as a Sinner

In comparatively recent times just as many have, on the one hand, lost faith in the supreme authority of God's word, so they have, on the other hand, become blind to the extreme gravity of their own sinfulness. There has been, as we all know, a period of humanistic optimism, a belief in natural evolution and inevitable progress. No wonder the relevance and the glory of the evangelical doctrine of the justification by God of the ungodly and the sinner ceased to be fully appreciated. In the last forty years, however, such hopes of human progress have been not only violently shaken but almost completely shattered. There is in consequence a new readiness to recognize the essential truth of the Christian insight concerning the inherent sinfulness and frustrating impotence of human nature. This new sense of depravity and proneness to despair provide just the field for the reinstatement of this doctrine of the salvation by God of the sinful and unworthy, this doctrine of a complete change in life's fundamental relations not only to things and people but above all to God Himself; a change offered, not as a reward of merit or as a prize to be won by good works, but as a free initial gift of divine grace to all who, confessing their need and unworthiness, cast themselves on the justifying mercy of God and the propitiating work of the God-given Saviour.

In contrast to the Englishman's inveterate Pelagianism, his persistent belief that God helps those who help themselves, there are fresh need and opportunity to make men aware and to proclaim that God helps those who cannot help themselves and who do not deserve to be helped either; and that our Lord Himself taught that it was the publican who acknowledged with shame his sinfulness and counted on God's provision of propitiation, who went home justified with God rather than the Pharisee, who could honestly enough protest, by comparison, how much he had done of righteousness or had not done of sin. This message of the free justification of the sinful is the distinctive glory of the Christian gospel. Also, as our Lord made equally plain, there are in the

---

[3] Ramsey, *Maurice*, p. 111.

end only these two alternatives – either condemnation or justification, either to exalt ourselves and be divinely humbled or to humble ourselves and be divinely exalted (see Luke 18:9-14). Such is the message which ought afresh to be clearly sounded forth.

The Substitutionary and Penal Death of Christ

It is no mere chance coincidence that at the time of the Reformation a penal and substitutionary doctrine of the atoning work of Christ and the full wonder and significance of the doctrine of justification by faith were appreciated and emphasized together. For the two doctrines are interdependent and complementary. The second rests upon the first as an indispensable and divinely ordained foundation. It was the Christ who was first delivered up for our offences, who was then raised again for our justification (see Rom. 4:25). He had first to be lifted up on the tree to bear the sinner's condemnation as one cursed of God, before He was lifted up to the throne in vindication to secure the sinner's acceptance in God's presence; and both happened to Him as our substitute or proxy or federal head. Again to quote significant New Testament words, 'Him who knew no sin God made to be sin on our behalf; that we might become the righteousness of God in Him' (2 Cor. 5:21).

Justification, therefore, is no empty pretence, no mere legal fiction, because although given to the sinner freely and apart from works, it does depend upon an objective work of propitiation wrought by Christ on the sinner's behalf and indeed in the sinner's stead. For Scripture does not teach that human sin can simply be pardoned. An objective work of redemption and remission is needed to set the sinner free from his burden and his guilt, and to give him a new standing of freedom and acceptance before God. This is exactly what is now ours because of what Christ has done for us. We cannot, therefore, reinstate the preaching of justification by faith without reinstating the preaching of a substitutionary and penal doctrine of Christ's atoning work. So it is of no small significance that, in spite of violent antagonism to the very idea on the part of many, there is a fresh readiness in more than one quarter to recognize that a substitutionary and penal doctrine of the atonement may, after all, be what Scripture teaches.[4]

---

[4] See J.P. Hickinbotham, 'The Atonement in St Mark's Gospel', *Churchman* vol. 58 (April 1944); F.W. Camfield, 'The Idea of Substitution in the Doctrine of the Atonement', *Scottish Journal of Theology* vol. 1 (December 1948); A.M. Hunter, *The Work and Words of Jesus* (London, 1950), pp. 91-100; Leon Morris, 'The Use of ἱλάσκεσθαι etc in Biblical Greek', *Expository Times* vol. 62 (May 1951).

The True Significance of Christ's Resurrection and Exaltation to the Throne

The doctrine of justification by faith, the certain fact of the sinner's full acceptance as righteous in God's presence only through faith in Christ, is not realized and preached as it ought to be by many, because they know no corresponding certainty that Christ's atoning work is finished and that He Himself as our High Priest is already fully accepted by God and enthroned at His right hand. They suppose rather that Christ is still making atonement by eternally presenting Himself to the Father as the Lamb that was slain. If, therefore, the Christ Himself in heaven is still only working towards our ultimate justification, justification can only be viewed and preached as a goal towards which believers are moving rather than as a God-given relation to God in which by grace they already and unalterably stand.

Such views, that the Christ in heaven and His church on earth, by the continual offering to God of His sacrifice, are making propitiation for sin and thus winning ultimate justification, sound devout and humble and are obviously attractive to the religiously minded, but they are not scriptural. Indeed, they involve a fundamental and God-dishonouring denial of the eternal sufficiency of Christ's one sacrifice, finished once for all; and they completely deprive believers of the proper evangelical assurance of present and permanent peace with God. What we need to reinstate, therefore, is the preaching to believers of the glorious gospel truth that at the very throne of God Himself none can deny our access or condemn us as sinners. For there on the throne we have God Himself in Christ as our justifier. He who died for us and was raised from the dead is now at God's right hand for this very purpose to intervene on our behalf as our Advocate, to pronounce us righteous in God's sight, and thus to secure the acceptance and full salvation of all who come unto God by Him (see 1 John 2:1-2, Rom. 8:31-34, Heb. 7:25). So in Christ we have already and eternally an inviolable status as holy and without blemish in God's sight.[5]

---

[5] On Colossians 1:22, 'to present you holy and without blemish', Professor C.H. Dodd has written: 'It is probably wrong to take the words *to present you holy* ... as referring to the ultimate issue of the divine purpose, in the final moral perfection of Christ's people. It is "justification by faith" of which Paul is speaking. It is not that the Colossians have attained, or are to attain in some remote future, a moral perfection which will secure their acceptance at the Last Judgment. It is that here and now by grace of God, who "justifieth the ungodly", they stand before him as his consecrated people to whom he "imputes" no fault.' *The Abingdon Bible Commentary* (London, 1929), p. 1256.

The Full Wealth of the Consequent Benefits and the Full Weight of the Accompanying Obligations

Neglect of the full significance and consequent implications of the doctrine of justification by faith has caused very many true believers in Christ to be completely unaware of the wealth of their Christian inheritance and of the weight of their Christian obligations. As a result, instead of possessing the possessions which are already theirs in title, instead of seeking to cease from sin and to perfect holiness by regarding themselves dead to sin and alive unto God, many seek some 'second blessing' as though they still needed God to do something more for them before holy living and full salvation can be theirs. Whereas actually once we are 'in Christ' all things are ours; and so not only our reconciliation to God but also our sanctification and our glorification are assured.

To quote the New Testament way of putting it: 'whom He justified, them He also glorified' (Rom. 8:30). 'Therefore, being justified by faith, we have peace with God through our Lord Jesus Christ: by whom also we have access by faith into this grace wherein we stand, and rejoice in hope of the glory of God' (Rom. 5:1-2). In other words, once we are reconciled to God through the death of God's Son much more can we be sure that we shall be continually kept safe by the power of His resurrection life, and finally saved through Him from God's wrath against sinners, and conformed in resurrection glory to the image of God's Son (see Rom. 5:9-10; 8:29).

The consequent obligation resting upon us is, therefore, so to live as those who are citizens of the heavenly Jerusalem and can no longer be earthly minded, as those who have the present available power of God's indwelling Spirit for holy living, and as those who have the sure future prospect of full redemption when we shall at Christ's coming be clothed upon with a new spiritual body, fashioned after the likeness of our exalted Lord's own glorious body. Such are the heritage and the high calling of the justified. The doctrines of justification, sanctification and glorification (or, 'the redemption of the body', see Rom. 8:23, 1 Cor. 1:30, Eph. 4:30) belong thus together. And in this connection it is the worthy exposition of the relevant scriptural promises and exhortations to the justified, which particularly needs in our day widespread reinstatement in the ministry of the word to Christian congregations.

The Proper Significance of the Two Sacraments of the Gospel

Christian baptism is the divinely appointed seal of our justification by faith. As an ordinance administered once for all it corresponds to the once-for-all character of the redeeming work of God in Christ. Just as the finished work of Christ is sufficient to procure the full salvation of all who are in Him, so baptism is not only administered once never to be repeated, but also it assures the recipient not only of initiation into Christ but also of every blessing of the justified life, including the final redemption of the body; as a sacrament it is thus eschatological as well as evangelical.

Adequate awareness of this comprehensive significance of the baptismal seal as pledging the sinner's full salvation from beginning to end is lacking in most Christian congregations. This is due, on the one hand, to the unworthy practice of infant baptism, to the failure frequently in the presence of the congregation both to baptize and to preach about baptism, and to the prevalence of mistaken views about baptismal regeneration. It is also due, on the other hand, to over-emphasis on the necessity of the candidate's personal confession of faith to the neglect of other and even more important truths about Christian baptism.

We all seem to have lost sight of the primary witness of baptism to God's justifying act, and still more to the full witness of baptism as pledging a complete salvation. For on the one hand, Christian baptism is not just an initiation or beginning only; still less is it simply a provisional admission into the visible church or local congregation. It is rather the visible seal of that incorporation into Christ which makes every blessing ours. All the promises of God which concern the sinner's full salvation, and not just the initial ones are therein visibly signed and sealed. At the same time, on the other hand, while emphasis on the necessity of faith on the part of the candidate is important and indeed indispensable, such emphasis is overdone if a person's baptism is regarded more as the occasion of his public confession of faith than as the visible seal given to the candidate in God's Name of God's one all-sufficient justifying act whose full benefit is thereby assured to the believer. We greatly need, therefore, first in our understanding and then in our exposition of the significance of Christian baptism, to reinstate the doctrine of justification by faith.

Similarly, in contrast to the widespread and grossly misleading use of the Holy Communion service as a Godward plea or sacrifice of the altar, we need more fully to realize and rejoice in its divine sanction as a manward pledge or gift of the Lord from His table to His people. Far from any further pleading or spreading before God of our Lord's sacrifice being necessary, these symbols given under His hand to His disciples are visible seals of the conveyance to His believing people of the innumerable benefits of His passion as an already and once-for-all finished work. Further, their repeated administration assures believers that the one sacrifice that has secured their initial cleansing and peace with God is sufficient both to make theirs fresh cleansing from sins of daily living, and to assure them of final preservation unto life everlasting of body as well as soul. In other words, the service challenges us to appreciate, and by faith either to appropriate or to anticipate, the full consequences and endless eternal blessings of being justified by faith. Also, many who devoutly use the service, desiring to find it a means of grace, need to be saved from the prevalent temptation to trust in the supposed virtue of partaking of the consecrated elements and taught to fix their faith and hope on the justifying Lord, who by these visible tokens seals the conveyance to His people of the benefits of His finished work. If, therefore, the significance of the Lord's Supper is to be properly appreciated, and its administration properly enjoyed, we need fresh and frequent preaching in its fulness of the doctrine of justification by faith.

Justification by Faith Only

The distinctive character and the sole-sufficiency of the faith which justifies continually need afresh to be both recognized and expounded. This can only be adequately done when attention is directed not towards faith but towards the person and work of Christ. The faith of the individual must be seen as having no value in itself, but as discovering value wholly and solely through movement towards and committal to Christ. It must be seen as simply a means of finding all one's hope outside oneself in the person and work of another; and not as in any sense an originating cause or objective ground of justification. For true faith is active only in the man who is wholly occupied with Christ; its practice means that every blessing is received from another. For this reason faith is exclusive and intolerant of company; it is only truly present when any and every contribution towards his salvation on the part of the believer himself or on the part of the church is absolutely and unequivocally shut out. Justification must be seen and received as a blessing dependent wholly and exclusively on Christ alone, on what He is and on what He has done – a blessing enjoyed simply through being joined directly to Him, through finding one's all in Him, through drawing one's all from Him, without the interposition of any other mediator or mediating channel whatever. The one sufficient cause and the distinctive character of the salvation consequently enjoyed can only be properly expressed if it is made abundantly plain that it is justification by faith only. Religious man is so incessantly prone to introduce some contribution of his own works or of the church's ceremonies and sacraments that this truth of justification by faith only unquestionably needs continual reiteration among those by whom it is appreciated, and frequent reinstatement among the many by whom it has all too often been lost.

True Evangelical Assurance

When hope is thus wholly and exclusively fixed outside oneself and outside one's fellow-men on another, and that other Jesus, the Son of God, the once crucified and now exalted Saviour, the believer finds a solid and unshakable ground of full and abiding assurance. He knows that his sins are forgiven and forgotten by God. He knows that by His grace all is and all will be well. Possession of such assurance is an intended heritage and should be a distinctive mark of all who embrace the Christian gospel.

Yet it is just this assurance which in our day so many lack and not least those who profess and call themselves Christians. What is more, for lack of it many are disturbed and sometimes tormented by inner misgiving. They resort for relief either to the psychoanalyst and his psychotherapy or to confession to and absolution by the priest. The widespread prevalence of both these practices provides objective evidence that men are still hungry for, and in many cases far from enjoying, inner assurance. It is ours to declare that such full assurance of peace with God, of sufficient grace to face the uncertainties of this life, and of sure hope in the life beyond, is only to be possessed and is meant fully to be enjoyed by those who are justified by faith. For none can give the heart of sinful man true peace except the justifying Saviour. This is exclusively His prerogative; and this glory He will not give to another. Is it not time, therefore, that over against the well-meaning but ultimately insufficient ministries of the psychologist and the priest those who know the truth of the gospel of saving grace should set the renewed preaching of justification by faith?

9

GOD BECAME MAN:
SOME CONSIDERATIONS OF THE QUESTIONS HOW? AND WHY? (1957)

The distinctive truth of Christianity concerns the Person and the work of Jesus Christ. For instance, not only Christians but Jews and Muslims also acknowledge one supreme God; they revere the patriarchs and prophets of the Old Testament; but they do not believe, as Christians do, that Jesus is God Himself become Man, and become Man to save men.

It has been characteristic of Christians from the first to seek to define and to be ready to confess this distinctive faith concerning Jesus. The first preachers of the Christian gospel were concerned to proclaim, and to persuade men to acknowledge, who Jesus was and what He had done for men. So Jesus was heralded as God's Christ, as the exalted Lord, as Himself sharing the throne and the worship of God. From God and His Christ all blessings flow; to God and His Christ all praise should be directed. Not only because of His earthly life and ministry, but more particularly because of His death and resurrection, Jesus was also heralded as able to save men, to give them repentance, remission of sins and eternal life.

Subsequently these convictions found brief concise expression in credal statements, which with the passing of the years were increasingly elaborated in order explicitly to express these two fundamental essentials of the Christian faith – who Jesus is and what especially He has done (see, for instance, the Nicene Creed and Article II of the Thirty-Nine Articles). Such credal statements are, in the first place, deliberately and directly based on the New Testament Scriptures. For from the days of the primitive church, Christians have also believed that God has by His Spirit inspired understanding and prophetic utterance of these truths for the enlightenment and profit of His people; and that such divinely

First published by Tyndale Press in February 1957.

inspired insight and verbal declaration are uniquely to be found in the New Testament. It is, therefore, a continuous duty of Christians, a task renewed with each fresh generation, to satisfy themselves first, that they properly understand the scriptural witness to these distinctive Christian truths; and, second, that credal statements of them in current use are wholly in harmony therewith.

In this sphere of right understanding the contribution of the scriptural witness is twofold. It first provides us with a record of the unique historical events connected with Jesus. It then adds significant indication both of the unique character of Jesus Himself and of the divinely ordered purpose and consequence of His earthly career. In this same sphere of right understanding each fresh age or generation – indeed each fresh individual student of the New Testament – is challenged by acquaintance with these things to come to a proper appreciation of their value. Rather than accept at once in faith the guidance of divinely inspired scriptural revelation, many prefer to be guided in their approach by their own powers of judgment and particularly by the prevailing standards and criteria both of philosophy and of natural science.

It is important, therefore, if we would hold fast to the Christian faith and not be persuaded to accept instead prevailing theories and philosophies essentially contrary to Christianity, that we should not be ignorant of present-day emphases in these two realms of scientific theory and philosophic speculation. We need rather so to understand their governing principles as to see clearly their relation to, and their harmony or inconsistency with, revealed Christian truth. The apostle Paul wrote to Timothy, 'O Timothy, keep that which is committed to thy trust, avoiding profane and vain babblings, and oppositions of science falsely so called: which some professing have erred concerning the faith' (1 Tim. 6:20-21). The aged apostle thus warned a young Christian worker against the presumptuous claim to know, a claim attractively but unjustifiably made in the name of some prevailing theory or philosophy not really worthy of credence; a claim which, once adopted, was bound to involve any who held it, and became held by it, in departure from the Christian faith.

There is still need of similar warning. For in the scholarly world prevailing theories are often treated as if they were fully established truths. In consequence individuals so accept them as to allow their whole outlook to be governed by them. This can create fatal prejudice against the Christian faith. Individuals may thus be tempted to prefer empty human speculation to substantial divine revelation; and may thus be made to lose their bearings as Christian believers, and to wander far from the truth. It is our intention in this essay to consider some particular dangers of this kind. For they are dangers of which all who would hold fast to revealed truth concerning the Person and work of God incarnate need deliberately to beware.

Christian Truth and the Scientific Method

We live in an age in which the increasing use of the scientific method of investigation and research has led to many fresh discoveries of far-reaching significance. By the unprejudiced, fearless, diligent and persevering use of this method man has reached in many directions a better understanding of the workings of nature. So men have progressed in ability to harness and use the workings of nature to further their own desires and to serve their own ends.

The startling successes so obviously achieved by the use of this scientific method have understandably given rise to the idea that every field of knowledge ought to be subjected to this same method of investigation. So, for instance, instead of taking biblical history and biblical doctrines for granted, as true and trustworthy, after the manner of former generations, many have felt that their study of them would only be impartial and properly rewarded if they started with no *a priori* assumptions and sought to discover that explanation which is demanded by the observable evidence itself. Particularly has there been a desire to submit to this kind of scientific enquiry anything in the Bible records which past generations of Christians have commonly treated as supernatural and miraculous. May it not be true, it is asked, that we are now in a position to discover that what has hitherto been regarded as miraculous and due to special divine intervention may be better understood and explained as due to the normal operation of some so-called law or manner of nature's working, a working which may be expected always to occur once certain conditions are fulfilled?

Such a suggestion, reasonable enough as it is, immediately faces us with a crucial issue. We are here bound to recognize that the Bible asserts, and that Christians have always believed, that the outstanding events of Bible history were brought about only by a special supernatural intervention of God. Such events, therefore, if that is so, can be properly studied by the scientific method only if this unique qualifying condition is fully recognized. To rule out, as some would, the occurrence of the unique event as impossible because it does not conform to the normal workings of nature, is to refuse to heed the very evidence of divine intervention which the unique features offer.

The Bible records of the birth of Jesus provide an illustration of this kind of crux. The scientific approach understandably makes an enquirer assert that, if a normal birth took place of a human mother, that is from the womb of a woman, there must have been a human father responsible for the procreation of the child and the initiation of the woman's pregnancy. We are, too, bound to admit that in all ordinary circumstances such reasoning would be compelling and conclusive. No one would wish to argue against it. But here the scriptural records bear witness to an abnormal, supernatural occurrence. This woman, we are told, became pregnant without sexual intercourse with a man, by the action of God the Spirit.

The issue now becomes one of faith or unbelief. Such a unique event, the more so because it happened so long ago, is beyond the reach of scientific confirmation. No similar event is now observable. No similar event can be experimentally reproduced. Either we let the measure of our scientific understanding shut out the possibility of such an occurrence from our minds; or else we become believers in the testifying word and in the corresponding unique work of an extraordinary divine agent, God the Spirit. This means, let us notice, that the scientific method cannot here help us to find the truth; and it may even keep some from embracing it. For here the condition of understanding is faith – faith in God, in His unique work and in His inspired word. So, at least, Christians are persuaded.

A much more important crux of the same kind is presented to us by the biblical records of the resurrection of Jesus. For this was no normal natural event like His birth of a human mother. Scientific investigation can lead only to the incontestable general conclusion that resurrections of the dead do not occur. Nor indeed, if a group of highly qualified present-day scientists could have examined the dead body of Jesus between the crucifixion and the resurrection, would they have been able to discover any evidence or indication of the impending transformation. The resurrection of Jesus was due to the unique supernatural intervention of God the Spirit. Jesus Himself was thus declared with power to be the Son of God. The event of resurrection itself was not normal to all dead sinful men, but uniquely appropriate to the one divine and sinless Man. It thus demands by its unique character, and for its fuller appreciation, faith in His unique person as God become Man.

The place of such doctrinal presupposition is significantly admitted by a modern critical scholar, who rejects the historicity of the empty tomb. In *The Historical Evidence for the Resurrection of Jesus Christ* Dr Kirsopp Lake makes this observation: 'The historical evidence is such that it can be fairly interpreted consistently with either of the two doctrinal positions ... but it does not support either. The story of the empty tomb must be fought out on doctrinal, not on historical or critical grounds.'[1] Commenting on this Archbishop Ramsey has written, 'These words of Lake are of the utmost significance. The author of the most scientific treatment of the historical problem that has been written, in this and perhaps in any language, admits that a decision cannot be made without recourse to religious presupposition.'[2]

Here, therefore, whether one is personally prepared to accept it or not, it must be openly acknowledged that from the standpoint of Christian faith an important presupposition of further profitable investigation is complete acceptance of the age-long Christian confidence that Jesus is God manifest in the flesh. Only those who allow themselves to be guided by this conviction will rightly interpret the evidence.

Here, too, so the present writer is at least himself persuaded, one must also recognize the complementary importance of faith in the scriptural records as themselves similarly produced by a special divine providence in history. For our knowledge of the unique events of the earthly life of God incarnate and our understanding of their true character and significance are dependent entirely on these Scriptures. This very fact makes it the more reasonable to believe that they have been specially given by inspiration of God to provide men of every age with this double enrichment. Certainly unless the authority of the Scriptures is thus accepted, it is impossible by any independent use of the scientific method to discover truths which Christians know only by revelation. For this is a realm in which repeatedly there is no general law, but only the unique particular instance, which is *sui generis* and a law unto itself. This, too, is not exclusively a realm in which we only accept conclusions logically induced, but rather one in which we believe in order that we may understand. Let us then pursue this study in this faith.

Some Kenotic Theories

Modern scientific investigation is particularly interested in discovering how nature works. It is therefore to be expected that this interest would lead students in the field of Christian evidence to seek to discern and to

[1] Kirsopp Lake, *The Historical Evidence for the Resurrection of Jesus Christ* (London, 1907), p. 253.

[2] A.M. Ramsey, *The Resurrection of Christ: An Essay in Biblical Theology* (second edition, London, 1946), p. 52.

define how the incarnation worked, or what happened to God when He became Man. Here there has been, to begin with, a sincere desire to do full justice to both sides of the truth; first, to acknowledge the Person who became Man as truly and essentially God, and then to recognize that He became genuinely and experimentally Man, that is, that He lived a true and real human life on earth and in history as a man among men.

It has then been understandably argued that a real experience of human life would not have been possible for God the Son unless He laid aside His distinctively divine attributes, such as omnipotence, omniscience and omnipresence, and lived wholly within the limits of finite human capacity. So, for instance, radical distinction has been drawn between the divine self-consciousness of the Pre-existent and Eternal Word and the human self-consciousness of Jesus of Nazareth. Also, because in Philippians 2:7 Paul speaks of Christ having 'emptied himself' (RV) in order thus to become man, this action of His has come to be described technically as His 'kenosis' or 'emptying', and hypothetical attempts to define the measure of His consequent limitations are often referred to as 'kenotic theories'.

Such theorizing has, however, been carried too far in one direction by many and has become both scientifically one-sided and theologically unbalanced; so at least the present writer believes, and is concerned to demonstrate. For in such theorizing it has been freely and frequently suggested that, as Man, the incarnate Son of God was so completely limited to the human awareness normal to His earthly contemporaries that He necessarily shared in their wholly uncritical and erroneous views. In consequence, so many have been prepared to think, some of His references to the Old Testament can be discounted as purely limited, human, first-century opinion, which was on some points mistaken and to which the conclusions of scholarly modern Old Testament criticism are much to be preferred.

Here interest in our Lord's human knowledge as limited and, as it is supposed, sometimes erroneous, clearly ceases to be purely and impartially scientific; for it is in measure stimulated by the desire thus to justify questionable modern critical theories concerning the Old Testament Scriptures. Not only so; in addition such theories concerning the limited and unreliable character of our Lord's human knowledge directly undermine the sanction of His authority as the Christian's supreme reason for believing in the Old Testament as the God-given word. So Professor R.V.G. Tasker has written:

It is not surprising that the extension of the 'kenotic' theory of the incarnation to our Lord's attitude to the Old Testament has led to a growing disinclination on the part of the Liberal-Catholics and Liberal-Protestants alike to use the Old Testament in preaching and in worship.[3]

On the other side, Professor Tasker also declares in the same context that in his view this theory of our Lord's uncertain knowledge of the origin and nature of the Old Testament is virtually irreconcilable with the way in which

> our Lord grounded His personal claims, His sense of a special vocation ... and the validity of much of His teaching on the belief that the Old Testament was not only a true self-revelation of His Father, but the incontrovertible expression of His Father's will for Himself, His Son. Here, if anywhere, we should expect our Lord to speak with divine authority and absolute truth. Indeed, if He could be mistaken on matters which He regarded as of the strictest relevance to His own person and ministry, it is difficult to see exactly how or why He either can or should be trusted anywhere else.[4]

In other words, much more is at stake here than a right scientific understanding of the limits of our Lord's human knowledge. For a mere theory or supposition is used, and unquestionably has been used, to undermine faith in the divine authority both of our Lord's own words and of the Old Testament Scriptures.

It is therefore of very great importance also to discern that such theories do not do full justice to our Lord's continuing deity. They are theologically unbalanced. For they suggest, in effect, that in order to become a true man Jesus temporarily ceased to be God, or at least to act and function as such. But such an idea is theologically untenable, as able modern scholars have fully recognized. For instance, Archbishop William Temple asked:

> What was happening to the rest of the universe during the period of our Lord's earthly life? ... To say that the Creative Word was so self-emptied as to have no being except in the Infant Jesus, is to assert that for a certain period the history of the world was let loose from the control of the Creative Word.[5]

Developing further the statement of what he declared to be 'insuperable objections' to the idea of divine self-emptying found in kenotic theories,

---

[3] R.V.G. Tasker, *Our Lord's Use of the Old Testament* (London, 1953), p. 19.

[4] Ibid., p. 19.

[5] William Temple, *Christus Veritas: An Essay* (London, 1924), pp. 142-143.

Professor D.M. Baillie wrote:

> Instead of giving us a doctrine of Incarnation in which Jesus Christ is both God and man, the Kenotic Theory appears to me to give us a story of a temporary theophany in which He who formerly was God changed Himself temporarily into man. ... For ... He has divested Himself of the *distinctively divine* attributes; which would imply, if language means anything, that in becoming human He ceased to be divine.[6]

Professor Baillie also went on to declare:

> The presupposition of the theory is that the distinctive divine attributes (of omniscience, etc) and the distinctive human attributes (of finitude) cannot be united simultaneously in one life, that is why the Incarnation is explained as a *kenosis*. ... Thus, on the kenotic theory ... He is God and Man, not simultaneously in a hypostatic union, but *successively* – first divine, then human, then God again. But that ... seems to leave no room at all for the traditional catholic doctrine of the *permanence* of the manhood of Christ.[7]

Full justice can, therefore, be done both to our Lord's full deity and to His true humanity only by recognizing that when, as Man, He acquired a finite mode of consciousness in which His knowledge and power and other perfections were limited to human measure, He also retained simultaneously, as God, an infinite mode of consciousness in which He knew all things and exercised all power.

First, it is important in our thinking to keep these two modes of consciousness properly separate and distinct. On this point Charles Harris has significantly written:

> These two modes, however close their union and intimate their interpenetration, as being modes of a single personality, must have remained *distinct*. For had the infinite mode at any time been merged in the finite, God would have been practically annihilated; and if, on the other hand, the finite mood had ever been merged in the infinite, the manhood of Jesus would have entirely ceased to exist, and the Incarnation would have been reduced to a Theophany.[8]

Next, it is equally important to recognize that since the two natures of deity and manhood were truly united in the one Person, these two

---

[6] D.M. Baillie, *God was in Christ: An Essay on Incarnation and Atonement* (London, 1948), p. 96.

[7] Ibid., p. 97.

[8] Charles Harris, *Pro Fide: A Text-book of Modern Apologetics for Theological Students, Ministers of Religion, and Others* (fourth edition, London, 1930), p. 584.

modes of consciousness must have been continuously and actively related. Admittedly this is to our finite minds very difficult to grasp. We cannot immediately see how such opposites as knowledge and ignorance can coexist in one person without contradiction. But it is surely of Christian faith to confess that their coexistence is an essential part of the truth and of the unique wonder of the incarnation.

When we try further to appreciate how two such apparently contradictory conditions may actively coexist in a single personality it is possible, for what it is worth, as Charles Harris indicates, to obtain some suggestive help to our thinking from inferior human analogies. For instance, while his conscious mind is otherwise engaged, a person's subconscious mind (without his conscious knowledge) may think out a problem of which it has previously been made aware; so that, when he returns later to his mental task, the solution of the problem instantly appears. Similarly, after being hypnotized, a person who returns to normal control may be said to be 'ignorant' of things experienced or learnt while in the hypnotic state. 'Nevertheless', writes Charles Harris,

> the knowledge is truly in his mind, and shows itself in unmistakable ways, especially by causing him to perform or to refrain from performing actions, which, but for the possession of this knowledge, he would not have performed or refrained from performing. What is still more extraordinary, a sensitive hypnotic subject may be made both to see and not to see the same object at the same moment. For example, he may be told not to see a lamp-post, whereupon he becomes (in the ordinary sense) quite unable to see it. Nevertheless he does see it, because he avoids it, and cannot be induced by any possible device to precipitate himself against it.[9]

In the unique case of God incarnate, therefore, we may at least reasonably suppose that our Lord's divine knowledge, while still personally possessed by Him as God, was deliberately kept below the threshold of His human consciousness, but could be drawn upon as and when His Father gave to Him to know, as Man, what eternally He knew as God (see John 8:47; 14:10, 24). Also, it is surely reasonable to assert, as J. Stafford Wright has done, that:

> The unity of His divine-human Person would prevent Him from teaching error, but unless His Father told Him to communicate a certain teaching, His consciousness would remain ignorant of it; such was the case with the date of His Second Coming (Mark 13:32).[10]

---

[9] Ibid., pp. 588-590.
[10] *The Life of Faith*, 3 November 1955, pp. 749-750.

Charles Harris has expressed the same general conclusion when he wrote:

> There is no contradiction, either logical or practical, in supposing (as orthodoxy does) that the finite or human consciousness of the Redeemer was compassed about by an infinite ocean of divine consciousness, belonging to the same personality, into which it could only partly penetrate, but by which it was nevertheless so completely guided and illuminated that the result was, for the Incarnate Life, not indeed omniscience (a thing impossible for a finite nature), but certainly real infallibility in matters of faith and morals.[11]

Nor do we see the need for the possible allowance of so-called unimportant error, which may be taken by some to be implied by this writer's limiting phrase – 'in matters of faith and morals'. It seems rather to us not only possible but proper to confess with equal conviction – 'and real infallibility in all other matters too'.

All this means that because Jesus was God as well as Man, He had still, as God, infinite resources of knowledge and power on which He could have drawn, had He wished, in a way completely impossible to other men. Some of the temptations which beset Him wrongly to draw upon such powers (for example, Matt. 4:3-4; 26:50-54) are only meaningful if this was true. What is significant for the understanding of His humanity and its genuine reality is the awareness that Jesus generally and deliberately refused to draw upon such supernatural resources, not available to other men. For He took upon Himself as man 'the form of a servant', 'he humbled himself and became obedient' (Phil. 2:7-8). So He who could say as God, 'I and my Father are one' (John 10:30), became able to say as Man, 'My Father is greater than I' (John 14:28). He thus entered fully into a true human experience within normal and natural human limits and conditions.

But we must also recognize the uniqueness of His humanity as well as its full similarity to our own. He was, for instance, as a man, both in nature and practice, wholly 'without sin' (Heb. 4:15). He was filled or possessed by God the Spirit without measure or restraint (see John 3:34). He enjoyed full and unhindered intercourse with God as His heavenly Father. Just as prophets and apostles in the discharge of special God-given missions were at times allowed to share in the exercise of special divine knowledge and power, so Jesus, as the continuous life-long prophet and the perfect ideal apostle, was allowed of God in the fulfilment of His unique mission, and in the expression in human living

---

[11] Harris, *Pro Fide*, pp. 590-591.

of His unique Person, to draw uniquely upon that divine knowledge and power which were already His own as God; but wholly in submission to His Father's pleasure and appointment and only as His Father granted such privilege to Him. So the authority of His divine Person, and the accompanying authority of both God the Father and God the Spirit, found full expression in the life of Jesus in both word and deed, without the genuine reality of His human experience being destroyed or violated.

Some Philosophical Speculations

In this so-called scientific age interest and enquiry are particularly directed towards the study of how things work. Students are eager to discover more of the laws of nature, to understand more fully the processes of nature's working. There is a complementary study which is much larger in its embrace, a study in which thinkers seek not so much to identify immediate natural causes and explanations of process as to discern more fundamental governing causes of all existence and possible interpretations of its ultimate purpose and intended or inevitable end. Just as natural scientists produce theories concerning the way in which nature works, so philosophers speculate and produce their systems of thought in the attempt to explain the first cause and the final meaning of all that is. One object of such philosophizing is to provide men with a way of looking at life as a whole in relation to which they may come to a better understanding of the place and purpose of life's manifold phases and experiences.

Here it is important to recognize clearly that there are two radically different ways for professing Christians to go to work in seeking to understand truth. On the one hand, we may accept the revelation of God's will and ways, which is afforded in the inspired and canonical Scriptures of the Old and New Testaments as our governing authority, and let that settle first what we believe and then how in consequence we act. This is the orthodox and, particularly since the Reformation, the protestant and evangelical way to proceed. This is why works of systematic theology are produced in an attempt to appreciate revealed truth as a whole, and to understand in relation to it the place and full significance of the different parts.

On the other hand, one may begin independently of Scripture, by accepting as axiomatic some philosophical principle which is then allowed to guide and to govern one's evaluation of the significance of the manifold details of evidence, which demand interpretation and systematization if one's understanding is ever to acquire the desirable characteristic of coherent wholeness. What is more, the details of evidence thus interpreted and systematized may still be predominantly, if not exclusively, scriptural. The result is that those who build up a system of thinking of this kind can understandably claim to be genuinely biblical, and thus to be furthering the proper appreciation of essential Christianity. They can argue with some plausibility that those who become learners in such a school will obtain a wholeness of view and a full-orbed theology usually not possessed by those who make tremendous appeal to the final authority of isolated scriptural statements, but have, so it is suggested, no corresponding, satisfying philosophy of Christian faith and life as a whole.

Let us in illustration of this, and in further pursuit of our specific interest in this essay, turn our attention once again to the great confession of the Christian faith that God became Man. Let us notice first, how possible it is to approach this central event of biblical and Christian revelation, that is, the incarnation of the Son of God, from the standpoint of an independent philosophical interest. It is possible thus to seek to postulate why God became Man and what was the ultimate objective in view or the chief result which it was intended would follow. Indeed, not only is such philosophizing possible, it has frequently been done and is still being done by Christian thinkers who make some governing philosophical idea fundamental and then seek to interpret the evidence accordingly.

What this present writer is concerned to demonstrate is that in the process of such philosophizing such thinkers, able and attractive as their systematization may be, sometimes depart from a proper balanced understanding of what the Scriptures reveal. Their complete acceptance of their governing philosophical idea makes them blind to parts of the scriptural witness which radically deny or seriously qualify it. They select and emphasize scriptural statements which can be made to fit into their own scheme of thought. In some cases they ultimately tend in principle to expose themselves to the condemnation of rejecting the plain word of God in order that they may hold fast to their own philosophy.

For instance, Archbishop William Temple and Professor O.C. Quick both objected to the 'kenosis' idea that in the incarnation God 'emptied Himself' and so virtually ceased to be God. But they did so not so much on scriptural as on philosophical grounds. They postulated that the essence of God Himself is self-realization through self-sacrifice, or living through dying; that is, Love. So God is to be thought of as realizing Himself through giving Himself, through becoming, as it were, less than God. The incarnate Word is therefore truly God just because He is truly human. Far from emptying Himself in order to become incarnate, in the incarnation God took a decisive step towards His own self-realization.

Now such ideas, however philosophically attractive and in measure theologically sound, also have tendencies which are unscriptural and theologically dangerous. For they suggest that God Himself is not eternally perfect, but needs participation in humanity for His own self-completion. The one safeguard against such wrong thinking is to submit to Scripture as the authoritative rule of faith, to let thought be genuinely governed by divine revelation rather than by human speculation. Otherwise the wisest and most devout of scholars may ultimately mislead us.

More recent Anglo-Catholic thinkers have struck a different emphasis in their contemplation of the incarnation and its purpose. They have become interested not so much in what happened to God when He became Man, as in what happened to humanity when it was thus united to God the Son. So, for instance, E.L. Mascall and L.S. Thornton have interpreted the significance of the incarnation in terms of human elevation and fulfilment. In Christ, so they suggest, through its union with God human nature is supernaturalized or taken up into a higher metaphysical perfection.

There is, particularly in the thought of L.S. Thornton, an attempt to combine orthodox doctrine with the philosophy of organism. In the universe man is the highest organism of an ascending series. Yet he shares the unfinished character of the cosmic series as a whole and needs for his complete fulfilment to be taken up organically into a higher principle of unity. These unfulfilled aspirations of humanity are satisfied only through the incarnation, in which human nature becomes the organ of that higher divine organism, which is Christ. Not only so; by such participation in elevation and higher fulfilment human nature does not become less human but rather more completely human. It thereby fulfils its own law of being. To be specific, what is needed to complete humanity is perfect filial response. This exists, to begin with, only in the divine Son and is achieved by the organic creation only when it is taken up into His activity. Redemption is then seen as an extension of these effects to us. Men may now share in the achievement of the incarnation through incorporation into Christ's human nature. This means a genuine metaphysical re-creation, an ontological change in contrast, so it is asserted, to the 'protestant' idea of atonement as a 'legal fiction' which leaves man essentially what he was.

The church provides, according to these thinkers, the sphere of participation. It is the extension of the new divine-human organism started in Christ. Men are saved or enter into fulness of life by incorporation into this organism of incarnation. This means that the church is the 'place' where reconciliation with God occurs, the 'sphere' into which individuals enter in order to share in the divine life. Protestants, we are told, are prevented from thus believing in a real ontological coherence of the church and the humanity of Christ by their doctrine of justification. The cross does not procure this new life. It is rather, on the one hand, 'a necessary passage through which the Incarnation must go to reach us',[12] and on the other hand, the crowning expression of the governing principle of the incarnation, namely, obedient self-sacrifice. The church, by being baptized into its spirit and into participation in its self-sacrificing offering, gives the incarnation not only extension but also true and necessary completion.

Christ's humanity is thus manifested under different forms or modes – through His earthly body, His glorified body, His body the church and the eucharistic body. So the church is metaphysically identical with the incarnate Lord. 'They are all', says E.L. Mascall, 'objective forms of expression of the manhood of the one Lord.'[13] (The present writer has tried to help his mind to grasp this strange idea by rather distant analogy that steam, water and ice are different modes of the same distinctive combination of hydrogen and oxygen.) Christ thus continues to offer Himself now in the humanity we share with Him. The eucharist is its externalization in ritual form. The church form of the incarnation thus finds in the eucharist the supreme occasion of the expression of its governing life-principle of self-sacrifice. In the eucharist

> offerers and offered are one, since both are modes of the body of Christ. When believers perform the eucharistic rite, they offer themselves in offering the elements. Further, Christ offers Himself as the believers offer the eucharistic sacrifice, since it is His humanity which the believers offer in offering themselves and the sacrifice.[14]

The eucharist is thus a making present in time of what is true in eternity.

---

[12] Lewis B. Smedes, *The Incarnation: Trends in Modern Anglican Thought* (Kampen, Holland, 1953), p. 82.

[13] E.L. Mascall (ed.), *The Church of God: An Anglo-Russian Symposium* (London, 1934), p. 17. Compare E.L. Mascall, *Christ, the Christian and the Church: A Study of the Incarnation and its Consequences* (London, 1946), p. iii; L.S. Thornton, *Revelation and the Modern World* (London, 1950), p. 127.

[14] Smedes, *Incarnation*, p. 115.

Let us now seek to offer a critical appreciation of such philosophizing in the light of the plain biblical witness. First, we may say in general that these views which we have mentioned are in places all hard to reconcile fully with the proper orthodox insistence upon the manner of the incarnation and the necessary distinction between the two natures in Christ of both deity and humanity. Also, they are all based upon unscriptural assumptions as to the purpose of the incarnation.

For instance, the Bible witness indicates unmistakably that what man needs is moral redemption, not metaphysical completion. For 'the Biblical doctrine of creation leaves us with an unavoidable impression that man created in the image of God was a completed being.' 'Man ... did not need an Incarnation of God in order to fulfil his vocation of total worship.'[15] This cancels out the prevailing premise of some of these writers as to the purpose of the incarnation – that it was required by the nature of creation and would have occurred even had not sin entered man's life. Also, according to the Bible, man's relation to God has been disrupted by the fall. So 'man's need of the Incarnation was religious, not metaphysical ... a need of reconciliation not of elevation, of mediation not of metaphysical completion.'[16]

In contrast to this scriptural emphasis we have in these modern Anglo-Catholic views consummation for man through the incarnation rather than salvation through atonement. So there has been (to quote William Temple) 'the development of a theology of the Incarnation rather than a theology of Redemption.' So Mary and the virgin birth become more fundamental and decisive than Calvary and the atoning sacrifice. 'The re-birth is a privilege granted by Christ as a result of His incarnation.'[17] The act by which God makes a man a Christian is 'incorporation into the human nature of Christ, an incorporation by which the very life of the Man Christ Jesus is communicated to us and we are re-created in him.'[18]

Also, evolutionary and optimistic humanistic ideas underlie some of these suggestions. Jesus Christ is represented as the crown and climax of all earlier development. The incarnation is not the divine remedy for evil but the fulfilment of the goodness of creation. There is a 'gospel' but it is Pelagian. It shows man not how to pass out of the sinner's death into the life of new creation in Christ risen from the dead, but how to become his true self by offering himself to die in and with and for Christ. We

---

[15] Ibid., pp. 136-137.
[16] Ibid., pp. 137-138.
[17] L.S. Thornton, *The Common Life in the Body of Christ* (London, 1942), p. 211.
[18] Mascall, *Christ, the Christian and the Church*, p. 77.

are encouraged to think of ourselves as incorporated into the human nature of the incarnate Son rather than into His death and resurrection. Existing things are supplemented and consummated, instead of old things having to pass away. Such views mean flattery of human nature as it is. Such views also mean flattery of the church, as itself the sphere of salvation and the body in which Christ is now incarnate. The sacrifice of the cross becomes an example or supreme expression of the principle or pattern of the incarnate life now manifested in the church, and indeed of the eternal activity of the divine Son. This is in complete contrast to the scriptural emphasis upon the once-for-all and finished character of the incarnate Son's personal offering of His human body to put away sin. For 'this he did once for all', says the writer of the epistle to the Hebrews, 'when he offered up himself' (Heb. 7:27, compare Heb. 9:11, 25-26; 10:10, 14).

So, while such views offer man fulfilment in Christ, fulfilment is offered to the natural man as he is. The incarnation is rationalized by taking it out of its biblical setting of creation, sin and redemption, and putting it within a semi-speculative setting of man's metaphysical incompletion.[19] Such an understanding of Christianity adds the practice of religion to what we already are and suggests that we can thus offer ourselves to God. It offers flattering philosophical idealism externalized in fascinating mystical ritual. It tends to give more prominence to participation in elaborate detached ceremonial rites than to proper concentration on walking in newness of life, in that daily obedience which is for us as Christians our proper worship or reasonable service.

What Scripture Teaches

Over against scientific theorization and philosophic speculation Christian believers set, and are prepared to give priority to, divine revelation. Also, as we have confessed already, it has from the first been an age-long Christian confidence that the Scriptures of the Old and New Testaments have been specially 'given by inspiration of God' in order to provide us with an adequate knowledge of the unique events of such divine revelation and with a proper insight into their divinely intended significance. To quote one testimony from the New Testament itself – St John the evangelist writes, 'And he that hath seen hath borne witness, and his witness is true: and he knoweth that he saith true, that ye also may believe' (John 19:35 RV, compare John 20:30-31). Here

---

[19] Smedes, *Incarnation*, p. 145.

John declares that his record is 'true' in a twofold way; on the one hand, as a trustworthy account by an eyewitness of events which actually happened; and on the other hand, as a perfect or 'ideal' interpretation of their divine meaning. Here he also declares that the purpose of such a record is to lead its readers and students, not to an understanding of all the answers to possible scientific or philosophic problems, but to personal saving and life-giving faith in the Person and work of Jesus, whom he desires his readers to acknowledge and to confide in as the Christ, the Son of God. Let us then seek thus to appreciate Christian truth, by the aid of the scriptural witness and praying for the help of the illuminating Spirit.

The full deity of Jesus

The New Testament is explicit and unmistakable in its witness that the Person who appeared in history as Jesus of Nazareth was none other than God Himself. He was One who shared essential unity and eternal fellowship with God the Father as the only-begotten Son. In His own absolute being, as the Word, He was eternally God with God; and it is none other than He, 'the true God' or genuine deity, who was from the beginning with the Father, of whom John writes, 'we have heard … we have seen with our eyes ... we have looked upon, and our hands have handled.' Also, as incarnate, He 'is' (not 'was'), says John, still in the most intimate communion with God – 'in the bosom of the Father' (see John 1:1-2, 18; 1 John 1:1-2; 5:20).

Over against influences of thought, both Jewish and Gentile, which tended to suggest that Jesus was only one of many mediating agencies between God and men – whether angels or emanations – the New Testament writers outspokenly assert that He is no mere higher creature or demi-god, but Himself one hundred per cent deity come down to earth as man. He is 'the image of the invisible God' (Col. 1:15), 'the effulgence of his glory, and the very image [or 'impress'] of his substance' (Heb. 1:3 RV), what the Nicene Creed describes as 'very God of very God', that is, 'genuine deity out from genuine deity', sharing in full measure as the only-begotten God the Son the nature or substance of God the Father.

The New Testament writers also assert that God the Son, or the Word, is the original agent, the present sustainer, the ultimate heir, and so the sovereign Lord, of the created universe. 'All things were made through him.' Nor is there any exception at all to this general truth. For apart from Him was not one single thing made that has been made; so St John writes (John 1:3, 10). Or the writer to the Hebrews declares that it was through His Son that God made the worlds (Heb. 1:2, 10-12). Similarly St Paul says 'in him were all things created'; and so He is 'the firstborn' or heir 'of all creation' (Col. 1:15-16). Nor is He Himself a creature. For 'before' the 'all things' of the created order came into being, He eternally 'is' (Col. 1:17). Or, as John the Baptist put it, 'for he was before me' (John 1:30). So, in contrast to the Arian dogma which made Him the chief of God's creatures, there never was a time when He was not.

Nor is God the Son only the originating cause of the created universe. He is also its present sustaining cause. He is continually 'upholding all things by the word of his power' (Heb. 1:3). Nor can this activity temporarily have ceased during the period of His human life on earth. For 'in him all things consist' or 'hold together' (Col. 1:17 RV). Were He to cease to be, or to cease thus to operate, the whole creation would fall to pieces.

In the third place, God the Son is the predestined heir of all things. The writer of the epistle to the Hebrews significantly mentions this first ('whom he appointed heir of all things') before he refers to His work in making and upholding the created order (Heb. 1:2-3). This means that before the universe was created, this was the predetermined purpose of God Himself that God the Son should possess it as His inheritance. Similarly Paul refers to the good pleasure of God's purpose in the fulness of times to 'sum up all things in Christ' (Eph. 1:9-10); for 'all things were created' not only 'by him', but also 'for him' (Col. 1:16). So the Son of the Father's love is the indispensable and all-sufficient key to the universe. It is impossible to suppose that He ceased to be this during the days of His flesh.

When, therefore, He, God the Son, became Man, He brought in His Person into humanity nothing less than the fulness – the one hundred per cent – of deity. Such is the explicit testimony of the New Testament writers. Our Lord Jesus Christ, say James and Peter, John and Paul, is 'the glory' or the visible manifested outshining of Jehovah Himself (see James 2:1, 1 Pet. 4:14, John 1:14, 1 Cor. 2:8, 2 Cor. 3:18, 4:6). What He was eternally as God the Son, He still was historically during His life on earth as Man – that is, the dwelling-place of the 'pleroma' or fulness of deity. Far from being deprived of some of His deity when He became man, it was 'the good pleasure of the Father' – in direct connection with the discharge on earth 'in the body of his flesh' of His reconciling work – 'that in him should all the fulness dwell' (Col. 1:19-22 RV).

In contrast to Gnostic ideas that only some greatly impoverished expression of deity could have any dealings with this material and evil world, Paul explicitly declares of the incarnate Son that 'in him dwelleth all the fulness of the Godhead bodily' (Col. 2:9). Also, in this immediate context and in this very connection, Paul warns his readers, 'Beware lest any man spoil you through philosophy and vain deceit, after the tradition of men, after the rudiments of the world, and not after Christ' (Col. 2:8). Such a warning may still have pertinent present-day application. Just as some first-century Christians needed to beware of Gnostic theories, so some twentieth-century Christians may need to beware of so-called kenotic theories.

Similarly Paul writes to the Corinthians, not only that 'God ... reconciled us to himself through Christ', but also that 'God was in Christ reconciling the world unto himself' (2 Cor. 5:18-19). So Jesus is without qualification to be acknowledged and worshipped as Himself God. Further confirmation of this is provided by the testimony and worship of the angels at the time of His human birth. For instance, not only did the angel tell Joseph, 'Fear not to take unto thee Mary thy wife; for that which is conceived in her is of the Holy Ghost.' He also said, 'And thou shalt call his name Jesus: for he shall save his people from their sins' (Matt. 1:20-21). The implication of these words is very remarkable indeed. For the people Jesus was to save were Jehovah's people. Yet the angel did not say of Jesus, as would have been said of any other deliverer, like the Old Testament Joshua, He shall save Jehovah's people. Instead the angel said, and said most emphatically, He shall save *His own* people. In other words, Jesus is none other than Jehovah Himself come to save His own people. This implied meaning the evangelist clearly recognizes and explicitly underlines by immediately referring to the prophecy of the child to be born of a virgin, whose name was to be called Emmanuel, 'which', he says, 'being interpreted is, God with us' (Matt. 1:22-23).

Consequently in Jesus nothing less than the character and the authority of God Himself were fully manifested. Of this manifestation Jesus Himself was personally conscious. To it, at times, He bore direct testimony. When Philip said unto Him, 'Lord, shew us the Father', Jesus answered, 'He that hath seen me hath seen the Father' (John 14:8-9). When the scribes reasoned in their hearts, accusing Jesus of blasphemy for claiming to forgive sin because none can forgive sin but God only, Jesus answered their thoughts by demonstrating that this exclusively divine authority to forgive sin was now present here on earth in His Person as the Son of man (see Mark 2:5-12). Jesus claims, therefore, to be acknowledged as the Man from heaven, as God become Man, who thus brings into the midst of humanity the full presence and power of deity. So while prophets of old gave supreme sanction to their words by saying 'Thus saith the Lord' (see Amos 1:3, 6, 9, 11, 13 etc), Jesus gave supreme sanction to what He said simply by saying, 'Verily, verily, I say unto you' (see John 3:3, 5 etc).[20] So when He speaks, His words, just because He is their author, have in themselves divine sanction. When, therefore, for instance, He declares of Psalm 110 that 'David himself' spoke its words 'in the Holy Spirit' (Mark 12:36 RV), that is for true believers in His Person sufficient evidence concerning its authorship.

Similarly there were occasions when in significant language Jesus openly claimed Himself to be the eternal I AM – Jehovah God. 'Before Abraham was', He said, 'I am' (John 8:58). And 'except ye believe that I am, ye shall die in your sins' (John 8:24 RV). Thus to confess Jesus to be Himself God, the Son of God, one who fully shares the divine nature and prerogatives, is therefore the crowning and the only complete Christian confession of His Person. To this truth the apostolic writers of the New Testament bear emphatic witness. So, writes John the evangelist, 'The Word became flesh, and dwelt among us (and we beheld his glory, the glory as of the only begotten from the Father), full of grace and truth. ... No man hath seen God at any time; God only begotten, which is in the bosom of the Father, he hath declared him' (John 1:14, 18 RV). Thus he declares that Jesus Messiah is the complete consummation of the revelation of God in history, because He is Himself 'Son' (Heb. 1:1-2) or 'God only begotten' and as such the very declaration or exegesis of God Himself. No one, therefore, can know the true God who denies the deity of Jesus. This is the Christian faith. 'Whosoever denieth the Son, the same hath not the Father: he that confesseth the Son hath the Father also' (1 John 2:23 RV).

The true humanity of Jesus

The Gospel records of the New Testament make abundantly plain that their chief character, Jesus of Nazareth, was a real man, an actual figure of earthly history. This truth is not open to doubt or to serious question. From the standpoint of the ordinary reader who comes to these records with no preconceived ideas, no so-called religious prejudices, the claim that is difficult to believe is not the claim that Jesus was a man, but rather the claim that this Man was God incarnate. For His appearance

---

[20] Compare Matt. 5:18, 20, 22, 28, 32, 34, 39, 44.

on the field of history is not just an abnormal passing theophany. He is not merely a man in superficial appearance only. Nor is He some superhuman spirit temporarily possessing a man other than Himself in order thus to manifest His presence in human deeds and human words. He is clearly Himself completely and naturally Man.

So we read, and there is no reason to doubt, that He was conceived in the womb of a woman, who gave birth to Him as His human mother. He began His earthly life as a dependent infant, needing to be carried and cared for by others. He passed through the stages of normal human growth and development. So Luke records 'the child grew' (Luke 2:40); and 'Jesus increased in wisdom and stature [or 'age']' (Luke 2:52 RV). He knew what it was to be weary, to sleep, and to rise early. He experienced hunger, thirst and temptation. He felt pleasure, anger and grief, even unto tears. He needed continually to seek God in prayer. Under extreme mental and spiritual stress His body was overcome with excess of sweat. At the end He died and was buried.

For the mind that is eager to know how things work – an interest so dominant in the present age of great scientific discovery – the problem is not to understand how Jesus functioned as a man; for that seems normal enough. The problem is rather to understand how He could still be functioning as God. Surely to make such a genuine human experience possible, He must have completely abandoned His supernatural divine powers? This is the problem which kenotic theories understandably attempt to answer.

Here Christian reverence, humility and faith prefer to recognize a mystery, which the enquiring human mind cannot thus scientifically penetrate and analyse. Just because it is unique, it is beyond logical definition. It cannot be classified or compared with similar phenomena; for there are none. It is *sui generis*. Also, because it is from above, a supernatural divine achievement, it is beyond the grasp of man's finite comprehension. Before this mystery, the superior scientific investigator, looking down on evidence which he is determined to analyse and explain, is forced to become a submissive worshipper, looking up in awe and reverence to acknowledge a mystery far bigger than his mind can grasp – but an unmistakable fact nonetheless.

Here, at any rate, men must choose between submissive faith and self-confident conceit. Here men must confess a mystery beyond the grasp of the human mind, or still hold fast to the fancy that the human mind is bigger than this mystery and well able accurately to theorize about it. Here all who would thus bring Jesus under their criticism must ultimately find themselves brought under His judgment. We sometimes do well not to forget that Jesus Himself said, 'For judgment I am come into this world, that they which see not might see; and that they which see might be made blind' (see John 9:39-41).

On this subject of the incarnation of God the Son the New Testament writers do offer some light to those who are minded thus to be taught of God. When God the Son became Man, it involved a new and special subordination of His Person to God the Father; with the result that He who could say eternally as God, 'I and the Father are one' (John 10:30 RV), could now say on earth as Man, 'the Father is greater than I' (John 14:28 RV). He who, as God the Son, was equal with God the Father and one with Him in substance or Godhead, in order to become true Man, like other men, took upon Himself the position of a slave or bond-servant in relation to God the Father. He humbled Himself in order to become as Man in all things both dependent upon His Father's giving and obedient to His Father's guiding. This is how, as Paul says, He 'emptied himself' (Phil. 2:7 RV). This is what His 'kenosis' meant.

As Man, the things He had to give were still the things of God, for He Himself was God, the One from above. But He did not and could not as Man give to men, or indeed use for Himself, all that was still His as God. He thus gave or used only as the Father allowed Him so to do. This complete dependence upon His Father's giving and guiding He personally recognized as Man, by continually seeking God the Father in prayer thus to gain fresh light and strength. This complete dependence upon His Father's giving and guiding He openly acknowledged in explicit testimony concerning His own speech and behaviour.

Let us quote some of His statements. 'I can of myself do nothing: as I hear, I judge' (John 5:30 RV). 'As my Father hath taught me, I speak these things' (John 8:28). 'I speak the things which I have seen with my Father' (John 8:38). 'The Father which sent me, he gave me a commandment what I should say, and what I should speak' (John 12:49). 'The things therefore which I speak, even as the Father hath said unto me, so I speak' (John 12:50 RV). This means, therefore, that, on the one hand, He lived a genuine human life within divinely controlled limits. But it means also, on the other hand, that what He did do and say as Man had the perfection, authority and infallibility of His own divine Person, and of the direct divine giving of His heavenly Father. Indeed He Himself said that if we dissociate ourselves from what He said, if we are ashamed of Him and of His words, He will disown us as His when He comes in His glory (see Mark 8:38).

Finally, while Jesus was unquestionably a real Man, it is important to recognize His radical difference from other men – just because other men are all sinners. For Jesus did not partake of the sinfulness of the human race. He 'did no sin, neither was guile found in his mouth' (1 Pet. 2:22). Such is the testimony of an eyewitness of long and detailed experience. Consequently Jesus never repented of sin. While He taught all other men to pray for forgiveness, He never asked forgiveness for Himself. In Jesus, therefore, we see revealed not only full deity but also perfect humanity. But this perfection of humanity is not man with some age-long deficiency now for the first time made good through the indwelling of deity. It is rather man as the Creator originally made him and meant him to be prior to the defilement and depravity due to Adam's fall into sin.

Jesus born to die

The assumption by God the Son of our humanity was not by itself alone the answer to man's need. There were first a conflict to be faced and a price to be paid, before men could be saved. God the Son became Man in order to face this conflict and pay this price, as Man for men. This is the explicit, reiterated, unmistakable teaching of the New Testament writers.

It is therefore a mistake and a misdirection of faith to look to the incarnation by itself as God's provision for man's need. God incarnate had also and first to die. Jesus as the Saviour of sinners does not share with us men the sinless humanity of which He partook, when He was born of the virgin Mary. He cannot extend and repeat in us the 'incarnation' which was realized in His human life, because our human nature is already defiled, and so defiled that salvation can be achieved only if this old nature is brought to an end in judgment and death, and a new man raised up in us. What, therefore, Jesus shares with men is the redemption He wrought by His death, and the new humanity which was raised up in Him at His resurrection.

We need, therefore, to recognize that the incarnation of God the Son found its purpose and its intended fulfilment in His death. The chief thing that was true of the Son of man was that He must suffer. In the eternal purpose of God He became Man with the cross plainly in view. His advent was related not to a naturally deficient humanity needing completion, but to an unnaturally defiled and an eternally doomed humanity needing redemption. He came not to raise the quality of man's present life by, so to speak, a 'blood transfusion' from His perfect human nature. He came to rescue men from the bondage and the penalty of the evil which had so successfully invaded their lives. This He could do not by 'blood transfusion' but only by 'blood-shedding'; that is, not by sharing with men the flesh and blood of His human nature, but only by sacrificing them in death for men's redemption.

So Jesus said of Himself that 'the Son of man came ... to give his life a ransom for many' (Mark 10:45). He knew that He had 'a baptism to be baptized with' (Luke 12:50) in order to secure for men the benefit which outward water baptism pledged, namely, remission of sins. Consequently all who are in true faith baptized into Christ are baptized not into a share in His human nature, but into a share in His death and resurrection (see Rom. 6:3-8).

What is more, because of His own sinless character as man Jesus had personally no need or liability to die. He could have gone to the glory of the life beyond by translation. But had He so departed from this world, as He had every right to do, at the time of His transfiguration, His incarnation would have afforded no salvation for His fellow-men. He knew, and His conversation with Moses and Elijah at the time of His transfiguration explicitly confessed, that if God's people were to be saved He must accomplish for them an 'exodus' at Jerusalem (Luke 9:29-31). So from that point onwards He set His face with fresh concentration of purpose to go to Jerusalem to die (Luke 9:51). He was fully persuaded that thus and only thus would He fulfil His mission and be fully glorified as the Son of man (John 12:23-24).

This truth might be confirmed at length by reference to many statements in the New Testament epistles. Let us quote from one passage only. In Hebrews 2:5-18 we are told that the 'glory and honour' divinely intended for man are now enjoyed by the human 'Jesus.' 'We see Jesus ... crowned with glory and honour.' Not only so; He was thus made perfect as 'the Captain of their salvation.' God's purpose is through His sufferings to bring the 'many' as 'sons unto glory'. To achieve this end God the Son not only became Man, He tasted death. Indeed, He was born as man with this death in view. He was, says this writer, 'made for a little while lower than the angels ... that by the grace of God he should taste death for every man' (RV). And again, since those whom He purposed to save were 'sharers in flesh and blood, he also himself in like manner partook of the same; that through death he might bring to nought him that had the power of death, that is, the devil; and might deliver all them who through fear of death were all their lifetime subject to bondage' (RV).

We cannot, therefore, properly appreciate the divine purpose of the incarnation unless we recognize that Jesus was born of Mary in order to die for sinners. Consequently our theology of the incarnation will only be properly related both to the mind of God and to the needs of men, if it finds its climax and completion – indeed its supreme *raison d'être* – in our theology of redemption. If, therefore, it is appropriate – as some do when they say the Nicene Creed – to kneel in wonder and worship at the contemplation of the divine condescension in the incarnation, surely they ought, when they go on to speak of His suffering and death, also to go on to fall prostrate on their faces in excess of wonder that God incarnate should deliberately stoop to such a depth of shame to save us sinners.

Jesus the firstborn of the new creation

If Jesus in His death was the Representative Man bearing in other men's stead the penalty of their sin, then the place to look to see whether this sacrifice has achieved its intended purpose is on its farther side. Did God accept what Jesus had done as sufficient to put away sin? Was Jesus as Man then given by God any reward or consequent benefits which He can now share with men? To these questions the answer of the New Testament writers is overwhelmingly, 'Yes'. For at the very moment when Jesus died the symbolic temple veil, which shut sinful men out from God's presence, was rent in twain from the top to the bottom. And on the third day the human body of Jesus was raised and glorified. So the atoning work, which God the Son became Man to do, was clearly finished, accepted and rewarded; and the benefits are for us men to share. This is the heart of the Christian gospel of salvation.

This means, on the one hand, that there is no longer need or place for any further offering for sin. Christ has already 'obtained eternal redemption for us' (Heb. 9:12). It is, therefore, nothing less than a denial of His finished work and of God's own indications of its sufficiency, as well as an improper human presumption, for men to suggest, however devoutly, that the church can and ought to continue and to complete Christ's atoning sacrifice.

This means, also, on the other hand, that the new creation in which we sinners may share is not found in the manger at Bethlehem in Jesus born of Mary, but at the empty tomb and in Jesus risen from the dead. For God 'hath begotten us again unto a lively hope, by the resurrection of Jesus Christ from the dead' (1 Pet. 1:3). We are not commissioned as preachers of the gospel to tell men that because God the Son was born of Mary, there is fulness of life for all who share in His humanity. It is rather part of faithful and exclusive gospel witness to declare that,

119

if Christ be not raised from the dead, our faith is vain and we are yet in our sins (1 Cor. 15:17). It is as 'the firstborn from the dead' (Col. 1:18, Rev. 1:5 rv) – not as the newborn infant in the manger – that Christ is divinely predestined to be 'the firstborn among many brethren' (Rom. 8:29-30). This is 'the image' to which we, who thus belong to Christ as His brethren, are 'to be conformed'. The life, which He now offers to share with those who believe in Him, is not the flesh-and-blood life of His days on earth, but His risen life as the glorified Man (see Rom. 5:10; 6:4-5, 8, 23); and He does this by His Spirit, which can quicken us as He quickened Him when He raised Him from the dead (Rom. 8:9-11). So Paul writes, 'The last Adam became a life-giving spirit' (1 Cor. 15:45).

The first Adam, we are told, 'begat a son in his own likeness, after his image' (Gen. 5:3). This son was born of his father's flesh and blood. But brethren of Christ, who are predestinated to be conformed to His image, are born not of Christ's flesh and blood, but of His Spirit. In this new order, as Jesus Himself explicitly taught, 'It is the spirit that quickeneth; the flesh profiteth nothing' (John 6:63). There is a sense, of course, in which Christian believers, particularly in their use of the Lord's Supper, do still 'eat the flesh of the Son of man, and drink his blood' (John 6:53); for it is of the very essence of saving faith to acknowledge that we owe these benefits, which the risen and living Christ makes ours by His Spirit, to the death which He once suffered in His earthly flesh and blood. They are ours to enjoy solely as consequences of His passion. But that does not mean that we partake physically of the actual flesh and blood of His earthly human nature, with which the unforgettable work of our redemption was once for all decisively wrought. Rather such graphic language and symbolism are used to keep us ever mindful of His one finished sacrifice, as the source from which all our present blessings flow.

Also, this new life which we thus enjoy in the risen and glorified Christ, is the life of the coming age which lies in its fulness beyond our present life of flesh and blood. This new life will only be fully enjoyed by Christ's people when they are glorified bodily at His second advent. Here and now this new life can be entered into and expressed only, so the New Testament teaches, if we appreciate and respond to the significance of our justification. We must by faith begin to reckon as true of ourselves what God already reckons to be true of us in Christ, namely, that we are dead to sin and free to live unto Him; so that we may here and now live accordingly, presenting ourselves unto God to live unto Him (see Rom. 6:11-13). The truth of our justification, therefore, far from preventing us from enjoying vital participation in the life of Christ, itself points the road to its realized enjoyment by the responsive believer.

Leaving us an example

Since some assert that Christ is still continuing His sacrifice and that Christians, particularly in the eucharist, are called to share as members of His Body, the church, in Christ's present offering of Himself to God, it is important to recognize clearly that what is taught by the New Testament writers is that Christ's sacrifice for sin on the cross was unique, and was then and there brought to a successful completion. What His people are called to do is not to share in its continuance, but to learn from it in principle the pattern for their own discipleship.

When Christ suffered for us, He also left us an example that we should follow in His steps (see 1 Pet. 2:21). We are challenged in the New Testament to enter into the spirit of Christ's self-sacrificing devotion both to the will of God and to the service of men. Jesus Himself repeatedly taught His disciples that He expected them to follow Him, and to find a pattern for their own discipleship and devotion in the path He trod of obedience to His Father's will, and of willing, patient, self-denying submission to reproach and suffering, and ultimately to a cross of shame (see, for example, Mark 8:31-38). So Peter, for instance, in his first epistle shows by repeated statement how fully he came to accept teaching which at its first hearing was so unacceptable. It is he who explains to believers in Christ, who were exposed to suffering for their faith, that such suffering is in this world part of our Christian calling (1 Pet. 2:20-21; 3:14-17; 4:12-16). Only by being willing to suffer in the flesh can we on the one hand have done with sin, and on the other hand be faithful to Christ (1 Pet. 4:1-2, 19).

So Christians may expect, and ought to desire, to know something of the fellowship of Christ's sufferings. We may in spirit and in principle, like James and John, expect in some measure to drink His cup and to be baptized with His baptism (Mark 10:35-40) – in other words, to share His lot of rejection and pain, sorrow and woe, in this world. By such devotion to Him, even if need be unto death, we ought as 'martyrs' or faithful witnesses to be prepared to prove our loyalty and to give our testimony to our divine Saviour. Indeed, it is those who most share in such suffering and self-sacrifice in this life, who will be the best able and the most qualified to share in Christ's glory in the coming day of its full manifestation (see Rom. 8:18, 2 Cor. 4:10-11, 17; 2 Tim. 2:12; 1 Pet. 4:13).

But it is also of even greater importance to make plain that such suffering and self-sacrifice for Christ, and with Christ, are no part of that atoning sacrifice by which the sin of man has been borne and put away. For this Christ did for His people once for all, when He offered up Himself (Heb. 7:27). Such offering of our lives in sacrificial devotion to God ought not therefore to be associated with what is done with the bread and wine in the Lord's Supper. It is wrong to suppose that we ourselves and these sacramental elements may both be offered together to God as an expression of Christ's sacrifice of His body. For in the Supper the bread and wine are not to be offered to God. They are given by the Lord to His people to be eaten and drunk. Also, they speak not of Christ's present offering of either His heavenly or His mystical body, but of the one past offering on the cross of the flesh and blood of His earthly body, by which our redemption has been fully and finally procured. So we ought, first of all, to use our partaking of the bread and wine to express outwardly and symbolically our appropriation by faith of the benefits procured for us by Christ's passion. It is such appropriation that is intended to be described by using the vivid metaphorical language of 'eating His flesh and drinking His blood'.

It is, however, possible, on the other hand, once we have first thus acknowledged afresh our complete dependence for every blessing on Christ's one sacrifice of the cross, also to use the act of partaking of the bread and wine to express our willingness and our determination to be openly associated with Christ crucified, and to share any suffering or shame in which this may involve us. So we may in responsive consecration in this second sense 'drink His cup', desiring thereby to pledge ourselves, whatever the cost, to follow His steps and to be faithful unto death.

Conclusion

The distinctive truth of Christianity concerns the Person and work of Jesus Christ. Christians believe that Jesus is God Himself become Man, and become Man to save mankind. So we wrote at the beginning. So we reiterate at the end.

This essay will not have been written in vain if it serves to make some who read it aware that we can only hold fast to this distinctive Christian faith, and enjoy its saving and eternal benefits, if in the light of the scriptural revelation, and in opposition to much modern theorization and speculation which are indulged in in the name of

Christian theology, we accept with no compromising qualifications the full deity of Jesus and acknowledge without evasive speculation the atoning purpose and the finished character of His sacrificial death. 'Who is he that overcometh the world, but he that believeth that Jesus is the Son of God?' (1 John 5:5). 'Faithful is the saying, and worthy of all acceptation, that Christ Jesus came into the world to save sinners' (1 Tim. 1:15 RV).

10

THE FINISHED WORK OF CHRIST
(1952)

The idea that Christ's atoning work is 'finished' is scriptural in origin; it is indeed based on a word uttered by our Lord Himself before His death on the cross. We read that Jesus said, τετέλεσται – It is finished: and he bowed his head, and gave up his spirit' (John 19:30). Clearly, therefore, when Jesus at last reached the point of departure from this present earthly life, the work to which this word τετέλεσται referred was already fully accomplished. Similarly the doctrine to which such plain scriptural witness gave rise, that Christ by His death has done all that was necessary to reconcile sinful men to God, was equally clearly a precious conviction of many of our Christian forebears. They gloried in 'the finished work of Christ'. It was to them the heart of their gospel, the foundation of all their hope. Nor, as we shall see, has its unqualified reassertion been completely lacking in recent times. But views which are fundamentally different are widely prevalent and are more far-reaching in their influence on Christian faith and worship than many are aware. It is our purpose in this study first to indicate briefly the distinctive features of these different views and then to show why they are to be rejected as unscriptural, and why we ought with renewed determination to embrace and to affirm the conviction of our forefathers concerning 'the finished work of Christ'.

In contrast to this view that Christ's atoning work was 'finished' at the cross, it is suggested by some that Christ's earthly passion was but an expression in time or history of something which happens only fully in eternity; and that the eternal Son of God is, therefore, to be thought of as continually offering Himself to God in order to secure our acceptance in God's presence. For instance, Bishop A.M. Ramsey writes:

The third annual Tyndale Lecture in Biblical Theology, delivered in Cambridge on 8 July 1952, first published by Tyndale Press.

Christ's priesthood belongs, as does His sonship, to the eternal world: for ever Son, He is also for ever priest. Priesthood means offering, and in the Son there is for ever that spirit of self-offering which the sacrifice of Calvary uniquely disclosed in our world of sin and death.[1]

Similarly, Professor D.M. Baillie, while he asserts that the idea of 'a divine sin-bearing', 'a costly atonement in the heart of God', arose out of the historical event of the death of Jesus Christ; and while he insists that, 'To reduce the importance of the historical event would be contrary to every instinct of Christian faith'; nevertheless goes on to write: 'and yet it seems impossible to say that the divine sin-bearing was confined to that moment of time, or is anything less than eternal.'[2] He also writes:

> As God was incarnate in Jesus, so we may say that the divine atonement was incarnate in the passion of Jesus. And if we then go on to speak of an eternal atonement in the very being and life of God, it is not by way of reducing the significance of the historical moment of the incarnation, but by way of realizing the relation of the living God to every other historical moment. God's reconciling work cannot be confined to any one moment in history. ... It is not that the historical episode is a mere symbol of something 'timeless': it is actually a part (the incarnate part) of the eternal divine sin-bearing.[3]

It is suggested by others that Christ's 'blood' or 'life', shed or rather 'released' through His death on the cross, is now being offered to God as a continual oblation; and thus that the decisive offering made once for all on the cross is in some way continued or 're-presented' before God, both by Christ in heaven and by the church on earth. Surveying the views and teaching of others, D.M. Baillie begins, indeed, by making the very questionable assertion that, 'As regards the idea that the divine sin-bearing, the atoning work, which appeared in history once for all on Calvary, goes on ever since in the heavenly sphere, there are hints of this in the Christian tradition from the beginning.'[4]

Certainly not a few modern writers have given expression to the view that the heavenly and the eucharistic offering complete and consummate the sacrifice of the cross. For instance, R.C. Moberly writes:

---

[1] A.M. Ramsey, *The Glory of God and the Transfiguration of Christ* (London, 1948), p. 94.

[2] D.M. Baillie, *God was in Christ: An Essay on Incarnation and Atonement* (London, 1947), p. 190.

[3] Ibid., p. 191.

[4] Ibid., p. 194.

Though Calvary be the indispensable preliminary, yet it is not Calvary taken apart, not Calvary quite so directly as the eternal self-presentation in Heaven of the risen and ascended Lord, which is the true consummation of the sacrifice of Jesus Christ. But of course, in that eternal presentation Calvary is eternally implied.[5]

Similarly E.J. Bicknell writes:

So our Lord, by His presence within the veil, is now making atonement for us. As the high priest uttered no spoken prayer but by his presentation of the blood made reconciliation for Israel, our Lord as our representative, clothed in our nature, having become all that He now is through His cross and passion, eternally presents Himself to the Father.[6]

Also, F.C.N. Hicks writes of Christ:

He has entered into the holy place – once for all, it is true. He does not need to re-enter every year like the Jewish priest; and there His work is to sanctify, by bringing His outpoured life before the face of God, as the blood was sprinkled on the mercy seat.[7]

This idea of the continued offering to God of Christ's one sacrifice is also said to find expression on earth through Christ's mystical body, the church, in the sacrament of Holy Communion. For instance, O.C. Quick writes: 'The Eucharist then is truly a sacrifice. For it is the perpetual externalization in human ritual of the self-offering of Christ, which was once for all in fact externalized on Calvary, but is ever real in the inward and heavenly sphere.'[8] 'In the Eucharist ... we make before God an offering which is one with Christ's present and eternal offering of Himself.'[9] Similarly in a chapter entitled 'The Eucharist as Sacrifice' W. Norman Pittenger of the General Theological Seminary, New York, writes: 'The Church is enabled to make its sacrificial action identical with the once-for-all event on Calvary because it is the same Christ who offered himself on Calvary and who gives himself in his Body the Church.'[10] 'The Eucharist is a sacrifice because it is that "offering of

---

[5] R.C. Moberly, *Ministerial Priesthood* (London, 1897), p. 246.

[6] E.J. Bicknell, *A Theological Introduction to the Thirty-Nine Articles of the Church of England* (second edition, London, 1925), p. 144.

[7] F.C.N. Hicks, *The Fullness of Sacrifice: An Essay in Reconciliation* (London, 1930), p. 238.

[8] O.C. Quick, *The Christian Sacraments* (London, 1927), p. 198.

[9] Ibid., pp. 199-200.

[10] W. Norman Pittenger, *The Christian Sacrifice: A Study of the Eucharist in the Life of the Christian Church* (New York, 1951), p. 109.

Christ once made", herein pleaded and offered to the Father, set between "our sins and their reward".[11] Pittenger thus asserts not only that the church in the eucharist continues Christ's atoning work, but also that only as she does do so is Christ's one oblation made effective for men's present benefit.

Over against all such views it is the conviction of this present writer that Christ's work of offering Himself for men's salvation is unmistakably represented in Scripture as exclusively earthly and historical, the purpose of the incarnation, wrought out in flesh and blood, in time and space, under Pontius Pilate; that by this once-for-all finished happening the necessary and intended atoning work was completely accomplished; that because of it Christ has been eternally rewarded and His people enjoy the benefits which unceasingly stream from it, without any necessity, indeed without any possible place, for its continuance and completion by Christ in His glorified or mystical body in heavenly or eucharistic offering. It is, therefore, the main purpose of this study to expound the grounds of this conviction and by implication to show the unscriptural and misleading character of the different views already illustrated.

Important Preliminary Considerations

The relation of Christ's work to sin

There is great need for a clear recognition of the definite and distinctive purpose of Christ's redeeming and reconciling work. Activity which may be eternally true of the divine Son in His relation to the Father, or activity which ought to be characteristic of sinless and perfect man in his relation to God, namely continuous devotion of self as a living sacrifice to glorify God and serve His pleasure, ought not to be confused with the special activity in which the eternal Son had to engage in order to redeem a lost race and reconcile sinful men to God. It is this latter activity that we are here to consider.

Since this special activity was called forth by man's fall into sin, it is impossible to appreciate its necessary character except in that connection. We need to appreciate that sin exposes those who commit it to immediate bondage and inevitable condemnation; such creatures rightly become objects of the divine wrath, deserving to be dealt with

---

[11] Ibid., p. 110.

in judgment. Also, such sin makes those involved in it totally unfit to approach God; they are inevitably excluded from God's presence and from the enjoyment of His company. They have deprived themselves of the true satisfaction and fulfilment of their God-given human nature – that is, to know God.

The special activity of Christ must, therefore, deal in particular with these two consequences of sin – exposure to the divine wrath and exclusion from the divine presence. Such consequences demand for their remedy a single decisive action rather than a continuous and eternal activity. Something needs to be done, and completely done – in other words 'a finished work' needs to be accomplished – to secure men's deliverance from the divine wrath, and men's free access to the divine presence. Such a 'finished work' Christ did when He died for our sins; and we propose to consider its 'finished' character in these two connections – first as 'The τελείωσις of Redemption', delivering us from God's wrath, and second as 'The τελείωσις of Reconciliation', securing our unhindered access to God's presence.

The performance of Christ's work in time as an event in history

Ideas that Christ's work is supremely achieved continuously or eternally in heaven sound philosophically attractive and spiritually good. Actually such ideas are unscriptural and irrelevant to man's need of redemption and reconciliation. For God has been pleased to deal with the situation which man's sin has created on the field of earthly history, in time and space, in flesh and blood, and particularly through suffering and death.

Valuable reassertion of this essential Christian truth has been made by Oscar Cullmann in his significant work published in an English translation under the title *Christ and Time*. One can scarcely do better than quote some of his statements which are, it is to be noted, not his own theorizing, but his scholarly evaluation of primitive Christian thought as it can be learnt from the witness of the documents of the New Testament. He insists that in order properly to determine 'the essential Christian kernel' it is necessary 'to renounce all standards derived from any other source than the most ancient Christian writings themselves.'[12] He warns us of the need deliberately to recognize the unique character of the Christian standard, namely, 'that the Christian

---

[12] Oscar Cullmann, *Christ and Time: The Primitive Christian Concept of Time and History* (London, 1951), p. 12.

norm is itself also history and is not, as is the philosophical norm, a transcendent datum that lies beyond all history.'[13] 'Here', he says,

> in the final analysis lies the 'offense' of the primitive Christian view of time and history, not only for the historian, but for all 'modern' thinking, including theological thinking: the offense is that God reveals Himself in a special way, and effects 'salvation' in a final way, within a narrowly limited but continuing process.[14]

Also, 'all points of this redemptive line are related to the one historical fact at the mid-point, a fact which precisely in its unrepeatable character, which marks all historical events, is decisive for salvation. This fact is the death and resurrection of Jesus Christ.'[15]

Again, this idea of a '*kairos*', or definite point of time especially favourable for an undertaking and central in the divine plan of salvation, is found connected with the work which the incarnate Christ performed not only in the subsequent faith of the church. 'Rather', says Cullmann, 'Jesus Himself, according to the Synoptic witness characterizes His passion as His "*kairos*".'[16] Similarly, 'in the numerous Johannine passages in which Jesus speaks of His "hour" … in every case the hour of His death is meant.'[17] So Oscar Cullmann would have us realize, on the one hand, that Jesus really 'regarded His own death as the decisive point in the divine plan of salvation',[18] and on the other hand, that what he calls the one great Christological heresy both of ancient and modern times is that wider Docetism which has at its root 'the failure to respect the historically unique character of the redemptive deed of Christ.'[19] Before we proceed further, therefore, we shall do well to take seriously to heart both this positive witness and this complementary warning.

The ΤΕΛΕΙΩΣΙΣ of Remission of Sin and of Redemption from Sin

Much might be said under this heading. We wish to concentrate thought upon this one point that Christ secured the remission of our sins, and our redemption from its bondage and its penalty, by His death as a decisive act once-for-all accomplished whose benefits endure for ever

---

[13] Ibid., p. 21.
[14] Ibid., p. 23.
[15] Ibid., pp. 32-33.
[16] Ibid., pp. 39-41.
[17] Ibid., pp. 43-44.
[18] Ibid., pp. 148-149.
[19] Ibid., p. 127.

and are available to be enjoyed by all for whom He died. In other words, the atoning and redemptive efficacy of His saving work, the necessary propitiation and ransom price, are to be found in His death; and it will be our object to show that this is explicitly indicated by significant utterances of our Lord and abundantly confirmed as the faith of the early church by the pointed testimony and dogmatic statements of the New Testament.

The significance of death

As an aid to fuller appreciation of what we understand the evidence to imply it may be helpful at this stage briefly to indicate what is, as we see it, the significance attached in the Bible both to death itself and to the voluntary submission to such death of the sinless God-Man Christ Jesus. For in the thought-world of scriptural truth, death is directly connected with sin as its consequence and penalty. To quote a recent writer: 'For man to die is unnatural. It is a punishment for sin (Romans 1:32 etc); and it is no arbitrary punishment, being bound up with it by an inner necessity.'[20] Over against this truth the unique, remarkable and indeed paradoxical truth about Christ's death is that while, on the one hand, He suffered the death due to men as sinners in all the grimness of its curse and shame, on the other hand, He did this not as Himself a sinner inevitably bound so to die, but in complete voluntary submission as one who freely chose thus to lay down His life (see John 10:18) to secure remission and redemption for sinners whose condition as under condemnation and judgment He thus completely made His own.

Christ's suffering was, therefore, penal – the kind of suffering due only to sin and to sinners. It was substitutionary because due actually not to the sinless Christ, but to us sinners in whose place He suffered as, so to speak, our 'proxy'. It was redemptive because by thus exhausting upon Himself the claims of sin and death against us sinners, without Himself becoming subject to their power as a sinner, He secured the possibility of our release, once we acknowledge Him as our Lord who did it in our stead. For once He was dead the ransom price was paid and the remission effected; in other words, the necessary atoning and redemptive work was finished.

No wonder it has appeared to some, particularly in the early centuries of the Christian era, as if the powers of evil were deceived. For the death due to us as sinners which He thus took upon Himself

---

[20] John A.T. Robinson, *The Body: A Study in Pauline Theology* (London, 1952), p. 34.

secured no proper hold upon Him, the sinless One. For Him death had no sting. Indeed, He died not 'in sin' or 'under sin' but 'unto sin' (see John 8:24, Rom. 6:10). 'It was', as Peter preached, 'impossible that He should be holden of death' (Acts 2:24); and He is now able to give release to sinners, who would otherwise be holden, because He thus died on their behalf. So sin and death are robbed of their prey. The stronger than the devil has taken possession of the devil's stronghold and is able to spoil his goods or free his captives; and all because the necessary work to make such results possible is already finished. The resurrection of our 'proxy' from the dead is the decisive proof that the sin He bore is remitted and that we are justified in God's sight (see 1 Cor. 15:17, Rom. 4:25).

Our Lord's attitude to His own death

The Gospel records themselves provide ample evidence that this is how Christ Himself during His life-time saw the death which He set Himself to face to be both absolutely necessary and abundantly worthwhile. Let us consider three significant illustrations.

a) Christ's submission to baptism by John

John gave baptism to the repentant as a solemn pledge and promise of remission of sins and of the baptism of the Spirit, a seal of that necessary cleansing and quickening which would give them entrance into the kingdom of God. Jesus came to be baptized, not because He needed remission and regeneration, but, as we believe, in order to consecrate Himself to the necessary work that would make such remission and regeneration possible for sinful men. His own explicit words later confirmed that it was His death which He saw plainly to be the true baptism with which he must be baptized (Luke 12:50). In submitting, therefore, to ceremonial baptism with water He was consecrating Himself to die to put away sin and make possible the gift of the Spirit.

This consecration was followed by three remarkable testimonies. First, the testimony of the Father's voice from heaven, indicating His delight in the Messiah who thus chose to fulfil the role of the Suffering Servant and bear the sin of many (Mark 1:11, Isa. 42:1, 53:10-12). Second, the testimony of the rent heaven and the descending Spirit, not only indicating that God Himself would empower Him for this very task, but also suggesting that when it was accomplished and

He emerged from His baptism of death the Spirit would be given to men (Mark 1:10). Third, the testimony of the Baptist's preaching. For John declared his awareness that through his water baptism 'the coming one' would be fully made manifest to Israel; and in the light of Jesus' consecration of Himself by baptism to the 'fulfilment of all righteousness' John proclaimed Him to be 'the Lamb of God which taketh away the sin of the world' and 'He that baptizeth with the Holy Spirit' (Matt. 3:13-17, John 1:29-34).

Yet further significant comment on John's baptism may be found in our Lord's discourse with Nicodemus (see John 3:1-14). To him Jesus made plain that the outward ceremony of water baptism alone would not suffice to give entrance to God's kingdom. There must be an accompanying inner renewal, a birth of the Spirit. And when Nicodemus asked how such a miracle could happen, Christ indicated plainly the decisive work that would make it possible for men who must otherwise perish as sinners, to become possessors of new God-given life. 'As Moses lifted up the serpent in the wilderness, even so must the Son of man be lifted up: that whosoever believeth may in him have eternal life.' Nor is it without complementary significance that as soon as Jesus' baptism of death was accomplished and He was risen from the dead, He at once made plain to His disciples that remission of sins and the gift of the Spirit can now be authoritatively offered to men (John 20:19-23, Luke 24:44-49); indeed, these are the great fundamental gifts of the gospel of which at Pentecost baptism in the name of Jesus Christ was declared to be the seal (Acts 2:38).

b) Christ's breaking of the bread to feed the hungry

In the familiar stories of the feeding first of the five thousand and then of the four thousand, the point at which the miracle happened is unmistakably clear: indeed, Jesus later rebuked His disciples for not remembering. It was when He broke the loaves that on each occasion there were enough broken fragments for all to be satisfied and enough over to fill several baskets (see Mark 6:34-44, 8:1-9, 14-21). The multitude was fed, first because Jesus was there, second because He condescended to take the loaves, third – and this was the decisive event – because He broke the loaves. Once that work was finished, there was plenty to give to all. Similarly the spiritual need of men has been met, first, because the eternal Son of God arrived on the human scene, He came down from above; second, because He condescended to take our nature, flesh and blood, to become man; third, and this is the decisive event, because He gave His flesh to be broken so that His blood was shed in death. Once that work was finished Christ could be offered to and received by men as the bread of life, that is, as the Saviour who died for them. For those who would have eternal life must, He said, 'eat my flesh and drink my blood'; and it is clear enough from the Old Testament that such phraseology as 'eating a man's flesh' and 'drinking a man's blood' meant to the Hebrew mind appropriating and enjoying as one's own benefits only procured at the cost of someone else's life (see Ps. 14:4, 27:2, 2 Sam. 23:15-17). In other words, eternal life is to be received solely and exclusively as a benefit of Christ's passion, as made available for us to enjoy by that one decisive event, the rending of His human body in death. This truth our Lord Himself indicated and enforced in the most dogmatic and conclusive fashion when He said, 'Verily, verily, I say unto you, Except ye eat the flesh of the Son of man, and drink his blood, ye have not life in yourselves' (see John 6:32-35, 47-58). Nor is it without complementary significance that the bread which we break according to Christ's ordinance in the Holy Communion, on the one hand unmistakably points to the decisive event of His death, and on the other hand, by what Christ commanded to be done with it (that is, 'Take, eat'), dramatically speaks of consequent benefits thereby made available to be received by men (1 Cor. 11:23-26). His finished work is thus visibly shown to make possible an unceasing feeding; it provides enough and more than enough to satisfy all the needs of all the people of God; or, as St Paul put it in appropriate passover language, 'For our passover also hath been sacrificed, even Christ: wherefore let us keep the feast' (1 Cor. 5:7-8).

c) Christ's declaration that He came to give His life a ransom for many (Mark 10:45, Matt. 20:28)

In biblical usage the word 'ransom' (Greek, λύτρον, Hebrew, *kôpher*) is clearly a price paid to deliver anyone from threatened or merited punishment, and particularly to secure release and rescue from death of a life otherwise forfeit (see Exod. 13:13, Num. 35:31). Psalm 49:6-8 declares of those who 'trust in their wealth' that 'none of them can by any means redeem his brother, nor give to God a ransom for him: for the redemption of their soul is costly, and must be let alone for ever.' Our Lord Himself emphasized the hopelessness of the human situation by two unanswerable rhetorical questions: 'For what doth it profit a man to gain the whole world, and forfeit his life? For what should a man give in exchange for his life?' (Mark 8:36-37). These words imply that once a man's life is forfeited, man has no means of redeeming it from loss. In relation to this situation Christ asserted that if He laid down His one life it would be sufficient to secure the release not only of one other, but of all the people of God – 'the many' – whose lives otherwise, so Christ implies, are all forfeited. Also, 'the giving of the λύτρον is certainly here the laying down of life in death.'[21] It is a reference to a work of redemption finished at and on the cross:

> It is not the presentation in heaven of blood shed on earth, nor the sprinkling in any sort of the Saviour's blood on earth or in heaven; but it is the blood-shedding, the dying, the death, which is here set before faith's view as the great work which the Son of man came into the world to do; and the doing of which is the paying of the ransom price for man's redemption, for his spiritual liberty and restoration.[22]

The very idea of paying a ransom demands, if it is to be successful, a decisive result, a complete consequent change in the condition of those for whose benefit it is paid. It is, therefore, completely out of place to think of Christ's redeeming work still being completed in heaven. For the reiterated testimony of the apostolic writers is that 'we have our redemption through his blood' (Eph. 1:7, compare 1 Pet. 1:18-19), that is, through His death, or to quote our Lord's own phraseology, through His human life given as a ransom. Also, His bodily resurrection as man was the proof that the redemption was already completely effected through His death.

The one finished work of Christ's voluntary submission to death is, therefore, to be viewed as a sufficient sin-offering or 'kôpher'. It is intolerable to think of this necessary payment of ransom as going on continuously or eternally.[23] Christ's own words indicate that He came into this world and became man in order to finish the necessary redemptive work here and now, by giving His earthly human life as the ransom. And in general the scriptural witness emphasizes that the necessary 'transaction' was all limited to and settled in one critical 'hour' or 'day' in which God thus allowed Him to be handed over to suffer in

---

[21] Nathaniel Dimock, *The Doctrine of the Death of Christ, in Relation to the Sin of Man, the Condemnation of Law, and the Dominion of Satan* (second edition, London, 1903), p. 48.

[22] Ibid., pp. 48-49.

[23] 'For it is one thing to believe that the moral government of God required an historic manifestation of the condemnation of sin through the earthly life and death of the Lord Jesus; but it is quite another thing to believe that God requires for man's forgiveness a continual process of propitiation through the ceaseless re-presenting to Him by our Lord of His sacrifice.' A.J. Tait, *The Nature and Functions of the Sacraments* (London, 1917), p. 89.

His person as man the inevitable outworking of the power and penalty of sin.

The decisive event itself

When we consider the New Testament records of the decisive event itself, together with the apostolic interpretation of its significance, there are noteworthy evidences that once this act of sin-bearing up to the death on the cross was finished the situation was completely changed and Jesus immediately began to enjoy the fruits of victory. For by Himself thus dying He did not become, like others, a victim and prisoner of death; rather, by dying voluntarily and not as one who must He, so to speak, stormed the stronghold of death and captured it. His purpose was by a human death in flesh and blood to 'bring to nought him that had the power of death, that is, the devil' (Heb. 2:14). 'God, sending his own Son in the likeness of sinful flesh and as an offering for sin, condemned sin in the flesh' (Rom. 8:3). Jesus 'realized' the eschatology of God's eternal judgment against sinful man by bringing it decisively to an immediate consummation and finish in the one completed act of earthly and temporal history – His death – which by its very nature as a freely chosen act of sacrifice took Him beyond the scene of sin and death not as their victim but as their victor, the one who had thus broken their otherwise invincible hold on men and inevitable doom for men.

Thus Jesus became the Lord of death and of the dead. Thus He was able freely Himself to open the gate back into life and came forth to proclaim: 'I was dead, and behold, I am alive for evermore, and I have the keys of death and of Hades' (Rev. 1:18). Thus, through such suffering, He was made perfect – a finished work – as the pioneer of salvation. For by this way of the cross He not only entered His own glory, but also opened up the road by which to bring the many as sons into glory – the destined glory of humanity of which men have come short through sin (see Heb. 2:10, Rom. 3:23). For when His flesh was rent in death He not only opened a way out for sinners from death and doom, He also consecrated a way in for believers into man's true home in God's presence (Rom. 4:25–5:2, 9; Heb. 10:19-20). As the redeemer He brings men out of sin and death, not back into physical, sinful, earthly life, but beyond it into spiritual, sanctified, eternal life and all because of the finished work of His own death and its endless consequences.

The hour, therefore, when the prince of this world was cast out, was the hour of Christ's death. The place where Christ was triumphantly lifted up as the king whose right it is to reign was on the tree (John 12:27, 31-33). There at the cross, to those who have the faith to see, He openly triumphed over the powers of evil. He cancelled out the legal charge sheet written against us as transgressors (Col. 2:14-15). He broke the hold that sin and the law, death and the devil, had upon us as guilty sinners (Rom. 6:6-7, 14; 7:4, 6). As soon as He was dead, all hell as well as all heaven knew that the decisive victory had been won. He went and proclaimed it to the rebellious spirits in prison, who await the judgment of the coming great day of God (1 Pet. 3:18-19, 2 Pet. 2:4, Jude 6).

Christ's burial and resurrection

The completely changed situation immediately following the death of Jesus may also be discerned in what happened to His dead body. For God providentially took over its proper care. Though Jesus suffered to the point of dying as though He were a sinner, as one numbered with transgressors and publicly bearing the curse due to sin, yet once He was dead His body was not roughly handled and thrown out like those of the other two malefactors. Not a bone of Him was broken; and by a sudden surprising intervention of two members of the Jewish Sanhedrin, His body was lavishly bound in linen cloths with spices and buried in a new rock-hewn tomb (see John 19:31-37). Neither did God suffer His holy one to see corruption (see Acts 2:27-32, 13:34-37). On the third day His body was glorified. Nor was His bodily resurrection just the condition of His going to heaven to complete the work which will avail to save sinful men. It was the proof of the success and the beginning of the reward of His finished work of propitiation and redemption. 'If Christ hath not been raised', wrote St Paul, 'your faith is vain; ye are yet in your sins' (1 Cor. 15:17). This means surely that because He has been raised we know that the hold of sin has been broken, that full propitiation has been made and that we are justified before God (see Acts 13:37-39, Rom. 4:25).

Similarly the writer of the epistle to the Hebrews says that 'the God of peace ... brought again from the dead the great shepherd of the sheep with ['by' RV margin, Greek ἐν] the blood of the eternal covenant' (Heb. 13:20):

> The force of ἐν here requires us to understand that it was in virtue of the blood of the covenant, because of its availing efficacy,

because, having been shed for many for the remission of sins it had accomplished its work, that the Lord Jesus was raised from the dead … [There is] evidence here that the blood of sacrifice … [was] effectual and … accepted as effectual, before the resurrection of Christ … also, an assurance that the New Covenant in that blood was, before the resurrection, already established and confirmed and in full force.[24]

Also, 'if the resurrection is the result of the Saviour's sacrifice offered in blood, it is impossible that the ascension of the Saviour can be in order to the offering of that blood of sacrifice in heaven.'[25] In other words, the necessary work of propitiation and redemption was finished at the cross where, in contrast to the hidden mercy seat of the holy of holies, Christ Jesus was openly set forth to be a propitiation by His death (see Rom. 3:24-26, note the Greek).

Christ's heavenly enthronement

The same writer to the Hebrews also says that the eternal Son of God 'when he had made purification of sins, sat down on the right hand of the majesty on high' (Heb. 1:3). If these two phrases are interpreted in their context, their grammatical form and their syntactical sequence emphasize two things: first, that the outstanding achievement of the incarnation was the purification of sins and, second, that the act of taking His seat in heaven at the right hand of God followed and was indeed a consequence of its completion. From repeated statements of a similar kind throughout this epistle it is abundantly clear that this writer regarded Christ's heavenly enthronement as itself the God-given proof and reward of a propitiatory work already successfully accomplished (see Heb. 1:13, 2:9, 10:12-13, 12:2). Also:

the force of Hebrews 9:22 lies especially in the fact that it does not say 'without sprinkling of blood is no remission' but it says χωρις αἱματεκχυσίας οὐ γίνεται ἄφεσις thereby showing the true subordination of the sprinkling as a means merely of applying the efficacy, which is to be viewed as resulting only from the blood-shedding.[26]

To return to the evidence of the Gospel according to St Luke, the conversation at the Transfiguration between Moses and Elijah and our Lord made plain that the decisive 'exodus', for the redemption of God's Israel from

---

[24] Dimock, *Death of Christ*, p. 58.

[25] Nathaniel Dimock, *The Sacerdotium of Christ as Taught in the Holy Scriptures* (London, 1910), p. 113.

[26] Dimock, *Death of Christ*, p. 62.

the bondage of sin, would be accomplished not in heaven after the ascension, but on earth at Jerusalem (Luke 9:30-31). That is where the necessary work of redemption was finished. That is where, as Peter wrote later, 'his own self carried up our sins in his body to the tree' (1 Pet. 2:24 RV).

The witness of the two sacraments of the gospel

That this is the truth on which all Christian faith and hope should rest is confirmed by that ordinance which the Lord ordained as the Christian passover, an ordinance in which we remember the redemption once for all accomplished by His death from which innumerable benefits unceasingly flow. For the sacrament of Holy Communion is not a means to repeat or re-present His sacrifice before God, but a visible and dramatic movement, directed by the Lord Himself towards His people, to make them aware that His one sacrifice already finished has so availed that unceasing benefits of it are continually available and may herewith be by faith appropriated and enjoyed.

Similarly in the other sacrament of the gospel all who are baptized into Christ are baptized into His death 'that the body of sin might be done away' (Rom. 6:3-7). They are thereby authoritatively made aware that the one sufficient ground and cause of redemption and release from sin, of acceptance in God's sight and freedom to live unto Him, is a finished act of the past – the death of Christ – into whose far-reaching consequences they are thus solemnly initiated and challenged actively to enter. It is here noteworthy that believers in Christ are not baptized into Christ's heavenly or eternal offering of Himself to God. For that would make salvation something only in the process of being won; that would deprive believers of the true evangelical assurance of sin forgiven; that would suggest that the church on earth must unite with the Christ in heaven to procure salvation by a continuing work of propitiatory offering. This is clearly not the gospel of the apostolic preaching in which the exalted Lord was proclaimed as one already put by God into that place of Lordship from which, without further atoning work, He can give repentance and remission of sins to all who call upon His name (see Luke 24:46-47, Acts 2:38, 5:30-31, 10:43, 13:38-39). 'The message of the gospel starts from the finished work of sacrifice.'[27] 'What ministers of the gospel have to offer of propitiation for acceptance is for acceptance not in heaven, but on earth; is offered not to the Holy God but to rebel hearts of sinful men.'[28]

---

[27] Dimock, *Sacerdotium of Christ*, p. 85.
[28] Ibid., p. 80.

In other words, only if we recognize and believe that Christ's atoning work is decisively finished, and He Himself exalted to give gifts to the sinful for whom He suffered, can we enjoy and proclaim the wonder of present full justification by faith only. Many of us lack assurance of sin forgiven, many of us have ceased to glory in the truth of justification by faith, because we have become weak in our conviction and certainty concerning the τελείωσις of redemption or the finished character of Christ's redeeming work. 'For the death that he died, he died unto sin once for all' (Rom. 6:10 RV). That is the point where sin and its doing and its doom are all left behind – at His cross; that henceforth in Him and with Him we may live eternally unto God.

The ΤΕΛΕΙΩΣΙΣ of Priesthood and of Reconciliation

As we have reminded ourselves in the introduction many hold the view that Christ is continually making propitiation in heaven by offering Himself to God as the Lamb that once was slain. What is more, this view is said to be unquestionably scriptural because, according to the ritual of the Day of Atonement, propitiation was made not by the killing of the animal but by the subsequent sprinkling of its blood in the most holy place (Lev. 16:15-17). Also, in the epistle to the Hebrews it is emphatically asserted that Christ functions as a priest not on earth, like the Levitical priests, but in heaven; and as a priest He must of necessity have something to offer (Heb. 8:1-4). Therefore it is right to think of Him in heaven making priestly and propitiatory offering for sin by offering Himself or His blood to God.[29]

It will be our aim in what follows to show that such a view represents a radical misunderstanding of the witness of Scripture through failure to give due consideration to certain new facts in the New Testament fulfilment of the Old Testament figure, which completely alter the situation. Such a view is, indeed, more Jewish than fully Christian, because it fails properly to appreciate the true τελείωσις or perfection and the consequent surpassing glory of the priesthood of Christ

---

[29] 'In every ordinary sin-offering ... not the slaying of the victim but the presentation of blood was the essentially priestly act; and if, therefore, our Lord ever performed what was the priestly function in its deepest meaning, it must have been when He presented Himself with His offering in the heavenly sanctuary.' 'The thought of "offering" on the part of our Lord is not to be confined to His sacrificial death: it is so to be extended as to include in it a present and eternal offering to God of Himself in heaven.' William Milligan, *The Ascension and Heavenly Priesthood of Our Lord* (London, 1892), pp. 7, 133.

compared with that of the Levitical system. For with the Levitical priests, although propitiation and the winning of full and free access to God for the people was the goal or τέλος of their service, this τέλος was never reached. 'There was no τελείωσις. The legal covenant knew no τετέλεσται'.[30] Whereas, to quote A.B. Bruce,'the didactic significance of Hebrews 7:11-28 is that in Jesus Christ, as the priest after the order or type of Melchizedek, the ideal of priesthood is realized.'[31] 'It is assumed that a priesthood worthy of, and destined to, perpetuity must make men "perfect" in the sense of bringing them really near to God, establishing between them and God a true unimpeded fellowship by the removal of sin.'[32] And it is shown that, because such 'perfection' could not be procured for men by the Levitical priesthood, it had to be superseded. It never became an effective and consequently an enduring priesthood; or, to use the scriptural way of putting it, it never became a priesthood 'for ever after the order of Melchizedek'.

The significance of the ritual of the Day of Atonement

As a figure of the true or a copy of heavenly things (see Heb. 8:5, 9:24) and as a shadow of good things to come (Heb. 10:1), the function of the ritual of the Day of Atonement was to suggest a method and to promise a divine provision that would do two things – secure access to God's presence for those otherwise shut out by sin, and so to provide for their sins' complete removal that they would be remembered no more. Both blessings were clearly shown by the ritual to lie beyond the decisive death of the sin-offering and to depend upon it (see Lev. 16:1-22). The stress in connection with the high priest sprinkling the blood on the mercy-seat is placed on the unique achievement of his thereby *securing entrance* into the most holy place, and not on his continuing to fulfil a work of offering the blood after entrance had thus been gained.[33] Indeed, his early reappearance from the sanctuary was eagerly awaited. For his coming out again alive was an explicit indication to the people of his acceptance in the most holy place; and he completed the indication of the benefits procured by the killing of the sin-offering by confessing the sins of the people on (its

---

[30] Dimock, *Sacerdotium of Christ*, p. 22. See also Heb. 7:11.

[31] A.B. Bruce, *The Epistle to the Hebrews* (Edinburgh, 1899), p. 262.

[32] Ibid., p. 263.

[33] 'A profound emphasis is laid upon both the secluded sanctity of the inner shrine ... and the sacrificial process by which alone the rare privilege of entrance into it could be obtained.' H.C.G. Moule, *Messages from the Epistle to the Hebrews* (London, 1909), p. 44.

'*alter ego*'[34]) the second live goat to be borne away into the wilderness. Thus there was in the figure of the ritual no continued offering in the sanctuary, but the immediate assurance of a completed atonement and of the present possibility of the taking away of sin. Though the writer to the Hebrews adds his significant comments that 'it is impossible that the blood of bulls and goats should take away sins' (Heb. 10:4); and that the very continuance of a tabernacle or temple, with the holy place permanently separated from the holy of holies by a dividing veil, was itself a Spirit-given witness that the true way into the holiest of all was not yet disclosed (Heb. 9:8). The whole ritual, therefore, represented a reaching-out after benefits never actually attained by it. There was in the figure an indication of the way of bringing to the birth, but there was no strength actually to bring forth. There was no τελείωσις either of priesthood or of reconciliation.

Corresponding fulfilment in Christ

All this should prepare our minds the better to appreciate both the character and the wonder of the actual τελείωσις in Christ. He was able to bring forth, to finish the work of propitiation, and thus to win through beyond it to the crowning fulfilment and ministry of priesthood into which the Levitical priests were never able to enter and which in the Old Testament could be found only figuratively suggested by the priesthood of Melchizedek (see Ps. 110:1, 4). Henceforth, instead of endlessly striving like the Levitical priests to fulfil the essential function of priesthood by the true achievement of reconciliation, Christ became able, as the one perfected priest, to minister to all who come to Him the endless and eternal benefits of His finished work of reconciliation (see Heb. 4:16, 5:7-10, 10:11-12). For in His offering of Himself by Himself, as the victim as well as the priest, He shed blood whose shedding could avail both to win entrance to God's presence and to cleanse all sin. Nor did His people have to wait long for His reappearance

---

[34] 'For it must be noted that there was here no second act of atonement. There were not two sin-offerings but one. And the reason that *two* goats were used for the *one* sin-offering lay in the fact that "the ritual of this exceptional sin-offering rendered it necessary that, after the slaughtering and sprinkling of the blood the animal should either still be living, or be brought to life again. And as this could not possibly be represented by means of one single goat, it was necessary to divide the role, which this sin-offering had to play, between two goats, the second of which was to be regarded as the *alter ego* of the first, as *hircus redivivus*" [J.H. Kurtz, *Sacrificial Worship of the Old Testament*, English translation (Edinburgh, 1863), pp. 395-396]. The second goat, therefore, carried to completion the work which the first had begun.' George Milligan, *The Theology of the Epistle to the Hebrews* (Edinburgh, 1899), pp. 164-165.

alive to administer the benefits of His finished work of atonement. For on the third day He appeared to His disciples, risen from the dead, and assured them that they could now become the dwelling place of God's Spirit, and that repentance and remission of sins could now be authoritatively proclaimed in His name to the ends of the earth (John 20:19-23, Luke 24:45-49). This surely is proof of the τελείωσις of priesthood and reconciliation. The pattern of the figurative ritual also suggests that those who would now know the peace of sins removed, have only to unburden them on One who was dead and is alive again, the Lamb once slain who takes away the sin of the world, because He has already 'made an end of atoning' (see Lev. 16:20-22).

How Christ finished the work of atonement

Let us now consider in more detail how Christ as high priest finished the work of atonement. To begin with, the Scripture states explicitly that every high priest is 'taken from among men' (Heb. 5:1) and that 'it behoved him in all things to be made like unto his brethren, that he might be a merciful and faithful high priest in things pertaining to God, to make propitiation for the sins of the people' (Heb. 2:17). Even so, because Christ's priesthood is clearly heavenly, some would regard not only His earthly life but even His death on the cross not as part of His priestly work but rather as necessary preliminaries. What we need to understand here is that because Christ's crowning act of priesthood, His offering of Himself, was done in relation to the actual presence of God and not in relation to the earthly figure sanctuary in Jerusalem, it was, as the writer to the Hebrews saw it, done in the true heavenly tabernacle and not in the shadow earthly one.[35] In other words, though Jesus died outside the city of Jerusalem, His deed as a priestly act was done in heaven, or in the heavenlies as Paul himself might have said, and not just on earth.

It was as man, in the flesh, that Christ was made sin for us and that God in Him condemned sin in the flesh (2 Cor. 5:21, Rom. 8:3). In this hour of judgment on the cross, His humanity, thus regarded and treated as sinful by God, became as it were itself the veil that shut men out of God's presence; and in the mystery of man's greatest darkness temporarily hid from Jesus His Father's face (Mark 15:33-34). But when His flesh

---

[35] 'In his view "true" and "heavenly" are synonyms; whatever is "true" is heavenly, belongs to the upper world of its realities ... If Christ's sacrifice of Himself be a true sacrifice, it belongs to the heavenly world, no matter where or when it takes place.' Bruce, *Hebrews*, p. 294. 'Heavenly things (Heb. 8:5, 9:23) are in contrast not with the earth as a locality, but with the tabernacle as a material building.' Milligan, *Ascension and Heavenly Priesthood*, p. 24.

was finally rent in death, it gave Christ not exit into outer darkness to await eternal judgment, but *immediate entrance* into God's presence (Heb. 9:24, 10:20). Christ's willing submission to such a death did not have to be followed by a separate, subsequent entrance into the heavenly sanctuary to sprinkle the true place of propitiation. For in the one act of offering Himself in death, He entered God's presence as Himself the now blood-stained propitiation (see 1 John 2:1-2), having already obtained eternal redemption for us (Heb. 9:12-14). Such entrance was itself evidence that His propitiatory and redeeming work was finished; it was not the preliminary only to its necessary and proper completion in heaven.

Christ offered Himself

Christ offered Himself, we are told, 'through the eternal Spirit' (Heb. 9:14). He was thus able, as undying deity, still to be active in the moment of the death of His humanity. In consequence He did what no other priest could do and, as simultaneously both priest and victim, 'offered Himself'. Accordingly He entered God's presence, not 'with blood' (Heb. 9:7, 25) as was necessary in the entrance of the Levitical high priest to provide evidence of the death of the sin-offering, but 'through his own blood' (Heb. 9:12), that is, through the very event of His own human death as the true sin-offering.[36] And where, in entering, the Levitical priest is said to have offered or brought near *blood* (Heb. 9:7), Christ is explicitly said through His own blood (that is, His death) to have offered or brought near *Himself* to God (Heb. 9:12, 14). Similarly later in a context, where the reference is explicitly defined as a reference to His earthly suffering and sacrifice, Christ's action in offering Himself is treated as corresponding to the action of the Levitical high priest in entering the holy place with blood (Heb. 9:25-26). Also, the very phraseology of Hebrews 9:12 and 9:14 indicates that Christ's blood shed in death was the ground of His entrance, and not that its subsequent atoning offering to God was the purpose of

---

[36] 'The statement that through death Jesus became *ipso facto* author of salvation is not falsified by the fact that the essential point in a sacrifice was its presentation before God in the sanctuary, which in the Levitical system took place subsequently to the slaughtering of the victim. ... The death of our High Priest is to be conceived of as including all the steps of the sacrificial process within itself. Lapse of time or change of place is not necessary to the accomplishment of His work. The death of the victim, the presentation of the sacrificial blood – all was performed when Christ cried τετέλεσται.' Bruce, *Hebrews*, pp. 190-191.

His entrance.[37] In other words, once He had *entered* Christ was no longer making atonement; He had begun to enjoy the benefits of full atonement already made.

The veil rent

What is more, by this sacrifice of Christ on the cross and by this entrance into God's presence through death, sin and the veil which shut men out from the sanctuary were not just temporarily and figuratively covered or by-passed; they were actually and eternally removed and done away. This fact is, of course, dramatically indicated in the Gospel records of both Mark and Matthew, who, immediately following the statement that Jesus yielded up His spirit, declare, 'And, behold, the veil of the temple was rent in twain from the top to the bottom' (Mark 15:38, Matt. 27:51). Christ, therefore, could never again find Himself, like the Levitical high priest, outside the veil as one needing still to continue or again to repeat the work of atoning for sin. For His propitiatory work and His entrance into God's presence were both accomplished once for all for ever; neither activity needs to be, or indeed can be, continued or repeated. Rather it is the blessed consequences of His finished work which continue for ever and repeatedly operate for the benefit of men.

Christ hailed and acclaimed by God

The amazing character of Christ's decisive achievement is indicated in Scripture, particularly in the epistle to the Hebrews, by the various ways in which we are told that as soon as by His obedience through suffering unto death he was 'made perfect' (Heb. 2:9-10, 5:7-9), He was immediately hailed and acclaimed by God. There are three relevant passages.

a) 'Sit thou on my right hand till I make thine enemies the footstool of thy feet' (Heb. 1:13, from Ps. 110:1)

First, Jesus was hailed as the victor who had done all that God required and who was worthy to be rewarded. So without being given more to do in heaven to complete His work, He was told by God Himself at once

---

[37] 'The writer [of Hebrews] uses language which can only fairly be understood as intimating that Christ enters heaven, not in order to offer His blood in sacrifice, but because of His blood already shed, and in virtue of the efficacy of His atoning death already offered upon the cross.' Dimock, *Death of Christ*, p. 56.

to occupy the seat of supreme power in the universe at God's right hand; and God Himself promised to see that all His enemies were brought into subjection to His Lordship. The same truth is as emphatically indicated by St Paul who says:

> Wherefore [that is, because of Christ's earthly obedience unto the death of the cross] God highly exalted him, and gave unto him the name which is above every name; that in the name of Jesus every knee should bow, of things in heaven, and things on earth and things under the earth, and that every tongue should confess that Jesus Christ is Lord, to the glory of God the Father (Phil. 2:9-11).

Paul also says when God displayed the strength of His might in raising Christ from the dead, not that He exalted Him to heaven to continue and complete His atoning work, but that He 'made him to sit at his right hand in the heavenly places, far above all rule, and authority, and power, and dominion, and every name that is named, not only in this world, but also in that which is to come; and he put all things in subjection under his feet' (Eph. 1:19-22).

b) 'Thou art a priest for ever after the order of Melchizedek' (Heb. 5:6, 10, from Ps. 110:4)[38]

Second, in contrast to the ineffective Levitical priests whose incessant offerings could never take away sin, as soon as Jesus had fulfilled the purpose of the incarnation, and had done the will of God on earth by offering His human body in sacrifice, He was hailed by God as the only true effective priest who, like Melchizedek, the scriptural figure of the true, would be able to occupy the throne for ever and henceforth give gifts of royal bounty to all who sought His priestly aid. He was, says the writer to the Hebrews, so 'named' or addressed by God as 'a high priest after the order of Melchizedek', as soon as through His earthly suffering He had been 'made perfect' and thus had become able to save men eternally (Heb. 5:7-10). Or again, the same writer says that it is because Jesus has successfully *entered* the sanctuary that He has clearly become a high priest for ever after the order of Melchizedek (Heb. 6:20). It was, therefore, by the propitiatory work which Jesus finished on the cross that He thus fulfilled His calling as the one true, heavenly and eternal high priest, and entered at once into its royal consummation.

---

[38] Compare Heb. 6:20, 7:17, 21.

c) 'Thou art my Son, this day have I begotten thee' (Heb. 1:5, 5:5, from Ps. 2:7)[39]

Third, Jesus, brought up from the dead, was immediately hailed as the Son to whom in His humanity God had given resurrection glory as the firstborn from the dead (see 1 Cor. 15:20, Col. 1:18, Rev. 1:5), the firstborn, that is, of the new creation, the redeemed community for whom He died whose similar resurrection was thereby assured. For it was God's foreordained purpose that the Son should not only Himself as man be begotten again from the dead, but also that He should be the firstborn among many brethren (Rom. 8:29; compare Heb. 2:12). His resurrection was the proof and the seal that He could and would raise or build a church, and that the gates of Hades or Death were no longer able to prevail against it or prevent it (Matt. 16:18). The same prospect of perfection for all the people of the new eternal covenant inaugurated by Christ's death is regarded by the writer to the Hebrews as assured by the fact that God has brought again from the dead 'our Lord Jesus' as the head of His people, 'the great shepherd of the sheep' (Heb. 13:20-21). Here, in one of the closing prayers of this epistle, there is no place given to any suggestion that further propitiatory work in heaven is necessary to win our full salvation. This exalted Jesus is obviously already and for ever able to save to the uttermost all who come unto God by Him (Heb. 7:25).

The additional wonder is that such coming by us into God's presence is now possible simply and solely on the ground of Christ's finished work. For when He entered God's presence by the road of suffering, He did so in our interest as our 'file-leader' (Heb. 2:10, 'the author', see Greek) or 'fore-runner' (Heb. 6:20). This is the outstanding achievement of His priesthood. His success was of such a kind that we now have inaugurated for us by His death a new and living way into the inmost sanctuary (Heb. 10:18-22). Because our great high priest has passed through the heavens, we are invited to come, and to come without misgivings in outspoken confidence, to what we shall now find to be a throne of grace; and when we come we find enthroned there the living and glorified Christ, 'Jesus, the Son of God', waiting and able to function as our great high priest by ministering directly and sympathetically to our need or speaking to God on our behalf (Heb. 4:14-16, 7:25).

[39] Compare Acts 13:33.

The place of offering in Christ's priestly ministry

Here some would contend that if Christ is, as the Scripture makes so plain, still our great high priest in heaven, He must have something to offer (see Heb. 8:1-3). Since any fresh sacrifice or repetition of Calvary is unthinkable, they imagine that the one sacrifice begun decisively at a point in time on the cross goes on without end in eternity; that Christ is always doing without cessation in heaven what He began to do in His earthly body, that is, offering Himself to God to make propitiation for sin. This action some also believe He sustains in His mystical body the church, especially through the oblation of the eucharistic elements.[40] But here there are both misunderstanding of and also major addition to what Scripture actually says. Admittedly the act of offering was necessary to constitute Christ a priest in fact, and not only in name, just as the act of child-bearing is necessary to constitute a woman a mother. But that truth does not mean in the case of motherhood that henceforth, to those who resort to her as 'mother', such a woman is always giving them birth. Her act of child-bearing is for them not only an indispensable but also a finished work. What they now enjoy are other complementary ministries of motherhood, which lie beyond the child-bearing. Similarly with Christ's priesthood His propitiatory offering is not only an indispensable but also a finished work. The appropriate sense to be given to Hebrews 8:3 is that it was necessary that He should perform an act of offering.[41] Indeed, it was because He was the only so-called 'priest' who has ever successfully offered, that He was hailed by God as the true abiding royal priest. For as with motherhood, beyond such successful discharge of the fundamental function of priesthood there lie other complementary throne ministries of grace, which the priest fulfils for the benefit of His already reconciled people.

---

[40] 'It [the Lord's Supper] is the Christian Sacrifice, for it is the continuation and the implementation, in the mystical Body of Christ which is the Church, of the "one oblation of himself once offered" in his physical body on the Cross.' Pittenger, *Christian Sacrifice*, p. 108.

[41] 'The only passage in the Epistle which could possibly lend itself to the idea of continual offering is Heb. 8:3, *it is necessary that this high priest have somewhat also to offer*. But the English translation does not and cannot exactly express the original. For in the Greek there is no equivalent of *it is*, and it would be equally possible and legitimate to use the rendering *it was necessary*. Again, the word for *to offer* is προσενέγκῃ, which can only mean *do an act of offering*. When the writer wishes to speak of continual offering he uses the tense which expresses it, προσφέρῃ (9:25). Finally, the context of this statement is one in which the writer emphatically denies continual offering (7:27, 9:25ff., 10:1lff.), on the ground that the completed act accomplished all that such offering was intended to accomplish (9:12, 10:10, 12, 14, 18).' Tait, *Sacraments*, p. 92.

This, says the writer to the Hebrews, is his 'chief point' that our Christian high priest is a priest of this sort, who has finished the indispensable offering to God and henceforth sits to dispense royal bounty to us (Heb. 8:1, compare 1:3). The bread and wine in Melchizedek's hands when he met Abraham,[42] like those in the hands of our Lord in the upper room, were offered not to God in propitiatory or eucharistic sacrifice but to men for their enjoyment and vital renewal. Also, in the case of the Christian sacrament of the Lord's Supper these very gifts evidence and seal the ratification of the new covenant by Christ's death. This covenant makes remission of sins ours; and once this blessing is being enjoyed there is no longer any need or place for sin-offering activity.[43]

The character of Christ's heavenly intercession

There is still one further point that may need explanatory comment. It concerns the character of Christ's heavenly intercession. For clearly, according to Scripture, the ascended Lord still intercedes for us (Heb. 7:25, Rom. 8:34). Does He not then still offer? In this connection William Milligan identifies the two activities. He writes: 'The intercession and the offering cannot be separated from each other. The offering is itself a continuous intercession, the continuous intercession implies the offering as a present thing.'[44] To this A.J. Tait answers: 'But it is just this separation that the writer of the epistle to the Hebrews insists on. He identifies the offering not with the intercession but with the death, and, because the death is accomplished and over, he speaks of the offering as a completed thing in the past.'[45] One has only to compare Hebrews 7:25 and 7:27 to see that this is so.

What then is meant by Christ 'making intercession for us'? 'The first thing to notice is that neither the word used by St Paul (ἐντυγχάνειν), nor the English equivalent, "to intercede", necessarily means "to offer petition". It has the much wider and more general significance of undertaking a

---

[42] See Gen. 14:18. The writer to the Hebrews 'purposely presents Melchizedek as priest, not in sacrificing but in blessing, that is, in communicating the fruits of an efficacious sacrifice already made.' B.F. Westcott, *The Epistle to the Hebrews: The Greek Text* (third edition, London, 1903), p. 203.

[43] 'Heb. 10:18, compare 9:12, 10:14; "no more" (οὐκέτι) expresses not class but time relation. It is the repudiation not merely of any other kind of offering or way of forgiveness, but also, and more particularly, of any continuance in time of the ministry whereby forgiveness is provided.' Tait, *Sacraments*, p. 92.

[44] Milligan, *Ascension and Heavenly Priesthood*, p. 160.

[45] Tait, *The Heavenly Session of our Lord: An Introduction to the History of the Doctrine* (London, 1912), p. 145.

person's affairs, looking after a person's interest, intervening in a person's favour.'[46] In the two places in the New Testament where the word is used to describe Christ's present activity, the contexts make plain that it is an activity which concerns our coming to God and our acceptance in His sight. In Hebrews 7:25 the writer declares, 'Wherefore also he is able to save to the uttermost them that draw near (τοὺς προσερχομένους) unto God through him.' 'Those who draw near' are in the Greek described by a present participle. The word indicates those who are continually or habitually coming. The reason then given for His ability completely to save them is 'seeing he ever liveth to make intercession for them'. The Greek word translated 'ever' is πάντοτε not ἄει. It means 'on every such occasion'; that is, in this context, 'every time someone draws near unto God through Him'. His intercession, therefore, is not something He is doing unceasingly. It is rather something which He does every time anyone comes. He then, so to speak, intervenes to speak to God on their behalf, to secure their acceptance with God, to see that they get all that they need. The same idea is expressed in 1 John 2:1 by saying 'we have an Advocate with the Father, Jesus Christ the righteous'.

Similarly in Romans 8:33-34, when the question is raised whether anyone can condemn the believer, the answer is given that in the very presence of God Himself, indeed at His right hand, we have Christ Jesus, who died and was raised from the dead, to support our case and to intervene on our behalf to ensure our justification, and effectively to gainsay all who would accuse us as unfit for God's approval and deserving to be condemned. Clearly, too, Christ is able to do this on the ground of His finished work, because He is the one who did die and has been raised from the dead, because He has thus become the sufficient 'propitiation for our sins' (1 John 2:2). No further offering or propitiatory work is necessary.[47] Also, He will never cease thus to be able to function, for He will never again die. Those who would draw near unto God through Him will never find Him no longer there at God's right hand to welcome and introduce them. Because He thus abides for ever His priesthood is unchangeable or inviolable. It can never be brought to an end or pass to another. He is, as the Lord sware, 'a priest for ever after the order of Melchizedek' (see Heb. 7:21-24 RV).

---

[46] Tait, *Sacraments*, pp. 90-91.

[47] 'The modern conception of Christ pleading in heaven His passion, "offering His blood" on behalf of men, has no foundation in this Epistle [to the Hebrews]. His glorified humanity is the eternal pledge of the absolute efficacy of His accomplished work.' Westcott, *Hebrews*, p. 232.

Our Lord's own statements about His Father's house

For yet more fundamental confirmation of the truth concerning the τελείωσις of priesthood and of reconciliation to God in the death of Christ it is possible to appeal to the significant implications of some of our Lord's own words with reference to His Father's house, particularly as they are recorded in the fourth Gospel. One may find here unmistakable indication that the barrier that both prevents men from entering God's presence and prevents God from abiding in men's midst, is completely and permanently removed by Christ's finished sacrifice of Himself.

The Greeks who asked to see Jesus were, we are told, 'among those that went up to worship at the feast' (see John 12:20-33). They had as Gentiles probably been impressed by Christ's cleansing of the court of the Gentiles. For here was a Jewish teacher who seemed concerned to give them a place to pray. They were, therefore, eager to see more of Him. It is certainly possible, if not probable, that they found it necessary to speak to one of the disciples, and not directly to Jesus Himself, because Jesus had gone in further to the inner court of the temple into which none but Jews could enter. We may imagine, therefore, that Andrew and Philip came from the outer court into the inner court and told Jesus that there were Greeks outside asking to see Him.

To this request Jesus made a surprising and significant response. He said – and, as the fourth evangelist pointedly indicates, it was in answer to their request – 'The hour is come that the Son of man should be glorified. Verily, verily, I say unto you, Except a grain of wheat fall into the earth and die, it abideth by itself alone; but if it die, it beareth much fruit.' A little later He added, 'And I, if I be lifted up from the earth, will draw all men unto myself'; and in comment the evangelist adds, 'But this he said signifying by what manner of death he should die.' In the probable setting of the temple courts all this suggests that Jesus implied that the way to answer the Greeks' request was not to go out to the outer court, but through His own blood shed in sacrifice to go in into the holy of holies, and by such entrance rend the veil and break down the middle wall of partition, and so through His 'lifting up' present Himself to the eyes of all as the Saviour of the world to whom the ends of the earth may henceforth look and be saved.

It seems equally possible to use thoughts of access to the inner shrine of the temple to interpret the meaning of our Lord's subsequent words about going into His Father's house to prepare a place where He could receive His own (see John 14:1-6). May He not have meant that, in contrast to the very limited size of the earthly holy of holies, there was in the true heavenly sanctuary of God's presence room for all; and that the purpose of His entering in through death was to open up a way for all men to come to God and to abide permanently in His presence? For in the same context Jesus immediately spoke of Himself as the way, the true and living way, whereby men may come to God and apart from whom none can come to God. And is it not our Lord's own statement here that underlies the exhortation in the epistle to the Hebrews, which tells us that having 'boldness to enter into the holy place by the blood of Jesus, by the way which he dedicated for us, a new and living way, through the veil, that is to say, his flesh', we should 'draw near' (Heb. 10:19-22)? Do not such words plainly imply that we can even now enjoy full access to God and abiding communion with God all because Christ's work of priestly reconciliation is already finished?

Significance of the gift of the Spirit

A similar consummation is suggested by our Lord's references to the gift of the indwelling Spirit to dwell in the hearts and in the midst of His disciples – references which significantly occur in St John's Gospel in the utterances of Jesus which immediately follow the passages (from John 12 and 14) which we have just considered. For such an incoming of the Spirit of God is the most decisive proof that the place thus occupied by the Spirit has become the sanctuary of God's presence, the dwelling-place of God most high. If such a consummation is already realized, then without question the work of priestly reconciliation is already finished.

In these utterances of Jesus recorded in St John's Gospel (see John 14:12, 16-18, 25-26, 15:26, 16:7-15) we find that Jesus said plainly that it was expedient that He should go to His Father – obviously by the way of the cross set before Him – because without such a going to God, the Spirit could not come from God to possess them. Jesus promised that once this going to God was accomplished, He would send the Spirit. This promise is confirmed later as no empty word, first by the declaration of the risen Christ and then by the experience at Pentecost of the company of believers. For on the very day of His resurrection, Jesus breathed on His disciples and said, 'Receive ye the Holy Ghost' (John 20:19-22); and on the day of Pentecost Peter declared of 'this Jesus' that 'being therefore by the right hand of God exalted, and having received of the Father the promise of the Holy Ghost, he hath poured forth this, which ye see and hear' (Acts 2:32-33).

Such a gift is surely final proof that the reconciling work is finished, that full atonement is already made. For the company of believers are no longer mere suppliants for mercy standing outside the sanctuary or drawing near to present and plead Christ's atoning sacrifice. They are already and henceforth for ever the temple of the Holy Ghost. Consequently the primary concern of the early primitive church was not, as in Old Testament times, to have a proper priesthood to offer propitiatory sacrifice for the people. For they knew by the witness of the God-given Spirit that they already lived in God's day of fulfilment, when the offering of such sacrifice was already finished and when its innumerable benefits were already to be enjoyed. They were, therefore, concerned rather to test the genuineness of every professed adherent of the believing company by asking, 'Did ye receive the Holy Ghost when ye believed?' (Acts 19:2). For if the answer to this question is 'Yes', propitiation is clearly already perfectly accomplished. Jesus meant nothing less when, as He was finally about to pass in death through the thereby once-for-all rent veil, He said in triumph 'τετέλεσται – It is finished: and he bowed his head, and gave up his spirit' (John 19:30).

Some outstanding Pauline statements

Let us now turn to consider briefly some of the outstanding statements of the epistles of St Paul. Here there is no mention whatever of any heavenly offering being still made or continued subsequent to the sacrifice of the cross in order to secure or ensure the completion of our salvation. Here it is stated, as plainly and emphatically as it can be put in words, that sinners are reconciled to God through the one finished work of Christ's human and earthly death.

a) Reconciliation already achieved and enjoyed

We quote Romans 5:10-11:

> For if while we were enemies, we were reconciled to God through the death of his Son, much more, being reconciled, shall we be saved by his life; and not only so, but we also rejoice in God through our Lord Jesus Christ, through whom we have now received the reconciliation.

Here reconciliation is spoken of as a work achieved decisively by one act already done, namely Christ's death; it is something the realized benefit of which we can and do now receive. It is not something still to be completed by anything which Christ is doing in heaven, or which the church must do on earth, in order to present or plead the one sacrifice before God.

That this is unquestionably Paul's meaning is made still more obvious by other and more detailed statements in the same context. For instance, he says that if we acknowledge that Jesus was delivered up to death for our trespasses and believe in God who raised Him as our Lord from the dead for our justification, then we are justified by such faith alone; we may without further hindrance or delay enjoy peace with God; we henceforth have before God a standing in grace and a sure hope of participation in the final glory (see Rom. 4:23–5:2). It is the wealth and wonder of this overwhelming evangelical assurance of which we are robbed, and of which we rob others, once we cease to believe in and to preach the finished work of Christ and begin instead to suggest that both in heaven and on earth continuation of propitiatory offering is still necessary to secure peace both for the living and the departed.

b) Reconciliation achieved through a finished work of earthly history

We quote Colossians 1:19-22:

> For it was the good pleasure of the Father ... through him to reconcile all things unto himself, I say, whether things upon the earth, or things in the heavens. And you, being in time past alienated and enemies in your mind in your evil works, yet now hath he reconciled in the body of his flesh through death, to present you holy and without blemish and unreprovable before him.

Here Paul declares it to be the Father's purpose to reconcile all things to Himself through Christ, including things in heaven as well as things on earth. But far from asserting that the reconciliation of this world to God depends for its completion upon a continued or eternal offering made in a spiritual realm beyond this one, that is, heaven or eternity, he asserts in phrases of grim bluntness that the whole work of reconciliation[48] was wrought out in this physical, material and earthly realm of flesh and blood, through the blood of Jesus as it was shed on the cross and

---

[48] 'It is probably wrong to take the words *to present you holy*, etc. (verse 22) as referring to the ultimate issue of the divine purpose, in the final moral perfection of Christ's people. It is "justification by faith" of which Paul is speaking. It is not that the Colossians have attained, or are to attain in some remote future, a moral perfection which will secure their acceptance at the last judgment. It is that here and now, by grace of God, who "justifieth the ungodly" they stand before Him as His consecrated people, to whom He "imputes" no fault.' C.H. Dodd, *The Abingdon Bible Commentary* (London, 1929), p. 1250.

through the death of His fleshly or natural human body; that is, through a finished work of earthly history.

c) Men exhorted in consequence to get right with God

We quote 2 Corinthians 5:18-21:

> But all things are of God, who reconciled us to himself through Christ, and gave unto us the ministry of reconciliation; to wit, that God was in Christ reconciling the world unto himself, not reckoning unto them their trespasses, and having committed unto us the word of reconciliation. We are ambassadors therefore on behalf of Christ, as though God were intreating by us: we beseech you on behalf of Christ, be ye reconciled to God. Him who knew no sin he made to be sin on our behalf; that we might become the righteousness of God in him.

Here the reconciliation of the world to God is declared to be an already accomplished act of God in Christ, on the ground of which God's terms of peace can be offered in Christ's name and stead by God's ambassadors to sinful men. Those who thus minister the word of reconciliation are explicitly to proclaim something which God has already done, because of which justification in God's sight can be enjoyed by all those who acknowledge Christ as their proxy or substitute. What God did was to let Christ, sinless though He was, occupy the place of sinners and be treated accordingly in judgment, in order that in Him we might be treated as His sinlessness deserves and become justified in God's sight. Not only is this reconciling act of God referred to as already finished; it is quite inconceivable to suppose that God could continuously, still less eternally, be treating Christ as a sinner in heaven. If He were, surely Christ would be excluded and not enthroned?

The unmistakable implications of this passage may be further emphasized by quoting P.T. Forsyth:

> God's reconciliation rested upon this, that on His Eternal Son, who knew no sin in His experience ... sin's judgment fell ... God by Christ's own consent identified Him with sin in treatment ... God ... judged sin upon His head.[49]

> Reconciliation was finished in Christ's death. Paul did not preach a gradual reconciliation. He preached what the old divines used to call the finished work. ... He preached something done once for all

---

[49] P.T. Forsyth, *The Work of Christ* (London, 1910), pp. 82-83.

– a reconciliation which is the base of every soul's reconcilement
... What the Church has to do is to appropriate the thing that has
been finally and universally done.[50]

For Christ 'turned the penalty He endured into sacrifice He offered.
And the sacrifice He offered was the judgment He accepted ...
The willing acceptance of final judgment was for Jesus the means
presented by God for effecting human reconciliation.'[51] And this is
a work which once-for-all and for ever was finished at the cross. It is
not being continued in heaven; nor is it happening eternally within
the Godhead.

In conclusion, there is perhaps no better final confirmation of these
truths than the emphatic and possibly abrupt witness of the primitive
church as it is reflected and recorded in the Gospel according to St Mark.
For here indication that the death of Jesus once accomplished secured
everything needful for full salvation is found in immediate brief factual
testimony to two decisive events – the rent veil (Mark 15:38) and the
empty tomb (Mark 16:1-8). For these concrete evidences testify to all
who will interpret them that redemption, remission and reconciliation
are fully achieved, and all on the sole and sufficient ground of the
finished work of Christ's death on the cross.

---

[50] Ibid., p. 86.
[51] Ibid., p. 163.

11

THE MEANING OF THE WORD 'BLOOD' IN SCRIPTURE (1948)

Introduction

The meaning of the word 'blood' in Scripture is obviously of great importance to all Christian students of the Bible because of its frequent use in connection with Christ Himself and with the Christian doctrine of salvation. First, it is essential to an understanding of the Old Testament sacrifices to appreciate the meaning of the blood ritual, and the whole significance attached to 'blood' and to what was done with it. Secondly, and still more, it is essential to understand rightly the use and meaning of the word 'blood' in the New Testament, if we are properly to grasp the doctrinal interpretation of the work of Christ which was adopted and preached by the apostles and evangelists in the first decades of the Christian church. What we need ultimately to discover and to be sure of is the theological significance of the word 'blood' in its use in the New Testament with reference to the sacrifice of Christ.

This is the more important because in this connection the word is used so often. As Vincent Taylor has pointed out, the 'blood' of Christ is mentioned in the writings of the New Testament nearly three times as often as 'the cross' of Christ and five times as frequently as the 'death' of Christ.[1] The term 'blood' is, in fact, a chief method of reference to the sacrifice of Christ, particularly in contexts which define its efficacy. Some adequate interpretation of the meaning of the term 'blood' cannot

The sixth annual Tyndale Lecture in the New Testament, delivered at The Hayes, Swanwick, Derbyshire on 31 December 1947, first published by Tyndale Press.

[1] See Vincent Taylor, *The Atonement in New Testament Teaching* (second edition, London, 1945), p. 177. The distribution is as follows: Matthew (1), Mark (1), John (4), Acts (1), Pauline epistles (8), Hebrews (6), 1 Peter (2), 1 John (3), Revelation (4).

therefore be avoided if we are to continue to hold fast to New Testament Christianity. For as Nathaniel Micklem has written, 'Not only the older form of evangelism, but every type of Biblical Christianity speaks of our salvation "by the blood of Christ".'[2]

A prevalent view – open to question

Interpretation is the more urgent because, as Dr Micklem goes on immediately to say in the same context, 'The phrase [the blood of Christ] is a stumbling-block to many in these days.' And in the judgment of the present writer this urgency is greatly increased because the line of interpretation commonly followed by the majority of modern writers is itself open to question as not true to the actual scriptural evidence.

According to this prevalent interpretation the phrase 'the blood of Christ' – to put it very briefly – stands not for His death but rather for His life released through death, and thus set free to be used for new purposes and made available for man's appropriation, particularly, as some would say, in the eucharist. Both the way in which this view is expressed and its prevalence among recent writers can best be indicated by some actual quotations. First, Dr Micklem says, in the same context as before, speaking of the Old Testament animal sacrifices:

> The blood of the victim is the life that has passed through death. When, therefore, we say that we are saved 'by the blood of Christ', we are ascribing our salvation, not to the death of Christ nor to some mysterious transaction on Calvary, but to the life of Christ, the life that has passed through death.[3]

Next, Vincent Taylor in several places in his books seeks to force upon his readers the acceptance of this view as alone adequate to explain the scriptural statements. Speaking of animal sacrifice he says:

> ... destruction [of the victim] is not the primary intention. The victim is slain in order that its life, in the form of blood, may be released, and its flesh burnt in order that it may be transformed or etherealized; and in both cases the aim is to make it possible for life to be presented as an offering to the Deity. More and more students of comparative religion, and of the Old Testament worship in particular, are insisting that the bestowal of life is the fundamental idea in sacrificial worship.[4]

---

[2] Nathaniel Micklem, *The Doctrine of Our Redemption* (London, 1943), p. 27.
[3] Ibid., p. 27.
[4] Vincent Taylor, *Jesus and His Sacrifice: A Study of the Passion-Sayings in the Gospels* (London, 1937), pp. 54-55.

In commenting on the teaching of St Paul and his use of the term 'blood' with reference to the death of Christ, Vincent Taylor writes, 'To explain the allusions to "blood" as synonyms for "death" is mistaken.'[5] In commenting on the epistle to the Hebrews, Vincent Taylor speaks of the writer's 'use of the word "blood" in relation to Christ in a sense entirely transcending the suggestion of a violent death'[6] and he adds later, 'it will be found, I think, that when he uses the term "blood" his main emphasis is upon the idea of life freely surrendered, applied and dedicated to the recovery of men.'[7] Writing of the fourth evangelist, Vincent Taylor says, 'the phrase "my blood" (in John 6:53-56) suggests the opportunity of life open to the appropriation of the believer'; and in the same context he incidentally observes, 'this thought of life released to be received is itself the vital concept without which no sacrificial theory can ever be adequately presented.'[8] Finally, in seeking to summarize the teaching of the New Testament on the doctrine of the atonement, Vincent Taylor writes, 'The sacrificial category is peculiarly suitable for this doctrinal presentation [of the work of Christ] because, in the use of the term 'blood' it suggests the thought of life, dedicated, offered, transformed, and open to our spiritual appropriation.'[9]

Similarly, C.H. Dodd writes, 'In speaking of the Sacrament of the Lord's Supper (1 Cor. 10:16), Paul can say, The cup of blessing which we bless, is that not participating in the blood of Christ? – i.e. participating in His life as dedicated to God.'[10] And O.C. Quick, commenting on the teaching of St John, writes, 'Blood represents the human life of Christ suffering, dying and sacrificed upon earth, which also cleanses Christians by being communicated to them in the Eucharist.'[11] Further, Bishop Hicks, writing on the development of sacrifice, asserts,

> Thus sacrifices are, in the first place, acts of fellowship between the god and members of the clan; and, later, are used for covenants, to create a blood brotherhood. ... In every case the blood is life released in order to be communicated.[12]

---

[5] Taylor, *Atonement*, p. 63.

[6] Ibid., p. 121.

[7] Ibid., p. 123.

[8] Ibid., p. 149.

[9] Ibid., p. 198.

[10] C.H. Dodd, *The Epistle of Paul to the Romans*, Moffatt New Testament Commentary (London, 1932), p. 56.

[11] O.C. Quick, *The Gospel of the New World: A Study in the Christian Doctrine of Atonement* (London, 1944), p. 56.

[12] F.C.N. Hicks, *The Fullness of Sacrifice: An Essay in Reconciliation* (London, 1930), p. 34.

If we go back a generation to writers of forty and fifty years ago we also find some prevalence of the same ideas. For instance, P.T. Forsyth wrote, speaking of animal sacrifice,

> The pleasing thing to God and the effective element in the matter is not death but life. The blood was shed with the direct object not of killing the animal, but of detaching and releasing the life, isolating it, as it were, from the material base of body and flesh, and presenting it in this refined state to God.[13]

And in their commentary on the epistle to the Romans, Sanday and Headlam said,

> The significance of the Sacrificial Bloodshedding was twofold. The blood was regarded by the Hebrew as essentially the seat of life (Gen. 9:4, Lev. 17:11, Deut. 12:23). Hence the death of the victim was not only a death but a setting free of life; the application of the blood was an application of life; and the offering of the blood to God was an offering of life. In this lay more especially the virtue of the sacrifice.[14]

It is also significant that in this context, and again later, Sanday and Headlam explicitly confessed their authority for such a line of interpretation. They wrote,

> The idea of Vicarious Suffering is not the whole and not perhaps the culminating point in the conception of Sacrifice, for Dr Westcott seems to have sufficiently shown that the centre of the symbolism of Sacrifice lies not in the death of the victim but in the offering of its life.[15]

This is an important confession. For it seems clear enough that it is Bishop Westcott who is chiefly responsible for the widespread modern prevalence of this idea. In his commentary on the epistles of St John, first published in 1883, there is an Additional Note on 1 John 1:7 entitled *The Idea of Christ's Blood in the New Testament*. It seems desirable to quote a selection of his statements to indicate his teaching. With reference to the Old Testament sacrificial system he observes,

> By the outpouring of the Blood the life which was in it was not destroyed, though it was separated from the organism which it had before quickened. ... Thus two distinct ideas were included in

---

[13] P.T. Forsyth, *The Cruciality of the Cross* (London, 1909), p. 186.

[14] William Sanday and Arthur C. Headlam, *A Critical and Exegetical Commentary on the Epistle of the Romans* (fifth edition, Edinburgh, 1902), p. 89.

[15] Ibid., p. 93.

the sacrifice of a victim, the death of the victim by the shedding of its blood, and the liberation, so to speak, of the principle of life by which it had been animated, so that this life became available for another end.[16]

After further discussion he adds,

Thus, in accordance with the typical teaching of the Levitical ordinances the Blood of Christ represents Christ's Life (1) as rendered in free self-sacrifice to God for men, and (2) as brought into perfect fellowship with God, having been set free by death. The Blood of Christ is, as shed, the Life of Christ given for men, and, as offered, the Life of Christ now given to men, the Life which is the spring of their life (John 12:24). ... The Blood always includes the thought of the life preserved and active beyond death.[17]

This conception of the Blood of Christ is fully brought out in the fundamental passage, John 6:53-56. Participation in Christ's Blood is participation in His life (verse 56). But at the same time it is implied throughout that it is only through His Death – His violent Death – that His Blood can be made available for men.[18]

It is no light task to set oneself against all this weight of scholarship. Yet it is the contention of the present writer that this view, thus eminently supported, is nevertheless open to question. And he is encouraged by the knowledge that in contending for a different interpretation he does not stand alone, nor is he advancing something new. Others have stood, and still stand, for the same interpretation as his. To mention three such writers. First, J. Armitage Robinson in his commentary on the epistle to the Ephesians, first published in 1903, says simply,

To the Jewish mind 'blood' was not merely – nor even chiefly – the life-current flowing in the veins of the living: it was especially the life poured out in death; and yet more particularly in its religious aspect it was the symbol of sacrificial death.[19]

Second, Kittel's *Theological Dictionary* is the most recent attempt to define the scriptural and theological meaning of Greek New Testament words. In the article by Johannes Behm on the word αἷμα

---

[16] B.F. Westcott, *The Epistles of St John: The Greek Text* (London, 1883), pp. 34-35.

[17] Ibid., p. 35.

[18] Ibid., p. 35. It is interesting and worthy of note that Bishop Westcott in a footnote virtually confesses his own indebtedness for some of his ideas to what he calls 'the very suggestive note' of William Milligan, *The Resurrection of Our Lord* (London, 1881), pp. 263-291.

[19] J. Armitage Robinson, *St Paul's Epistle to the Ephesians* (London, 1903), p. 29.

there is no reference whatever to the idea of life released. Behm gives a straightforward interpretation of the evidence of the New Testament usage itself and declares that 'blood', in the connection in which we are most interested in its use, stands for 'death'. Writers who speak of 'the blood of Christ' are interested not in the material substance but in the shed blood, that is, in the death of Christ. For the shedding of blood involves the destruction of the seat of life. And so the phrase 'the blood of Christ' is 'only a more vivid expression for the death of Christ in its redemptive significance'.[20]

Third, James Denney is particularly worth quoting because, in a book first published in 1902, he shows an awareness of Westcott's interpretation and an outspoken refusal to be fascinated by it. He says,

> It is by no means necessary, for the understanding of the evangelist [John] here, that we should adopt the strange caprice which fascinated Westcott, and distinguish with him in the blood of Christ (1) His death, and (2) His life; or (1) His blood shed, and (2) His blood offered; or (1) His life laid down, and (2) His life liberated and made available for men. No doubt these distinctions were meant to safeguard a real religious interest; they were meant to secure the truth that it is a living Saviour who saves, and that He actually does save, from sin, and that He does so in the last resort by the communication of His own life; but I venture to say that a more groundless fancy never haunted and troubled the interpretation of any part of Scripture than that which is introduced by this distinction into the Epistle to the Hebrews and the First Epistle of John. ... He [Christ] did something when He died, and that something He continues to make effective for men in His Risen Life; but there is no meaning in saying that by His death His life – as something other than His death – is 'liberated' and 'made available' for men.[21]

Such quotations are enough to indicate the issue which we have to face, and to anticipate the conclusion that we hope to justify. So bringing our introduction to a close, we must now get to grips with a detailed examination and considered evaluation of the actual scriptural evidence.

---

[20] See Gerhard Kittel (ed.), *Theologisches Wörterbuch zum Neuen Testament* (10 vols, Stuttgart, 1932-78), vol. 1, pp. 171-175, article on αἷμα by Johannes Behm. See also Taylor, *Atonement*, p. 24.

[21] James Denney, *The Death of Christ: Its Place and Interpretation in the New Testament* (revised edition, London, 1911), pp. 196-197.

Examination of Scriptural Usage in the Old Testament

General

The Hebrew word for 'blood', as the name for the red or purple fluid which circulates in men's arteries and veins, also had in the common speech of the people of Old Testament times a further significance which is readily understandable. When Joseph's brethren sold him to the merchantmen who were going to Egypt, they took Joseph's coat and dipped it in blood and sent it to Jacob. The sight of the blood made Jacob say, 'An evil beast hath devoured him' (Gen. 37:31-33). So blood directly suggested death, particularly a violent death. For when blood becomes visible and begins to flow it means that damage has been done to someone's life; and when the blood is poured out in quantity and, so to speak, thought of in isolation as now separated from the body in which it flowed, it means that a life has been taken. So 'blood' became a word-symbol for 'death'. When the psalmist says, 'What profit is there in my blood?', he means, 'What profit is there in my death?' (Ps. 30:9).

Also, after a life has been taken by someone else it is signs of the blood that may reveal the murderer. Someone with blood visibly upon him is immediately open to suspicion. And details of this kind, doubtless originally true in actual concrete cases, passed as pictures and thought-forms into the speech of the people and produced many vivid metaphorical phrases. A murderer was said to have upon him the blood of the person he had killed. Also, since murder demanded punishment or provoked revenge, the man who retaliated or inflicted the penalty was said to be avenging the murdered man's blood (see Num. 35:19, 26-27, Ps. 79:10). Such action was said to take the blood away from those responsible to take vengeance and to return it upon the head of the murderer (1 Kings 2:29-34). So in Proverbs we read of 'A man that is laden with the blood of any person' (Prov. 28:17 RV). Jonathan declared to Saul that to slay David without a cause would be to sin against innocent blood (1 Sam. 19:5). Jeremiah said, 'If ye put me to death, ye shall bring innocent blood upon yourselves, and upon this city, and upon the inhabitants thereof' (Jer. 26:15 RV). Further, if a person deserved to be put to death, or if his death was the result of his own folly, his blood was said to be on his own head and not on someone else's (Josh. 2:19, 2 Sam. 1:16, 1 Kings 2:37).

What is more, such metaphorical use of vivid word pictures involving 'blood' was apparently often resorted to, and sometimes in a surprisingly dramatic form, especially to indicate people's connection with someone's death. Judah said to his brethren about Joseph, 'What profit is it if we slay our brother, and conceal his blood?' (Gen. 37:26). Joab who 'shed the blood of war in peace' is said to have 'put the blood of war upon his girdle ... and in his shoes' (1 Kings 2:5, compare Jer. 2:34). When the righteous are to rejoice at the sight of vengeance on the wicked, the psalmist says they will wash their feet in the blood of the wicked (Ps. 58:10). To drink someone's blood (or to eat up his flesh, Ps. 27:2) meant not only to take his life, but to gain some advantage as a result of his death or at the price of taking away his life. So David, even when his three mighty men had done no more than put their lives in peril to fetch him water from the well of Bethlehem, said, 'Shall I drink the blood of these men that have put their lives in jeopardy?' (1 Chron. 11:17-19, 2 Sam. 23:15-17). Surely such metaphorical phraseology, and not least the fact that it is only metaphorical, must be of some significance to the Bible student in interpreting such New Testament statements as 'They washed their robes, and made them white in the blood of the Lamb' (Rev. 7:14), or 'He that eateth my flesh and drinketh my blood hath eternal life' (John 6:54 RV). Already we seem to see that in such phraseology 'blood' is a vivid word-symbol for referring to someone's violent death and for connecting other people with the consequences resulting from it.

Special: the language of religion

The significance of the word 'blood' in the Old Testament becomes even more interesting and important once we recognize the inevitable Godward reference of the thought of all its writers; and still more when we consider the solemn ceremonies of religious worship. For it was what was done with 'blood' in the first Passover and in the regular sacrificial ritual, in putting it on places, things and people together with the recognition that nothing else but 'blood' would avail, which must have most influenced the development of the metaphorical phraseology of the everyday speech of the people, of which we have just instanced some examples.

In three places in the Old Testament the truth is dogmatically stated that the blood is the life (Gen. 9:4, Lev. 17:11, Deut. 12:23). This statement is emphatically quoted by those who assert that 'blood' stands for 'life' not 'death', because it seems at first sight to endorse that interpretation. But a careful examination of the contexts reveals that in each of the three cases these statements say not that 'blood' is 'life' in isolation, but that the blood is the life of the flesh. This means that if the blood is separated from the flesh, whether in man or beast, the present physical life in the flesh will come to an end. Blood shed stands, therefore, not for the release of life from the burden of the flesh, but for the bringing to an end of life in the flesh. It is a witness to physical death not an evidence of spiritual survival.

Further, the conviction that underlies the Old Testament Scriptures is that physical life is God's creation. So it belongs to Him not to men. Also, particularly in the case of man made in God's image, this life is precious in God's sight. Therefore, not only has no man any independent right of freedom to shed blood and take life, but also if he does he will be accountable to God for his action. God will require blood of any man that sheds it. The murderer brings blood upon himself not only in the eyes of men but first of all in the sight of God. And the penalty which was due to God and which other men were made responsible to inflict, was that the murderer's own life must be taken. Such a man is not worthy to enjoy further the stewardship of the divine gift of life. He must pay the extreme earthly penalty and lose his own life in the flesh. Further, the character of the punishment is also significantly described by the use of the word 'blood'. 'Whoso sheddeth man's blood, by man shall his blood be shed' (Gen. 9:5-6).

Again, human blood thus wrongly shed is said to pollute the land (Num. 35:33, Ps. 106:38). It is witness of a wrong done which must be visited upon the wrongdoer. Only so can innocent blood be put away from Israel (Deut. 19:11-13). It needs expiation, 'and no expiation can be made for the land for the blood that is shed therein, but by the blood of him that shed it' (Num. 35:33 RV). Also, until something is done to avenge such blood and to vindicate justice in God's sight, such blood can be said to cry out to God from the ground for something to be done (Gen. 4:10). It has, so to speak, the power to shout to heaven. For the taking of physical life is in God's sight so serious that it cannot rightly be overlooked. It raises an issue that demands settlement.

It is here in this realm of thought in which the right of shed blood to demand recompense is recognized, that Bishop Westcott in his influential Additional Note begins to go wrong.[22] For he misunderstands

---

[22] Westcott, *Epistles of John*, pp. 34-37. Since (as previously indicated) Westcott acknowledges the suggestive character of a note by Dr Milligan, it is perhaps worthy of note that Milligan makes this very suggestion that shed blood is alive because of the way in which it 'cries' to God. He says of the blood shed in sacrifice, 'No reflecting person can imagine for a moment that blood, simply as blood, could be acceptable to God. What made the blood

the vivid metaphorical phraseology and suggests that statements that blood already shed can cry to God are witness that the blood is still alive after death. This surely is a serious misunderstanding of metaphorical language and a completely unjustified attempt to suggest a very far-reaching conclusion on wholly inadequate grounds. How can 'life' in the full personal, rational and responsible sense be attributed to blood, which has no power of independent personal action? True, according to Scripture the 'blood' of a man after he is dead may cause things to happen. But that is not because the blood itself is still alive. The compelling cause is not the literal blood, not some persistent activity of the life that was in the blood, but the fact of the death or the life taken which the blood represents in the sight both of God and of men.

Next, there is in the Old Testament explicit indication that not only human life but animal life was equally recognized as God's. It could, therefore, only be taken by divine permission; and when it was taken God's ownership of the life that was taken had to be solemnly acknowledged. So, before their flesh could be rightly eaten, animals had to be slain before the Lord as unto Him; and their blood, which represented the life that had been taken, had to be either poured out on an altar or poured out to God on the ground and reverently covered. Any drinking of the blood was strictly forbidden (Gen. 9:4, Lev. 17:3-7, 10-14, Deut. 12:15-16, 20-28, 1 Sam. 14:32-35).

Such convictions and precepts gave all eating of animal flesh a religious significance, because the taking of the animal's life was something that had to be done unto God, as a 'sacrifice' unto Him and not just a slaying for men. Eating animal flesh, therefore, assumed the character of a sacrificial feast.[23] It was a meal only possible because God, to whom the life belonged, had allowed the life to be taken. It was a meal

---

acceptable was that, as it flowed, it 'cried', confessing sin and desert of punishment. It thus could not be dead. It was alive. Not indeed that it was physically alive. It was rather ideally alive – alive with a life which now assumed its true attitude towards God, with a life which confessed, as it flowed forth in the blood, that it was surrendered freely and in harmony with the demands of God's righteous law. We know that the idea of the blood thus speaking was familiar to the Jew (Gen. 4:10, Job 16:18, Ezek. 24:7-8, Heb. 12:24), but what speaks either must be, or must be thought of as being, alive. ... The blood is a conventional hieroglyphic labelled as the life' (Milligan, *Resurrection*, pp. 277-278). Here there seems to be obvious confusion between the vivid meaning or significance attributed to shed blood by men, and the actual persistence in the shed blood of the living power to act or 'cry' on its own. The shed blood was not still alive, but to intelligent and morally responsible men it did visibly 'speak' of a life either violently taken or freely offered.

[23] Compare the idea, prevalent in idolatry and witnessed to in 1 Corinthians 8-10, that meat was commonly not available to be eaten by men until it (as part of the animal slain to get it) had been offered to the idols first.

only possible by God's gift to men of part of the slain animal – that is, the flesh, which also was His. Such eating, therefore, was an occasion for thanksgiving to God. Such eating, too, was only possible at the cost of the animal's death. It was not a feeding upon the animal's life, but a feeding made possible by the animal's life being taken. The meal was a consequence of the animal's death. And the blood, which is the life of the flesh, was not released for men to partake. Rather, as a witness of animal life brought to an end, it was something too precious and too sacred to God for men to appropriate. So it had to be poured out unto God. A similar attitude not only to drinking blood as divinely forbidden, but also to the solemn significance of enjoying a benefit procured at the cost of the sacrifice of life, in this case human life, is expressed in David's unwillingness to drink water procured at the risk of men's lives. He said, 'My God forbid it me, that I should do this: shall I drink the blood of these men that have put their lives in jeopardy?' And he did with the water what he would have done with blood. He poured it out unto the Lord (1 Chron. 11:17-19 RV).

What may now be seen in all its outstanding significance is the remarkable fact that the shed blood of animals, which it was otherwise forbidden to men to drink or in any way to use as theirs, was, so we read, given by divine appointment to be used to make atonement for sin and to effect expiation and cleansing (Lev. 17:11). Such were the virtue and value of a life laid down, particularly as a ransom for a life otherwise forfeit. Here instead of expiation by the blood of the guilty there was expiation by the blood of a guiltless substitute, a lamb without blemish and without spot.

The first and decisive example of this principle explicitly given in Scripture is in connection with the institution of the Passover (Exod. 12, compare Heb. 11:28). Here the blood of a lamb slain was appointed to be used by the Israelites to sprinkle on their doorposts to provide shelter and protection from divine judgment. The animal life thus to be taken had to be without blemish and, so to speak, not itself liable to death. Only so could its life be sacrificed as a substitute for another life under judgment that otherwise ought to have been taken. Once this spotless life was brought to an end and its blood shed, the value of the sacrifice was capable of being extended to shelter those in danger. This extension of the virtue and saving power of the animal's death was expressed by the sprinkling of the blood on the doorpost. The blood was not a 'release of life' for either God or men to partake. It is expressly said to be 'a token', which God would 'see' (Exod. 12:13). What mattered was its significance. And as a token it was a visible sign of life already taken. Those within the house who sheltered from judgment beneath the blood of the lamb, and feasted on its flesh, were not partakers in the animal's released life, but people enjoying the benefits of the animal's death. Also, such a provision by God of life given in sacrifice to ransom those whose lives were otherwise forfeit purchased the beneficiaries. They were redeemed by blood; and redeemed not only from judgment but to be a people for the Lord's own possession.

There is a further application of this same principle in the ceremonial law and the sacrificial system of the Old Testament. Here we learn that the blood of animals, which man may not drink nor use for himself, has been given by God to men upon the altar to make atonement for their souls (Lev. 17:11). Such animal blood may, therefore, not only be shed and poured out to God as His upon the altar; it is also there to be regarded as given by divine appointment to cover sin; and it may, therefore, actually be appropriated for use and sprinkled upon things and people to secure ceremonial purification (see Exod. 29:1, 10-12, 15-16, 19-21, Lev. 3:2, 8, 13, 4:4-7, 15-18, 22-25, 16:14-19 etc). Such action was not the completion of the making of the sacrifice, but the application of the virtue and the appropriation of the benefits of the sacrifice. Such blood could, so to speak, give access to God's presence. It could purify from defilement, at least symbolically, the holy place, the altar and the worshippers. For it was a witness to, or a token of, a spotless life sacrificed, which was more than a sufficient compensation in God's sight for the death due to the sinner, and which ultimately symbolized the spirit of utter obedience unto death and complete devotion to God which were all well-pleasing to Him. Such blood, therefore, far from crying out for investigation and vengeance cried out rather for acknowledgement and reward. It spoke better things than the blood of the murdered Abel. And just as the blood of someone wrongly slain could be on a person for condemnation, involving him in inevitable penalty, so this blood could be on a person or between him and God for expiation and cleansing, securing both his ransom and release from sin's penalty and his acceptance with God. It made him, ceremonially at least, fit for God's presence. Also, such benefits were all made available not through release of the animal's life and participation in it, but through the applied virtue and value of the animal's life freely poured out in death in devotion to God, of which the animal's blood and what was done with it were adequate and intelligible symbols.

Before we close our survey of the Old Testament evidence, mention ought also to be made of the use of blood in covenant making, particularly at Sinai in the covenant between Jehovah and Israel when Moses took blood and sprinkled both the altar and the people and said, 'Behold the blood of the covenant which the Lord hath made with you' (Exod. 24:4-8). Here, as with the custom of passing between the divided pieces of slain animals in covenant making (see Gen. 15:7-21, Jer. 34:18-19), the intention of the symbolism seems clearly to have been to introduce in figure, and for purposes of solemn pledge, the death of the covenant maker. So the blood, particularly as sprinkled on the people, was a sign of death not a vehicle for the communication of life.

To sum up thus far, the general witness of the Old Testament is, therefore, that 'blood' stands not for life released, but first for the fact and then for the significance of life laid down or taken in death.

Examination of Scriptural Usage in the New Testament

General

In the New Testament the word 'blood' (Greek αἷμα), while it is sometimes used in its direct literal sense to describe actual blood, is much more often used, as in the Old Testament, in a metaphorical sense as a way of referring to violent death and of connecting other people with it.

The word 'blood' first suggests the kind of damage to human life which threatens and results in death. So to 'resist unto blood' (Heb. 12:4) means to resist unto death, to die rather than yield. And when 'the souls of them that had been slain for the word of God, and for the testimony which they held' are said to cry, 'How long, O Master, the holy and true, dost thou not judge and avenge our blood?' (Rev. 6:10 RV), they obviously mean by avenge 'our blood' avenge 'our death', or rather the causing of our death and the shedding of our blood; or, as we might say, 'our murder'.

Similarly, to do something to endanger and to bring to an end someone's life is to have dealings with his blood. So after Judas had handed our Lord over to the chief priests, he confessed, 'I betrayed innocent blood'; and the money which he got for doing it was described by the chief priests as 'the price of blood' (Matt. 27:3-8 RV). Later Pilate, in his unwillingness to be responsible for giving sentence for Christ's crucifixion, said, 'I am innocent of the blood of this righteous man: see ye to it'. And all the people answered and said, 'His blood be on us, and on our children' (Matt. 27:24-25 RV). Again, after Pentecost the high priest said to Peter and the other apostles, 'Ye intend to bring this man's blood upon us' (Acts 5:28). This obviously means, 'You intend to hold us responsible and punishable for His death.' There is still more vivid language in the Apocalypse where Babylon is said to be a woman 'drunken with the blood of the saints, and ... martyrs of Jesus.' 'And in her was found the blood of prophets and of saints, and of all that have been slain upon the earth' (Rev. 17:6, 18:24 RV). Such phraseology is obviously metaphorical. It connects people with responsibility for someone's death. What really rests upon them is not actual blood, nor some virtue or vengeance of 'life released', but the defilement and guilt of blood shed, that is, of murder.

Blood thus shed by men may also be required of them, or come upon them, in judgment. So our Lord said that there shall 'come upon this generation' 'all the righteous blood shed on the earth, from the blood of Abel the righteous unto the blood of Zachariah son of Barachiah' (Matt. 23:34-36, Luke 11:50-51). In this statement it is significant that there occur the phrases 'the blood of Abel' and 'the blood of Zachariah', because they are phrases directly parallel in form to the phrase 'the blood of Christ'; and here the 'blood' of these men 'coming upon' the Jews of our Lord's day means, not the conveyance to the Jews of the released life of Abel and Zachariah, but the imposing on them of the consequences of their violent deaths.

We read, also, that on one occasion our Lord said to the scribes and Pharisees, 'Woe unto you', because they said, 'If we had been in the days of our fathers, we should not have been *partakers with them in the blood of the prophets*' (Matt. 23:29-30).[24] This description of men as 'partakers in the blood of' others is worthy of the more particular attention because of the somewhat parallel phraseology in 1 Corinthians, where Paul writes, 'The cup of blessing which we bless, is it not *a communion of the blood of Christ?*' (1 Cor. 10:16).[25] Clearly the phraseology used by our Lord describes men as sharers in the guilt of slaying the prophets, sharers, that is, in responsibility for their death and so men faced with the prospect of sharing in the punishment due in consequence of it. So we may in anticipation suggest that Paul meant of Christ that those who share in a communion in His blood are partakers, not in His released life, but in the consequences of His death – and, in this case, in its benefits and not in liability to judgment as those responsible for causing it.

---

[24] The significant words are κοινωνοὶ αὐτῶν ἐν τῷ αἵματι τῶν προφητῶν.

[25] Here the somewhat parallel phrase is κοινωνία τοῦ αἵματος τοῦ Χριστοῦ.

Special: the blood of Christ

In turning now to consider passages in the New Testament which refer to the blood of Christ, one or two general comments seem desirable first, in order to suggest the main line of interpretation. This will also afford, in passing, welcome opportunity to refer to occurrences in the New Testament of the word 'blood' in the phrase 'flesh and blood' (see Matt. 16:17, 1 Cor. 15:50, Gal. 1:16, Eph. 6:12, Heb. 2:14). This phrase 'flesh and blood' stands for man's living body in its present earthly state. It indicates the condition and weakness of man's present physical nature as opposed to God and created spirits, and in contrast to the body that shall be in the resurrection. When the eternal Son of God became man He took a share in flesh and blood. So when the New Testament writers speak of 'the days of his flesh' (Heb. 5:7) or of knowing 'Christ after the flesh' (2 Cor. 5:16), the reference is to His earthly life – that is, the days of His flesh and blood, the days when like other men He had flesh kept alive by the blood that was in it. Similarly, when the New Testament writers speak of 'the blood of Christ' they are equally referring to His earthly life in the flesh and particularly to its violent end, that is, to what Paul specifically calls 'the blood of his cross' (Col. 1:20). Indeed, it is the more certain that the term 'the blood of Christ' can only refer to His earthly death. For although our Lord spoke of His glorified body as having flesh and bones (Luke 24:39), there is no indication that it had any blood. Nor, indeed, is it likely; for the corruptible had put on incorruption (see and note 1 Cor. 15:50-53).

Also, there is in heaven no blood ritual such as there was in the Levitical tabernacle. For in the fulfilment of these divinely-ordained 'figures of the true', Christ Himself does not do things after His sacrifice with His blood, as something material and outside Himself which He comes before God to minister. He entered in not with, but 'through his own blood', that is, by means of or because of His death as Man when His human blood was shed (see Heb. 9:7, 11-12, 24-26). So in the heavenly glory He does not sprinkle and never has actually sprinkled blood upon some heavenly mercy-seat.[26] Rather He is Himself, so to speak, the mercy-seat or propitiation, being Himself already sufficiently 'blood-stained' by reason of His death on the cross. He partook of flesh and blood to 'taste death for every man' and 'that through death he might bring to nought him that had the power of death, that is, the devil'; and it is 'because of the suffering of death' that we now behold

---

[26] Some fuller exposition of this point follows below.

Jesus 'crowned with glory and honour' and able as the pioneer of man's salvation to bring His many brethren as sons of God into the same glory (see Heb. 2:5-17). He is for ever accepted and enthroned, worshipped and honoured, and assured of final and complete triumph, because He is the 'Lamb as it had been slain' (see Rev. 5:6). So the term 'the blood of Christ' is a metaphorical or symbolical way of referring to His earthly death in a human body upon a cross of shame, and to its innumerable and eternal consequences. And it is these benefits of His passion that are meant to be conveyed to and enjoyed by all who are said either to be sprinkled by His blood or to drink symbolically of it.

We now pass to a more detailed examination of passages in the New Testament in which explicit reference is made to the blood of Christ, together with a few closely allied passages in the epistle to the Hebrews which refer to the ceremonial uses of blood under the old covenant.

a) Romans 3:25 RV: 'Whom God set forth to be a propitiation, through faith, by his blood' (ὃν προέθετο ὁ Θεὸς ἱλαστήριον διὰ τῆς πίστεως ἐν τῷ αὐτοῦ αἵματι).

Here προέθετο may convey the sense of 'set forth openly' or 'made a public spectacle', in contrast to the Levitical sprinkling of the mercy-seat which was hidden from the sight of the people. In that case it means that on the cross, Jesus was openly displayed as propitiatory in the suffering of death or by the shedding of His blood. Some would, of course, translate ἱλαστήριον as 'mercy-seat' and thus make Christ the mercy-seat. Sanday and Headlam say, 'There is great harshness, not to say confusion, in making Christ at once priest and victim and place of sprinkling.' And they add, 'The Christian ἱλαστήριον or "place of sprinkling", in the literal sense, is rather the Cross.'[27] This thought corresponds, too, to the foregoing interpretation of the verse, an interpretation which focuses all attention on Christ's death, on the shedding of His blood on the cross. If, however, προέθετο means 'purposed' or 'foreordained' and we do translate, 'whom God foreordained to be the mercy-seat – in His blood', the suggestion then is not that after His death Christ sprinkled blood on some heavenly mercy-seat, but that He Himself is the true, eternal mercy-seat of the divine purpose 'by his blood', that is, because of His death as Man for men. This corresponds to the statement in 1 John that, in the presence of God, Christ Himself and not some further sprinkling of His

---

[27] Sanday and Headlam, *Romans*, p. 87

blood is the propitiation for our sins (1 John 2:1-2). Also, whichever interpretation we prefer, the phrase 'in his blood' refers equally to the event of His death as Man on the cross.

b) Romans 5:9 RV: 'Much more then, being now justified by his blood (δικαιωθέντες νῦν ἐν τῷ αἵματι αὐτοῦ), shall we be saved from the wrath [of God] through him.'

In this context the three previous verses all refer exclusively to dying and emphatically to Christ's death for us sinners. The sequence of thought demands, therefore, that the words 'his blood' must refer to His dying for us. Also, while in this verse and the next there are double references to complementary aspects of full salvation, the parallelism demands that 'being justified by his blood' in verse 9 should be regarded as more or less equal to 'while we were enemies, we were reconciled to God through the death of his Son' in verse 10; and not with the idea that we shall be 'saved by his life'. In other words, justification is a benefit made ours through His death for us. Again to quote Sanday and Headlam, 'He [Paul] ... clearly connects the act of justification with the bloodshedding of Christ.'[28]

c) Ephesians 1:7 RV: 'In whom we have redemption through his blood (διὰ τοῦ αἵματος αὐτοῦ), the forgiveness of our trespasses.'

1 Peter 1:18-19 RV: 'Knowing that ye were redeemed ... with precious blood (τιμίῳ αἵματι), as of a lamb without blemish and without spot.'

Acts 20:28 RV: 'The church of God, which he purchased with his own blood' (ἣν περιεποιήσατο διὰ τοῦ αἵματος τοῦ ἰδίου).

Revelation 5:9 RV: 'For thou wast slain, and didst purchase unto God with thy blood (ἐν τῷ αἵματί σου) men of every tribe, and tongue, and people, and nation.'

In these passages the reference is to 'blood' as the 'ransom' or 'purchase price'. Commenting on 'through his blood' in Ephesians 1:7, Bishop Lightfoot wrote, 'This is the ransom-money, the λύτρον (Matt. 20:28; Mark 10:45), or ἀντίλυτρον (1 Tim. 2:6, compare Titus 2:14), the price, τιμὴ (1 Cor. 6:20, 7:23), for which we were bought.'[29] Such a ransom was

---

[28] Ibid., p. 128
[29] J.B. Lightfoot, *Notes on Epistles of St Paul from Unpublished Commentaries* (London, 1895), p. 316.

under the law some equivalent compensation and in this case obviously 'life' for 'life' or 'blood' for 'blood'. Since the sinner's life was forfeit and subject to death, Christ could only redeem the sinner and break the hold of sin and give release (what Paul calls τὴν ἄφεσιν τῶν παραπτωμάτων, Eph. 1:7) by His blood; that is, by Himself as Man suffering death in the sinner's stead. This act also purchased the redeemed as His own property. The church is His because He laid down His life for it. As Paul indicates in Titus 2:14, Christ secured both our redemption from iniquity and the rights of possession over us by giving Himself for us. 'His blood' therefore – described possibly in Acts 20:28 as 'the blood of God' or 'God's very own blood' – means the outpouring in death of that human life which He had made His own by becoming Man. It is a reference to His one act of final sacrifice on earth in the days of His flesh and blood, when He gave up His human body to be nailed to the tree.

d) Ephesians 2:13 rv: 'But now in Christ Jesus ye that once were far off are made nigh in the blood of Christ' (ἐν τῷ αἵματι τοῦ Χριστοῦ).

This verse comes in a paragraph which refers to the bringing in of the Gentiles, who had been complete outsiders, to become fellow-citizens with the saints and full members of the family or household of God. Hitherto, as the dividing wall of the Jewish Temple courts symbolized, they had been both shut out from nearer access to God and separated from full fellowship with Israel. Now they are reconciled both to God and to man; and, says Paul in the same context, Christ abolished the enmity 'in his flesh', or through His incarnation and earthly life; and He actually achieved the full victory and slew the enmity by means of the cross. It is, therefore, 'through the cross' that He reconciles them both unto God (see Eph 2:11-22, especially verses 14-18). When, therefore, Paul said previously that those once afar off are made nigh 'in the blood of Christ' he unquestionably means, as he immediately explains, that they are made nigh as a consequence of Christ's death upon the cross.

e) Colossians 1:19-20 rv: 'For it was the good pleasure [of the Father] that in him should all the fulness dwell; and through him to reconcile all things unto himself, having made peace through the blood of his cross' (εἰρηνοποιήσας διὰ τοῦ αἵματος τοῦ σταυροῦ αὐτοῦ).

Again, the thought is of reconciliation of all things to God, and of doing away with the enmity and estrangement caused by sin. It is those who in time past were alienated and enemies in their mind in their evil works that Christ has now reconciled to present them holy and without blemish and unreprovable before Him (see Col. 1:19-22). How then has He done this? Paul says first not only 'through his blood' but 'through the blood of his cross'; and he makes his meaning doubly and unmistakably plain by adding 'in the body of his flesh through death'. There were in Colossae Gnostic tendencies to despise things earthly, fleshly and material, and to believe that the holy things of God, and much more His personal appearing and activity, could not be fully of or in this world. Paul's answer to such heresy was direct and emphatic. He declares that the universal reconciliation has been effected through something done in history, in a human body of flesh and on a cross of shame; and it was done through physical dying. So 'the blood of his cross' can mean no other than the pouring out in death of His earthly human life by crucifixion on a common gibbet. That is the deed that avails to put men right with God.

f) Hebrews 9:7 RV: 'but into the second went the high priest alone, once in the year, not without blood (οὐ χωρὶς αἵματος) which he offereth for himself, and for the errors of the people.'

Hebrews 9:11-14 RV: 'But Christ ... through his own blood (διὰ δὲ τοῦ ἰδίου αἵματος) entered in once for all into the holy place. ... For if the blood of goats and bulls, and the ashes of a heifer sprinkling them that have been defiled, sanctify unto the cleanness of the flesh: how much more shall the blood of Christ, who through the eternal Spirit offered himself without blemish unto God, cleanse your conscience from dead works to serve the living God?'

Hebrews 9:22: 'And, according to the law, I may almost say, all things are cleansed with blood (ἐν αἵματι), and apart from shedding of blood there is no remission' (καὶ χωρὶς αἱματεκχυσίας οὐ γίνεται ἄφεσις).

Hebrews 9:25 RV: 'as the high priest entereth into the holy place year by year with blood not his own' (ἐν αἵματι ἀλλοτρίῳ).

Hebrews 10:4 RV: 'It is impossible that the blood of bulls and goats should take away sins.'

Hebrews 10:19-20, 22 RV: 'Having therefore, brethren, boldness to enter into the holy place by the blood of Jesus (ἐν τῷ αἵματι Ἰησοῦ), by the way which he dedicated for us, a new and living way, through the veil, that is to say, his flesh; ... let us draw near ... having our hearts sprinkled from an evil conscience.'

These verses deserve much more detailed attention than we can here give them. Further, in this paper their significance has already been partly anticipated. To comment briefly: the main objective of the priestly ministry was clearly to remove the barriers and estrangement caused by sin and to gain access to God's presence. Under the old order of the Jewish tabernacle the true way in was not yet made manifest (see Heb. 9:8). The high priest, who did enter once a year into the most holy place, could only do so 'not without blood' and 'with blood not his own'. This taking of blood into the holy place was a token of blood already shed and of a life laid down in expiation for sin. But Christ did not enter 'with blood' or taking blood at all. He entered 'through his own blood', that is, by way of His own death; in which way He did not cease to act when as Man He died, because as God He was also eternal and undying Spirit. He could, as none else could, offer Himself in the act of dying. When His blood was shed He made a present immediate offering or sacrifice of Himself to God in 'the greater and more perfect tabernacle' (see Heb. 9:11-12, 23-26). His flesh (made sin for us) became as it were the separating veil and was rent; and as His blood flowed forth in death a new and living way to God was opened up and consecrated for us; as, also, in the very hour in which He yielded up His spirit, the veil of the symbolical temple was rent in twain from the top to the bottom (Mark 15:37-38). Thus He entered into the true immediate Presence of God 'through his blood', when He offered Himself to God on the cross; and He thus entered once for all, never again needing to offer anything further to secure entrance either for Himself as man's high priest or for His people.

For Christ's resurrection and ascension, which are significantly not mentioned in this whole context, were not stages in the sacrificial presentation of Himself or of His offering to God. Rather they were subsequent stages of triumph and exaltation for His humanity, consequent upon a work already finished and a victory won. It was the enthronement of the high priest whose work of making propitiation was already finished. Christ did not offer His glorified body to God, but the body of His flesh in death, the body of flesh and blood in which He bore our sin. And just as He entered into God's Presence 'through his blood', or by reason of His human death, so all His people are bidden to have boldness to enter into the holy place by the same blood of Jesus, appropriating for themselves the benefits of His death and walking in the way which because of His dying for us now stands open. 'By the blood of Jesus' means, therefore, through the death of Jesus and its realized significance.

Again, under the old Levitical order the blood of goats and bulls and the ashes of a heifer were sprinkled upon men to secure for them ceremonial purity. This reference to ashes of a burnt corpse suggests that what is being signified is not the released life of the victim but its accomplished death. It was this that had virtue to atone and to sanctify; and this virtue, be it noted, could continue to operate after and indeed because the animal's life had been taken. Participation in this virtue or benefit from the animal's sacrifice already accomplished, was symbolized by sprinkling men with its blood or with its ashes mixed with water. Similarly, and much more, Christ's one act as Man of offering Himself to God in death for sin has an abiding value and efficacy. It continually avails to secure not just ceremonial cleansing but inner moral purification and release from bondage. Its power thus to cleanse is inexhaustible and still available. This continuing efficacy of the one past act of sacrifice to give men present cleansing is expressed in language provided by the Old Testament by describing the cleansing as done by the blood of Christ. The cleansing is a present benefit which is made available and actual because of the one sufficient sacrifice made when the incarnate Son of God shed for men His human blood. So, as this writer to the Hebrews also says, it is by this one offering of His human body once for all that He has perfected for ever them that are sanctified (see Heb. 10:10-14).

g) Hebrews 12:24 RV: 'and to Jesus the mediator of a new covenant, and to the blood of sprinkling that speaketh better than that of Abel'.

1 Peter 1:2: 'unto obedience and sprinkling of the blood of Jesus Christ'.

1 John 1:7: 'and the blood of Jesus Christ his Son cleanseth us from all sin'.

These verses all pursue the thought just commented on above. Sacrifice of life is so significant in God's sight that the blood thus shed has, so to speak, power to cry out afterwards either for recompense or reward; and to secure a share in these consequences for those either involved in it or sprinkled by it.

> Abel's blood for vengeance
> Pleaded to the skies;
> But the blood of Jesus
> For our pardon cries.

Oft as it is sprinkled
On our guilty hearts,
Satan in confusion
Terror-struck departs.

'The sprinkling of the blood' in the case of Christ's sacrifice means the extension to the persons sprinkled of the value and the benefits of the death of which it is the token.[30] So the phrase and the idea continue to be a metaphorical way of referring to the application of and the participation in the saving benefits of the death of Jesus.[31] This efficacy of the one sacrifice already made is continuous and all-sufficient. So Christians can still prove, as they walk in the light, that the blood of Jesus cleanses them from all sin; that is, that Christ's death avails to purge away any and every fresh defilement. Here, too, in 1 John it is significant that John, who is often so occupied in thought with the believer's participation in Christ's life, attributes to the blood of Jesus not the power to quicken but the power to cleanse. For the quickening or regenerating work which gives men new life is done by the Spirit, not by the blood.[32]

h) Matthew 26:27-28 RV: 'And he took a cup, and gave thanks, and gave to them, saying Drink ye all of it, for this is my blood of the covenant, which is shed for many unto remission of sins.' (See also Mark 14:24, Luke 22:20, 1 Cor. 11:25-27.)

Hebrews 9:15-20 RV: 'And for this cause he is the mediator of a new covenant, that a death having taken place for the redemption of the transgressions that were under the first covenant, they that have been called may receive the promise of the eternal inheritance. For where a testament is, there must of necessity be the death of him that made it.

---

[30] Compare: 'He [Paul] conceives of that Death as operating by a sacrificial blood-shedding. The Blood of that Sacrifice is as it were sprinkled round the Christian, and forms a sort of hallowed enclosure, a place of sanctuary, into which he enters. Within this he is safe, and from its shelter he looks out exultingly over the physical dangers which threaten him; they may strengthen his firmness of purpose but cannot shake it.' Sanday and Headlam, *Romans*, p. 119.

[31] For its connection also with the new covenant note Heb. 12:24a, compare Exod. 24:7-8 and see following section on covenant blood.

[32] Compare John 6:52-63. It is noteworthy that when our Lord spoke of gaining life through eating His flesh and drinking His blood, He added, 'It is the spirit that quickeneth; the flesh profiteth nothing.' This seems to mean that there is no life actually transmitted through the material flesh and blood; but rather that, as a result of His atoning death and as a benefit of His passion, the Spirit is given to give men new life. Compare John 7:37-39.

For a testament is of force where there hath been death: for doth it ever avail while he that made it liveth? Wherefore even the first covenant hath not been dedicated without blood. For when every commandment had been spoken by Moses unto all the people according to the law, he took the blood of the calves and the goats, with water and scarlet wool and hyssop, and sprinkled both the book itself, and all the people, saying, This is the blood of the covenant which God commanded to you-ward.'

Hebrews 10:29: 'and hath counted the blood of the covenant, wherewith he was sanctified, an unholy thing'.

Hebrews 13:20-21: 'with [or 'by'] the blood of the eternal covenant' (ἐν αἵματι διαθήκης αἰωνίου).

There are more references to 'the blood of the covenant' than we can here examine in detail. Covenants seem clearly to have been dedicated with blood (note Heb. 9:18) as a symbolic representation of the death of the covenant-maker. In ordinary human transactions such symbolism was presumably a vivid witness before God to what the individuals concerned condemned themselves to suffer if they failed to fulfil their covenant undertakings. They swore by their lives; if they failed – let their blood be shed. But in the perfect eternal covenant in Christ's blood there is more than this. For the death that actually took place was the death of the incarnate Son of God. And so the blood with which this new covenant was dedicated affords 'cover' to give actual remission of sins. It can make men clean from all defilement. For, as the writer to the Hebrews says, 'a death' has 'taken place for the redemption of the transgressions that were under the first covenant' (Heb. 9:15 RV). So Christ is the mediator of a new covenant 'which hath been enacted upon better promises' (Heb. 8:6 RV) and by which, as did not prove true under the old covenant, reception of the promised inheritance by those called is absolutely sure. For in this new covenant, because of Christ's blood that was shed, there is guarantee that those who share in it will not fail in the middle nor be found wanting at the last. The God of peace, who showed His acceptance of what Jesus had done for men by bringing Him as the great Shepherd of the sheep again from the dead, will for the same reason do more and do all. Because of Christ's accomplished sacrifice and by the blood of the eternal covenant thus sealed, God Himself can be counted on to make all the sheep for whom the Shepherd laid down His life perfect in every good thing to do His will (Heb. 13:20-21). Nor is any further offering of His sacrifice for their sins necessary, even though they commit fresh sins. For where remission of sins is – and that is what, according to Christ's own words, the blood of the covenant assures us of when we drink the cup[33] – there is no more offering for sin (Heb. 10:18).[34] So the cup of the covenant blood is not a means of participation in life released to be communicated, but a visible seal of eternal redemption fully obtained for us by Christ's death and now available to be enjoyed and offered for faith's appropriation.[35]

i) John 6:54-58 RV: 'He that eateth my flesh and drinketh my blood hath eternal life .... For my flesh is meat indeed, and my blood is drink indeed [or 'true drink']. He that eateth my flesh and drinketh my blood abideth in me and I in him.'

Revelation 1:5 RV: 'Unto him that loveth us and loosed [or 'washed'] us from our sins by his blood' (ἐν τῷ αἵματι αὐτοῦ).

Revelation 7:14 RV: 'These are they which come out of great tribulation, and they washed their robes, and made them white in the blood of the Lamb' (ἐν τῷ αἵματι τοῦ ἀρνίου).

Revelation 12:11 RV: 'And they overcame him because of the blood of the Lamb' (διὰ τὸ αἷμα τοῦ ἀρνίου).

We have surely surveyed enough scriptural quotations already to see that for those who have entered into the heritage of Scripture there is every justification for the most vivid metaphorical use of the word 'blood' in phrases that express the benefits that become ours through Christ's death for us. Such metaphorical language is found nowhere more vividly applied than on the lips of Christ Himself. He spoke of the necessity of 'drinking his blood' and said, 'My blood is true drink.' And we venture to assert that our previous study has made it abundantly clear that such language describes not participation in His life but appropriation of the benefits of His life laid down. To eat His flesh and to drink His blood is to confess that only through His death can I live. As the familiar Prayer Book language asserts, it is 'The blood of our Lord Jesus Christ which was shed for thee' (not 'which is now being given to thee') which can 'preserve thy body and soul unto everlasting life.'[36] We drink the cup

---

[33] Note Matt. 26:28 RV, 'unto remission of sins.'

[34] Alternatively, for those who deliberately reject this one sacrifice there is no other second sacrifice held in reserve; they have no prospect but judgment. See Heb. 10:26-31.

[35] Of course, this redemption includes Christ's gift of life and life more abundant. The point here is that this new life is not directly signified by, released in, or communicated through 'the blood of Christ.'

[36] Words used in the administration of the cup in the Holy Communion.

in remembrance of the one act of sacrifice – His blood shed – and in appropriation of its benefits.

Similarly, in the Apocalypse there are vivid metaphorical phrases which are not an indication of some crude 'religion of the shambles', but a purely figurative method of rejoicing in salvation through Christ's death. So we give Him honour who has 'loosed [or 'washed'] us from our sins by his blood'. The multitude of the redeemed, who stand before God's throne, are they who 'washed their robes and made them white in the blood of the Lamb'. The Christian brethren overcome the devil who would accuse them before God, 'because of the blood of the Lamb'. Such language attributes freedom, cleansing and final triumph over all condemnation all to the virtue of Christ's one sacrifice for His people when as Man He shed His human blood.

What the writers of the New Testament thus began, the Christian worshippers in song – the hymn-writers of the church – have ever since sustained. They still know, as some so-called theologians apparently do not know, how to glory in the blood of the Lamb and thus to sing the praise of Him who died. For Christ's death for us is 'the sinner's hope', the unending cause of all our blessings. It can, therefore, even in heaven itself, never cease to be the central theme of all the worship. 'Worthy is the Lamb that hath been slain to receive the power, and riches, and wisdom, and might, and honour, and glory, and blessing' (Rev. 5:12 RV). Let him who can, refrain from saying 'Amen'.

Conclusion

Some attempt must now be made to sum up our findings and to make some final comments. Before we do this, let us notice two general considerations essential to a right understanding of the meaning of the word 'blood' in the Bible. First, there is nothing in the ideas of the Bible about 'blood' which is at all comparable to the modern practice of blood transfusion. Nowadays one man can sometimes say of another, 'He gave his blood to me.' This is not a right thing for the Christian to say of Christ. To talk of 'the drinking of his blood' with reference to participation in the Holy Communion, or thus to describe the response of appropriating faith, is something entirely symbolical or metaphorical. And it is well for us to note that the Jewish abhorrence of all actual blood-drinking was recognized and respected in the early church (see Acts 15:28-29). Clearly, therefore, none thought that Christ had given them His actual blood to drink as the way of being renewed by His life.

Second, we are very prone to forget that the shedding of blood is in man's experience wholly a consequence of sin. Man was not originally intended by God to die in this way. Apart from sin man would have entered into glory by translation and transfiguration, as is suggested in the cases of Enoch and Elijah (Gen. 5:24, 2 Kings 2:11) and made finally plain by our Lord's own transfiguration. As sinless Man Jesus could have gone to heaven that way; but He chose to accomplish a different kind of 'exodus' in Jerusalem and to shed His blood as the Passover lamb for the redemption of His people (see Luke 9:28-36). To speak, therefore, of Christ's shed blood is to acknowledge the amazing fact that He, the sinless Son of God, actually as Man died the kind of death which only sinners ought to die. All our references to 'Christ's blood' ought therefore to involve the significant recollection that His human life in this world came to an end by the violent rending of His flesh and that, as though He Himself were a sinner, He died the sinner's kind of death (that is, a blood-shedding death); and it is because He died the kind of death that sinners ought to die, that sinners can by faith in Him and Him crucified be saved from sin and all its dire consequences.

For, 'being found in fashion as a man, he humbled himself, becoming obedient even unto death, yea, the death of the cross' (Phil. 2:8 RV). This is the amazing condescension to which the New Testament writers bear witness when they say that 'Christ died for us', and that we are 'justified by his blood'. This is equally the amazing condescension which still inspires the unceasing wonder and worship of His people. It is, therefore, when the redeemed sing the praise of the Lamb who died, that the word 'blood' is spontaneously given its true scriptural meaning. So, for example, it is that one has written,

> Bearing shame and scoffing rude,
> In my place condemned He stood;
> Sealed my pardon with His blood:
> Hallelujah! What a Saviour!

Now, let us seek to sum up more generally and more comprehensively the main significance of the word 'blood' as we have seen it to be used throughout the whole Bible. Blood is a visible token of life violently ended; it is a sign of life either given or taken in death. Such giving or taking of life is in this world the extreme, both of gift or price and of crime or penalty. Man knows no greater. So, first, the greatest offering or service one can render is to give one's blood or life. 'Greater love hath no man than this, that a man lay down his life for his friends' (John 15:13).

Second, the greatest earthly crime or evil is to take blood or life, that is, manslaughter or murder. Third, the great penalty or loss is to have one's blood shed or life taken. So it says of the blood-shedder, 'by man shall his blood be shed'; and so Paul says of the magistrate, 'He bareth not the sword in vain: for he is a minister of God, an avenger for wrath to him that doeth evil' (Rom. 13:4 RV). 'The wages of sin is death' (Rom. 6:23). Fourth, the only possible or adequate expiation or atonement is life for life and blood for blood. This expiation man cannot give (see Ps. 49:7-8, Mark 8:36-37). Not only is his own life already forfeit as a sinner. But also all life is God's (see Ps. 50:9-10). So man has no 'blood' that he can give. This necessary but otherwise unobtainable gift God has given. He has given the blood to make atonement (Lev. 17:11). Atonement is, therefore, only possible by the gift of God. Or as P. T. Forsyth expressed it, sacrifice 'is the fruit of grace and not its root.'[37] What is more, when our Lord claimed to have come 'to give his life a ransom for many' (Mark 10:45), He was implying His deity as well as His human sinlessness and indicating the fulfilment of that which the shed blood of animal sacrifices merely typified. Here in Jesus, the incarnate Son, was God come in person to give as Man the blood which only can make atonement. The church of God is, therefore, purchased with His own blood (Acts 20:28).

All these four significances of 'blood' as shed meet in the cross of Christ. There the Son of Man in our flesh and blood for us men and for our salvation made the greatest offering. He gave His life (see John 10:17-18). Second, He became the victim of mankind's greatest crime. He was vilely and unjustly put to death. Third, 'He was reckoned with transgressors' (Luke 22:37 RV, from Isa. 53:12) and endured the extreme penalty of the wrongdoer. The hand of the law and of the Roman magistrate put Him to death. By man was His blood shed. Fourth, He as God made flesh gave, as He alone could do, His human blood to make atonement. Repentance and remission of sins can, therefore, now be preached in His Name. We are justified by His blood.

So, 'the blood of Christ' speaks to us, as Archbishop Cranmer said of the bread and wine in the Lord's Supper, of Christ 'ut in cruce non in caelo'. 'To drink his blood' means not to appropriate His life, nor to feed upon His glorified humanity, nor to draw upon the power of His resurrection

---

[37] William Sanday (ed.), *Different Conceptions of Priesthood and Sacrifice: A Report of a Conference Held at Oxford* (London, 1900), p. 93. Compare, 'The atonement did not procure grace, it flowed from grace.' The positive truth is that the sacrifice is the result of God's grace and not its cause. It is given *by* God before it is given *to* Him.' Forsyth, *Cruciality of the Cross*, pp. 78, 185.

– with the cross put into the background as but a necessary preliminary to release the life. Rather does it mean consciously, and by faith alone, humbly to appropriate all our blessings and not least redemption and cleansing from sin as wholly and solely the benefits of His death.

Further, this one act in history of the death of Jesus – the offering of His body and the shedding of His blood – is of such value that it avails to reconcile all things unto God and to perfect for ever those whom it sanctifies. Such is the value in eternity of the Lamb slain. This one offering has an all-sufficient efficacy to cover the sins passed over before Christ came, and to cleanse completely all those who are being brought in until the church is complete. The 'broken pieces' which (as in the feeding of the five thousand) are more than enough to satisfy the whole multitude, all come from His one breaking of the bread. So William Cowper was right and truly scriptural both in doctrine and in language when he taught us to sing:

> Dear dying Lamb, Thy precious blood
> Shall never lose its power,
> Till all the ransomed Church of God
> Is saved to sin no more.

In conclusion, therefore, we regretfully disagree with Bishop Westcott (to whose exposition of Scripture we owe so much) and with his many modern disciples, when they say that 'the blood of Christ' signifies His life released through death and thus made available for new uses; and we endorse as right the exegesis and the judgment of those who have said that the phrase 'the blood of Christ' is, like the word 'cross,' only a more vivid expression for the death of Christ in its redemptive significance.'[38] 'It connotes the sacrificial death of Christ and all its remedial issues.'[39]

---

[38] Johannes Behm in Kittel, *Theologisches Wörterbuch*.
[39] W. Saumarez Smith quoted by Nathaniel Dimock, *The Doctrine of the Death of Christ* (second edition, London, 1903), p. 63.

12

THE BIBLE AND THE PULPIT (1953)

Much modern preaching is weak and ineffective, disappointing and unconvincing, because of a lack in the preacher of adequate conviction concerning the place of the Bible in the pulpit. Those of us who are called to this task of preaching greatly need a new awakening to, and a consequent compelling awareness of, the character of our stewardship. For 'it is required in stewards that a man be found faithful' (1 Cor. 4:2). The Christian preacher has something unique to offer to men – the proclamation that God has acted in human history both to reveal Himself and to redeem mankind. So our gospel for men ought not to be found in human philosophy and man-made ideas, and still less in our personal preferences and prejudices, but in the declaration of God's self-revealing and saving acts.

These acts of God, because they are acts in history, possess the character of particularity and once-for-all-ness. God is not repeating them in each fresh generation. If therefore they are to fulfil their universal and age-long purpose of speaking to all men and bringing to them light and hope, worthy record, appropriate interpretation and effective announcement of them are indispensable. Nor has God left such necessary complementary ministries to chance. Prophets and apostles were raised up of God to provide both the record and the interpretation, and preachers are continually being called to utter the word of God thus entrusted to them in living application to the present generation – and all under the compulsion and enlightenment of the inspiring Spirit.

'Surely the Lord God will do nothing, but He revealeth His secret unto His servants the prophets'; so Amos saw (3:7). 'The Lord God

First published in *The Churchman* vol. 67 (December 1953).

hath spoken, who can but prophesy?' so Amos spoke (3:8). Such particular confessions indicate and illustrate the general method of divine revelation. God's special acts in history to reveal and to redeem have also been accompanied by the raising up of prophets to record and to interpret. Their words, significantly fixed in permanent written form, are for all subsequent generations doubly indispensable. Without them the acts of God would not be known; still more without them the acts of God would never be understood and appreciated in all their unique and supernatural significance.

What was true of the preparatory disclosures of God in Old Testament times when He spoke to men 'by divers portions and in divers manners' (Heb. 1:1), here a little and there a little, is still more true of the crowning act of revelation and the final work of redemption through the incarnation of God the Son. Through special chosen witnesses God, acting in sovereign providence, secured the writing down of a record of these events of revelation and redemption in ways which throw into relief their true significance, together with a fuller interpretation for the responsive of truths concerning God and man therein revealed. The writings thus inspired also provided manifold indication both of the dynamic outworking of the benefits of this gospel in the lives of men, and of the final consummation in which it will inevitably issue. Thus the New Testament Scriptures were added to the Old.

It is through these Scriptures and through these alone that the true God can now be known and His saving purposes for men discerned. Here only can we find the true Christ in all the fulness of both His divine person and His saving work. To quote Dr Alan Richardson, 'The Christian understanding of historical revelation is that it was given through certain historical events as interpreted by the faith and insight of the prophets and apostles of the Bible'. 'Christians believe that the perspective of biblical faith enables us to see very clearly and without distortion the biblical facts as they really are.' 'The interpretation of the biblical facts, as it was given to them by those who recorded them in the biblical history and apostolic witness, is necessary to a true seeing of the facts themselves.'[1]

What is more, it is God's further complementary purpose that in each fresh generation and in every Christian congregation this written testimony should fulfil its illuminating and saving ministry among men through the present confirming witness of God the Spirit, and through

---

[1] Alan Richardson, *Christian Apologetics* (London, 1947), pp. 92, 105.

the Spirit-enabled exposition and relevant practical application of the written word by the faithful preacher. So these three should agree in one common witness to convince the hearer – the written word, the illuminating Spirit and the faithful preacher. But here, too, since the preacher is the appointed 'voice' to give utterance, if he does not fall into proper line in his ministry, not only is the word of God not heard, but men are compelled to listen to a disappointing counterfeit. 'The hungry sheep look up and are not fed.'

It is, therefore, for the man who would worthily occupy the Christian pulpit to recognize, first, that he is called to serve God and to promote God's glory and men's good by preaching Christ; second, that he is called to serve Christ and to present Him truly and fully to men by preaching that word which has been written to set Him forth; third, that he is called to serve God the Spirit by seeking His guidance, and following His illumination and leading, both in discovering within the written word the truth of God which is relevant and in declaring its relevance to his waiting audience; and fourth, that he is therefore called by the whole Trinity, Father, Son and Spirit, to serve God by becoming a servant of the written word, a man whose utterances are wholly determined both in content and aim by the written word's plain statements and not by his own independent prejudices and preferences.

Would that the many who enter Christian pulpits week by week could be made to feel the amazing wonder of their high privilege, and the full burden of their solemn responsibility, as ministers of the God-given word. Then they would unquestionably give a new priority to the worthy discharge of their stewardship. Nor is there any one accession that many congregations need more than the advent of a preacher who, in the face of all the temptations to do otherwise, can but re-echo the apostle Paul's words, 'Necessity is laid upon me, yea, woe is unto me, if I preach not the gospel' (1 Cor. 9:16).

Such use of the Bible in the pulpit by the preacher is not likely to be adopted, and still less to be faithfully maintained in season and out of season, unless the preacher is convinced of and compelled by certain fundamental truths and consequent obligations with regard to his task. Let us, therefore, seek to make ourselves aware of some of these more in detail.

The preacher ought always to be constrained by the recollection that the church is 'a witness and keeper of Holy Writ' (Article XX of the Thirty-Nine Articles). To quote the late Professor E.J. Bicknell, 'The Church exists to propagate certain beliefs ... Her message is sufficiently set forth in Scripture. … Her primary function is that of *witness*. … As witness, she cannot alter or add to the truth: she is the servant and not the mistress of her message.'[2] Before a congregation of Christian believers the preacher who would be faithful has, therefore, no right to choose what he will say according to his own fancy or personal interest, nor to make brief quotations from the Scriptures serve as pegs on which to hang his own ideas. In the pulpit, if he is to be true to his calling, he must be a minister or servant of the God-given word. He should make it his business solely to set forth for men's edification what can be got out of God's word written rather than what can be independently devised by the initiative of his own reasoning or imagination.

In this connection there is arresting and appropriate significance in the custom which obtains in some Reformed churches, that before the minister enters the pulpit the Bible should be solemnly carried in and placed upon the rostrum, as a visible sign and freshly acted witness that the Holy Scriptures are the one authoritative text-book that is reverenced and that is to be read and expounded in this congregation.

On the other hand, with us 'a text' has come to mean something short, something which belongs to the preacher – '*his* text' – something which, because it is more or less just an indication or introduction of his subject, he can use or depart from as he will. Such a preacher makes the word serve his ends instead of himself becoming a true servant of the word. Whereas originally and properly the word 'text' (as in the reference to the text of ancient manuscripts) describes simply the actual statements to be found in the Holy Scriptures in any particular passage, whether short or long; and the proper business of its preacher is to stick to that passage, and to set forth exclusively what it has to say or to suggest, so that the ideas expressed and the principles enunciated during the course of the sermon are plainly derived from the written word of God, and have its authority for their support and enforcement rather than just the opinion or enthusiasm of their human expositor.

It is thus the preacher's privilege and responsibility continually to bring his hearers into the light and under the judgment of the God-given word. To quote Professor Oscar Cullmann:

> The written witness of the Apostles is for us the living element which continually sets us anew face to face with Christ. If we realize the magnitude of this miracle … we can no longer speak of the dead letter of the Bible. Yet this presupposes that we share the faith of the

---

[2] E.J. Bicknell, *A Theological Introduction to the Thirty-Nine Articles of the Church of England* (second edition, London, 1925), pp. 317-318.

first Christians that the Apostles are not writers like other authors of antiquity, but men set apart by God for the execution of His plan of salvation by their witness, first oral, then written.[3]

The apostolic witness has a double role: it engenders inspiration and acts as its controller, since in all inspiration there is a risk of other spirits putting themselves in the place of the Holy Spirit.[4]

Here we sometimes need deliverance from prevailing but misleading traditional interpretation of Scripture. For instance, in His condemnation of the rabbinic interpretation of the commandment to honour father and mother (Mark 7:9-13), as well as in the antitheses of the Sermon on the Mount, our Lord was significantly indicating 'the necessity of returning to the Word itself to get from it the divine intention.'[5]

On the other hand, we equally and more often need deliverance from the temptation to impair the distinctive witness of the God-given word through following some prevailing fashion of academic scholarship or popular thought. For instance,

If the texts have to be manipulated previously, when historical witnesses are interpreted as myths, or when the scholar decides beforehand how much of the text he is to regard as 'eternal truth' and how much as 'historically conditioned' and therefore valueless material, the experience he looks forward to will not be related to the God of our salvation but rather to the theologian's own views of what salvation ought to be.[6]

Or again, 'In our eagerness to evangelize, we may actually distort the Gospel by identifying it with a program or ideology which is already acceptable'. 'To make the Gospel relevant *according to our views of relevancy* is to manipulate God's revelation to suit ourselves – but then we do not allow *God* to speak *to* us in *his* own way.'[7] If, therefore, God's voice is to be properly heard in the congregation of His people the preacher must be a wholehearted and uncompromising servant and expositor of the God-given word.

The preacher should believe and become increasingly aware that there is a vital Christian significance for present-day hearers to be

---

[3] Oscar Cullman, 'Scripture and Tradition', *Scottish Journal of Theology* vol. 6 (June 1953), p. 119.

[4] Ibid., p. 121.

[5] Ibid., p. 123.

[6] Otto A. Piper, 'Mysticism and the Christian Experience', *Theology Today* vol. 10 (July 1953), p. 168.

[7] Hugh T. Kerr, 'Revelation and Relevancy', *Theology Today* vol. 10 (July 1953), pp. 145, 147.

found in Scriptures written long ago. This particularly applies to the Old Testament – as the apostle Paul explicitly and repeatedly testifies (see Rom. 15:4, 1 Cor. 10:11, 2 Tim. 3:15-17; compare 1 Pet. 1:10-12). These Scriptures can and should mean more to us than they did or could to the men of Old Testament times; for we live in the light and experience of their Christian fulfilment. Also, they were written for our instruction; they have been divinely prepared and provided for our benefit, to help our understanding and enjoyment of salvation through faith in Christ. For instance, 'St Paul (1 Cor. 10:11) says that the events of the Exodus happened to Israel τυπικῶς – by way of type.' 'For the exodus-theme (with its associated thoughts) provides the clue for the interpretation of each successive stage in God's redeeming acts.' 'The earlier story not only shows a correspondence with the later; it provides the imagery, the authoritative categories by which alone the true meaning of the later can be understood.'[8] Therefore the Old Testament stories ought to be used and expounded as divinely provided material for the better preaching and appreciation of Christ and the gospel.

In this connection, as Professor C.H. Dodd has significantly shown, striking illustration of this method of exposition is to be found in the use of the Old Testament which is made by the New Testament writers. According to their judgment through the ancient Scriptures the Holy Spirit speaks to us 'today' (see, for example, Heb. 3:7). They appealed to the ancient scriptural history and statement to confirm the divine origin of, and to interpret the divine purpose in, the events of the gospel or the experience of Christians. Paul thus 'found a securer basis than his own "experience" for the theology he taught'. 'He expressly bases his theology upon the kerygma as illuminated by the prophecies of the Old Testament; or, in other words, upon the historical facts which he had "received" from competent witnesses, set in the larger historical framework, witnessed, both as fact and as meaning, by the prophetic writers.'[9]

Appreciation of the place and need for this kind of preaching use of the Old Testament in our pulpits is the more urgent because the literary and historical criticism of the Old Testament, engaged in by ordinands-in-training more than by others, has developed in the preachers-to-be of our churches a critical scientific attitude to the Old Testament documents, and has actually inhibited rather than encouraged their use

---

[8] W.M.F. Scott, 'The Christian Use of the Old Testament', *The Churchman* vol. 61 (December 1947), pp. 177-178.

[9] C.H. Dodd, *According to the Scriptures: The Sub-structure of New Testament Theology* (London, 1952), p. 135.

of these Scriptures in the way in which a Christian preacher should handle them. For 'the Bible has become too much a book for specialists; a book on the serious discussion of which men are hesitant to embark, lest they trespass on some technical preserve, and be condemned out of hand for some highly technical errors'. 'It is the great immediate loss produced by the historical study of the Bible that it has destroyed the old common believing use of the Bible.'[10]

Preachers, therefore, need to return to a proper Christian attitude to the Old Testament, and to a proper believing use of it in Christian preaching and teaching. What is more, to get to the root of the matter, men being trained as preachers in the theological colleges need to be set free from absorption in the study of the prevailing scientific and historical criticism of the Old Testament, which is for them not only so largely profitless but also so grievously deadening, and encouraged to study the Old Testament with its Christian application and use fully in view.

The preacher ought to prepare for his task as one who believes that it is within the Canon of the Old and New Testament Scriptures that God's present word for men is still to be found and heard; and that it is through the faithful exposition and vital application of these Scriptures to the congregation that this present word of God is to be expressed and made living and intelligible to men by the quickening and illuminating Spirit. This means in practice that when considering what to preach, the preacher-to-be will prayerfully wait upon God with and in His word. In other words, it is to the Scriptures that he will turn; it is in them he will tarry; it is at them he will toil; constrained by the belief and encouraged by the unfailingly renewed experience that God still has much light waiting to break forth from and through His written word.

Not only so; he will seek in this way the more exclusively and diligently to discover the message to be preached, because he knows it to be his calling thus to minister the God-given word rather than to give to men what they may imagine or what he may think they need. For neither the people in the pews, nor the man in the pulpit are the best judges of what is truly relevant to the needs of the congregation. Men and women, living as we all do so sinfully and selfishly, need the breaking in from outside of a word announcing a staggering objective truth, relevant to us because we are inevitably related to it and of such a kind as will alter our whole present circumstance and our whole future behaviour. The Christian preacher should be like a telegraph messenger

---

[10] Hubert Cunliffe-Jones, *The Authority of the Biblical Revelation* (London, 1945), p. 35.

bringing to the hearer in person, and not least to the wholly indifferent and unsuspecting, the kind of news that completely alters his position and his prospects – like the bringing to light of evidence making one chargeable with a capital offence, or the news of the death of a relative by whose will one is richly to benefit, provided one goes to live on his estate. Such is the news which the preacher is called to find for men in the God-given word, and commissioned authoritatively to give to men in God's Name.

The preacher can only adequately discharge his responsibility if he recognizes that he is called to preach the whole Bible and the Christ of all the Scriptures. There is no justification for deliberately leaving some out or carelessly disregarding its witness. In a sermon on 2 Timothy 3:16-17, John Calvin wrote:

> That no man might take the liberty to choose what he pleaseth and so obey God in part, St Paul saith the whole Scripture hath this majesty of which he speaketh, and that it is all profitable. ... When he speaketh of the Holy Scripture ... he doth mean the Old Testament. ... Thus we perceive that his mind was that the law and the prophets should always be preached in the Church of Christ.

Or, to quote two modern writers:

> In any merely human system of truth ... obsolete ideas are discarded, new ideas are incorporated in the light of fresh discoveries. But no part of the divine revelation can ever become out of date, nor does it need to be supplemented from outside. Hence the place assigned to Scripture.[11]

And again, 'The Bible is a vehicle of revelation, and it is not open to a believer to select from it only such passages as suit his personal taste'.[12] So the faithful steward of the mysteries of God must preach the Scriptures, the whole Scriptures, and nothing but the Scriptures.

One last word needs to be added. Such preaching requires in the preacher personal qualifications of a moral and spiritual order in the realm of his own faith in Christ and his own obedience to God's word. To the proclamation of the message the effective preacher, whom the Spirit uses to enlighten and to inspire men, commonly sets the seal of his own testimony that God's word is true. This he does both by the confession of his lips and by the correspondence of his life. For the God-

---

[11] Bicknell, *Theological Introduction*, p. 317.

[12] W.J. Phythian-Adams, *The People and the Presence: A Study of the At-one-ment* (London, 1942), p. 86.

given word is made by the Spirit present saving gospel to the hearer who believes, as it is preached with conviction and urgency by the man who himself believes it and has experienced its power. Similarly the God-given word becomes challenging and compelling teaching to the hearer who is prepared to obey, as it is presented in exposition and exhortation by the man who has himself worked out its meaning and entered into its practical application in his own daily living.

By all means, therefore, let us preach the word, in season and out of season. In other words, in the pulpit let us confine ourselves to biblical exposition. For we are stewards of divinely revealed truth and 'it is required in stewards that a man be found faithful'. But to our faithful stewardship let us add faith in our divine Fellow-Worker and the obedience of wondering fellow-workmen. Let us, as we preach, ourselves be doers of the word and not preachers only. Let us, as we preach, never cease to believe that if the word be God-given He will cause it to prosper in the thing whereto He sends it. Such labour cannot be in vain.

13

The Ministry of God's Word (1960)

The Weapon of God

'Take ... the sword of the Spirit, which is the word of God' (Eph. 6:17)

The words quoted above come in a passage which indicates that there is a war in progress, a war in which, if we are Christians, we have to fight; a war not against physical forces but against spiritual foes; a war for which God Himself has provided us with armour to wear and a weapon to wield. This weapon, the sword of the Spirit, is the word of God. In 2 Corinthians 10:3-5 RV we read:

> For though we walk in the flesh, we do not war according to the flesh: (for the weapons of our warfare are not of the flesh, but mighty before God to the casting down of strongholds); casting down imaginations, and every high thing that is exalted against the knowledge of God, and bringing every thought into captivity to the obedience of Christ.

These words of St Paul not only repeat the idea that Christians are involved in inevitable warfare; they also explicitly affirm that in this warfare we cannot fight with physical weapons. The weapons which must be used are spiritual, because the enemies to be overcome are the wrong thoughts and ideas, the human imaginations and reasonings, which men presume to set up in direct opposition to the truth of God and to the God of truth. It is these hostile and rebellious thoughts which have to be subdued, so that those who think them may be brought into captivity to Christ and to His obedience.

First published by the Church Pastoral Aid Society in February 1960.

A war of ideas

This warfare is the world's fundamental conflict, a fight not between physical forces, nor with atom and hydrogen bombs, but between ideas or, as they are nowadays sometimes called, ideologies. This war is waged not by material weapons of steel but by words, words in which ideas find forceful and possibly explosive and destructive expression. Such words can like anti-aircraft shells bring down some from their flights of fancy; or they may, like torpedoes, sink some who sail on oceans of their own conceit.

In such conflict the stronghold to be captured is the mind or, in Bible language, the heart; that is, the place within himself where a man thinks and decides. When in the book of Proverbs we read, 'Keep thy heart with all diligence; for out of it are the issues of life', it is very important to recognize that here 'the heart' does not just mean the seat of one's emotions. It also means, as the context in Proverbs makes plain, the mind, the part of us with which we retain and give heed to God's words (see Prov. 4:20-23).

Men cannot, like animals, live properly simply on food for their bodies; they also need food for their minds. Because we are creatures to whom He has given minds, God ministers to our need through His word (see Matt. 4:4). That also is how the enemy of men's souls deceives us and leads us captive – by words, by the propagation of misleading ideas. So we find ourselves involved in *a battle of words*, a war of ideas, a combat in which truth and error are in mortal conflict.

This battle for man's soul began in the garden of Eden. Here God first put right ideas into man's mind through His word. He told him plainly what to do, and what not to do, in order to enjoy life and to avoid death (see Gen. 2:16-17). Then the adversary put wrong ideas into man's mind, through subtle, malicious propaganda, directed to persuade man to rebel against God. So man was tempted first to doubt God's word, next to deny God's word, and finally to defy God's word (see Gen. 3:1-6). So Adam and Eve were misled into believing the lie and following the liar: and this is still how the enemy of men's souls perverts and corrupts men's lives, by possessing their minds with wrong ideas, ideas propagated by words.

We find this battle of words, this war of ideas, again being actively waged in our Lord's temptations in the wilderness (see Matt. 4:1-11). But this time the liar and the deceiver did not win. We read of his clever devilish onslaughts, full of guile and malice, superficially so specious and enticing. We see him trying to put wrong ideas into the mind of Jesus in order to mislead Him into wrong action. Every time Jesus countered the wrong ideas by right ideas from the words of God. He answered: 'It is written'; and quoted words which both exposed the error of the devil's suggestions and indicated the true way to please God. This is still the only way of victory over subtle temptation and enticing propaganda. We need minds well acquainted with God's word and able to use it like a sword in decisive counter-thrust (see Ps. 119:11).

The power of propaganda

The same battle of words was also waged by our Lord in His public ministry. He went forth to reach and to rescue men. Words were His weapon. Similarly, later, when He sent forth His followers, He sent them to preach. The sword which He put into their hands with which to overthrow error, destroy delusion and liberate captives, was the sword of truth, the sword of His word. Consequently, just as the enemy of souls leads men captive by a subtle campaign of enticing words, so the Christian evangelist goes forth to set captives free by wielding the sword of the Spirit, which is the word of God. It is here in the propagation of the gospel of Christ and in the rescue of the slaves of sin that the battle of words is most decisively joined.

This conviction that men can be reached and rescued, that they can be persuaded to act differently and their lives completely changed, *by words*, is fundamental to Christianity. Preaching and propaganda as a dynamic practice for winning new adherents started within the Christian church. It began with the ministry of the word of God and the propagation of the gospel of Christ. Only in the last generation or two has the world learnt from the church the effectiveness of this method. So the modern world is full of advertisement and propaganda, of attempts to use words and visual aids to capture men's minds and men's obedience.

What is more, since the twentieth century began, the power of words to penetrate to the ends of the earth and to influence the minds of the masses has been vastly increased by printing and the circulation of books and pamphlets, newspapers and magazines, and finally by radio and television, using the staggering power of broadcasting to confront millions of people all at once with the same sights and words. Much of this influence is unworthy, godless, impure, provocative of licence and self-indulgence. It needs to be countered and gainsaid and defeated by the weapon which God has put into our hands to wield – by the word of God, preached, printed, propagated. We can take our share in the fight against the penetration and prevalence of wrong ideas and corresponding wrong behaviour by encouraging people to read God's word, by circulating good literature, by openly taking sides – and the right side – in this war of ideas, by ourselves actively engaging in the ministry of the word of God.

God's Use of Messengers

'Behold, I will send my messenger, and he shall prepare the way before me.' (Mal. 3:1)

'How shall they hear without a preacher? and how shall they preach, except they be sent?' (Rom. 10:14-15)

God has not only made man dependent upon His word, and chosen to use words to reveal Himself and His purposes to men; He has also chosen to use human messengers to carry His words to men and to confront men with His messages. In Old Testament times such messengers of the Lord of hosts were commonly called *prophets*. In New Testament times and in the subsequent Christian era they are more usually called *preachers*. Such messengers are stewards of divine revelation, charged with the responsibility of declaring to men what God has made known to them. The work which they are commissioned to discharge is evidence of the very important and strategic place occupied by the ministry of God's word in the outworking of God's purposes for mankind.

The call of Samuel to be a prophet

In 1 Samuel 3 we read of the call of Samuel by God Himself to become such a messenger of His words to others. The record opens by declaring that there was a dearth in the land of the God-given word. It goes on to indicate how God acted to meet the need by appointing a new minister of His word to the people. What is significant and often overlooked concerning the first message which God gave to Samuel, was that it was a message not for himself but for Eli. It was a message which had to be declared. It became a burden upon his spirit until it was delivered. Also, this experience of receiving from God a message to be publicly declared to men was an experience which from then on was frequently renewed in Samuel's life. Thus he became openly established in the eyes of all

Israel as a divinely commissioned prophet of the Lord. Repeatedly he was used as a minister of God's word to the people. 'For', on the one hand, 'the Lord revealed Himself to Samuel in Shiloh by the word of the Lord.''And', on the other hand, 'the word of Samuel came to all Israel' (1 Sam. 3:21, 4:1).

Similarly we learn from the Old Testament that it was one of the regular responsibilities of the priest in the community to be a teacher of God's ways to the people. 'They should', wrote Malachi, 'seek the law at his mouth: for he is the messenger of the Lord of hosts' (Mal. 2:7). So his privilege as a special minister was not only occasionally to lead the worship of the sanctuary, but also regularly, as a true pastor of God's flock, to be a minister of His word to enquiring individuals.

The call of Paul to be a preacher

One truth about his life and work as a Christian of which St Paul was absolutely sure, was that God intended him to be a preacher, and a preacher not to Jews but to Gentiles. He came to see that in the purpose of God he was set apart to this task from his birth (see Gal. 1:15-16). He knew his apostleship involved him in the responsibility to preach and to teach. Twice he explicitly writes with reference to the gospel and the testimony which must be given to it: 'Whereunto I am appointed a preacher, and an apostle, and a teacher of the Gentiles' (2 Tim. 1:11; compare 1 Tim. 2:7). This was to Paul a great wonder, a crowning proof of the divine mercy, that 'the glorious gospel of the blessed God' had been committed to his trust; and that he, 'who was before a blasphemer and a persecutor', had been put into the ministry – 'to preach among the Gentiles the unsearchable riches of Christ' (see 1 Tim. 1:11-13; Eph. 3:8).

Paul saw that the way of salvation by faith, by simply calling upon the name of the Lord, extends the opportunity of embracing God's blessing to all alike, without distinction between Jew and Gentile, provided that they learn of Christ crucified and risen through the God-given word. He indicates, in addition, that it is part of God's purpose not just to cause men to read His word, but to cause them to *hear* it (see Rom. 10:10-15). So in this present gospel age God is still working out this purpose and adding to the saved community of Christ's church by sending *preachers*. This is the continuing apostolic ministry which God Himself still commissions. Those belong to it who are divinely sent to preach 'the gospel of peace' (Rom. 10:15). This is the primary ministry of God's word in a sinful world.

The Method Christ Chose

'The seed is the word of God.' (Luke 8:11)

'The sower soweth the word.' (Mark 4:14)

'And he ordained twelve, that they should be with him, and that he might send them forth to preach.' (Mark 3:14)

The ministry of the word was the chosen method of our Lord Himself. He fulfilled His public ministry chiefly by *preaching and teaching*. St Mark opens his record of it by saying, 'Now after that John was put in prison, Jesus came into Galilee, preaching the gospel of God' (Mark 1:14). St Matthew gives a summary statement: 'And Jesus went about all Galilee, teaching in their synagogues, and preaching the gospel of the kingdom' (Matt. 4:23). True, there were also healing miracles. But this work was deliberately kept subordinate and treated as an endorsement of His calling as a prophet or God-sent teacher to whose words men ought to give heed.

A seed and a sword

Significant evidence of the priority given by our Lord Himself to prayer and the ministry of the word is provided by Mark 1:32–2:13. The people, we are told, pursued Jesus with their sick folk, desiring healing. Jesus sought escape to a solitary place to pray. When He was found and told that the crowds wanted Him, He says, Let us go elsewhere, where I can preach; for that is the real purpose of my present mission. 'And he preached in their synagogues throughout all Galilee.' When He did return to Capernaum He deliberately stayed indoors where, because of the crowds, the sick could not be brought to Him; and there 'he preached the word unto them'. Later, when 'he went forth again by the seaside; and all the multitude resorted unto him', the one description given of His activity is 'and he taught them'.

It is not surprising, therefore, that when Jesus began to preach by parables, He depicted the work which He was doing in terms of a sower sowing seed; and pointedly declared, 'the seed is the word of God'. By the parables and by the subsequent explanation He implied that by this method of giving men God's word, He was both bringing His hearers under judgment, and ensuring in due time the production and ingathering of a satisfying harvest. Doubtless His Jewish contemporaries looked for a Messiah who would establish God's kingdom by quicker and more violent methods. But, to change the metaphor, His only chosen sword was the sword that proceeded out of His mouth, the sword of the word of God.

Workers to preach and to teach

In addition, our Lord chose the same method of the ministry of the word, first for the training of His followers and secondly for their continuance of His work. The twelve whom He specially selected for intensive training were clearly chosen to become full-time disciples, learning continually in private as well as in public, both from the teaching which He gave to them alone and from His preaching and ministry to the people. Also, His ultimate intention is at once indicated; He desired in due time to send them forth *to preach*; and they were given initial experience of such ministry while still with Jesus in Galilee. After His death and resurrection, Jesus defined the work which He was now sending them to do for Him in terms of preaching and teaching – preaching the gospel to every creature and teaching converts and responsive disciples to observe all things whatsoever He had commanded them (see Mark 16:15; Matt. 28:19-20). So their ministry, like His, both in order to bring men to repentance and faith in Christ, and in order to build them up in consistent Christian living, was *a ministry of the God-given word*. This is the Lord's own appointed method.

The Early Church

'So mightily grew the word of God and prevailed.' (Acts 19:20)

'We will give ourselves continually to prayer, and to the ministry of the word' (Acts 6:4). These words give us the twelve apostles' conception of their task and of their bounden duty. This was, as they saw it, in the light of the Lord's own injunctions, the work to which they were called; and it was therefore to this they were determined to give themselves. This was indeed the task which was already fully occupying their time. For 'daily in the temple and in every house, *they ceased not to teach and preach* Jesus Christ' (Acts 5:42). This was the work from which they refused to be turned aside and in comparison with which they regarded other tasks, however urgent, as work which they had no freedom nor right to undertake. To the assembled company of believers they said emphatically and at once, 'It is not fit that we should forsake the word of God, and serve tables' (Acts 6:2).

Concern to fulfil this ministry

The apostles' consequent concern in prayer was that they might fulfil their ministry without wavering and not be silenced by opposition. 'Now, Lord', they prayed, 'behold their threatenings: and grant unto thy servants, that with all boldness they may speak thy word' (Acts 4:29). Similarly St Paul, a prisoner for the gospel's sake in Rome, asked for special supplication for himself 'that utterance may be given unto me, that I may open my mouth boldly, to make known the mystery of the gospel, for which I am an ambassador in bonds: *that therein I may speak boldly, as I ought to speak*' (Eph. 6:19-20).

Nor was this ministry of the word a task wholly reserved for a select few. When believers other than the apostles were scattered abroad by the persecution which followed the witness and martyrdom of Stephen, it is recorded that 'they ... went everywhere preaching the word' (Acts 8:4). Indeed, such ministry of the word provided all Christians alike with their chief means of helping others to enjoy the same salvation. So St Paul regarded it as the calling of all the saints in Philippi to 'shine as lights in the world, holding forth the word of life' (Phil. 2:15-16).

It was consequently in these terms that the apostles measured the success of their work. St Paul was satisfied if only 'the word of the Lord' could 'have free course and be glorified' (2 Thess. 3:1). He coveted to be thought of by others simply as one of the ministers through whom they believed (see 1 Cor. 3:5). Similarly St Peter testified that 'God made choice ... that by my mouth the Gentiles should hear the word of the gospel and believe' (Acts 15:7). This is apostolic success; this is the hallmark of the true apostolic succession – to be a minister who by preaching the word leads men to faith in the Saviour. This is the crowning joy of the minister – to have men say of him, 'it was through your ministry of God's word that I believed, that my faith was strengthened'.

How the work spread

It is in similar terms that the spread of the work and the consequent growth of the church are described in the New Testament. In the Acts of the Apostles, the only authentic history of the early church which we possess, there is frequent and emphatic reference to the preaching and reception of the word of God as events of major importance. Luke sums up the progress of the work in this way: 'The word of God increased; and the number of disciples multiplied in Jerusalem greatly' (Acts 6:7); 'The apostles and brethren that were in Judea heard that the Gentiles had also received the word of God' (Acts 11:1); 'The word of the Lord was published throughout all the region' (Acts 13:49); 'So mightily grew the word of God and prevailed' (Acts 19:20).

In his epistles St Paul more than once refers to the spread of the work in the same way. The Christians in Thessalonica, he says, became followers of the Lord when they received the word (see 1 Thess. 1:6). Writing from imprisonment in Rome, he gives thanks to God because *the word of the truth of the gospel* is bearing fruit and increasing in all the world (see Col. 1:5-6). For it is by hearing the word of truth, the gospel of their salvation, that men are brought to trust in Christ (see Eph. 1:13). St Paul thus proved, in his work of preaching, a truth which St Peter first experienced in the house of Cornelius, that it is by the hearing of faith that men receive the Spirit and become newborn members of the family of God (see Gal. 3:2; compare Acts 10:44).

The vital power of the word of God

The writers of the books of the New Testament undoubtedly regarded the word of God as possessing inherent power to change lives. 'For the word of God is living and active' (Heb. 4:12 RV); it has, as it were, in itself vital energy. It is capable of activity. It can produce far-reaching results. This is, of course, always true in some measure of any word which is or claims to be a revelation of truth. It is much more true of that word which is the truth and which unlike men's utterances abides for ever. As we have already seen, our Lord Himself used the illustration of seed. As seed, the word of God has power to germinate and to produce fruit. So Luke records, 'The word of God grew and multiplied' (Acts 12:24).

It is as *the Spirit quickens the word* and makes it a living, active force in men's minds, that things happen. It was, for instance, the word of God, the dynamic energy of revealed truth, in the mind and soul of Martin Luther that made him take the stand he did – 'The just shall live by faith' (Rom. 1:17). This is the word that burst out into life and fruit, and like a sapling cracking masonry in the energy of its growth, forced its way through the dead weight of medieval corruption.

The word from God had God-given power to work in the heart and to produce fruit in the life. Such was the conviction of the apostles. St Paul says of the word of God that it effectually worketh in those that believe; it has, or is accompanied by, an energy which operates in men (see 1 Thess. 2:13). St Peter asserts that it is *through the seed of the word of God* that men are born again. And the word which God uses to produce this result is no passing ephemeral thing like the grass of the field, which soon withers. For like begets like; God is eternal; His word lives and abides for ever; and the life which he begets through His word is eternal life. This, too, is the word which by the gospel is preached unto men (see 1 Pet. 1:23-25). Yet again – to add a third witness – St James in his epistle speaks of the implanted word, received with meekness, as able to save the soul (James 1:21).

In addition, the same word of God which has power to germinate and produce life, also has power to make life grow and fructify. The initial minister of the word, the evangelist or preacher of the gospel, is like a sower who plants the seed; the subsequent minister of the word, the pastor and teacher, who brings exhortation and instruction, is like one who waters the soil where the seed is sown to make it grow (see 1 Cor. 3:5-7). Or again, the God-given word is like milk; it has power to nourish life and promote growth (1 Pet. 2:2). It is the instrument by which believers in Christ are established. So when bidding farewell to the Ephesian elders St Paul commended them 'to God and to the word of his grace, which', he said, 'is able to build you up' (Acts 20:32). Finally there is the crowning witness of our Lord's own example and prayer. In His concern for His disciples He acted as one who believed that it is His word which God uses to promote purity and holiness in men's lives. 'Now ye are clean', He said, 'through the word which I have spoken unto you' (John 15:3); and later He prayed to God for them, 'Sanctify them in the truth: thy word is truth' (John 17:17).

Providing food for the mind

It is also worthy of special notice that this milk which promotes spiritual growth is described in 1 Peter 2:2 as rational or intellectual ('reasonable', or literally 'logical') milk. In other words, such milk is food not for the body but for the mind. This means that its profitable digestion is impossible without the appropriating activity of man's powers of thought. In feeding us by His word God deals with us as rational creatures. We cannot feed upon His word without using our minds and exercising the right of private judgment. The spiritual growth of young Christians is therefore to be promoted, not by encouraging a superstitious reverence for quasi-magical rites, but by encouraging each individual believer to use his own powers of thought in the personal appropriation and application of revealed truth.

Consequently, wherever Christian missionaries have gone, they have taught men to read, they have translated the Scriptures into the vernacular and given them to the common people. Christian missionaries who are true to New Testament principles have inevitably become the pioneers in, and the promoters of, popular education. For the word of the gospel which they preach challenges men to use their minds and to think for themselves. True response to its appeal expresses itself not in ritual conformity and multiplied ceremony but in 'reasonable' or 'rational' service (Rom. 12:1-2), in voluntary and intelligent obedience.

A challenge to our day

The age in which we live is one in which this word of God is not preached and taught as once it was. It is more than time that those called and ordained to the ministry of the word should awaken to the peril of such neglect:

> Retrograde tendencies of the Christian Church from its primeval purity are always tendencies to the disuse of preaching. A sliding scale might be constructed by which one might gauge the degree of corruption in the Church of the Middle Ages by the progressive decline of the pulpit ... While the symbols of Christian worship multiplied in number, and increased in splendour, the symbol of Christian thinking and persuasion sunk into imbecility.[1]

On the other hand: 'Revivals of religion go hand in hand with a deepened reverence for the Scriptures, and a multiplied use of the pulpit.'[2] There are, therefore, need and occasion for us to face the challenge to give proper priority in both the worship and the witness of the church to the ministry of God's word.

---

[1] Austin Phelps, *The Theory of Preaching: Lectures on Homiletics* (London, 1882), p. 5.
[2] Ibid., p. 5.

A Personal Responsibility

'And these words, which I command thee this day, shall be in thine heart: and thou shalt teach them diligently unto thy children.' (Deut. 6:6-7)

Since God thus deals with us as rational and responsible creatures, to whom He has spoken in His word, this places upon every individual who comes within the sound and knowledge of God's word the opportunity and the obligation to do something with it. Once others have fulfilled their ministry in bringing God's word to his notice, the individual must become, so to speak, *its minister to himself*. This is the most intimate and the most influential form of the ministry of God's word in the life of every man. None but he can heed it and store it up in mind and memory for subsequent use in faith and obedience.

Ministry to oneself

When God fed His people in the wilderness by giving them manna from heaven to eat, He ordained that every individual should collect his own personal portion every day (see Exod. 16:4). Similarly God-given spiritual nourishment can only be fully gained from God's word by those who learn to feed themselves from it daily. Just as food needs preparation and mastication before it becomes eatable and digestible, so God's word demands diligent enquiring study and detached prayerful meditation, if it is to be received and responded to with full profit. In these matters it is for every man to seek to become his own minister, counting always on the cooperating aid of the illuminating Spirit. So Moses enjoined Joshua: 'This book of the law shall not depart out of thy mouth, but thou shalt meditate therein day and night, that thou mayest observe to do according to all that is written therein: for then thou shalt make thy way prosperous, and then thou shalt have good success' (Josh. 1:8; compare Ps. 1:1-3).

Ministry to our children

There is a complementary sphere of individual personal responsibility in the family and the home. While children are still children, unable as yet fully to use God's word for themselves, they ought to be given elementary and detailed instruction in it by those responsible for their care, particularly by their parents. This is best given frequently, in small quantities, and spontaneously and informally, by the use of the passing occasion or circumstance to teach some relevant God-given promise or prayer, precept or prohibition – here a little and there a little. So we read: 'And thou shalt teach them diligently unto thy children, and shalt talk of them when thou sittest in thine house, and when thou walkest by the way and when thou liest down, and when thou risest up' (Deut. 6:7). This injunction also suggests – and any faithful personal ministry of God's word must surely include – the practice of daily family prayers and the reading of God's word, with brief, simple comment on its meaning and application.

The Unceasing Task

'Preach the word; be instant in season, out of season.' (2 Tim. 4:2)

Most of all does this responsibility to minister the word of God rest upon those who are specially called to serve God and their fellow-Christians as ministers in the local churches. Whether in their public preaching in the congregation, or in their teaching of groups and classes who need instruction, or in their private and personal pastoral care of individuals, what they should always unmistakably be is *ministers of the God-given word*. They should, so to speak, regularly do their work with the Bible in their hands, or with its statements on their lips. Their responsibility so to act is solemnly and visibly enforced in all three of the ordination services of the Church of England by the presentation to every candidate on each occasion of a copy of the Scriptures.

Similarly we find the apostle Paul solemnly charges Timothy, as one who will be answerable to Christ as the Judge at His appearing, to preach the word, to stick to this ministry through thick and thin without faltering, to be always on the job, to fulfil his ministry, to do the work of an evangelist, to give heed to reading, to exhortation, to teaching (see 2 Tim. 4:1-2, 5; 1 Tim. 4:13.)

Preaching the gospel

These exhortations of St Paul's all refer to aspects of the ministry of God's word. First, the gospel must be frequently and faithfully preached from the Scriptures, Old Testament as well as New Testament, which are able to make even children wise unto salvation through faith which is in Christ Jesus (2 Tim. 3:15). God has committed to men the word of reconciliation; and it is the minister's responsibility to set forth from God's word the work of the Saviour and the way of salvation, and to urge men to embrace the opportunity thus offered to find peace with God. It is also his responsibility to exhort those already familiar with gospel truth not to receive the grace of God to no purpose, but to appropriate its benefit while the present day of salvation lasts (see 2 Cor. 5:18–6:2). In addition, true believers in Christ need establishing in an informed awareness of what Christians believe and why; so that from the Scriptures they may be able to give a reason for their confidence and hope.

Teaching disciples

Next, the people of God must be instructed in Christian living. Our Lord left behind Him much teaching and commanded that it should be given to all who become His true disciples; not just for their intellectual acquaintance but for their practical observance (see Matt. 28:19-20). If Christians are to make progress both in understanding and in right living, they must learn to discern between good and evil and to act accordingly, to refuse the evil and to choose the good. For such instruction all Scripture is profitable and ought to be preached and taught, in order that God's people may grow in mature and balanced Christian judgment, and in disciplined and worthy Christian behaviour.

Providing reproof and encouragement

Finally, the faithful pastor and teacher must, as the minister of God's word, apply its challenge to the hearers in both admonition and exhortation. The Scriptures were written, on the one hand to afford warning, and on the other hand to provide encouragement and foster hope (see 1 Cor. 10:11, Rom. 15:4). The minister of God's word should use it to achieve these practical ends.

As St Paul reminds us, the Scriptures are profitable for reproof and correction (2 Tim. 3:16), for pointedly showing us where we are wrong, and for effectively setting us right. The faithful minister of this word must therefore 'reprove, rebuke, exhort' (2 Tim. 4:2). Like a surgeon, as Chrysostom suggested, he must uncover the unpleasant seat of trouble, insert the lance, and then apply the soothing and the healing balm. This should be done, says the apostle, 'with all long-suffering and doctrine'; with endless patience and sympathetic, understanding fellow-feeling, and with helpful, positive and constructive teaching. Such ministry, too, may obviously need to be done privately and personally during a pastoral interview rather than in a public pulpit utterance.

Always using the Bible

For such ministry the Scriptures are the one adequate and indispensable text-book. The faithful evangelist, pastor and teacher must become an unceasing and unfailing servant and minister of the God-given word, giving himself to its ministry and to accompanying prayer as his primary task, always quoting it as his authority, and proving as he does so that the living God is still active by His Spirit to use His word to do His saving work in the hearts and lives of men and women.

May God inspire many of His people in the local churches of our land to value, to desire and genuinely to encourage in their midst, this kind of ministry; and as they pray accordingly, may God in answer give us an increase of ministers thus steadfastly devoted to this one task – the ministry of God's word.

14

THE WORD OF FAITH WHICH
WE PREACH (1957)

At the beginning of September, 1918, when I was just seventeen, I spent my first Sunday in London. I was taken on the Sunday evening to Highbury Quadrant Congregational Church to hear Campbell Morgan preach. Dr Morgan was on that Sunday beginning a special pastorate of one year at that north London church. His text on that Sunday evening was Matthew 11:28, 'Come unto me, all ye that labour and are heavy laden, and I will give you rest.' He said, I remember, that this was not the first time that he had preached on this text. Indeed, he confessed, that ever since he had been a preacher, he had preached on this great word of our Lord's at least once every year. At the end of his sermon, deliberately, as I remember, without request for any evidence of response visible to men, he invited hearers quietly and personally to respond direct to the Saviour's invitation. The impression left clearly upon my mind was that here was a preacher who had for souls in need a present word from God, a word to be responded to here and now by coming to Christ.

This recollection, which I am particularly happy on this occasion to be able to recall, simply and vividly illustrates the principles of the theme which I desire to use this opportunity to expound – a theme which so markedly found outworked fulfilment in the public ministry of George Campbell Morgan. The theme is this – that the Christian preacher is called and sent by God to speak to men's deepest needs, and to lead them to faith not in himself but in Christ and the gospel of saving grace, by offering them not his own ideas but the God-given word. Simple

The ninth Dr Campbell Morgan Memorial Lecture, delivered at Westminster Chapel on 19 June 1957. George Campbell Morgan (1863-1945) was minister at Westminster Chapel 1904-17 and 1934-43, where he exercised an influential preaching ministry.

and obvious as this may seem to those who are already persuaded that it is so, it is right that we should recognize that it requires a personal commission from God Himself and an accompanying activity of the divine providence to produce such a preacher. For circumstances have to be overruled and the responsive human will has to be specially disciplined before such a messenger of the Lord fulfils his God-given ministry.

It is appropriate on this occasion that we should let Campbell Morgan himself testify afresh to these fundamental truths; and first of all to the primary necessity of the personal divine call. 'Men cannot choose', wrote Dr Morgan,

> to become ministers of the Word. This calling is differentiated from all others, in this very fact. While a man can, upon the ground of natural ability, decide whether he will be a doctor, lawyer, or commercial man, he cannot so choose to become a minister. The words of our Lord are of abiding application, and must be taken in their fullest sense; 'Ye have not chosen Me, but I have chosen you'. So strongly do I feel upon this matter, that I never ask men to enter the Christian ministry. The only men who can really enter this ministry are those whom the Lord chooses, calls, and equips, by the bestowment of gifts according to the wisdom of His will.[1]

The same truth is pointedly emphasized by the Apostle Paul in Romans 10:15 when he asks, 'And how shall they preach except they be sent?' In the second place, the Christian preacher is sent to minister to men's deepest needs, not to his own pride or ambition. Dr Morgan himself recorded how at the age of sixteen he was helped by a faithful friend to face this issue. 'David Smith', he wrote,

> conducted the meeting and I preached. I do not think that I dare now quote my text, but I will tell you where it may be found. Let those interested refer to Isaiah 51:6. I have not preached from it recently. The walk home was by moonlight, and six miles long. It seemed longer, for David Smith made full use of it to point out to me the uselessness of speaking before people, merely that they might be given an opportunity to discover my ability. I rebelled at first but, finally, I was convinced. A few weeks later, I went again with the selfsame man, and spoke in the selfsame cottage – this time from the words of Jesus, 'Come unto Me, all ye that labour and are heavy laden, and I will give you rest.' There had been much searching of soul in the intervening time, and much prayer. In the

---

[1] G. Campbell Morgan, *The Ministry of the Word* (London, 1919), pp. 200-201.

middle of that address, I broke down utterly; but ere we left two or three had obeyed the call of Christ. It was to me an experience, the effect of which has never left me. One day, in the Land of Light, I expect to thank David Smith.[2]

In the third place, the true Christian preacher must proclaim the word of the Lord, not his own ideas. Again Dr Morgan himself related how, when he was twenty-nine, he was finally made to choose between being either a popular preacher of his own making or the Lord's messenger. 'God was speaking to me', he wrote,

that I knew, and the crisis in which His voice rang out clearly, almost peremptorily, making known to me His will, came at Rugeley, one Sunday night, after service. I had preached, and we had held an after-meeting, in which men and women had decided for Christ. At the end of the day I went home to my own study, and sat there alone. As clearly as though it had sounded in the room, a voice put this question, 'What are you going to be, a preacher, or My messenger?' For a moment I knew not what it meant, except to realize that the Spirit of God had created a crisis. I stood at the parting of the ways. Presently I began to ponder that night's sermon – to review my ministry. To my dismay I discovered that the desire to become, and to be known as a great preacher, was beginning to get the upper hand.

'What are you going to be, a preacher, or My messenger?' For hours I sat, vainly endeavouring to answer the question, but not until the night had died down, and the light of morning glinted through my study window, did I arrive at a decision. It was a night of conflict between a man and his God. It was my brook Jabbok – the place where God met me, face to face. Just as the light of morning scattered the darkness of the night, so did the light Divine stream into my soul, and joyously I cried out, 'Thy messenger, my Master – Thine!'

But the victory was won, only when the ashes of a bundle of sermons lay in the study fireplace. The work of many years was destroyed on that golden morning, when I stepped out to follow God at all costs, determining to do so without the sermons. During the night hours I came to see that they had been moulded and made so as to include a large element of self. For that reason they were destroyed. As they burned, I said to my Master, 'If Thou wilt give me Thy words to speak, I will utter them, from this day

---

[2] John Harries, G. *Campbell Morgan: The Man and his Ministry* (New York, 1930), pp. 32-33.

forward, adding nothing to them, taking naught away. Thine whole counsel I will declare, so help me God.' So did the Lord prevail.[3]

It was out of such personal awareness of the divine commission, it was out of such personal experience of divine constraint, that Dr Morgan later wrote:

> We are facing today the biggest hour the world has ever known for preaching. The miseries of theological controversy that are blighting our age cannot satisfy. The mass of men are waiting for preaching of the New Testament kind, with a great message of grace to meet human need, delivered by men who realize that they represent a Throne, and have the right to claim submission to it.[4]

The God-Given Word

The first thing that is fundamental, both to the ministry of the preacher and to the faith of the hearer, is the God-given word. Without it the preacher has nothing proper to proclaim; without it the hearer has nothing proper to believe.

Here we do well to pause, and to consider the decisive and indispensable function of words, as a means not only of man's but also of God's personal self-expression and communication. Without God-given words God's presence, God's purpose and God's performance would all be unappreciated. God makes His presence known by His words. God makes others aware of His purpose by His words. God promises His action, He records His action, He interprets His action, all by His words. So, as Amos was inspired to declare, 'Surely the Lord God will do nothing, but he revealeth his secret unto his servants the prophets' (Amos 3:7).

A witness to God's presence

At the burning bush Moses realised that he was in God's presence, not because he saw any visible form, but because he heard words which declared, 'I am the God of thy father, the God of Abraham, the God of Isaac, and the God of Jacob' (Exod. 3:6). The same was true later at Sinai, when God made His presence known to all the people. They saw no image or similitude, no visible figure or form; only they heard a voice (see Deut. 4:12). Words thus spoken are a decisive witness to the actual existence and living presence of their author. Similarly at our Lord's

---

[3] Ibid., p. 46.
[4] G. Campbell Morgan, *Preaching* (London, 1937), pp. 17-18.

baptism, and again at His transfiguration, a cloud was seen. This was a recognizable symbol of the divine presence. So at the transfiguration the three disciples 'feared as they entered into the cloud'. But what made the divine presence unmistakably certain was the spoken words which came out of the cloud. They heard God say, 'This is my Son, my chosen: hear ye him' (see Luke 9:34-35).

Nor does it end there. The apostle Paul plainly declares that in the Christian congregation, when the spiritual gift of prophetic utterance is truly exercised, words thus spoken can and should make the visitor to the meeting fall down on his face in worship acknowledging the presence of God in the midst (see 1 Cor. 14:24-25). Somewhat similarly some of our own ancestors who went to great pains and faced death itself to make the Bible available to be read in a language which the ordinary man could understand, believed that by such means the earnest reader could draw near to God in personal communion and hear God speak to his own soul. It is, therefore, by His word that God is pleased to bring Himself near and to make men aware of his presence. It is the preacher's solemn privilege, as he is used to proclaim the God-given word, to make hearers aware that God is here and that the opportunity to have dealings with Him is near at hand.

A witness to God's purposes

Again by His words God not only makes known His presence; He also makes known His purposes. Such words of revelation both complement, and are themselves completed by, God's performance. By His words God predicts and promises what He is going to do. By His words God records and interprets what He has done. While full divine revelation and fulfilled divine redemption are accomplished only by God's personal intervention in deeds, awareness and appreciation of His doings and responsive appropriation of their benefit depend upon God's words. It is only through the divinely inspired words of the prophets, evangelists and apostles that we know what God has done, and that we discern its significance both in revealing Him and in saving us.

The word to be preached

These God-given words, therefore, and none others, are the words to be preached and taught in all their fulness, without addition or subtraction. Only those who faithfully do this are truly God's messengers. It is to the understanding and proclamation of these words that the divinely commissioned preacher must give his whole mind. Here it is once again very relevant to quote Campbell Morgan. There is something very pertinent to be learnt from the confessed detail of his personal self-discipline and of his deliberate choices as he prepared himself to preach. 'For many years', he confessed, 'I have observed this rule, that when I am at work, preparing either sermons or Bible work of any kind, I never allow myself to open a newspaper until after one o'clock of the day.'[5] 'I would rather have', he wrote, 'on my study shelf one book of scholarly exegesis than forty volumes of devotional exposition.'[6]

The word made available in the Scriptures

There is something deeper and more fundamental still to be learnt from Campbell Morgan's confessed faith in the divinely inspired Scriptures, and in his submissive acknowledgement of their supreme authority. 'In order', he wrote,

> that men might know and profit by the Speech of God, whether in the divers portions and manners of the past, or in the Son, it was necessary that the expressions should be preserved in such form that they might be at the disposal of men for all time. This was accomplished in the sacred Scriptures. In the second letter of Peter we have a statement which reveals, so far as it is possible, the method by which these writings were produced: 'Men spake from God, being borne along by the Holy Spirit' (2 Pet. 1:21). In that statement we discover the natural and the supernatural elements. Men spake from God. That is the natural in the highest sense of the word. As they spake, in their own languages, in conformity with their own mental powers, influenced by their own surroundings, so also they wrote. But they were borne along by the Holy Spirit. The figure is that of a vessel with all sails stretched to the winds, and carried out beyond all the limitations which hold it, apart from that action of the wind, into the deeps. So these men, speaking and writing with all the simplicity of a perfect naturalness, were supernaturally guided into the most profound deeps; being thus inspired to say and write what should be said and written, and equally to omit the things which should be omitted. The result of this method, at once human and Divine, we have in our Bible.[7]

---

[5] Ibid., p. 96.
[6] Ibid., p. 99.
[7] Morgan, *Ministry of the Word*, pp. 53-54.

So it is the Scriptures which must be preached

It is, in consequence, the Bible to whose authority Dr Morgan submitted in all his preaching. 'Preaching', he said,

> is nothing else than bringing God's message, as it is found in the Oracles Divine. When the sermon has a text which is authoritative, all the rest is to be tested by it. That is the value of the text. I read a text to my congregation. That is the message. That is the one thing that is absolutely and finally authoritative. My sermon has no authority in it at all, except as an interpretation or an exposition or an illustration of the truth which is in the text. The text is everything. That is the point of authority.[8]

Here let us also remind ourselves that these words do but re-echo and reaffirm the teaching of the apostles and the conviction of the Reformers. When Paul, the aged, wrote to Timothy to give him counsel concerning the discharge of ministry, he solemnly charged him to preach the word (see 2 Tim. 3:14–4:2). It is worthy of notice that the Scriptures here explicitly referred to in the immediate context are the Old Testament Scriptures.

In order to add the confirming testimony of the Reformers on this point may I quote from a sermon on this very passage by John Calvin, a sermon entitled, *The Proper Use of Scripture*. John Calvin says,

> And that no man might take the liberty to choose what he pleaseth, and so obey God in part, St Paul saith, the whole Scripture hath this majesty of which he speaketh, and that it is all profitable. To be short, St Paul informeth us that we must not pick and call the Scripture to please our own fancy, but must receive the whole without exception. Thus we see what St Paul's meaning is in this place; for when he speaketh of the Holy Scripture, he doth not mean that which he was then writing, neither that of the other apostles and evangelists, but the Old Testament. Thus we perceive his mind was that the law and the prophets should always be preached in the Church of Christ.

Also, in the same sermon, John Calvin speaks more generally of the divinely inspired Scriptures as a whole. 'Thus we see', he says, 'St Paul's meaning is that we should suffer ourselves to be governed by the Holy Scripture, and seek for wisdom nowhere else.' 'Whosoever will not show himself a rebel against God, and set Him at nought, must submit

---

[8] Morgan, *Preaching*, pp. 61-62.

himself to the Holy Scripture.' 'Let us always remember that the Holy Scripture will never be of any service to us, unless we be persuaded that God is the author of it.' 'Therefore the Holy Scripture will be lifeless and without force until we know it is God that speaketh in it, and thereby revealeth His will to man.' 'St Paul requireth us to confine ourselves to the Holy Scripture because God speaketh there, and not man. Thus we see he excludeth all human authority ... When we go into the pulpit, we ought to be assured that it is God that sent us, and that we bring the message which He committed to us.'[9]

Such then is the unique, fundamental, indispensable function of the God-given word, and particularly of the divinely inspired Scriptures. This is the word to be preached. Dr Campbell Morgan fully devoted himself to this ministry and desired to preach none other. May God give us more of such preachers and teachers.

The Response of Faith

The second truth that gives far-reaching significance to the God-given word and its faithful ministry is that these are the two essentials which God uses to bring men to faith. Without them faith is impossible. For 'faith cometh by hearing, and hearing by the word of God' (Rom. 10:17). 'And how shall they believe in him whom they have not heard? And how shall they hear without a preacher?' (Rom. 10:14 RV).

Faith made possible

All words from God, which reveal His character and declare or promise His action, bring their hearers into immediate potential relation with God and particularly with the person and work of God in Christ. Also, it is these – that is, God Himself and what God does – and not the words heard nor the faith exercised by themselves, that make ours both assurance and benefit. For when God's words are seen or heard they always give their readers or hearers something, or rather Someone, to believe; and they often give them some fulfilment to expect. So they invite responsive acceptance and committal, confidence and hope.

This truth may be illustrated at the commonplace human level. The would-be traveller by train or bus only begins to believe and to act when words seen or heard tell him the time of a train's departure or the route

---

[9] John Calvin, *The Mystery of Godliness and Other Selected Sermons* (Grand Rapids, 1950), pp. 129-133.

and destination of a bus. Then he trusts those who operate these public services and issue timetables, to be true to their declared intention and to fulfil it for his benefit. His faith, therefore, is not something which he himself can produce or make possible by his own work. It is only called forth by the announcements or declaration of intention made by the transport services.

Similarly words from God call forth faith in Him. They bring faith to the birth, they make its exercise possible. It is the divinely commissioned preacher who is used to cause men to hear them and to understand them, as a present message from the living God in relation to their personal need. Once such words have been heard, there is Someone to believe and something to expect. Such faith, therefore, and still more its ground of confidence and its appropriated benefit, are all the gift of God. Also, once decisive words from God are thus heard, faith is no longer a mere pious hope or theoretical supposition. It becomes a sure confidence and a certain expectation. It becomes 'the substance of things hoped for' and the evidence of the living presence of the One unseen (see Heb. 11:1). Thus do simple believers count in quiet confidence on the great unseen Doer and on His faithful doing.

So, for instance, was the Gentile widow of Zarephath moved to responsive faith in the God of Israel, when Elijah gave her in her dire distress God's word of hope and said, 'For thus saith the Lord God of Israel, The barrel of meal shall not waste, neither shall the cruse of oil fail, until the day the Lord sendeth rain upon the earth'. So 'she went and did according to the saying of Elijah; and she, and he, and her house, did eat many days' (1 Kings 17:14-15). Similarly, the apostle Paul, on the storm-tossed ship in the Mediterranean, was assured by the God-given word that neither he nor his fellow-travellers were to perish in the sea. So in responsive heart faith and in open public confession he exhorted all those on board the ship 'to be of good cheer'. 'For', said he, 'there shall be no loss of any man's life among you. ... *For I believe God, that it shall be even as it was told me*' (Acts 27:21-25). Thus did the God-given word make new faith possible and bring new hope to the birth.

Faith made easy and sufficient

The full truth of the New Testament gospel goes further still. For 'the word of Christ' (see Rom. 10:17 RV) – words, that is, which speak of Christ as well as words spoken by Christ – not only makes faith possible; it also makes it easy and all-sufficient. For Christ has Himself already done all that is necessary to bridge the gap between men and God, and to triumph over the depths of sin and the grave. In order to get reconciled to God we do not have ourselves to climb to heaven to bring Christ down. For the gospel tells us plainly that the eternal Word has already become flesh, that the Man Christ Jesus is the one available and all-sufficient Mediator between God and men. It is enough to believe in Him.

Or again, on the other hand, in order to free ourselves from the power and the penalty of sin we do not have to storm the depths of Hades. For by dying Christ has already broken the power of the prince of death and delivered us. Christ is already risen from the dead. Death can have no more dominion over Him. He has the keys of Death and of Hades. He is the Lord of death as well as of life. So the word of this gospel brings eternal salvation immediately within our reach where we are and as we are, as frail mortals and vile sinners. It asks of us faith, and faith only – faith in the person and in the work of the God-Man crucified and exalted.

So salvation is within easy and immediate reach. It can be embraced by the appropriating activity of our hearts and our mouths. Such, so St Paul asserts, 'is *the word of faith, which we preach*; that if thou shalt confess with thy mouth the Lord Jesus, and shalt believe in thine heart that God hath raised him from the dead, thou shalt be saved. For with the heart man believeth unto righteousness, and with the mouth confession is made unto salvation' (Rom. 10:8-10). This means that because of the amazing word which God has spoken in Christ, salvation can be embraced and enjoyed by sinners solely through the obedience of faith. It is this simple sufficient response which the God-given word invites, inspires and informs.

So when the Philippian jailor asked Paul and Silas, 'Sirs, what must I do to be saved?' he was not told to do anything by his own personal achievement, but to trust wholly to the person and work of another. 'Believe', they said, 'believe on the Lord Jesus Christ, and thou shalt be saved, and thy house' (Acts 16:31). Such good tidings make faith easy and faith all-sufficient, or rather they proclaim that Christ is all-sufficient. They thus bring salvation within the reach and embrace of all who hear. They make no distinction between Jew and Gentile. 'For whosoever shall call upon the Name of the Lord, shall be saved.' Thus 'the apostle', wrote Dr Morgan (commenting on Rom. 10:13), 'again quoting from the Old Testament ... shows by the use of the great word "Whosoever" that salvation is at the disposal of all who believe'.[10] Indeed (in commenting further on Rom. 10:16-21), Dr Campbell Morgan went on to write, 'The truth which is brought out here with great clearness is that God elects those who believe to salvation, rather than that those believe whom God elects'. 'This', he wrote, 'does not ... clear away all the mystery that surrounds the subject. It does, however, place the emphasis at the right point, as it reveals the fact that responsibility rests upon those who hear.'[11] So important is the place which Dr Morgan understood Scripture to give to the faith of the hearer.

The believer justified

The word of Christ which thus brings salvation within the embrace of the believer, is a word of creative power because it is a word possessing divine authority and giving expression to the mind and will of God. It is this mind and will which determine what is and what is to be. By His word and at His pleasure God can and does quicken the dead and call the things which are not as though they are, and henceforth so they are.

This is the truth about God which underlies the doctrine of justification, namely that a man's standing before God is primarily determined and finally fixed by God's mind towards him, by God's will for him and by God's word about him. So if God Himself has declared by word and deed that sinners who trust in Christ, and in Christ crucified for sinners, share His acceptance before God and are counted righteous in God's sight, then they are righteous in God's sight. This decisive word of God none can either deny or defy. It is this word of God's justifying grace which the sinner believes when he embraces the gospel, that is, 'the word of faith which we preach'.

The believer given assurance and hope

The same word of God which we are given to preach, gives the simple believer assurance of much more than present acceptance in God's sight. By faith in this word, or rather in God who can be counted on to fulfil it, the believer gains entrance into either the outworked experience or the joyful anticipation of all that it promises. Thus the present blessings of the new covenant and the certain hope of a personal share in the coming heavenly glory become his in realized possession.

---

[10] G. Campbell Morgan, *The Epistle of Paul the Apostle to the Romans*, The Analysed Bible (London, 1909), pp. 163-164.

[11] Ibid., p. 165.

This enjoyment of benefit and embrace of hope by faith in Christ's word are significantly illustrated in the records of some of the miracles wrought by our Lord during His earthly ministry. Then the word that He spake made faith possible, easy and sufficient because to the responsive it was complemented by His creative deed. Thus hope was not only born; it also became strong and found fulfilment. Thus at the wedding in Cana of Galilee, to the servants Jesus said, 'Draw out now, and bear unto the governor of the feast'. And they bare it. So did the ruler of the feast taste not water but wine (John 2:1-11). Similarly, on what Luke calls 'the lake of Gennesaret', Jesus said to Simon, 'Launch out into the deep, and let down your nets for a draught'. And Simon answering said, '*At Thy word I will*'. 'And when they had this done, they inclosed a great multitude of fishes' (Luke 5:1-11). Again, later to ten lepers who cried for mercy, Jesus said, 'Go shew yourselves unto the priests'. 'And it came to pass, that, as they went, they were cleansed' (Luke 17:11-19). So the word of Christ spoken to men in their need and in their defilement makes faith possible, easy, sufficient, and abundantly worthwhile. 'And this is the word which by the gospel is preached unto you' (1 Pet. 1:25).

The Task of the Preacher

We come, in conclusion, to the place and task of the preacher. God Himself has ordained that the word He has spoken shall be brought near to men in present living utterance and in urgent exhortation by preachers.

The preacher's authority and appeal

Such preachers speak with a twofold authority. On the one hand, their message is God-given. The word they have to proclaim is not their own ideas, nor the opinions of men, but the word of God. On the other hand, they themselves are God-sent. They possess a divine commission. A stewardship in the gospel is entrusted to them. Woe is unto them if they preach not the gospel.

Such preachers also beseech men with a twofold appeal. On the one hand, they speak as themselves sinners, saved by God's grace in Christ. They invite other men to share in the response of faith which they themselves have made. Their own personal experience of God's saving grace, of its peace and joy, its liberty and hope, its constraint and power, is itself a living testimony confirming the truth of their words and giving warmth and earnestness to their appeal. So when they preach the gospel, the offer of righteousness from God that is therein revealed is by such preachers offered 'from faith to faith' (Rom. 1:17).

The preacher as God's fellow-worker

On the other hand, since they are divinely commissioned, true preachers of the gospel of Christ beseech men 'in Christ's stead' (see 2 Cor. 5:18-20). It is as though through them Christ Himself urged men to be reconciled to God, to embrace God's terms of peace. So true is this that those who reject such preachers reject Him who sent them. Nor is that all. Since the preaching of the gospel is a work divinely originated, God Himself works in and through the human preaching. The preachers become in vital deed God's fellow workers. While they plant or water, it is God who gives the increase. For it is this activity of proclaiming the truth of Christ crucified and exalted which God Himself is pleased actively to use to save those who believe.

No wonder Paul said that he owed the proclamation of this gospel to all men, that he was ready to preach it everywhere, that he was not ashamed to preach it anywhere. For he knew that God would make such preaching the instrument and the occasion of the manifestation of His power to save men. So when Paul says, 'I am not ashamed of the gospel of Christ: for it is the power of God unto salvation to every one that believeth', by the word 'gospel' he refers not only to the message preached, but also to the dynamic activity of preaching it (see Rom. 1:14-17). 'The word *gospel* denotes here', writes Godet on Romans 1:16,

> as in verses 1 and 9, not the matter but the *act* of preaching; Calvin himself says: *De vocali praedicatione hic loquitur*. And why is the apostle not ashamed of such a proclamation? Because it is the mighty arm of God rescuing the world from perdition, and bringing it salvation ... No one need blush at being the instrument of such a force.[12]

Or let me (from a translation) quote in full John Calvin himself. He says, 'But observe how much Paul ascribes to the ministry of the word, when he testifies, that God thereby puts forth His power to save; for he speaks here not of any secret revelation, but of vocal preaching.'[13] It is

---

[12] F.L. Godet, *Commentary on St Paul's Epistle to the Romans*, translated by A. Cusin (2 vols, Edinburgh, 1880-81), vol. 1, p. 151.

[13] John Calvin, *Commentaries on the Epistle of Paul the Apostle to the Romans*, translated by John Owen (Edinburgh, 1849), p. 62.

such an announcement of the good tidings, it is such evangelization of men by preaching, that becomes by the divine co-operation 'the power of God unto salvation to every one that believeth'.

The importance of preaching

It is, therefore, of primary importance that this preaching of the gospel of Christ should be maintained in every generation and carried in its discharge to the uttermost parts of the earth. It is those who belong to this order of divinely sent preachers of the gospel, whether at home or overseas, who belong to the true apostolic succession which God Himself never allows to die out in His world. It is the work that such preachers do that is particularly beautiful in God's eyes, and the more so when to reach some with their message they travel on foot over the mountains to places difficult of access or remote from large centres of population. Even as it is written, 'How beautiful upon the mountains are the feet of him that bringeth good tidings ... that publisheth salvation' (Isa. 52:7 and Rom. 10:15). This work is fundamentally so simple that it requires no elaborate accompanying paraphernalia of ecclesiasticism. This gospel, as Charles Spurgeon acknowledged with thanksgiving to God, can be carried to the ends of the earth by a man on his two feet.

Earthly life's supreme privilege

This gospel of Christ offers to 'whosoever believeth' the greatest privilege of eternity – to have one's name written in heaven as one of God's redeemed people. For those who have thus embraced the heavenly blessings of the gospel, there is no higher privilege to be enjoyed in one's earthly life as a Christian than to be a divinely commissioned herald of this same gospel and thus to be used to lead others to believe in it, or rather to believe in Christ and to confess Him as Lord.

It is, therefore, no surprise that the apostle Paul confessed with wondering awe, 'Unto me, who am less than the least of all the saints, is this grace given, that I should preach among the Gentiles the unsearchable riches of Christ' (Eph. 3:8). Nor is it any surprise either that George Campbell Morgan wrote, 'To serve the Word is to fulfil the highest function of which man is capable. Let those called to its holy privilege halt in awe, worship in wonder, and go forward with glad confidence.'[14]

---

[14] Morgan, *Ministry of the Word*, p. 58.

'The supreme work of the Christian minister', he wrote, 'is the work of preaching. This is a day in which one of our greatest perils is that of doing a thousand little things to the neglect of the one thing, which is preaching.'[15] 'Given the preacher', he said, 'with a message from the whole Bible, seeing its bearing on life at any point, I cannot personally understand that man not being swept sometimes right out of himself by the fire and the force and the fervour of his work.'[16]

Nothing surely would please Dr Morgan more than that God should use such a lecture as this to call young men to this same ministry, to be preachers of the God-given word of faith. This is a task before which none can rightly say on his own initiative, 'Yes, I will undertake it'. But before the divine call and commission to 'Go ... *preach*', it is life's highest privilege, whatever the cost or the sacrifice, joyously to cry out with George Campbell Morgan, 'Thy messenger, my Master – Thine!' 'If Thou wilt give me Thy words to speak, I will utter them, from this day forward, adding nothing to them, taking naught away. Their whole counsel I will declare, so help me God.'[17]

---

[15] Morgan, *Preaching*, p. 12.
[16] Ibid., p. 56.
[17] John Harries, *Campbell Morgan*, p. 46.

15

TAKING THE CHURCH SERIOUSLY (1948)

'There is in Protestantism an inherited inability to take the visible Church with due seriousness.' These words occur in a report called *Catholicity*, prepared by a group of Anglicans of the 'catholic' school of thought, and published last year.[1] The chief danger about such statements is lest protestants should believe them and be content to reply, 'We glory in Christ and the gospel. Let catholics glory in the church, if they will.'

It is time that some of us realized afresh that the 'catholics' are wrong, indeed doubly deceived. For, on the one hand, they think that they do take the church seriously. Yet their emphasis on institutionalism (that is, on one or more of the following – the papacy, apostolic succession, monarchical episcopacy and a special sacerdotal order of clergy) is not taking the true visible church seriously at all. It is attributing a seriousness to forms which are not of the original essence of the New Testament church. Whereas, on the other hand, those who really take the visible church seriously are not the 'catholics' but those protestants who recognize worthily the place of the laity or whole people of God in God's purpose, and the consequent significance and God-given authority of the local congregation.

Yet the 'catholic' taunt, mistaken as it is, is not without some present-day justification. They think they are obviously right when they accuse protestants of not taking the visible church seriously, because so many zealous and spiritually minded evangelicals seem to attach such little importance to church membership and regular attendance at the meetings of the local congregation. Unquestionably some protestants

First published in *The Christian Graduate* vol. 1 (September 1948).
[1] *Catholicity: A Study of the Conflict of Christian Traditions in the West; Being a Report Presented to His Grace the Archbishop of Canterbury* (London, 1947).

are nowadays open to charges of this kind. The 'catholics' may be right in their judgment, as far as some of us are concerned. What then is the reason?

To answer such a question effectively it is necessary to draw an important distinction. The plain truth is that many keen and orthodox evangelical laymen have been forced by bitter and disappointing experience not primarily to cease taking the visible church seriously (for they would much like to be active church members), but to cease taking the ordained ministry seriously. For in so many of our local churches the ordained minister has ceased to be worthy of the evangelical layman's full respect and loyalty. So in many cases the layman is no longer willing to support a local congregation that is so dominated by such a minister. The causes of this grievous state of affairs are mainly to be found in the way in which our ordained ministers have been trained. For as a result of this training most ministers have been influenced to a greater or less degree either by biblical criticism or by sacerdotalism or by both. Evangelical laymen are only too conscious of the far-reaching consequences of this.

On the one hand, ministers in both the Free Churches and the Church of England alike have ceased to be faithful preachers of the apostolic gospel, and diligent expositors and teachers of the inspired and authoritative word of God. Consequently many evangelical laymen find themselves not only not satisfied by the spiritual food which is offered them from the pulpit, but also deeply offended and distressed by the attitude that is sometimes adopted towards the Holy Scriptures. As a result they have little desire to go regularly themselves to endure such 'preaching', and still less are they willing to encourage new converts and young people to sit and hear such misrepresentation of the truth. So they are driven by dire necessity, and quite contrary to their natural preference, both to look for and possibly to help provide some more satisfying ministry of the word in meetings which are independent of the disappointing minister and the congregation which he serves. It is therefore the ordained minister and not the local congregation which such laymen are not willing to 'take seriously'.

On the other hand, the 'catholics' in the Church of England have specialized in training men both to accept their non-evangelical views of a special sacerdotal ministry and to adopt the corresponding forms of a sacerdotal sacramentalism. The Church of England is in consequence flooded with far too many clergy of this type, who tend to introduce everywhere they go both their views and their practices. Nor do they always treat the local congregation sufficiently seriously to seek its cooperative good will. Often their innovations are unwanted and opposed, and that not by unenlightened unbelievers, but by converted and spiritually minded laymen who have for many years been members of the very congregations into which they bring such changes.

It is such ministers whom many Christian laymen are quite unwilling to 'take seriously', in spite of the fact that they would much like to support their local church. The real hindrance is not therefore protestant failure to take the visible church seriously, but the imposition by the ordained ministers on an unwilling laity of non-evangelical and sacerdotal ceremonies. Nor is the situation helped by the fact that many ministers, who are by no means extreme critics of the Bible or definite 'catholics' (and who would indeed in many cases still call themselves 'evangelicals') have been so far influenced in these undesirable directions that, in ways of which they are scarcely themselves aware, they are no longer able to give the lead, take the stand and fulfil the ministry for which not a few keen evangelical laymen are looking. So the situation in the local churches is confused by the unsatisfactory condition of many of the ordained ministers.

The situation is often made still worse by the fact that many ministers, often all unknowingly, take themselves and their office too seriously. They consequently presume because of their position that they can settle the teaching and the practices which are to prevail in the congregation which they are called to serve. It is therefore such ministers, and not least those of the 'catholic' type, who actually refuse to take the visible church with due seriousness. For they afford no scope for things to be told to the church and for the church as a corporate fellowship to discover and to declare the will of God. Rather they tend to keep the settlement of such matters in their own hands and to keep the laity in tutelage, dependent on, if not subservient to, their ministry. Whereas if they really took the visible church seriously, they ought to seek to welcome all the lay members of the local congregation to the realized maturity of full stature and true equality in Christ; and they ought to seek to equip, encourage and exhort the local congregation by the worship, fellowship and witness of all its members to function fully and worthily as a corporate unit.

This surely is the only way in which the encompassing community of the on-looking world can be made properly aware of the presence in its midst of the visible church. In other words, society will take the visible church seriously only when the visible church of the local congregation speaks and acts publicly in true unity as a corporate body which has come to a common mind in the Lord and by the one Spirit. This in its turn is likely to happen only if evangelical laymen will make it their Christian business and the constant burden of their prayers to see that suitable young men, truly called of God, are so trained for ministry in our local congregations that they may serve to help and not to hinder the achievement of this end. We shall not see local church life revived unless we first see a transformed and a renewed ordained ministry. 'Pray ye, therefore, the Lord of the harvest that He will thrust forth labourers into His harvest' (Matt. 9:38).

16

New Testament Teaching
Concerning The Church (1950)

The Greek word ἐκκλησια, which is commonly translated into English as 'church', occurs in only two passages in the four Gospels. These passages are both in the Gospel according to St Matthew. In both the word 'church' occurs in sayings of our Lord Himself. On the first occasion, after Simon Peter had confessed Jesus as the Christ, our Lord said to him, '... thou art Peter, and upon this rock I will build my church: and the gates of hell shall not prevail against it' (Matt. 16:18). On the second occasion our Lord was giving instruction to the individual how to act if his brother should trespass against him. First, he should speak to him about it alone; then, if that failed to produce the proper response, he should raise the matter in the presence of two or three others; and, finally, 'if he shall neglect to hear them, tell it unto the church: but if he neglect to hear the church, let him be unto thee as an heathen man and a publican' (Matt. 18:17).

It is at once worthy of note that in these two instances of the use of the word 'church', on the first occasion the word refers to the one church of God's eternal purpose, the blessed company of all believing people; and on the second occasion the same word is used to refer to the local congregation or church meeting to which it is assumed that the individual disciple will belong.

In the rest of the New Testament, apart from the four Gospels, the same word 'church' occurs over one hundred times. Here the same two different spheres of reference may be clearly distinguished. On the one hand, the word in some places obviously describes the one church of God, the universal and eternal company of all believers, past, present

First published in *Inter-Varsity Magazine* (Summer Term 1950).

and future. On the other hand, the word in other places explicitly refers to a particular company of believers associated together in one particular place, such as Antioch or Corinth, or even in someone's house. In this second sense only the word sometimes occurs in the plural, so that we read of 'the churches' (see Eph. 1:22-23, 5:23-27, Acts 11:26, 1 Cor. 1:2, Rom. 16:5, Acts 15:41, 1 Cor. 11:16). Let us then examine these two uses more in detail.

Our Lord's words, 'I will build my church', are very revealing. They make plain that of the church He is the Beginning and the End, the Author and the Owner; He is its Builder and it is His. Put simply this means that men enter the church only by His doing and wholly for His glory. These same words of our Lord also make plain the fundamental fact that He had in view the establishment of such a community. This community began to be constituted as He called men to follow Him and to devote themselves to Himself as Lord in discipleship and obedience. Such men, like Simon Peter, definitely reached the point where they were ready for incorporation into the building, when in personal faith they confessed Jesus as the Christ, the Son of God. It was then that our Lord said to Simon, 'Now you are Peter'; that is, 'a stone'. The Lord also went on to imply that there were to be many other similar stones with which He intended to build a whole church. In his first epistle, Peter recalls this thought when he says to his Christian readers that by coming to Christ as the chief cornerstone they also as living stones are to be built up into a spiritual house in which God is to be worshipped (see 1 Pet. 2:4-6).

The community of the church, therefore, is built up by our Lord as He brings individuals by faith into living relation with Himself. So He described individuals as 'sheep' who were to find a new unity as 'one flock' around Himself as the 'one Shepherd' (John 10:16 RV). Or He spoke of Himself as the true Vine and His disciples as the branches; and He taught that they were to find their place and fulfil their function in the one organic whole by abiding in Himself (John 15:1-5). In other words, men do not establish contact with Christ by joining the church; they can rather belong to the true church only by being joined to the Christ and by being indwelt by His Spirit. This gift or baptism of the Spirit is the indispensable and sufficient hall-mark of true membership (Rom. 8:9, 1 Cor. 12:13). But this is not an immediately visible mark; and so in the last analysis only the Lord Himself knows who actually are His (2 Tim. 2:19).

Our Lord's additional words, 'And the gates of hell shall not prevail against it' are no less significant. The gates referred to here are the gates of Hades or death. For the church began actually to exist only when Christ broke the power of sin and death by His own resurrection; and the whole church will not be completely glorified and made perfect until, after the completion of the number of the elect, all share in the final resurrection of the body. The true church is therefore God's new creation. It does not exist in the natural visible order of this world but only in the unseen spiritual order, the order of the world to come. As 'the first-begotten from the dead' Christ is the first-born of the new creation and one destined of God to be 'the first-born among many brethren' (Col. 1:18, Rev. 1:5, Rom. 8:29). Only those enter the true church who are spiritually quickened and raised in Christ to a new life (1 Cor. 15:26, 54). This church exists, therefore, only in 'the heavenly places' (Eph. 2:5-6, 3:10). For true believers in Christ, crucified and risen, have thus come in Him to 'the heavenly Jerusalem', and belong to the 'church of the first-born which are written in heaven'; that is, in the realm or city to which they now belong (Heb. 12:22-23). It is with this unseen company that they now have fellowship; it is together with them that by faith they serve and worship God.

In the other statements made by our Lord concerning the church, His command, 'Tell it unto the church' is equally significant. For here the word 'church' (RV margin, 'congregation') clearly refers to a local meeting, that is, to a number of believers meeting together and acting corporately in one particular place. The essentials of such a 'church' are surprisingly simple. For immediately following his reference to 'the church' in this way, our Lord said, 'For where two or three are gathered together in my Name, there am I in the midst of them'. In contrast to this the Jews apparently required that in order properly to constitute a new local synagogue it was necessary to have at least ten or twelve men (that is, circumcised males) met together. Here without any distinction of male or female, our Lord says that 'two or three' are enough. What makes such a meeting a 'church' meeting is on the human side the acknowledgment by those who meet of Christ as Lord – they must gather together in his Name – and, on the divine side, the Presence of Christ Himself in their midst. In other words, the indispensable and sufficient essential is believing and vital, personal and corporate relation to Christ as the living and present Lord (see Matt. 18:15-20).

It is very important to recognize, as the use by our Lord and by the New Testament writers of the unqualified name 'the church' explicitly indicates, that what is thus locally constituted and made visible and functioning is genuine 'church'. One may find a suggestive illustration in our common method of reference to the moon. When one sees a thin crescent only in the sky, one says not 'there is part of the moon' but, 'there is the moon'. For the part that is visible is genuine moon; and, what is more, it is actually, though to us invisibly, united with all the rest of the moon. Similarly, a local Christian congregation is genuine church become visible. It is, as Paul says of the local group of Christians at Corinth, essentially 'body of Christ' and invisibly one in Him with the whole of his body (see 1 Cor. 12:27).

We ought also to note carefully that in the reference which He made to the meeting and functioning of the local congregation our Lord explicitly indicated some of the great spiritual benefits to be gained by thus meeting together. He mentioned three. The one of greatest importance is a special assurance and experience of His own manifested Presence. 'There am I', he said, 'in the midst of them'. This provides a supreme reason why Christians should regularly meet together in Christ's Name, in order to renew and deepen their experience of fellowship in and with the present living Lord.

The other two benefits of meeting together, which Christ mentioned, both arise in the same way. They are a direct consequence of the God-given agreement in the Spirit of the minds of the Lord's people met together. One of these benefits is Godward and the other manward. One is a God-given confidence that He intends to answer our united prayer, because by the common witness of the one Spirit in more than one heart we know that what we are asking is according to the will of God. The other similar and complementary benefit is manward in its operation. It has to do with the right settlement by the local church of personal differences and moral issues referred to it for decisive judgment by one or more of its members. For our Lord indicated that when the local church functions properly, and comes in the Spirit to agree as to what is the mind of the Lord, its decisions and judgments so made will have a divine sanction (see again, Matt. 18:15-20).

To sum up the two sides of our Lord's teaching about the church, we may say, on the one hand, that the one great church of God exists invisibly in the heavenly places. It is to Christians an object of faith, not of sight. On the other hand, the only thing that exists visibly in the world as an earthly counterpart to this heavenly fellowship is the local churches, the meeting together in many places of those who profess the faith of Christ. But such meetings are in their membership inevitably mixed. Not all who belong to them belong to the true church of God. Also, they are by their limitation in size, and by their measure of separation and even estrangement from one another, obviously incomplete and imperfect. Nor is there any scriptural promise that complete purity of membership or full unity of fellowship is realizable in this life or in these visible earthly forms. We have all yet to come together to a perfect man, a goal finally to be realized only in the consummation of the life beyond after the resurrection of the body.

It is, therefore, surely of some significance that the New Testament writers never use the word 'church' in the singular to suggest one great visible earthly organization. In contrast to any such idea, the Apostle Paul speaks deliberately and in some ways very surprisingly in the plural of 'the churches'. When, for instance, he speaks of his burden of concern for the spiritual well-being of the groups of Christians, for whose existence he was under God mainly responsible, he does not speak of oversight in the one great church of God in the world, but of 'the care of all the churches'. When he wishes to give guidance to the Corinthian Christians on matters concerning the ordering of worship in the congregation, he does not say, 'This is not the practice of the great world church', but 'We have no such custom, neither the churches of God' (see 2 Cor. 11:28, 1 Cor. 11:16).

There is, therefore, no scriptural ground for looking for the emergence of one ecumenical or worldwide church as a visible earthly organization, having like an earthly empire a geographical centre and a human head. The great invisible church's one mother-city is the heavenly Zion, not Rome, nor Canterbury, nor Geneva. The great invisible church's one Head is Christ Himself, not some human pope or primate or moderator. True Christian loyalists, or as we may call them, proper biblical churchmen, believe in and not a few have been prepared to die for the Crown Rights of the Redeemer.

17

THE PLACE OF SACRAMENTS (1948)

Sacraments are essentially an expression of relations between people. They are a form of personal communication, of giving and receiving. They involve the use of material things and physical actions as outward and visible signs of personal intention, donation and reception. They afford assurance, providing seals to guarantee and confirm words of promise. They facilitate conveyance, because the visible handling of and symbolic action with deliberately chosen elements or material things provides a formal means between people both of handing over and of taking possession. So, rightly used, they complement words of promise and profession, providing actions in which the parties concerned participate, which are a symbolic expression of the performance or fulfilment of the giving or responding which is verbally indicated by the words of promise and profession.

The full place and highest use of sacraments in connection with the gospel of Christ cannot be appreciated without some preliminary recollection of the nature and destiny of man, and of the primary and final place in human experience of man's relation to God Himself. Man has been made by God, in God's image and for God's company; his chief end is 'to glorify God and to enjoy Him for ever'. As indispensable to this high calling man is a rational and morally responsible creature – a being to whom God can speak in words, a being capable of understanding the meaning of such words, and a being who by his own free choice and obedience, and in co-operation with his fellows, can and ought to respond to God and find his constant delight in doing God's will.

First published in *The Churchman* vol. 62 (March 1948).

These truths about man's nature and destiny inevitably give outstanding importance to words. For words, as our own experience of life continually evidences, are essential to communication and cooperation between persons. The words of first importance are the words of God to men which tell man what he ought to do and how rightly to use his freedom to act. It is very significant therefore that when our Lord was tempted as Man to act wrongly He quoted, as His reason for not so acting, words which express the governing principle of right human living; namely, 'Man shall not live by bread alone, but by every word that proceedeth out of the mouth of God' (Matt. 4:4, from Deut. 8:3). Only if he can be sure of God's words, that they are true and trustworthy in the guidance they give, and only if he devotes himself to act accordingly, can man live rightly.

Further, God's words are not all precepts telling man what he must do. Many of them are promises or warnings telling man what God will do. Such words cease to be of full value and true worth unless man can be sure that God is faithful and will always keep His word and do what He says. Again, in making response to the offers and demands of others, and most of all of God Himself, man is so made that, being spoken to in intelligible words, he answers first by giving his own words of assent and promise and then by acting to fulfil all that such words imply. It is important therefore that in his use of words man also should be faithful and should not say what he does not intend to do.

It is in this fundamental relation to God's words that man has failed and become a sinner. The record of Genesis 3 makes it abundantly plain that things first went wrong in human life when man disobeyed God's word. Such action, to say no more, immediately cast man's faithfulness into complete uncertainty. He could no longer be counted on to keep God's word. Also, as one who had broken faith, he could no longer be counted on to keep his own word. He became a liar and a deceiver, a person who often said things that he did not do.

This fallen state of man as a sinner who has disobeyed God's words has thrown man's whole use of words into uncertainty. Since man is a person who does not keep his own word he finds it hard, if not impossible, to believe that other people will keep theirs. Likewise he looks at history and sees that it is strewn with broken promises. So man, the sinner, is with good reason a natural doubter and unbeliever. Yet men still go on making pacts and agreements because they are equally conscious that there can be no hope of peace and freedom from conflict in international affairs, nor can there be the necessary cooperation between individuals in social life and in all the wide variety of human affairs, unless men will pledge their word and then stand by it, so that others can trust both them and it, and not be taken unawares by underhand and deceitful dealing or by failure to fulfil promises given.

For their reassurance, therefore, men have from the earliest times sought to have added to the bare words of another man some solemn sign or confirmatory pledge, which might be a special and more trustworthy witness of good faith; and so that they might be the more sure that in this particular case the words thus pledged could be trusted and their fulfilment confidently expected. So there grew up the practices of oath-taking and of covenant-making, many references to which can be found, for instance, in the Bible in the book of Genesis.

When men thus took an oath or sealed a covenant they commonly did one or both of two things. Either they swore by God, as by One greater who could deal with them in judgment if they failed to keep their word; or they swore by their own lives (possibly saying 'upon my life', or dramatically drawing a knife across their throats, and such like), thereby indicating that they were prepared for their own lives to be taken if they failed to fulfil the undertaking thus solemnly pledged. These two methods of solemn pledging were combined in the ancient ritual of slaying animals and passing, as one gave one's promise, between the divided pieces (see Jer. 34:18-20). For violent death was thus visibly represented, and the person making the covenant probably called upon God to treat him similarly if he failed to keep his word. This possibly explains the underlying significance of the words, 'The Lord do so to me and more also' – that is, if I fail to perform the intention or undertaking thus solemnly declared (see Ruth 1:17, 1 Kings 19:2, 20:10, 2 Kings 6:31).

Such visible confirmations of verbal undertakings and such additional pledges of personal good faith are still required in acts of social contract. Men commonly require important statements to be made not only in words but upon oath, or in writing and duly signed and sealed. For instance, in the making of a marriage covenant the words of promise made by the two parties are visibly confirmed by the giving and receiving of a ring. This particular article (the ring) and what is done with it (the giving and receiving) are regarded as a token and pledge of the vow and covenant betwixt them made. Or when property changes hands, the parties concerned get a lawyer to prepare a proper deed of conveyance. Only when this has been properly stamped, sealed and signed is the transaction regarded as formally effected and legally confirmed. The deed then becomes tenable and, if need arise, presentable to others by the new landlord as formal proof of ownership.

Thus confirming signs and evidences of this kind obviously have an important social significance. They afford easily recognisable visible witness. They are valuable not just for their own sake but for what they indicate or imply. It is, for instance, by the ring on her finger that one knows that a woman is married. It is by drinking the loyal toast or by saluting the national flag that men openly profess their devotion to king and country.

Further, in their highest connection signs of this kind involve reference not only to one's fellow men but also to God; they have, that is, a religious significance. For instance, when men take an oath they commonly swear by Almighty God. This means that they appeal to the Supreme Being as One greater, calling upon Him to be the witness and the judge of their good faith (see Heb. 6:16). It is now for God to see that they keep their word and to deal with them if they fail. Their obligation is to Him; and so the assurance and the sanction that they give to others is in God's Name. Similarly in ancient times when Jacob and Laban made a covenant together they set up a heap of stones in witness, they ate together a meal of fellowship, and they swore by the God of their fathers, saying, 'The Lord watch between me and thee' and 'judge betwixt us' (see Gen. 31:44-55).

This method of solemn confirmation used by men to assure their fellows of the trustworthiness of their word God Himself also has condescended to use. Not that in His case such assurances were necessary. For His word is always to be trusted. But because men are slow to believe and in order to help their faith, God has confirmed His word by an oath, thus giving us for our confidence a double ground of assurance – two immutable things; first, His word, and second, His oath or covenant with its solemn pledges and visible seals (Heb. 6:17-18). So, after the flood, when God promised to Noah that there should not again be a similar flood to destroy the earth, God established a covenant and appointed the bow in the cloud as a visible token of the covenant between Him and mankind (see Gen. 9:8-17).

Such establishment of a covenant and the appointment of confirming seals was particularly used by God in connection with His special choice of Abram and His promise of blessings to him and his descendants. For instance, when Abram wanted assurance and asked concerning the land which God said was to be his, 'Whereby shall I know that I shall inherit it?', God gave Abram a visible and acted covenant pledge. He told Abram to slay animals and to divide the pieces as in covenant-making. Then, after dark, 'Behold a smoking furnace, and a flaming torch that passed between these pieces.' And we read that, 'In that day the Lord made a covenant with Abram saying, Unto thy seed have I given this land' (see Gen. 15:7-21).

Later God went further and made a covenant with Abram to give him a child, to multiply his seed and Himself to be their God, thus making them in a special way His people. As pledges of what God would do Abram's name was changed to Abraham and Sarai's to Sarah, as a witness that they were together to be the father and mother of a multitude of nations (Gen. 17:5, 15-16). As a further continuing pledge, in which all male children were to share, God appointed circumcision as a token of the covenant between Himself and Abraham's seed. So every male child born into Abraham's family was at eight days old to have his body solemnly marked with a sign of covenant relation to God. Only those thus marked were to count as belonging to God's people (see Gen. 17:1-14).

Some hundreds of years after in Egypt the promised descendants of Abraham, the Israelites, were solemnly constituted for the first time as the assembly of God's congregation when they met in their houses under the shelter of the blood sprinkled on the doorposts and feasted upon the flesh of the passover lamb. By participation in these acts they appropriated the promised redemption and were visibly marked off as God's people. Moreover, this passover feast was to be solemnly observed year by year as a perpetual ordinance – a thankful remembrance of the one great act of divine redemption by which they were saved from judgment in Egypt and brought out to be separated unto God as His people (Exod. 12). This relationship to Him as His peculiar people was further sealed at Sinai when Moses read the terms of the covenant, when the people assented to them, and when Moses sprinkled blood on the people and said, 'Behold the blood of the covenant which the Lord hath made with you concerning all these words' (Exod. 24:6-8).

These things resulted in the practice of circumcision and the celebration of the passover becoming among the Israelites the recognized witnesses of their individual and corporate covenant relation to the God of Israel. One was the mark of membership in the people of God, the other the evidence of continuing participation in the God-given privileges and blessings of being God's people. Also, as Paul makes plain in his exposition in the epistle to the Romans about Abraham (see Rom. 4:9-12), it was not the act of circumcision which made Abraham the actual possessor of the God-given blessing. In his case, for instance, he was justified by simple faith in God and His word before he was circumcised. He was given circumcision afterwards as a visible seal of the fulfilment to him of God's word, a fulfilment which he had already appropriated by faith alone. Similarly when Abraham's descendants were circumcised in infancy, the circumcision was simply a divinely-appointed seal guaranteeing God's promises as applying to them and available to be appropriated. But they could and did only enjoy the actual blessings thus certified as theirs to possess, if they followed in the steps of Abraham's faith and (when they became old enough so to act) themselves believed in God.

The possibility of radical difference between individuals alike circumcised in infancy in their subsequent personal response to the pledges of covenant grace is illustrated in the cases of Esau and Jacob. They were both circumcised in infancy. But Esau despised his birthright; and as a result he lost the corresponding blessing. Jacob regarded it as a prize to be coveted; and at Peniel he laid hold of the angel of the Lord to be blessed. 'And he blessed him there' (Gen. 32:24-30). So we see that while covenant signs and actions do pledge and seal the corresponding blessings as genuinely 'given', these blessings can only be actually 'received' and enjoyed by those who make the response of faith. 'For', as Paul says, 'circumcision indeed profiteth if thou be a doer of the law; but if thou be a transgressor of the law, thy circumcision is become uncircumcision ... For he is not a Jew, which is one outwardly; neither is that circumcision, which is outward in the flesh: but he is a Jew, which is one inwardly; and circumcision is that of the heart, in the spirit, not in the letter; whose praise is not of men but of God' (Rom. 2:25, 28-29).

Some such understanding as this of the seals and pledges of God's covenant with the Israelites seems essential to a proper appreciation of the corresponding seals and pledges of God's new covenant with men in Christ. For the two sacraments of the gospel, baptism and Holy Communion, are seals of the new covenant; and in the life of God's new Israel they do directly supersede and take the place of circumcision and the Passover feast under the old covenant.

Baptism, like circumcision, is a visible mark of distinction put upon the body of the individual. It is a formal seal solemnly given in God's Name and under the hand of a minister acting in God's Name. It is a pledge or effectual sign both of donation and initiation. It is an adequate assurance to the individual who receives it that in Christ, and through His death and resurrection, forgiveness of sins and quickening into new life by God's Spirit are together given to him on the simple conditions of repentance and faith; and assuming that these are present it outwardly incorporates him into Christ as a member of God's people or church, His true Israel.

Similarly Holy Communion, like the Jewish Passover, is a commemorative feast in which those who partake solemnly call to remembrance the one decisive act of dying for men on the cross by which Christ secured their redemption. It is, therefore, a continually renewed thanksgiving or'eucharist'. Further, its symbols and the accompanying words and deeds challenge all who use them to realise that by His death Christ secured for His people benefits which, like food and drink, they are meant to appropriate for their own continual strengthening and renewal. Also, by His death He ratified the new covenant, which promises to all who share in its benefits the full remission or divine forgetting of sins and the putting within each heart of God's own transforming Spirit of grace. Such are the benefits which all who eat this bread and drink this cup can rightly rejoice in and appropriate as theirs. These, too, are gifts to be received as from Christ's own hand, according to His own solemn testamentary disposition and as sealed to His people by His own shed blood.

For it is, finally, Christ Himself who appointed these two covenant seals of Baptism and Holy Communion thus to be used by His believing people. They are, therefore, clearly meant to provide help and to be realised means of grace to every individual Christian and to companies or congregations of Christians acting together. They are divinely ordained corporate acts by which believers in Christ first seal and then sustain their vital fellowship both with Christ and in Him with one another.

In conclusion, let us consider still further the application to the administration of baptism of the general principles already recognised, and particularly with reference to the familiar form of service appointed in the *Book of Common Prayer*. It is of fundamental importance to recognise that Christian baptism is not something the candidate does to or for himself. Nor is it primarily a method whereby a convert to Christianity confesses his faith in Christ. Baptism is something done to the candidate by another and something done in the Name of God. It visibly expresses not man's movement Godwards, but God's movement manwards in grace – to cleanse from sin and to quicken by the Spirit. It is a sure witness and an effectual sign of grace and of God's goodwill towards us (Article XXV of the Thirty-Nine Articles).

Baptism is the initiatory rite of the new covenant of the gospel. Put simply it may be said to do three things:

+ to confirm the promises of God

+ to confer a status

+ to convey an inheritance.

One may again compare a man's gift to a woman of a wedding ring. By this ring put on the bride's finger the bridegroom does three things:

+ he confirms and pledges his promises

+ he confers upon the woman a status – as married, and married to him, while she consequently becomes known as a member of his family and is called by his name

+ he conveys an inheritance; he formally makes her the fellow-sharer of his wealth, saying, 'With all my worldly goods I thee endow.'

With regard to Christian baptism these same three ideas are all explicitly expressed in the statements of the Articles and the Prayer Book of the Church of England:

+ It confirms God's promises; by it 'the promises of forgiveness of sin and of our adoption to be the sons of God by the Holy Ghost are visibly signed and sealed' (Article XXVII).

+ It confers a status. In it 'I was made a member of Christ and the child of God' (Catechism). By it I was marked off as different from those not christened (Article XXVII) and given a Christian name (Catechism). By it I was 'grafted into the Church' (Article XXVII) and 'received into the congregation of Christ's flock' (Baptism Service).

+ It conveys an inheritance. In it 'I was made ... an inheritor of the kingdom of heaven' (Catechism).

These blessings thus pledged in baptism are offered to those who make a twofold response. This involves, on the negative side, an act of repentance and renunciation of sin, and on the positive side an act of faith and committal to God in Christ. So in the Catechism there is the question, 'What is required of persons to be baptized?' and the answer, 'Repentance, whereby they forsake sin; and faith, whereby they stedfastly believe the promises of God made to them in that Sacrament.' Further, in the Baptism Service itself, it is only after a candidate has personally (or, in the case of an infant, by proxy) professed repentance, faith and obedience that he is baptized in the Name of God, Father, Son and Holy Ghost, and the minister makes the declaration, 'this person is regenerate'. For baptism witnesses to the gospel of God-given salvation for sinful men and to the simple essential conditions of benefit. Provided only that any individual is truly penitent and believing, the minister of the gospel has authority to declare in the Name of God that such an individual is saved. 'For God so loved the world, that He gave His only-begotten Son, that whosoever believeth in Him should not perish, but have everlasting life.' And what the word of grace declares the covenant seal formally conveys to the person to whose body it is applied, thus confirming him and other Christian believers who pray for him in the assured possession of the divine gift of grace – that is, salvation. It is, therefore, for those who are baptized thereby to be assured, and on this account to believe and to confess that the full double gift of forgiveness and of the Spirit is theirs on the simple condition of personal repentance and faith. Such awareness, too, should move them to lifelong thanksgiving to God and unceasing devotion to His will.

18

SACRAMENT, SACRIFICE AND EUCHARIST:
THE MEANING, FUNCTION AND USE OF THE LORD'S SUPPER (1961)

In the first place, this essay is unmistakably an essay written by an Anglican to his fellow Anglicans, to awaken them to the urgent issues which confront them in days of impending Prayer Book revision, and to remind them of positive scriptural truths which deserve fresh appreciation and demand steadfast preservation in the ordering and use of the sacrament of the Lord's Supper.

But, in the second place, it is equally true that these issues concern all Christians and concern the future of evangelical Christianity in our own island and far beyond it. On the one hand, dangers continue to beset our loyalty to evangelical truth and our enjoyment of Christian liberty, from the encroachment in fresh ways of sacramentalism and sacerdotalism. On the other hand, the sacrament of our common redemption by Christ's blood and of our unity as fellow-members of Christ's body, still waits to be better understood and more worthily used – particularly as an expression of a loyalty to Scripture, of a faith in the gospel and of a unity in the Spirit that transcends all denominational barriers. So there is reason why non-Anglicans also should be interested in what follows and eager to be better informed in this sphere.

So the author's prayer is that the Lord may use what he has written for the vindication of His truth and for the benefit of His people.

Introduction

In the matter of the meaning of the Lord's Supper, and of its consequent intended function and use in the Christian church, there are not only

First published by Tyndale Press in June 1961.

long-standing radical differences of theological conviction among us, but also much prevailing confusion of thought, not least in the use or misuse of terminology with regard to it. There is, therefore, obvious urgent need for clarification and for better understanding.

Those whose thought and practice in this matter do fundamentally differ often need to appreciate more clearly than they do where and why this is so. This is the more necessary today because changes in interest and in interpretation have made some of the older distinctions no longer fully appropriate and applicable. For instance, 'the eucharistic sacrifice' is a concept quite different from 'the Sacrifice of the Mass', and if the unscriptural purpose of the latter involves a radical abuse of the sacrament, perhaps the preferable ideas of the former may best be described as involving an unauthorized new use of the sacrament. In either case what is needed by many is a better understanding of the meaning and purpose which govern such varying uses.

There are, too, fresh practical reasons why better understanding is desirable. For the sacrament of the Lord's Supper is in many places being given fresh prominence and changed usage. The so-called Liturgical movement finds the obvious focus of its activity in its celebration. Rightly or wrongly many feel with new awareness that in the early church it was not only regularly observed, but was also itself the central act of worship. The significant modern ecumenical movement has made Christians of the different churches sensitively conscious that common participation in it is the chief visible way in which to express and realize our unity in Christ; and that inability to come together in this way is itself an exposure and a condemnation of our failure to obey the truth of God and of the gospel.

Also, the Lord's Supper is a subject with regard to which many are often more aware of developed church teaching than of the basic biblical and evangelical truths which ought to determine both its interpretation and its use. We do well, therefore, to remember that in the Church of England our forms of worship are as scriptural and as evangelical as they are, because the Reformers of the sixteenth century were not unwilling to reject current church doctrines and practices which involved departure from revealed truth, and to seek to return to a faith and a use more in harmony with the plain teaching of the word of God. For in our day and generation, and in our own land and Church of England, there is fresh need again to submit prevailing ideas and practices to the searching judgment of the word of God. Only so will our scriptural heritage be preserved, our evangelical purity maintained and true fellowship at the Lord's table with Christian brethren everywhere rightly and freely enjoyed.

It is to further such ends, as well as chiefly to aid some to better understanding, that this essay has been written. One prays that, when more come to see the truth, the Spirit of God who enlightens them will also stir them to contend valiantly for it. It will be a sad day for England if the candle lit by Latimer and Ridley is ever allowed to go out.

The Old Difference in Doctrine: The Sacrifice of the Mass or a Sacrament of the Gospel

According to the Council of Trent, the eucharist is a propitiatory sacrifice which the priest offers up on behalf of the living and the dead. According to authoritative statements of the Church of England, the sacrament of the Lord's Supper was ordained 'for the continual remembrance of the sacrifice of the death of Christ, and of the benefits which we receive thereby'.[1] Also,

> The Offering of Christ once made is that perfect redemption, propitiation, and satisfaction, for all the sins of the whole world, both original and actual; and there is none other satisfaction for sin, but that alone. Wherefore the sacrifices of Masses, in the which it was commonly said, that the priest did offer Christ for the quick and dead, to have remission of pain and guilt, were blasphemous fables, and dangerous deceits.[2]

Here is the old difference in faith and practice: either the deliberate use of the consecrated elements in the Lord's Supper to make an offering to God, propitiatory in character and intention; or the complete disowning of any such idea or Godward movement, and the exclusive concentration in the sacrament proper on a movement manwards, by which Christ's death for us is vividly brought to mind and its enduring benefits symbolically offered for actual present appropriation by the believing recipient.

There can be no mistaking or denying the deliberate intention of our Anglican Reformers to make this clear-cut distinction, and radically to alter in relation to it the essential character and purpose of the sacramental action. The very title of the service in the Prayer Book makes this plain. What is there provided for use is 'The order of the administration of the Lord's Supper, or Holy Communion'.

---

[1] The Prayer Book Catechism
[2] Article XXXI of the Thirty-Nine Articles.

Commenting on this Bishop E.A. Knox wrote, 'A Sacrament may be administered, but who could speak of administering a Sacrifice?' In the familiar Prayer of Consecration 'there is no hint that we are making any offering to God'.[3]

This difference in both doctrine and use was emphatically indicated by Archbishop Cranmer himself in the treatise which he called *A Defence of the True and Catholic Doctrine of the Sacrament of the Body and Blood of our Saviour Christ, with a confutation of sundry errors concerning the same*. He identified, as one of the chief roots of error to be pulled up, the doctrine 'of the sacrifice and oblation of Christ made by the priest for the salvation of the quick and the dead'.[4] Such doctrine, he wrote, 'is contrary to the doctrine of the Gospel, and injurious to the sacrifice of Christ'.[5]

This same difference is unmistakably still with us, and with us within the Church of England. Such a state of affairs has become widely prevalent only within the last one hundred years. Preaching in 1958 at the centenary service of the Eucharistic Congress, the then Archbishop of York, Dr A.M. Ramsey, said:

> The Tractarians recovered the doctrine ... that in the Eucharist the sacrifice is that of Christ himself. … Having nothing of our own to offer, trusting only in Christ's one offering of himself, it is *that* which we re-present to the Father, as ourselves members of Christ's body, accepted only in him.[6]

Unquestionably, too, there are many Church of England clergymen today who would go much further than the Archbishop in associating themselves with the Roman doctrine and practice which the Reformers disowned. They would argue that Article XXXI condemns only 'sacrifices of Masses', not 'the Sacrifice of the Mass'; and when they celebrate the eucharist the full intention of the Mass confessedly dominates their thought and determines their action – and the vestments which they choose to wear. This is obvious, for instance, in their use of Requiem Masses for the benefit of those who have departed this life.

Not only is the old doctrine of the Sacrifice of the Mass thus held and acted on by many: the practice is now justified by new forms

---

[3] E.A. Knox, *Sacrifice or Sacrament? Which is the Teaching of the Anglican Communion Office?* (London, 1914), pp. 36, 39.

[4] *Archbishop Cranmer on the True and Catholic Doctrine and Use of the Sacrament of the Lord's Supper* (London, 1928 edition), p. xxviii.

[5] Ibid., p. 239.

[6] A.M. Ramsey, 'He Took' in *The World for God: Addresses Delivered at the 1958 Eucharistic Congress* (London, 1958), p. 18.

of theological exposition. A fully developed example of this is to be found in *The Christian Sacrifice* by W. Norman Pittenger of the Episcopal Church in America. He argues that by the guidance of the Spirit the church came to understand the divinely intended use of the actions ordained by our Lord at the Last Supper, an intention not fully known at the time to the limited human mind of Jesus; which is, of course, why any reference to it is not to be found in the New Testament records of the institution. Developing this contention he suggests that the ritual oblation in the eucharist is necessary to declare before God the intention of Christ's immolation on the cross, and to offer it and its virtue to the Father. Let us quote some sentences in illustration:

> The Lord's Supper ... is the Christian Sacrifice, for it is the continuation and the implementation in the mystical Body of Christ which is the Church, of the 'one oblation of himself once offered' in his physical body on the Cross.[7]

> What the critic fails to see is that the Eucharist as sacrifice is not a substitute for the perfect sacrifice of Calvary, as if there were anything lacking in the utter completeness of that act of Christ's. It is not a substitute for, or a sacrifice in addition to, Calvary; it is, rather, an entrance into and a pleading of 'the merits' of that sacrifice, made possible because the Church is the mystical Body of the Lord and thereby can make that sacrifice its own. The Church is enabled to make its sacrificial action identical with the once-for-all event on Calvary because it is the same Christ who offered himself on Calvary, and who gives himself in his Body the Church.[8]

> The Eucharist is a sacrifice because it is that 'offering of Christ once made', herein pleaded and offered to the Father, set between 'our sins and their reward'.[9]

So Christ is said to do in His church body what He could not do or complete in His earthly physical body. He thus Himself offers to the Father the atoning sacrifice made by Him on the cross. This means that there are extension and completion in and through the church not only of His incarnation but also of His atoning work. This is not the gospel of the New Testament; nor is it the gospel to whose already available benefits for sinners the sacrament of the Lord's Supper was ordained to

---

[7] W. Norman Pittenger, *The Christian Sacrifice: A Study of the Eucharist in the Life of the Christian Church* (New York, 1951), p. 108.

[8] Ibid., p. 109.

[9] Ibid., p. 110.

bear witness, in order to stir responsive faith and thus to convey to the believing recipient present realized enjoyment.

These two approaches which regard the consecrated elements either as a sacrifice to be offered to God, or solely as a sacrament to be administered to men, are also illustrated in the difference between the Communion offices in the 1549 and the 1552 Prayer Books. For in the former the priest is instructed, immediately after the consecration and while still turning to the altar, to say: 'Wherefore, O Lord and heavenly Father, according to the instruction of Thy dearly beloved Son, our Saviour Jesus Christ, we Thy humble servants do celebrate and make here before Thy divine Majesty; with these Thy holy gifts, the memorial which Thy Son has willed us to make.' Whereas, in the latter, as in the 1662 Prayer Book which we still use, administration immediately follows consecration and the prayer of oblation is not said until afterwards, nor is it said with any reference to the consecrated elements spread upon the table; for they are either all consumed, or significantly already covered over.

What is more, this form of the difference in doctrine and practice is not just of historical interest. For although the 1662 pattern is the only authorized use in the Church of England, not only do many use the other pattern (as expressed, for instance, in the 1928 Prayer Book), but also the authorized use in churches outside England, here of one form and there of the other, does now seriously divide the Anglican Communion. This situation has been explicitly recognized and commented on in recent important reports. In a 'Memorandum of the Church of England Liturgical Commission', entitled *Prayer Book Revision in the Church of England*, the following statements are made:

> When we come to the Eucharist proper ... we meet in its acutest form the question of the Book of Common Prayer as a standard of doctrine. A survey of Lambeth utterances on the subject would seem to suggest that the Lambeth Fathers hitherto have regarded the 1662 Book as the norm of Anglican doctrine, and the Prayer Books of the other parts of the Anglican Communion as merely making explicit in various ways that which is implicit in the 1662 Book. In fact, however, this supposed agreement has covered a substantial cleavage. For, if the matter be examined at a deeper level, many Low Churchmen would be found to claim that the 1662 Communion Service, no less than that of 1552, excludes the element of Godward commemorative offering which was a feature of 1549, and which has been restored in most of the Anglican eucharistic rites outside England.

This other

> stream of teaching ... has continuous representation, not only in a succession of Anglican theologians, but also in the 1549 rite, in the short-lived Scottish liturgy of 1637, in the later Scottish liturgy of 1764, and in the rites that have followed the same general pattern in the United States of America and South Africa, in the 1927-1928 English Canon, and in the proposed revisions at the present time in the Church of India, Pakistan, Burma, and Ceylon, in Japan, and in Canada.[10]

Similarly in *Principles of Prayer Book Revision*, which is 'The Report of a Select Committee of the Church of India, Pakistan, Burma and Ceylon', 'the fact' is noted 'that the Anglican Communion possesses two types of eucharistic Liturgy, the one stemming from the rite of 1552, and the other from that of 1549'.[11]

In correspondence with this, and doubtless influenced by these Reports, the 1958 Lambeth Conference registered a radical change of attitude concerning 'The place of the Book of Common Prayer of 1662 in the Anglican Communion'. On this subject its relevant Committee Report declares:

> When in the past, there has been discussion on the place of the Book of Common Prayer in the life of the Anglican Communion, the underlying assumption, and often the declared principle, has been that the Prayer Book of 1662 should remain as the basic pattern, and, indeed, as a bond of unity in doctrine and worship for our Communion as a whole... Yet now it seems clear that no Prayer Book, not even that of 1662, can be kept unchanged for ever, as a safeguard of established doctrine.[12]

The same Report also quotes the following words of Dr Massey Shepherd, uttered in 1954 at the Anglican Congress at Minneapolis: 'Our Communion with its two types of liturgy, expressive of two approaches to the problem [of the eucharistic sacrifice], may be able to hold its various facets in tension. Sooner or later, however, it must be resolved.'[13]

---

[10] *Prayer Book Revision in the Church of England: A Memorandum of the Church of England Liturgical Commission* (London, 1957), p. 37.

[11] *Principles of Prayer Book Revision: The Report of a Select Committee of the Church of India, Pakistan, Burma and Ceylon* (London, 1957), p. 34.

[12] *The Lambeth Conference, 1958: The Encyclical Letter from the Bishops, Together with the Resolutions and Reports* (London, 1958), part 2, p. 78.

[13] Ibid., part 2, p. 83.

This, then, is the issue which afresh confronts the Church of England. Serious pressure from without is now openly added to pressure from within to change and adapt our authorized liturgy. The danger is lest the biblical and evangelical truth to which our present Prayer Book has borne uncompromising witness for so long should be superseded in the Anglican Communion as a whole, and so in the Church of England as part of it, by the universal acceptance of a pattern and practice of worship which on scriptural grounds the Reformers rightly abandoned. The inevitability of far-reaching decisions being made in the years immediately ahead concerning the Church of England Prayer Book and its revision makes adequate understanding of the issues at stake in connection with the Communion office the more urgent and indispensable.

The New Emphases in Interpretation: Not a Propitiatory Sacrifice, but a Eucharistic and Intercessory One

While the old difference in doctrine is, in principle, very much still with us, the new prominence given to such a term as 'eucharistic sacrifice' indicates a changed centre of interest and a new line of interpretation. The old assumptions, we are told, are now rejected by both Roman and Anglo-Catholic theologians. 'Any idea that in the Eucharist we offer a sacrifice to propitiate God' is repudiated as a medieval development.[14] A new theology of sacrifice is being taught. The belief has even been expressed that 'the time has come to claim that controversies about the Eucharistic Sacrifice can be laid aside'. Such a claim is said to be 'the result of new knowledge gained from biblical and liturgical studies'.[15]

Let us then seek briefly to appreciate some of the governing elements in this new type of interpretation. What is clearly basic is the meaning to be attached to the concept of sacrifice. In his able and informed treatment of this subject, in which he deals both sympathetically and critically with the central theological problem of interpretation, Gustaf Aulén has rightly said: 'The character and form of the eucharistic service depends on the position taken in regard to the element of sacrifice.'[16] On this point we are told that the category of sacrifice includes much more than the sin-offering; and that in any full appreciation of sacrifice at its highest level the part played by death is neither central nor indispensable.

---

[14] Ibid., part 2, p. 85, quoting A.G. Herbert.

[15] Ibid., part 2, p. 83.

[16] Gustaf Aulén, *Eucharist and Sacrifice*, translated by Eric H. Wahlstrom (Edinburgh, 1958), p. 6.

The error, for instance, of late medieval eucharistic theology is said to lie 'not in the view that the Eucharist was a sacrifice but in an inadequate and restricted view of sacrifice itself'; and particularly 'in its exclusive identification of sacrifice with death'.[17] Such an attitude means – let us notice at once – that primary and distinctive features of the sacrifice of the cross are thus to be treated as secondary to a larger and more compelling conception of sacrifice itself.

Admittedly the sin-offering is first necessary to remove disqualifications from worship in the would-be worshipper. But its offering is not the worship itself and therefore not the chief sacrifice. According to Hebrews 9:13-14 the function of the blood of Christ is to make the service of the living God possible for the defiled; and it is into this activity of serving or worshipping God by offering sacrifice that Christians are meant to enter in the properly appreciated eucharist. In this connection a comment made by Dr E.L. Mascall on the lack of reference to the eucharist throughout the epistle to the Hebrews is illuminating. 'Surely, we feel', he writes,

> if the Eucharist had anything like the importance for the first Christians that it has held in subsequent Catholicism, the writer, after describing what the Son of God has done in the past, how he became incarnate, suffered, died, rose again and entered into the heavenly places, would go on to tell us what this same Saviour does now in the Eucharistic rite. But in fact nothing of the kind is said. And why? Not, I would suggest, because for the writer the Eucharist was unimportant, but because it was not for him another event in the Saviour's life. It was for him – though he would not of course have used these words – a sacramental, not a biographical, fact. It was not another incident in the Messianic biography, something happening to Christ *after* the Ascension in the way in which, for example, the temptation in the wilderness or the crowning with thorns happened *before*. It was something in which the *whole* biography, the *whole* life of self-oblation to the Father, beginning in time with the Incarnation in the womb of Mary and culminating in the eternal order at the Ascension, was made present, not as a new event in history, but as a permanent reality communicated to the Church under the sacramental signs. Thus, if from one point of view we are bound to say that there is nothing about the Eucharist in the Epistle to the Hebrews, from another point of view we might almost say that the Epistle is about nothing else. For *everything* that

---

[17] E.L. Mascall, *Corpus Christi: Essays on the Church and the Eucharist* (London, 1953), p. 84.

the Epistle describes is given to us in the Eucharist; it would be a pitiful weakening of the theme to make the Eucharist *one item* in the series.[18]

Also, the other and richer meanings of true sacrifice are exemplified in the sacrifice of the cross. For it was an act of willing obedience, 'an offering and a sacrifice to God for an odour of a sweet smell' (Eph. 5:2 RV), and not only a bearing of the curse upon sin from which God Himself hid His face. So we can apparently learn here what true eucharist means. Christ, it has been said, 'fulfils in the Cross the thanksgiving of man to God.'[19] Consequently the service which is the appointed memorial of that sacrifice can be made a vehicle for Christians to express the same outgoing Godwards in the self-oblation of eucharistic sacrifice. Indeed, the eucharist is to be understood as an activity of Christian worshippers who are united with Christ or possessed by Him, in the expression of such offering, offering which finds its proper ritual counterpart and consummation in the presentation of the consecrated elements before God on the altar.

In addition, it is said of Christ's earthly sacrifice that 'though it cannot be repeated, it is not merely a past fact; it is not only an event in history but the revelation of eternal truth.'[20] So apparently, from the standpoint of eternity, Christ's sacrifice may be thought of as continually being offered. Thus it becomes possible and appropriate for His people to join in and with Him in offering it. Indeed, Christ is to be thought of as Himself offering it in and through them; and the eucharist affords the occasion and the divinely-ordained ritual for its corporate expression by the church.

An alternative approach to much the same conclusion is found by suggesting that the eucharist and our participation in it ought to be immediately associated with the sacrifice which our exalted High Priest continually presents in God's presence at the heavenly altar. For it is contended that in Hebrews 10:19-22 baptized believers, who through Christ's death have access to the sanctuary of God's presence, are invited to join in such sacrificial worship with the ascended Christ as participants in the offering of the one sacrifice which Christ makes at the heavenly altar; and again, the eucharist and the offering in it to God of the consecrated elements are the intended means for its present realization.

---

[18] Ibid., p. 109.

[19] Louis Bouyer, *Life and Liturgy* (London, 1956), p. 131, quoted in *The Lambeth Conference, 1958*, part 2, p. 84.

[20] *The Lambeth Conference, 1958*, part 2, p. 84.

A complementary idea, already implied, ought also to be explicitly indicated. It has been expressed by saying that while 'Christ's sacrificial work on the Cross was *for* us; he died as our Redeemer'; yet 'He who once died, and is now alive for ever more, is also *in* us; he dwells in our hearts by faith'.[21] This means, at least so some would deduce, that we are not now in the position of the apostles at the Last Supper when we partake in the eucharist. The Christ gave to them; now He lives in and acts through us. The eating and drinking in which they shared anticipated the atonement, but we live after its fulfilment and in its realized enjoyment. These differences, it is suggested, must affect the way in which we interpret our present participation in the eucharist, and what Christ and we express in and through it.

Another way in which to indicate this change of emphasis in interpretation is to assert that only the baptized can rightly participate in the eucharist. Thus all who do so have, so to speak, got beyond experiencing the benefit of Christ's death for sinners and realizing that they are justified by faith in the Saviour. For their baptism has already related them to the cross. They have been baptized into Christ's death. Now as sharers in Christ's resurrection they act, so to speak, like the risen Lord Himself on the heavenly side of the cross. Consequently the eucharist, while it still rightly reminds us of the cross as the great earthly expression of utter self-oblation, is itself to be more directly related in its present use by the church to the heavenly sanctuary and to participation in Christ's present offering of Himself to the Father.

This means, in other words, that in terms of the two sacraments our baptism unites us to Christ as the sin-offering, and the eucharist is the consequent acceptable offering to God which our baptism into Christ enables us to offer. Because we are already baptized and come to the Communion service as acceptable offerers in Christ, there is nothing incongruous in our offering before we receive. Rather, since our baptism has to do with our repentance from sin and our reconciliation to God, and particularly with the remission of our sins and our regeneration by God the Spirit, the eucharist is to be regarded as the divinely ordered complementary rite by the use of which we may complete and consummate our response Godwards, both by pleading Christ's sacrifice as the ground of our approach and our intercession, and by expressing the offering of our own sacrifice of thanksgiving and self-offering – and all by what is done with the bread and wine.

---

[21] Ibid., p. 84.

A Canadian Rector, the Rev. Paul Gibson, has recently put it this way:

> Baptism and the eucharist are together the ground of the church; they are the two points at which the fellowship of redemption is created. We might say that we are baptized in order to do the eucharist and we do the eucharist because we are baptized.[22]

> The eucharist is the worship of the new creation: the showing forth of the Lord's death by and in the Body of Christ. We are always stepping from baptism to the eucharist; we approach the eucharist on the strength of our baptism; in the eucharist we experience that which God has made us in baptism.[23]

> For St Paul the eucharist seems to be a showing of the Lord's death by and in that community which is already dead and buried with Christ in baptism and which already lives in the life of the risen Christ.[24]

So the sacrifice which we offer in this way in the eucharist is not to be thought of as propitiatory. Indeed, we can only share in offering it because propitiation has been made and because, now accepted in Christ, we are able to join with Him in the heavenly sanctuary in the worship of pure sacrifice which is 'not a propitiation but a homage'. This is a phrase of E.L. Mascall's. Let us quote from the context. He there writes of Christ: 'As the loving and obedient Son, who delivers himself back to the Father in joyful and filial self-oblation, he is the eternal priest who offers himself as the archetypal sacrifice.' He also adds in a footnote: 'There is, of course, no suggestion that this eternal sacrifice is a sacrifice for sin; it is not a propitiation but a homage. Nor does it involve destruction; it is self-giving not destruction.'[25] Let us also quote, as the 1958 Lambeth Committee Report has done, Dr A.G. Herbert on this matter:

> The Eucharistic Sacrifice, that storm centre of controversy, is finding in our day a truly evangelical expression from the 'catholic' side, when it is insisted that the sacrificial action is not any sort of re-immolation of Christ, nor a sacrifice additional to His one Sacrifice, but a participation in it. The true celebrant is Christ the High Priest and the Christian people are assembled as members of His Body to present before God His Sacrifice, and to be themselves offered up in Sacrifice through their union with Him. This, however, involves a

---

[22] Paul Gibson, 'Liturgical Revision and a Theology of Incorporation', *Theology* vol. 63 (June 1960), p. 228.

[23] Ibid., p. 229

[24] Ibid., p. 230.

[25] Mascall, *Corpus Christi*, p. 32.

repudiation of certain medieval developments, notably the habitual celebration of the Eucharist without the Communion of the people; or the notion that the offering of the Eucharist is the concern of the individual priest rather than of the assembled church; and, above all, any idea that in the Eucharist we offer a sacrifice to propitiate God. We offer it only because He has offered the one Sacrifice, once for all, in which we need to participate.[26]

There is, nevertheless, in the minds of many a significance in the offering before God of the consecrated elements which, if not propitiatory, is intercessory. True, the church does not now make the propitiatory sacrifice; for Christ made that once for all upon the cross. But many hold that in the eucharist we do present before God, we do plead or offer before Him, as the ground of our approach and our prayer, the one sacrifice of Christ, or rather the Christ Himself who has been sacrificed; just as, at other times, without the accompanying ritual of the sacrament, we make request to God in Christ's Name or through His merit and blood. So it is believed that in the eucharist we may rightly still speak of the offering of Christ or of offering His sacrifice. Consequently Archbishop Michael Ramsey (as previously quoted) has apparently himself endorsed the Tractarian doctrine which he was expounding when he said: 'in the Eucharist the sacrifice is that of Christ himself. ... Having nothing of our own to offer, trusting only in Christ's one offering of himself, it is *that* which we re-present to the Father, as ourselves members of Christ's body, accepted only in him.'[27]

Points which are raised by these various statements will be dealt with in more detail later. Here, in conclusion, let it simply be said that among these contentions there are unquestionably worthy scriptural ideas to which it is right that Christians should give expression in worship. Such worship ought to be sacrificial, eucharistic, intercessory. But the one fatal objection to the offering before God of the consecrated bread and wine in order to express this worship is that the Lord's Supper has not been ordained to be used in this way. So it ought not to be transformed into the vehicle for making our sacrifice to God. To do this is to follow the doctrines of men rather than the word of God. To do this is to misuse the sacrament and to divert it from its intended exclusive reference to the one, unique, atoning sacrifice, once offered by Christ alone to secure remission of sins for us. To do this is improperly to introduce into its use a purpose additional to, and very different from, its one declared

---

[26] *Ways of Worship: The Report of a Theological Commission of Faith and Order* (London, 1951), quoted in *The Lambeth Conference, 1958*, part 2, p. 85.

[27] Ramsey, 'He Took', p. 18.

purpose of reminding believers in Christ of His redeeming death for them, and conveying to those who worthily receive present assurance and enjoyment of its endless benefits.

It also seems relevant to note the following contrast. While, on the one hand, in the Lord's Supper a ritual with visible symbols has been ordained to help us to remember with thanksgiving a past event which cannot be repeated, and to realize and appropriate its still operative benefits; yet, on the other hand, present offering Godwards by Christians is, according to the explicit instruction and urgent exhortation of the New Testament, to be substantial not symbolical. We are not told to offer tokens of our thanksgiving and self-oblation. We are rather enjoined actually to present ourselves, our souls and bodies a living sacrifice, and to make substantial gifts in ministry to the needs of others. And it is spiritually dangerous to prefer ritual to reality, to do the office rather than render true obedience.

The Basic Issue: Biblical and Evangelical

If we are to assess ritual practices and the underlying doctrines which they are said to express, we need to recognize and apply proper standards of judgment. We here appeal to two which Christians surely must acknowledge as supreme and decisive. These are the Bible and the gospel.

There are the highest precedents for this attitude. Our Lord Himself during the days of His public ministry contended with Jewish religious leaders and teachers, and condemned some of their practices because, as He said, they gave their own tradition or the doctrines of men priority over the word of God; and by so doing made the word of God of none effect. Instead of obeying God they contradicted His revealed will by preferring their own ideas and by using corresponding man-devised practices. So our Lord quoted, and endorsed in reference to them, the words of Isaiah which speak of divine worship being made vain or worthless by the teaching of men (see Matt. 15:1-9, Mark 7:5-13; compare Isa. 29:13).

Such perverse religious development is clearly an ever-recurring peril within the professing church of God. The words of Isaiah, which Christ quoted, indicate that it was a peril in Old Testament times. Christ's own words show that it was a peril in the days of His earthly ministry. In the sixteenth century the Reformers had to make the same kind of protest, to disown ecclesiastical teaching and tradition and to root out corrupt practices in order to be loyal to the God-given word. In the twentieth century we are still exposed to this age-long danger, a danger which besets us not from outside but from inside the church, the danger lest obedience to God's revealed truth may be superseded by conformity with undesirable prevailing ecclesiastical teaching and practice. If we are to discern rightly between truth and error, the same criterion must be applied – the witness of God's written word.

The second criterion is the gospel itself, the revealed truth of God's saving grace in Christ. For our appeal to this as a decisive standard of judgment we have explicit apostolic precedent. In his epistle to the Galatians we find that the apostle Paul has recorded how he resisted the imposition of ritual practices and ceremonial requirements in the declared interest of 'the truth of the gospel'. He withstood the demand in Jerusalem to have a Gentile convert circumcised as something necessary to salvation, in order, as he says, 'that the truth of the gospel might continue with you', that is, with the Gentile Christians of Asia Minor to whom he was writing (see Gal. 2:1-5). He was aware that an improper surrender to such pressure in the home church would directly affect the liberty in Christ of the younger churches overseas. The same is still true. Also when at Antioch Peter withdrew from table fellowship with Gentile believers, Paul 'withstood him to the face' for the same reason; because, as Paul says, he saw that Peter and those who followed him 'walked not uprightly according to the truth of the gospel' (see Gal. 2:11-16). For it is, as Paul saw it, a grave menace to the spiritual well-being of the whole church, if leaders use their position of influence to set an unworthy example, and if not only ordinary or uninstructed church members, but experienced ministers like Barnabas, are carried away by such pressure to follow the official ecclesiastical lead rather than the revealed truth of God.

This same governing principle still applies to every situation in which we may find ourselves. Teaching and practice which we are asked to accept must be judged as right or wrong to follow, not simply in the light of the extent of its adoption by the churches and their theological teachers, but rather by asking whether it is according to the truth of the gospel. Let us then seek to evaluate current ideas about the true meaning and the proper function and use of the sacrament of the Lord's Supper by direct reference to these two decisive standards of judgment – the Bible and the gospel.

Let us begin by quoting a welcome statement of governing principle made in their Memorandum by the Church of England Liturgical Commission in connection with possible future Prayer Book revision.

They say, 'Where Scripture gives positive guidance in regard to any rite that guidance must be followed. Thus the use of water in Baptism, and the use of bread and wine (the fermented juice of the grape) in Holy Communion are essential.'[28] Here let us also add a complementary principle, which is of direct relevance to our whole subsequent discussion. It has been well stated in his discussion of this very subject by Gustaf Aulén. He writes: 'The tradition of the ancient Church cannot be regarded as a norm, and still less as an authority on a par with the Bible.'[29] When we ask whether ideas about the eucharist, which we have seen to be current, are clearly supported by positive biblical evidence, the answer at several important points seems to be 'No'; and certainly 'No' rather than 'Yes'. Let us mention these.

First, is the sacrifice of Christ 'not only an event in history, but the revelation of eternal truth'? Can it, in some sense, be thought of as being offered continually? Was the cross an expression in time of an activity which happens fully only in eternity? For instance, Professor D.M. Baillie wrote, 'It seems impossible to say that the divine sin-bearing was confined to that moment of time, or is anything less than eternal.'[30] 'God's reconciling work cannot be confined to any one moment in history. ... It is not that the historical episode is a mere symbol of something "timeless": it is actually a part (the incarnate part) of the eternal divine sin-bearing.'[31]

The question is, Is this what Scripture teaches? To this question the right answer would seem to be 'No'. Rather in the Bible eternity is represented as somehow looking forward or looking back to a single event in time – the slaying of the Lamb. And according to what Paul says in Colossians 1:20, even 'things in heaven' are reconciled to God through what is bluntly described as 'the blood of his cross'; that is, through the value of a work done and finished here on earth. So at this point, and at others like it, the basic issue is a choice between submission to scriptural statement or the introduction of unsupported philosophical supposition. Here some prefer what appears philosophically attractive; we prefer what is explicitly biblical.

Second, let us ask, Is there a continuous offering by Christ in heaven? On this point we may quote Gustaf Aulén. He asks, 'Is it biblically legitimate to maintain a continuous offering of Christ in

---

[28] *Prayer Book Revision in the Church of England*, p. 30.

[29] Aulén, *Eucharist and Sacrifice*, p. 177.

[30] D.M. Baillie, *God was in Christ: An Essay on Incarnation and Atonement* (second edition, London, 1955), p. 190.

[31] Ibid., p. 191.

heaven?'[32] Here are parts of his answer: 'The resurrection is God's Yes to the sacrifice fulfilled in death. The ascension is the coronation of Christ (Eph. 1:20-21). In view of these facts it seems difficult to find any meaning in the statement that the resurrection and ascension belong to the sacrifice.'[33] Or, if Christ's heavenly intercession is a sacrifice, then '"sacrifice" is used in a different sense from the atoning sacrifice of Christ.'[34] 'What the New Testament primarily wants to say is that the sacrifice of Christ was finished in His death.'[35] 'The Son does not continue as the suffering Servant of the Lord to give Himself as He did during His earthly life.'[36] It is also appropriate here to quote Dr A. J. Tait's exposition of Hebrews 8:3. He wrote:

> The only passage in the Epistle which could possibly lend itself to the idea of continual offering is Hebrews 8:3, *it is necessary that this high priest have somewhat to offer*. But the English translation does not and cannot exactly express the original. For in the Greek there is no equivalent of *it is*, and it would be equally possible and legitimate to use the rendering, *it was necessary*. Again, the word for *to offer* is προσενέγκη which can only mean *do an act of offering*. When the writer wishes to speak of continual offering, he uses the tense which expresses it, προσφέρῃ (9:25). Finally the context of the statement is one in which the writer emphatically denies continual offering (7:27, 9:25ff, 10:11ff), on the ground that the completed act accomplishes all that such an offering was intended to accomplish (9:12, 10:10, 12, 14, 18).[37]

Or, if we wish to recognize that, as the glorified Man, Christ must be thought of as continually devoting Himself to the Father, just as those redeemed and regenerate in Him are exhorted to present their bodies a living sacrifice to God; then we must also recognize that such a living sacrifice – the Godward devotion of the whole life in unceasing obedience – is something very different from the propitiatory sacrifice which involved death or blood-shedding, and the forfeiting or laying down of the life as a ransom price. The latter Christ is certainly not doing continually. He did it once for all on the cross. The two activities are distinguished in Romans 6:10, where Paul says, 'For in that he died, he died unto sin once for all: but in that he liveth, he liveth unto

---

[32] Aulén, *Eucharist and Sacrifice*, p. 149.

[33] Ibid., p. 150.

[34] Ibid., p. 153.

[35] Ibid., p. 190.

[36] Ibid., p. 191.

[37] A.J. Tait, *The Nature and Functions of the Sacraments* (London, 1917), p. 92.

God'. And it is the once-for-all death to sin which the Lord's Supper commemorates. So it ought not to be associated in thought with any present continuous heavenly self-offering.

In the third place, we would ask, Can the church offer Christ to God? Again, the proper scriptural answer is 'No'. Commenting on A.G. Herbert's contention that we may rightly speak of 'presenting before God', 'pleading' or 'offering' before Him the one sacrifice of Christ, Gustaf Aulén writes:

> All this is in reality nothing else than a vivid and concrete interpretation of the meaning of prayer 'in the Name of Jesus'. ... But having said all this, there is really no positive reason for the assertion that we offer the sacrifice of Christ, and much less for the statement that we offer Christ. ... In reality no man has ever 'offered' the sacrifice of Christ. Christ's sacrifice is and remains His own act.[38]

> We look in vain for any New Testament statement to the effect that we offer Christ.[39]

> The sacrifice of Christ is and remains His own sacrifice, eternally valid, present in the eucharist, but entirely His own, not the Church's sacrifice.[40]

Also, it is surely impossible for sinful men to join in making Christ's one indispensable atoning sacrifice. Our imperfection would mar His perfection. 'Thus', writes Professor C.F.D. Moule,

> it seems to me impossible fully to identify an act of obedience in a Christian (including his participation in the sacrament of obedience) with the absolute and perfect act of obedience by God incarnate in Christ. Each Christian act of obedience is indeed Christ's obedience in us; but not therefore identifiable with His own one-hundred-per-cent obedience in His own person.[41]

We ought not, therefore, in the service which is a memorial of Christ's one sacrifice to think that we can share in offering the sacrifice which He alone could and did offer.

Fourthly, we must ask, Was the ordinance of the Lord's Supper meant to be so used? Is there any scriptural indication that the consecrated elements were or ought to be offered Godwards? Again, the unavoidable

---

[38] Aulén, *Eucharist and Sacrifice*, p. 37.
[39] Ibid., p. 166.
[40] Ibid., p. 182.
[41] C.F.D. Moule, *The Sacrifice of Christ* (London, 1956), p. 40.

biblical answer is 'No'. Indeed, according to the New Testament records of its institution our Lord did not say the significant sacramental words, which give the bread and wine their distinctive character, until He had already handed them to His disciples and commanded them to eat and drink. So neither did He, nor did they, offer the sacramental bread and wine Godwards. It is, therefore, plainly unscriptural and wholly improper that we should do so. 'It would be completely foreign to the biblical conception', writes Gustaf Aulén, 'if we should regard the Lord's Supper as our offering of Christ.'[42] It is, in fact, the exact opposite. It is His offering of Himself and of the benefits of His passion to us. Consequently, the only proper way to participate is to receive, to eat and to drink, not to present the consecrated elements before God.

Similarly, we must ask about some current eucharistic ideas and uses whether such teaching and practice are true to the gospel; and again there are points at which the unavoidable answer is 'No'. For instance, it is unmistakably a double denial of the gospel of salvation for sinners by grace, through faith apart from works, to teach that we have ourselves to offer Christ's sacrifice in order to accomplish propitiation for sin and to secure remission. For this suggests not only that we have to do something, but also that we can do something to procure salvation. Both of these ideas are radically wrong and misleading. For as sinners needing salvation we can ourselves do nothing to procure it; nor does the gospel demand that we should. Yet this teaching, that in the eucharist we 'offer Christ' or 'offer His sacrifice', implies that what Christ has done is incomplete and does not by itself make present salvation available to be embraced as a free gift by faith alone. 'The greatest blasphemy and injury that can be against Christ', wrote Archbishop Cranmer, 'is this, that the priests make their mass a sacrifice propitiatory, to remit the sins as well of themselves as of other, both quick and dead.'[43] 'Wherefore it is an abominable blasphemy to give that office and dignity to a priest which pertaineth only to Christ; or to affirm that the Church hath need of any such sacrifice.'[44]

We must, of course, recognize that many including the bishops at Lambeth in 1958 have disowned any propitiatory intention in the eucharist. Their aim in offering Christ's sacrifice is rather intercessory – to plead Christ's merit. Yet in critical comment on the use in this connection of such phraseology as to 'offer Christ' or to 'offer Christ's sacrifice', Gustaf Aulén has written:

---

[42] Aulén, *Eucharist and Sacrifice*, p. 166.

[43] *Archbishop Cranmer on the True and Catholic Doctrine and Use of the Sacrament of the Lord's Supper*, p. 232.

[44] Ibid., p. 240.

The formula does not occur in either the New Testament or in the documents of the primitive church. ... In reality it is contrary to the fundamental conception of the sacrifice of Christ which we find in the New Testament. The sacrifice of Christ is entirely and solely His sacrifice – and God's. This is the one essential point: God was in Christ reconciling the world to Himself. Through this sacrifice, perfected once for all, He abolished all man-made sacrifices. A formula such as this that we 'offer Christ' turns the biblical kerygma upside down. It is not strange therefore that all kinds of erroneous associations have become attached to it.[45]

Our contention is therefore that certain ideas and practices concerning the eucharist ought to be rejected, because they are neither biblical nor evangelical. To make the reasons for this clearer we propose in what follows to seek more positively to expound what the Bible evidence indicates about the eucharist, and how this ordinance of the Lord's Supper may be properly appreciated and used as a sacrament of the gospel.

The One Sacrifice for Sins

At the very heart or foundation of the Christian gospel is the fact of an atoning sacrifice offered by the incarnate Son of God as a propitiation for the sins of men. It is this unique finished event, together with all its far-reaching consequences, which the sacrament of the Lord's Supper has been ordained to commemorate. The New Testament itself explicitly encourages us to regard the Holy Communion service as the Christian Passover. It is a memorial of one sacrifice once offered, which makes ours for enjoyment a continual feast (see 1 Cor. 5:7-8). The Passover association thus forcibly suggests that one decisive event in the past, to which we owe our very existence and freedom as God's people, provides ground for unceasing thanksgiving and enjoyment of benefit. The true eucharist is expressed by saying grace and partaking.

This efficacious atoning sacrifice, which we thus commemorate and whose benefits we still embrace, was made by the death, not the life, of our Lord Jesus Christ. Our Lord Himself declared that it was the purpose of His coming into the world to secure release for all the people of God by the laying down of His one life (Mark 10:45). This means that by giving up His life in death He would provide a ransom, a substitutionary exchange, and thus secure a consequent release for the lives of men which were otherwise forfeited because of sin.

---

[45] Aulén, *Eucharist and Sacrifice*, pp. 198-199.

This all-important redeeming death took place not in eternity nor in heaven, but in time and on earth. For it was God's pleasure that men who had fallen into sin here on earth should be redeemed in the same sphere, by action taken in time and space, in flesh and blood, and particularly through suffering and death. So the writer of the epistle to the Hebrews asserts that any repetition of His offering would involve repeated incarnation and fresh suffering. 'Nor yet that he should offer himself often ... for then must he often have suffered' (Heb. 9:25-26). Commenting on this Canon W.M.F. Scott wrote: 'To him the offering was the suffering. This rules out the idea of continuous offering.'[46]

Such a giving up of Himself to death to make atonement for sin and to provide a ransom for sinners was possible for the eternal Son of God only because, first, He became man. So 'once at the consummation of the ages hath he been manifested to put away sin by the sacrifice of himself' (see Heb. 9:26). Second, it was possible for Him to undertake this only because, as Man, He Himself lived a sinless life. For only a life not itself forfeited because of sin could be freely offered as a ransom or substitutionary price to secure the release of those whose lives were forfeited. Also, and still more fundamentally, our Lord's ultimate achievement on the cross of the necessary propitiation depended upon His deliberate self-consecration to the task. So by His own free choice He came from heaven to do God's will; and became Man, a partaker of flesh and blood, in order that as Man He might die for sinners (see Heb. 2:14-17, 10:5-7). Similarly when, as Himself sinless, He could as Man have been glorified without seeing death, as the vision granted to the chosen three disciples at His transfiguration made clear, yet again by His own free choice He came down from the mountain of glory back into the world of sinful men and steadfastly set His face to go to Jerusalem – to die (Luke 9:28-31, 51).

It is this ultimate giving of Himself to die which alone could secure men's redemption. While His coming down from above, and His going to Jerusalem, involved self-offering, as also did His whole earthly life of daily obedience to God, yet the freely chosen laying down of His life was an action special and unique, necessary only to save others from sin. It is this unique act of self-sacrifice in which He gave Himself to die, to bear the penalty of our sins in His body, that the Lord's Supper commemorates. The whole interest and emphasis are concentrated there – on the breaking of His body and on the shedding of His blood.

---

[46] W.M.F. Scott, 'The Eucharist and the Heavenly Ministry of our Lord', *Theology* vol. 56 (February 1953), p. 44.

This staggering climax to His earthly life did not and could not occur until His hour, or God's time for it, was come. Then He was handed over, or betrayed, into the hands of wicked men. This happened not merely by the treacherous human action of Judas, but also and chiefly according to the foreordained purpose and pleasure of God the Father and by the deliberate and submissive consent and self-consecration of Jesus Himself. The night on which He was betrayed was supremely the night on which He handed Himself over, a willing victim. It was the night when God the Father, who up to that hour had shielded Jesus from violence, Himself as it were took His hands off and left Him exposed to the powers of evil that He might bear it and break it in His own Person.

So Jesus entered the agony and the darkness of Himself becoming the sin-offering. He publicly bore sin's penalty right up to its final extremes, of shameful execution and of exposure to the curse of heaven, as though He Himself were the worst of wrongdoers. What the scriptural witness emphasizes is that the necessary 'transaction' was all limited to and settled in one critical 'hour' or day. It is intolerable to think of this necessary payment of ransom as going on continually or eternally. In healthy protest against any idea that the atoning sacrifice must be continuously offered to God, Dr A.J. Tait wrote:

> For it is one thing to believe that the moral government of God required an historic manifestation of the condemnation of sin through the earthly life and death of the Lord Jesus; but it is quite another thing to believe that God requires for man's forgiveness a continual process of propitiation through the ceaseless re-presenting to Him by our Lord of His sacrifice.[47]

It is, therefore, of the very essence of the gospel of God's saving grace that the sacrifice necessary to make atonement for sin is completely finished; that there is no more offering of any kind to be done to secure remission of sins; and that the benefits of full salvation can now be freely enjoyed by penitent and believing recipients, as the sacrament of the Lord's Supper when it is properly administered visibly confirms.

The truth of this has been finally evidenced by decisive acts of God which followed the finished sacrifice. Immediately, as Christ breathed His last on the cross, 'the veil of the temple was rent in twain from the top to the bottom' (Mark 15:37-38). Access to God's presence was thus declared open to sinners hitherto shut out by the barrier of sin. Also, on the third day, our Lord's tomb was found empty (Mark 16:1-8). God

---

[47] Tait, *Nature and Functions of the Sacraments*, p. 89.

raised Jesus from the dead and gave Him glory. Clearly no more offering or petitioning had to be done by Christ to secure God's acceptance either of Himself or of His sacrifice. Rather God acted to give Him the throne of the universe, from whence He can save to the uttermost all who make Him their confidence and call upon His Name.

Canon W.M.F. Scott wrote in comment on Hebrews 10:11-12: 'Our Lord's session evidently means that, unlike the Levitical priests still standing at the altar, his sacrifice for sins had been offered and was complete.'[48] Also Hebrews 9:12 records of Christ that He 'through his own blood entered in once for all into the holy place, having obtained eternal redemption'. On this Canon Scott wrote: 'Notice that the writer holds that our Lord had obtained redemption for us before he entered into the heavenly sanctuary. In other words, his sacrifice was offered and accepted on the Cross.'[49]

So, when we respond to the invitation of Christ and the gospel, particularly as it is visibly extended to us in the administration of the Lord's Supper, we do not find ourselves called to stand before an altar to continue offering Christ's sacrifice. Rather are we summoned to sit at His table and to share in the feast which His finished sacrifice has permanently provided. This is the gospel which the sacrament is intended visibly to proclaim. Any offering Godwards at an altar of the consecrated elements contradicts this intended emphasis and deprives the worshippers of the full assurance which the sacrament was ordained to provide. In the blunter words of the Reformers, ideas often associated with such Godward offering are 'blasphemous fables, and dangerous deceits.'[50]

The risen Lord indicated the same evangelical truth in His instructions to His disciples. As the Christ who had suffered and risen again, He commissioned them to preach in His Name repentance and remission of sins (Luke 24:45-47). He made plain that forgiveness could now be offered freely to all who would acknowledge and believe in Him. There was no more offering of Christ's sacrifice to be done first. Nor ought expression of such offering to find any place in the worship of the church. For Hebrews 10:18 says about sins and their forgiveness, 'Now where remission of these is, there is no more offering for sin.' So Dr A.J. Tait wrote: 'The argument of the New Testament is not merely that there is remission of sins because Christ offered Himself once

---

[48] W.M.F. Scott, 'Priesthood in the New Testament', *Scottish Journal of Theology* vol. 10 (December 1957), p. 402.

[49] Scott, 'The Eucharist and the Heavenly Ministry of our Lord', p. 45.

[50] Article XXXI of the Thirty-Nine Articles.

for all; it is also that there is no more offering for sin because there is remission.'[51] Any offering of Christ in the eucharist with propitiatory intention involves, therefore, a radical denial of the truth of the gospel.

Some will nevertheless still wish to ask whether, as our great High Priest, Christ is not offering in heaven now. On this point, W.M.F. Scott wrote:

> Appeal, however, is sometimes made to Hebrews 8:3, which in the RV runs, 'Every high priest is appointed to offer both gifts and sacrifices: wherefore it is necessary that this high priest also have somewhat to offer.' Here it is said that the continuance of our Lord's offering is plainly implied. If so, the writer must be contradicting himself in successive sentences. For he draws a contrast between the repeated offerings of the Levitical priests and the completed offering of our Lord symbolised by His session.[52]

Elsewhere, also, Canon Scott wrote:

> Some perhaps would agree that our Lord is not offering his sacrifice, but would maintain that the truth is that he is pleading it. They would probably quote such passages as 'He ever liveth to make intercession for us' (Heb. 7:25) and 'Christ entered into heaven itself, now to appear before the face of God for us' (Heb. 9:24). In English we can speak of a lawyer appearing in a court to plead for his client. But the Greek word ἐμφανισθῆναι contains no such idea, but means rather to be fully visible. There is an implicit contrast with the High Priest who could enter the holy of holies only hidden in a cloud of incense, 'that he die not' (Lev. 16:13). Our Lord needs no such protection. He is fully manifest. In other words, he is in perfect communion with the Father into which we can enter.[53]

What the writer to the Hebrews says is his 'chief point' (Heb. 8:1 RV) is that our Christian High Priest is, like Melchizedek, a royal priest, a priest who having finished the indispensable offering to God henceforth sits on the throne able to dispense royal bounty to us. This is how the Bible encourages us to think of our ascended Lord, not as now offering to God, but as able and waiting to give gifts to men (see Ps. 68:18, Eph. 4:8, Heb. 4:14, 16). Similarly the bread and wine in Melchizedek's hands when he met Abraham (Gen. 14:18), like those in the hands of our Lord in the upper room, were offered not to God in propitiatory

---

[51] A.J. Tait, *The Heavenly Session of our Lord: An Introduction to the History of the Doctrine* (London, 1912), p. x.

[52] Scott, 'Priesthood in the New Testament', p. 404.

[53] Scott, 'The Eucharist and the Heavenly Ministry of Our Lord', p. 46.

or eucharistic sacrifice, but to men for their enjoyment and vital renewal. This surely is the way in which Christ ought to be thought of as personally active still in the sacrament which He ordained; that is, as therein giving to believing recipients the benefits consequent upon His already finished sacrifice, and not as inviting participants in the sacrament to join with Him in therein offering His sacrifice to God.

Proclaiming the Lord's Death

The greatest theme of all the Scriptures is the Lord's death. The central object of all worship in the universe of God's creation, and alongside the worship of the sovereign Creator Himself, is the Lamb that was slain (Rev. 5:13). To the saints who constitute His church it is given not merely from outside as wondering spectators, like the angels, but rather from inside as those personally experiencing salvation, to sing as no others can sing: 'Worthy art thou ... for thou wast slain, and didst purchase unto God with thy blood men of every tribe, and tongue, and people, and nation ... Worthy is the Lamb that hath been slain to receive the power ... and blessing' (Rev. 5:9, 12 RV).

Christ's sacrifice of Himself to save them is the event which His people can never forget. All their blessings stream from this source. Ever and again they have occasion to acknowledge their utter dependence on His redeeming work and their recurring need of its cleansing power. It is the cross of Christ, His finished sacrifice to atone for sin, that has turned their darkness into light and has made it possible for them to pass out of death into life. So to it they repeatedly return in mind and thought, in praise and prayer, to thank God afresh for His amazing grace, and to appropriate its endless benefits of which the first is remission of sins.

What is most staggering about it is that it is *the Lord's death*; that Jehovah God, deity Himself, should not only become man, but also that as man He should taste of death, the consequence and penalty of sin; and that He should do it for sinners like us. It is the sheer overwhelming surprise of it all that made Charles Wesley write, and has made thousands join him in singing:

And can it be, that I should gain
An interest in the Saviour's blood?
Died He for me, who caused His pain
For me, who Him to death pursued?
Amazing love! how can it be
That Thou, my God, shouldst die for me?

Lest we should forget His sacrifice for us and in order to keep us aware of its actual fulfilment, and to provide us with means to realize and to enjoy the benefits of its accomplishment on our behalf, our Lord Himself instituted this ordinance of the Lord's Supper. This sacrament is to be observed or participated in, to quote the Prayer Book Catechism, 'for the continual remembrance of the sacrifice of the death of Christ, and of the benefits which we receive thereby'. So in our understanding and use of this sacrament our whole interest should be focused on the one sacrifice for sins once made for us all by Christ alone; and not on any subsequent or complementary sacrifice of His which may be continuous in heaven or in which through His redeeming grace we may now share. The Lord's Supper speaks exclusively of the one sacrifice which only Christ could and did make; in relation to which, as a sinner, I must come in penitent faith and humble thankfulness, with empty hands, to receive its consequent benefits; and not by any Godward movement with the bread and wine to suggest that I can take any share in its offering to God. For this sacrifice, the one great sin-offering here commemorated, we sinful men never can offer. Nor is there place or need for any more of such offering. For the one sacrifice once made has availed to secure forgiveness of sins. 'Now where remission of these is, there is no more offering for sin' (Heb. 10:18).

This means that the older type of view expressed, for instance, in the doctrine of the sacrifice of the mass, is nearer to the truth than some modern views concerning the eucharistic sacrifice. For the old view did concentrate interest at the right points – on Christ's sacrificial death and on the making of propitiation for sin as its primary objective. In contrast to this some modern views give their main attention to the worshippers' supposed participation, both in Christ's heavenly and eternal self-offering, and in feeding upon His glorified humanity. On the one hand, the former view involves a radical abuse of the sacrament, because it suggests the necessity of using it ourselves to procure salvation by offering Godwards, instead of finding in it God-given pledges that salvation has been procured and is hereby offered to us for our appropriation by faith. On the other hand, some modern views involve a serious misuse of the sacrament, because they pervert it to express ideas which are fundamentally different from those indicated in the New Testament and by our Lord Himself as the explanation of its institution and appointed use.

For this sacrament, as originally ordered, is an unmistakable memorial of Christ's earthly physical death – of the breaking of His body and the shedding of His blood on the cross, as the one sacrifice for the remission of sins. The immediate object of participation in it is not to share in Christ's present heavenly self-offering, or ourselves to feed on His glorified humanity, but rather with praise and thanksgiving to God to recall His earthly sacrifice for us and to receive afresh of the unending benefits of His passion.

In this sacrament not only is our Lord Himself the Giver and His people the recipients – that is, not only is the movement of the bread and wine wholly manwards – but also what Christ gave, and what He still gives to His people in this service, speaks explicitly and exclusively of His death upon the cross. For the consecrated elements speak not of Christ's living body and blood, either as they were in Palestine then or as they may be in heaven now, but of His body broken and of His blood shed.

In the institution in the upper room, there was a significant prolonged interval between Christ's giving to His disciples first of the bread and later of the wine. It was not until 'after supper' that 'in like manner also he took the cup' (see 1 Cor. 11:25). So the bread and wine were deliberately separated, just as the pieces of slain animals were divided in covenant making – to represent the violent death of the covenant maker (see Gen. 15:9-10, 17-18). It would help us to appreciate this when we partake and to realize that what we receive are solemn covenant pledges, if we all returned to the explicit original pattern and New Testament practice of a separate administration to all communicants, first of the bread by itself and subsequently of the wine separately.

The consecrated elements are not, therefore, in any sense to be thought of as the tabernacle of Christ's present indwelling; for Christ cannot be spiritually divided as He was physically rent asunder. Nor do the elements become associated in some mystical way with our Lord's glorified humanity (which it seems scriptural to regard as possessing no corruptible blood in it, see 1 Cor. 15:50-53, compare Luke 24:39). Rather they represent, as Cranmer said, Christ's flesh and blood as they once were on the cross and not as they now are in heaven. So when we eat this bread and drink this cup, what we declare is Christ's death, His one finished sacrifice for sin.

That this is the right understanding of our Lord's own meaning has been carefully indicated by Dr Joachim Jeremias in his detailed and scholarly treatment of *The Meaning of the Eucharistic Words of Jesus*. He argues that 'body' and 'blood' on the lips of Jesus in this context constitute a twin concept, to which the only possible Aramaic equivalent must be 'flesh' and 'blood'.[54] Jesus, he says, using this twin concept 'explained

---

[54] Joachim Jeremias, *The Eucharistic Words of Jesus* (Oxford, 1955), pp. 140-141.

both elements ... in reference to His own person.'[55] This expression 'flesh and blood' signifies here, he says, 'the two component parts of the body, especially of a sacrificial victim, which are separated when it is killed ...A New Testament instance of the same cultic meaning of the twin concept σωμα-αἷμα is found in Hebrews 13:11.' Thus 'Jesus speaks of Himself as a sacrifice.' 'Above all', he adds, 'the words about the "outpouring of the blood" (Mark 14:24) taken, as they are, from the language of sacrifice, hardly allow of any other explanation.'[56] 'We therefore have', Dr Jeremias continues,

> a twofold parable by Jesus here ... Its meaning is quite simple. Each one of the disciples could understand it. Jesus made the broken bread a parable of the fate of His body, the blood of the grapes a parable of His outpoured blood. 'I must die a victim's death', is the meaning of the last parable of Jesus.

Also, 'By comparing Himself with the paschal lamb, Jesus describes His death as redemptive.'[57] So the one proper centre of interest in this service, the event to be recalled, whose benefits are to be appropriated, is Christ's death on the cross.

What our Lord thus instituted, He commanded to be done in remembrance of Himself (see 1 Cor. 11:24-25). Here some would insist on a Godward movement with the consecrated elements is intended, by asserting that our Lord's injunction means 'Offer this sacrifice as a memorial before God'. But neither the language used, nor the whole context of this command, justifies such an interpretation of our Lord's meaning. Since many nevertheless insist that a Godward movement is not only appropriate but divinely intended, it seems necessary to state the many reasons against any such understanding of our Lord's words.

First, then, let us ask, Can the words 'Do this' mean 'Offer this'? The simple answer is 'No'. In more detailed support of such an emphatic denial, let us quote the points listed and the inescapable deduction drawn by Dr A. Plummer. He wrote concerning τοῦτο ποιεῖτε:

> The proposal to give these words a sacrificial meaning, and translate them 'Offer this, Sacrifice this, Offer this sacrifice' cannot be maintained. It has against it (1) the *ordinary meaning* of ποιεῖν in NT, in LXX, and in Greek literature generally; (2) the authority of all the *Greek Fathers*, who ... understood the words as having the ordinary meaning, 'Perform this action'; (3) the authority of the

---

[55] Ibid., p. 143.
[56] Ibid., p. 144.
[57] Ibid., pp. 145-146.

Early Liturgies, which do not use ποιεῖν or *facere* when the bread and wine are offered, but προσφέρειν or *offerre*, although the words of institution precede the oblation, and thus suggest ποιεῖν or *facere*; (4) the authority of *a large majority of commentators*, ancient and modern ...[58]

So the right translation of our Lord's words is 'Do this thing'.

Next, let us ask whether the 'remembrance' intended by the Greek word ἀνάμνησις is a sacrificial memorial before God. Again, the simple answer is 'No'. Professor C.F.D. Moule has briefly expressed it by saying, 'For myself I remain wholly unconvinced by the attempts to make the *anamnesis* ("this do in remembrance of me") mean that God is here reminded of what Christ has wrought',[59] that is, as though Christ's words meant 'Do this to remind God of me'. On this point Mr Douglas Jones has declared after a careful survey of the evidence, 'that the liturgical, Godward meaning is not inherent in any of the instances of the word ἀνάμνησις in the LXX' and 'that the use of the word ἀνάμνησις in the LXX involves too many ambiguities to provide authority for any particular interpretation of New Testament passages.'[60] After a complementary examination of 1 Corinthians 11:25 he concludes:

> The sum of the matter is this: that the objection to the usual translation of 1 Corinthians 11:25 does not withstand scrutiny; that common usage would suggest the usual translation while analogies for the alternative translation are found to be inadequate; that the Passover context would at once suggest the usual translation and require explicit redirection to permit any other.[61]

So the best translation of our Lord's words is still 'This do in remembrance of me'; or 'Continually do this in order to bring Me to mind', that is, 'to remind yourselves and others of the redemption which I have won by My death'.[62] Mr Douglas Jones also adds this significant theological comment:

> With some relief one feels freed of an interpretation which, if regarded as the primary and exhaustive meaning of our Lord's command, seems to come near to transforming the community of

---

[58] Alfred Plummer, *A Critical and Exegetical Commentary on the Gospel According to St Luke* (fourth edition, Edinburgh, 1901), p. 497.

[59] Moule, *Sacrifice of Christ*, p. 47.

[60] Douglas Jones, 'ἀνάμνησις in the LXX and the Interpretation of 1 Corinthians 11:25', *Journal of Theological Studies* vol. 6 (October 1955), pp. 183, 187.

[61] Ibid., p. 191.

[62] Plummer, *Luke*, p. 498.

disciples and therefore the Church into some sort of mediator between God and his Christ, presenting to the divine memory at every Eucharist the story of his obedience and sacrifice that God may remember him and so effect his vindication at the last day.[63]

More positively, the Greek word ἀνάμνησις expresses the idea of a calling to mind, a recalling or recollection, exactly similar to the way in which the Jews at the celebration of the Passover recalled their deliverance from Egypt. To the Semitic mind thus to commemorate a past event was personally to realize and experience its present operative significance as an event with abiding consequences. So Canon W.M.F. Scott wrote: "'Do this in remembrance of me" can now be seen to mean that as we "eat this bread and drink this cup" our Lord's sacrifice becomes here and now operative in our lives.'[64]

Thirdly, let us ask, What is meant by 'proclaiming' the Lord's death? Can this mean, 'Show it to God'? Again, the simple answer is 'No'. On this point of interpretation Dr W.H. Griffith Thomas wrote: "'Ye do show forth" means actual oral announcement and not representation by action. It is "showing forth" or "proclaiming" by words rather than by deeds (compare Acts 4:2). The object of the verb is obviously not God but man.'[65] Also, Canon Scott aptly commented:

> The word is commonly used in the Acts and Pauline Epistles (seventeen times) for the proclamation of the Gospel before men. It is never used in the New Testament in any other sense. Indeed its structure forbids any other, as the prefix κατὰ means 'down'. καταγγέλλω therefore can no more mean show up to God than a cataract can mean a fountain, or a catacomb a skyscraper.[66]

In this connection it is relevant also to recognize that Christian faith and hope show themselves to be alive and active by spoken confession (see Heb. 3:6, 4:14, 10:23). Open confession, with the mouth, of Jesus as Lord is essential to the enjoyment of His salvation (see Rom. 10:9-10). Similarly it is good that we should renew and increase our experience of Christ and of His saving grace as the crucified and exalted Saviour by fresh acknowledgment of what we owe to His atoning sacrifice. So to "show" His death is solemnly and in His Name

---

[63] Jones, 'ἀνάμνησις in the LXX', p. 191.

[64] Scott, 'The Eucharist and the Heavenly Ministry of Our Lord', p. 44.

[65] W.H. Griffith Thomas, *A Sacrament of our Redemption* (second edition, London, 1920), p. 29.

[66] Scott, 'The Eucharist and the Heavenly Ministry of Our Lord', p. 44.

to tell ourselves and one another, in and by His ordinance, that He died for us.[67]

Participation in the Lord's Supper, therefore, should be for all who share in it a dramatic or acted proclamation of the gospel. In such 'oral announcement' the scriptural record suggests that all who communicate should share. For the apostle wrote,'as often as ye eat this bread, and drink the cup, ye proclaim the Lord's death till he come' (1 Cor. 11:26 RV). One may compare in possible illustration what happens when the loyal toast is proposed. In response not only do all stand to drink, but also audibly they all proclaim 'The Queen'. Similarly, it may be, when at Corinth the Lord's Supper was eaten, not only was the story of Christ's passion retold, but also every communicant shared in confessing his faith by declaring audibly the significance of his action. Certainly it would make our own worship more fully corporate and confessional if when the sacrament is administered every recipient proclaimed the Christian significance of his participation; and said, for instance, as he received the bread:'I take and eat this in remembrance that Christ died for me, and I feed on Him in my heart by faith with thanksgiving.' And similarly later on at the reception of the cup.

Finally, whatever 'remembrance' and 'to proclaim' may mean, according to the Lord's injunction and the scriptural evidence they are both done by all eating the bread and drinking the wine, and not by the celebrant spreading or presenting the consecrated elements before God. The necessary sacramental movement with the bread and wine is, therefore, exclusively manwards not Godwards. For such recollection and proclamation of Christ and of His death are activities in which we need to share, not to remind God, still less to persuade Him to remember His Christ; but rather to awaken and to encourage our own faith and active response, so that we may be moved afresh to appreciate the wonder and purpose of Christ's sacrifice for us, to appropriate all that He offers us through His death for us, and to give to God and to Christ the sacrifices of our praise and thanksgiving and of ourselves and our substance.

Obtaining the Benefits of Christ's Passion

At the Last Supper in the upper room our Lord was fully aware that His own death was imminent. It is, therefore, not inappropriate to think of

---

[67] R.B. Girdlestone, H.C.G. Moule and T.W. Drury, *English Church Teaching on Faith, Life and Order* (London, 1897), p. 126.

Him as like a man making a will to dispose of what he has to give. Here we see Jesus solemnly assigning His last bequests to His friends. He has no material wealth acquired during His earthly life to leave them. What He formally pledges and symbolically hands over to them for their enjoyment are benefits which are to become available through His death for them. So He invites them to eat and to drink; and says of the bread as it is distributed, 'This is my body, which is broken for you', and similarly of the wine, 'This cup is the new covenant in my blood' (1 Cor. 11:24-25).

'To Orientals', writes Joachim Jeremias, 'the idea that divine gifts are communicated by eating and drinking is very familiar.' Here 'the meaning is that by eating and drinking He gives them a share in the atoning power of His death.'[68] 'This is Christ's last and greatest gift: He can give nothing greater than a share in the redeeming power of His death.'[69] It is to express this, and to invite our responsive reception, that this sacrament was instituted.

According to ancient Semitic ritual a man turned a promise into a solemn covenant and visibly ratified it, by passing as he made his promise between the divided parts of slain animals. The governing idea was that he was swearing by his life and invoking God thus violently to rend him asunder if he failed to keep his word. Hence the phraseology, 'The Lord do so to me, and more also, if ...' (Ruth 1:17, 2 Sam. 19:13, 1 Kings 2:23). In His institution of this sacrament of the gospel our Lord similarly used the bread and wine to symbolize His own violent death – His body broken and His blood shed. Also, by a deliberate interval between their distribution, He formally divided the pieces. Then as He gave them the cup, He spake of His shed blood as a covenant pledge. Those therefore who receive this bread and take this cup as from His hand or, so to speak, under His seal, may rightly find in them tangible pledges of His solemn undertaking to make certain benefits theirs.

Nor is that all. For these pledges do more than the divided pieces of slain animals ever did or could. For those pledges simply asked for the life of the defaulter to be violently taken if a man failed to keep his promise. They did not assure the other party, to whom the promise was given, that any failure would be made good. Whereas in the Lord's Supper, the pledges give witness to a substantial and not a mere symbolic death which has already taken place, which not only makes fulfilment of God's promises certain but is sufficient to

---

[68] Jeremias, *Eucharistic Words of Jesus*, p. 154.
[69] Ibid., p. 159.

cover, and to secure from penalty for default, sinful men who by these pledges know themselves brought by God's grace into covenant relation with God.

So every time I partake of these pledges, I receive renewed God-given assurance that He will fulfil His promises in me and that all my sins and shortcomings, since I became a Christian as well as before, are covered by His violent death for me. Hereby I know that although I fail to keep my covenant pledges, I shall not on that account become liable to a violent penal death because Christ has already died such a death in my stead. Also, I am hereby certified by these very presents, that under the new covenant hereby sealed to me the Lord Himself undertakes by His Spirit to work in me to cause me to do His will and ultimately, at the resurrection of the body, to make me to be fully conformed to His likeness as the glorified Man. It is to make such peace and hope ours that these covenant seals are given to Christ's people according to His own explicit ordinance and injunction. It is, therefore, on such benefits that thought and thanksgiving and appropriating faith ought to be concentrated when we receive this sacrament.

Our Lord's action and words at the institution indicate that He desired His disciples to become partakers of His body and of His blood. He had also spoken much earlier in His teaching of the necessity of eating His flesh and drinking His blood as indispensable to the enjoyment of eternal life (see John 6:53-58). Let us, therefore, seek to understand more fully exactly what such ideas and phraseology mean.

First, let us indicate what some think they mean. For instance, Darwell Stone in an article on the Lord's Supper wrote: 'The gift contemplated in the rite instituted must be viewed in the light of the spiritual nature and powers of the risen body of Christ.' He claimed that 'Exegesis of our Lord's words at the Institution, as recorded by St Paul, indicates that the gift in the eucharist is the spiritual food of the risen and ascended body of our Lord'. Consequently the communicant feeds 'on the living, risen body and blood of the Lord which have passed through death'.[70] Such a view means, as for instance Bishop H.C.G. Moule understood it, that

the Incarnation is (if we may say it with reverence) thus, as it were, infused into the communicant. A New Humanity, which is to come out in the life of glory, is thus deposited and built up in the man by successive gifts of the 'real' Manhood of the glorified Christ.

---

[70] James Hastings (ed.), *A Dictionary of Christ and the Gospels* (Edinburgh, 1906-8), vol. 2, pp. 72-73.

... This gift of infusion is regarded as what is meant specially by 'grace'.[71]

Over against such ideas, which we cannot find to be taught in or supported by the New Testament, let us now set the original emphasis of our Lord's own expressive phraseology. He was unquestionably concentrating attention by such words on His earthly physical death, and on the necessity of appropriating benefits derived exclusively therefrom and obtainable in no other way. When, for instance, our Lord spoke of Himself as 'the bread of life', He said that 'the bread that I will give is my flesh, which I will give for the life of the world' (John 6:35, 51); and in His subsequent declaration of the absolute necessity of everyone eating His flesh and drinking His blood (John 6:53-58), the reference to flesh and to blood separately clearly points to His death. Commenting on John 6:53 Bishop B.F. Westcott wrote: 'A violent death is presupposed'.[72] Also, 'flesh could only be eaten by a Jew after the blood had been drained from it, and the multitude therefore ought to have had no great difficulty in perceiving the meaning of the allusion'.[73] In addition, according to Old Testament usage, 'to eat a man's flesh' or 'to drink his blood' means to enjoy benefits or to acquire advantages consequent upon his death; that is, either through his own willing self-sacrifice or through others violently murdering him (see Ps. 14:4, 27:2, 2 Sam. 23:15-17).

In his exposition of the significance of such phraseology Bishop J.C. Ryle wrote:

> I believe that by 'flesh and blood' our Lord meant the sacrifice of His own body for us, when He offered it up as our substitute on Calvary. I believe that by 'eating and drinking' He meant that communion and participation of the benefit of His sacrifice which faith and faith only conveys to the soul. I believe His meaning to be 'Except ye believe on Me as the one sacrifice for sin, and by faith receive into your hearts the redemption purchased by My blood, ye have no eternal life and will not be saved'. The atonement of Christ, His vicarious death and sacrifice, and faith in it – these things are the key to the whole passage.[74]

Similarly Bishop H.C.G. Moule wrote:

> The Body and the Blood, as presented to our faith in the Lord's Supper, are things which literally exist no longer; for in the Calvary

---

[71] Girdlestone, Moule and Drury, *English Church Teaching*, p. 11.

[72] B.F. Westcott, *The Gospel According to St John: The Authorized Version with Introduction and Notes* (London, 1882), p. 107.

[73] Griffith Thomas, *Sacrament of our Redemption*, p. 9.

[74] J.C. Ryle, *Expository Thoughts on the Gospels* (London, 1883), St John, vol. 1, p. 402.

state that most sacred Body is now no more. They are not existing things to be infused into our being; they are an infinitely precious Fact to be appropriated by our faith. Thus, 'faith', faith in Christ, in His work and word, is, as the Article says, 'the means whereby the Body of Christ is received and eaten in the Supper'.[75]

The same interpretation of the distinctive phraseology, and the same complementary emphasis on the spiritual conditions essential to the enjoyment of the benefits, are to be found in a noteworthy rubric which follows the order for 'The Communion of the Sick' in the 1662 Prayer Book. This states:

> If a man ... by reason of ... any just impediment, do not receive the Sacrament of Christ's Body and Blood, the Curate shall instruct him, that if he do truly repent him of his sins, and stedfastly believe that Jesus Christ hath suffered death upon the Cross for him, and shed his Blood for his redemption, earnestly remembering the benefits he hath thereby, and giving him hearty thanks therefore, he doth eat and drink the Body and Blood of our Saviour Christ profitably to his soul's health, although he do not receive the Sacrament with his mouth.

This corresponds closely to Archbishop Cranmer's statement in his *Defence of the True and Catholic Doctrine of the Sacrament of the Body and Blood of our Saviour Christ.* He thus expressed his conclusion:

> These things before rehearsed are sufficient to prove that the eating of Christ's flesh and the drinking of his blood is not to be understood simply and plainly, as the words do properly signify, that we do eat and drink him with our mouths; but it is a figurative speech spiritually to be understood, that his flesh was crucified, and his blood shed, for our redemption. And this our belief in him, is to eat his flesh and to drink his blood, although they be not present here with us, but be ascended into heaven. As our forefathers, before Christ's time, did likewise eat his flesh and drink his blood, which was so far from them that he was not yet then born.[76]

Such evidence all emphasizes that the proper interest of the informed recipient of the sacrament should be in Christ's death for him, and in the present personal appreciation and appropriation of the benefits made available thereby.

---

[75] H.C.G. Moule, *The Pledges of His Love: Thoughts on the Holy Communion Devotional and Explanatory* (London, 1894), p. 53.

[76] *Archbishop Cranmer on the True and Catholic Doctrine and Use of the Sacrament of the Lord's Supper*, pp. 135-136.

Next, let us ask what these benefits are. There is scriptural witness for stating in answer that the first of these is remission of sins. Indeed, this is the benefit explicitly mentioned by our Lord in the words of the institution when He spoke of His blood as 'shed for many for the remission of sins' (Matt. 26:28). In correspondence with this, in the familiar post-communion prayer in the 1662 Prayer Book we ask that we 'may obtain remission of our sins, and all other benefits of his passion'. It is, therefore, in the reception of the Holy Communion that the Christian believer ought to gain fresh and present assurance of complete remission of sins, including the remission of sins committed since last he received the sacrament.

This proper function and use of the Lord's Supper have great practical relevance because they concern the urgent problem in the Christian life of post-baptismal sins and their absolution. In this connection some present-day scholars are prepared to see in our Lord's words recorded in John 13:10 ('He that is washed needeth not save to wash his feet') an intended indication that while baptism is administered once for all without repetition as a sign and seal of full salvation in Christ, the Lord's Supper is to be received subsequently and repeatedly to assure us of fresh cleansing from the fresh defilements of daily living – also as a benefit of Christ's one sacrifice for sins.[77] And even if such exegesis may rightly be regarded as by itself inadequate to support such a fundamental doctrinal deduction, yet the idea herein expressed about fresh assurance of cleansing as one purpose of our participation in the Lord's Supper, seems from our Lord's explicit mention of remission of sins at the institution to correspond with His intention. In this context of thought the sacrament is seen to fulfil its double function, both of adding a visible seal to God's word of promise and of witnessing to the one all-sufficient sacrifice for sins. It is thus capable of giving to the instructed and believing recipient strong assurance of present forgiveness. Such profit in its reception depends upon understanding and faith.

In this connection the wording of the 'Prayer of Humble Access' in the Prayer Book is very remarkable and noteworthy: 'Grant us therefore, gracious Lord, so to eat the flesh of thy dear Son Jesus Christ, and to drink his blood, that our sinful bodies may be made clean by his body, and our souls washed through his most precious blood.' In using these words we treat the eating and drinking as symbolical of appropriating the benefits of Christ's passion; and in it we pray, through right reception, not for strengthening but for cleansing. So there is no need of the confessional,

---

[77] See A.J.B. Higgins, *The Lord's Supper in the New Testament* (London, 1952), p. 84.

nor of special absolution by a 'priest' in a so-called sacrament of penance, to assure the penitent Christian of cleansing from post-baptismal sin. Rather the way for the Christian to appropriate and to find assurance of fresh cleansing to the end of his earthly life is in worthy partaking of Christ's body and blood in the Communion service.

Here some contend that the very suggestion that Christians should thus approach the eucharist as penitents seeking fresh cleansing is wholly inappropriate. They argue that only the baptized can come to the eucharist and that remission of sins is assured to us by our baptism. They seem virtually to assert that by those who are justified by faith, and acceptable to God in Christ and His righteousness, no further appropriation or application of the virtue of Christ's atoning work is necessary; and that we can and ought to enter the sanctuary to offer sacrifice. Also, they wish to make what is done with the bread and wine the ritual expression of such Godward offering. In expression of such a protest Paul Gibson has written:

> The act of participating in the offertory is the act whereby the individual asserts that he is a member of the redeemed community; thus the whole eucharistic action is the crown and completion of the Christian life and not a means of restoration to the Christian life.[78]

Or again,

> To say that we are not able to recite the Lord's Prayer or to offer ourselves as members of the Whole Christ until after communion is to regard sin as normal to the Christian life, baptism as an important but transitory event in the past and the eucharist as a medicinal remedy rather than a real participation in the glorious sacrifice of the Risen Lord by the redeemed community.[79]

Also, 'the place for solemn, corporate expressions of deep penitence and for solemn declarations of absolution is outside the context of the eucharistic liturgy in recognition of the fact that sin "excommunicates" us and deprives us of the right to offer.'[80]

As these quotations indicate, such thinkers argue from church history and practice that believers defiled by gross transgression have commonly been excommunicated; and that penitence, confession and absolution or the assurance of forgiveness ought to take place as a preparation to make one fit to share in the eucharist, rather than themselves to form part of the activity of participation in this sacrament. But such ideas are

---

[78] Gibson, 'Liturgical Revision and a Theology of Incorporation', p. 230.
[79] Ibid., p. 231.
[80] Ibid., p. 231.

determined by church tradition and natural conjecture rather than by the revealed truth of God and the explicit teaching of Christ, as these are made available to us in the Spirit-inspired Scriptures.

Or alternatively, in as far as such ideas concerning eucharistic sacrifice are scriptural and worthy of a place in Christian worship, those who are thus dominated by them are guilty of misusing the bread and wine and perverting the sacrament which Christ ordained in order to give them ritual expression. It would help to clarify current confusion of thought and practice, if they would distinguish what they wish to do from what Christ told us to do with the bread and wine; and if they ceased from calling their activity the sacrament of the Lord's Supper. Then others, who wish to be true to the Bible and to the gospel, might disapprove of them less; and the Lord's Supper could be properly observed and appreciated and used by us all according to Christ's ordinance.

If remission of sin is the first benefit consequent upon Christ's death for us, the gift of the indwelling Spirit is the second. These two benefits are both pledged and symbolically given in Christian baptism. Its water speaks, on the one hand, of cleansing from sin and, on the other hand, of quickening by the Spirit. The same two benefits are explicitly mentioned in the promises of the new covenant (Jer. 31:33-34, Ezek. 36:25, 27); and the second sacrament of the gospel, the Lord's Supper, has been ordained by the Lord Himself afresh to pledge and to convey to us a share in these benefits. So those who, with understanding and faith, rightly receive this sacrament may not only find in doing so fresh assurance of sin forgiven, but may also thereby appropriate and claim for themselves the outworking in their daily lives of the new life in Christ which is already theirs by the Spirit. For God's promise is: 'I will put my Spirit within you, and cause you to walk in my statutes'; and the seals of the covenant given to me in the Lord's Supper are witness that I may, through Christ and His death for me, count upon God by His Spirit to fulfil this promise in me. It is, indeed, 'through the blood of the everlasting covenant' that we are assured that God Himself will make us 'perfect in every good work to do his will' (see Heb. 13:20-21). Also, such scriptural understanding of the character of the benefit to be enjoyed will lead me to look for fulfilment not to the outward symbols but to the unseen and indwelling Spirit, that He will produce such progress in holiness in my life, first in heart and will, and then in word and deed. It is, therefore, the life-giving Spirit rather than portions of Christ's glorified humanity of whom I thus partake in consequence of Christ's death for sinners like me.

Nor do the benefits of Christ's passion end there. For because of His accomplished sacrifice, we are invited to share in a continual feast. We thus become 'partakers of the Lord's table' (1 Cor. 10:21). This makes ours three consequent blessings. First, we are hereby assured of our acceptance in God's sight, of our full welcome in His presence and of our unhindered enjoyment of His gifts. So our justification is confirmed by visible proofs. Second, we find ourselves herein united in a divinely created fellowship and unity with all who like ourselves have received and responded to the same gospel invitation. As partakers of the one loaf broken for us, we realize that through our common relation to the one Lord we are constituted one body (see 1 Cor. 10:16-17). So participation is not only His seal to us of our fellowship with Him; but also it becomes, as we understand the full embrace of its significance, the seal of our fellowship through Him with one another.

Finally, we remember that at its institution the Lord looked forward and spoke of a coming day of fulfilment and of the triumph feast in which He, obviously alive again from the dead, would join with them in fellowship (Matt. 26:29, Mark 14:25). So our eating and drinking at His table are the occasion to realize spiritual fellowship with the risen and present Lord, to rejoice in His triumph over sin and death, to appropriate our share here and now of the outworked fulfilment of His victory through death, and above all to anticipate with exultation the crowning day of final consummation yet to come, in whose glory and fulfilment of hope we know 'by these presents' that we are to share. For this sacrament and our partaking of it are but provision for the pilgrimage of the church through the world and its tribulation. They are only 'till he come'.

Since, therefore, to the end of our earthly lives participation in this sacrament should make us freshly aware, first, of the Saviour's once-for-all gift of Himself for us, and second, of the Saviour's continual giving to us of Himself and of all the benefits of His passion, it is a very misleading perversion and misuse of the sacrament and its movement to suggest that what is done with the bread and wine is meant to express an act of giving to God by us, or an act of Christ's own giving through or in us. For at the Lord's table still, as at Emmaus or in the upper room, He is to be recognized as distinct from us, the only Saviour, whose personal self-oblation for us and whose continual gracious giving to us are the source of every blessing we enjoy. So here, in the handling of the bread and wine, He is the one Giver and there is room or welcome for us only as empty-handed, grateful recipients.

True Eucharist

The words 'eucharist' and 'eucharistic sacrifice' are terms often used, and sometimes improperly used, to refer to the sacrament of the Lord's Supper. The use of these words has become a sphere of misunderstanding and confusion of meaning with regard to the sacrament itself. Consequently clarification of meaning and more exact reference in use are highly desirable. Let us, therefore, attempt to improve our own understanding and our own practice in this matter.

First, let us recognize explicitly and without qualification that in the proper sense of the words 'eucharist' and 'sacrifice', the sacrament itself which our Lord instituted in the upper room is neither the one nor the other. For the movement in which He engaged, with the accompanying explanatory words indicative of its significance, was in itself neither a thanksgiving nor an offering to God. It was rather a donation to men. There is no more reason for calling this action eucharistic or sacrificial than there is for calling the similar action of baptizing someone in God's Name either a eucharist or a sacrifice.

On the other hand, we must admit without question, first, that our Lord Himself, before He distributed the bread and the wine, did twice engage in thanksgiving; and, second, that reception of such gifts on the part of His disciples should be both expressive of and accompanied by thanksgiving. Indeed, since in this context disciples express their utter dependence and thankful indebtedness simply by receiving, the very act of receiving can, almost paradoxically, be described as the most appropriate form of thank-offering; and so it may itself be called a 'eucharistic sacrifice'.[81] But these words thus used describe the character not of what our Lord did in initiating the sacrament, but only of what we do in responsive reception.

Consequently, if we use the term 'eucharist' or 'eucharistic sacrifice' to describe the sacrament as a whole, we conceal thereby its primary character as the Lord's Supper or the gospel feast, and give prominence to proper characteristics of worthy reception at the cost of failing explicitly to name the divinely ordained occasion of such response. We ought rather, therefore, to speak not of 'going to the eucharist' nor of 'offering the eucharistic sacrifice', but of sharing in an administration of the Lord's Supper. For there can be no proper sacramental eucharist or eucharistic sacrifice except in this context of becoming recipients in a meeting with the Lord, in which the primary movement is His towards us, not ours towards Him.

---

[81] Compare Ps. 116:12-13: 'What shall I render ...? I will take ...'

Similarly in participating in this sacrament we ought to speak not of going to the altar, as though the primary interest is our offering to God, but rather of going to the Lord's table, because the primary and distinctive action in this service is His giving to us and our chief personal cause for wonder and thanksgiving is that we are invited to be His guests. Admittedly such giving by Him to us could not happen if there had not been first His sacrifice on the cross. But this service in which we share is not the occasion for us to offer His sacrifice to God. Rather it is the feast consequent upon His sacrifice, a feast in which He functions as the Lord at His table giving to men and not as a priest at the altar offering to God. This is the biblical and evangelical truth which ought at all costs to be preserved and proclaimed in our ordering of this sacrament.

In the context of such reception of the Lord's gifts to His people from His table there are three points at which, and three ways in which, 'eucharist' or thanksgiving may rightly find expression. Indeed, participation and response would, of course, be incomplete and unworthy without such eucharist. The first thanksgiving is in words and should be said, like the 'grace' before a meal, before the elements are administered in exact correspondence with our Lord's action in the upper room. For the first thing that He did, both when He took the bread and later when He took the cup, was to bless God the Giver. Such was the character of the customary Jewish grace before meals. The 'thanksgiving' or 'blessing' uttered did not ask God to bless the food, but it blessed God for the food. The second eucharist, and the one distinctive of participation in the Lord's Supper, is expressed in response to the Lord's sacramental movement towards us by receptive action. We gratefully acknowledge our debt and dependence, and show our gratitude for blessings made available for us by Christ's sacrifice and gift, simply by receiving; that is, by eating the bread and drinking the wine. The third eucharist, which completes the expression of our gratitude, is made after reception in responsive thank-offering; that is, in the giving of ourselves and of our substance to the Lord. This involves substantial deeds and donation on our part, though it finds immediate outlet and confession in words of devotion and dedication.

Similar careful distinction needs to be made with regard to the description in this same context of our thanksgiving as sacrificial. Such description is scriptural and proper. We are exhorted in Scripture to offer such 'sacrifice of praise to God continually, that is, the fruit of our lips giving thanks to his name' (Heb. 13:15). So our spoken expression of thanksgiving may rightly be called a eucharistic sacrifice.

The important point to be recognized, however, in this context of participation in the Lord's Supper, is that the term sacrifice does not apply to the consecrated elements or to what is done with them. It is completely foreign to the simple pattern of the sacrament which Christ ordained to offer them to God. Also, while they do bear witness to the one sacrifice of Christ made once for all on the cross, and testify that it is still operative in making benefits available to men, that sacrifice was not eucharistic but atoning. So this is not the place to talk or think of Christ's eucharistic sacrifice, as though participation in the sacrament is an intended way for us to be united with Him in offering it to God. Rather is the sacrament His appointed way of offering to us the benefits of His unique atoning sacrifice, accomplished once for all by Him alone on the cross. It is the present remembrance of this sacrifice, and the Lord's consequent gifts to us for our present and eternal good, which in the context of this sacrament should call forth our unending eucharist.

In this sphere of eucharist or thanksgiving there is scope for the recognition of a more scriptural view of consecration than at present obtains in the minds of many. For we tend to associate the consecration of the elements with the saying of the distinctive sacramental words, 'This is my body' etc, whereas it ought properly to be associated with the previous thanksgiving or saying of grace. On this point Dr J. E. L. Oulton, formerly Regius Professor of Divinity in the University of Dublin, wrote:

> The Prayer of Consecration as found in the Book of Common Prayer of the Church of England from 1552 on labours under the defect of appearing to adopt 'an extreme and even exaggerated acceptance of the scholastic view of consecration in its most exclusive form' – namely that the words, *Hoc est corpus meum*, are the form of consecration for the bread, etc.[82]

Whereas, the truth is that

> The words 'This is my body', 'This is my blood', were not words of consecration spoken immediately after he had blessed the bread and wine; they were words of administration spoken as he was delivering to the disciples fragments of the broken bread and the cup, or after (note especially Mark 14:23-4) he had delivered to each his portion and had passed the cup round to all.[83]

---

[82] J.E.L. Oulton, *Holy Communion and Holy Spirit: A Study in Doctrinal Relationship* (London, 1951), p. 29, quoting W.H. Frere, *The Anaphora* (London, 1938), p. 201.

[83] Ibid., p. 26.

Professor Oulton added:

> It seems to be not unnecessary to underline the point ... since the familiar prayers and actions and their sequence in the Book of Common Prayer tend so to substitute in our minds something different from the evangelical order that we are recalled to it with a measure of surprise. To show that this is not an overstatement, I venture to quote the following from a fairly recent work: 'He took the bread that was before him; he called it his body; he gave thanks for it; he broke it; he gave it. ... How would the disciples think of those strange words "This is my body"? Inevitably they would see that as in that moment he treated the bread, so in that moment he was treating his body: "He brake it and gave it." He was offering a sacrifice; the victim was himself.' Clearly, this is not the sequence of words and actions that we find recorded in the Synoptists or St Paul; it appears to be written from the point of view of a communicant today, who before he receives the elements has already heard in the Prayer of Consecration the words of mysterious import which the Lord used in delivering the bread and the wine. It is noteworthy that, though the Evangelists differ much among themselves in other details about the Institution of the Sacrament, they are agreed that at its most significant moment the Lord's actions were in the following order: (1) He took the bread (or the cup) into His hands; (2) He blessed it; (3) He brake (the bread); (4) He gave the bread and the cup to the disciples; (5) He said 'This is my body', or (in some form or another) 'This is my blood of the covenant'.[84]

The 1958 Lambeth Conference also gave welcome and explicit recognition to the truth that consecration of material things like food for use by us is, according to the ancient biblical idea and persistent Jewish practice, accomplished by giving praise to God the Giver; not, be it noted, by any prayer for the objects themselves or by any invocation of the Spirit upon them. So the Lambeth Committee Report declares:

> We desire to draw attention to a conception of consecration which is scriptural and primitive and goes behind subsequent controversies with respect to the movement and formula of consecration. This is associated with the Jewish origin and meaning of *eucharistia* and may be called consecration through thanksgiving. 'To bless anything and to pronounce a thanksgiving over it are not two actions but one.' 'Everything created by God is good, and nothing

---

[84] Ibid., pp. 27-28, quoting William Temple, *Thoughts on Some Problems of the Day* (London, 1931), p. 142.

is to be rejected if it is received with thanksgiving; for then it is consecrated by the word of God and prayer' (1 Tim. 4:4-5).[85]

This means that, just as at an ordinary meal the food is consecrated for use by blessing God the Giver, so in the Lord's Supper the consecration of the bread and wine should be associated with a proper thanksgiving or blessing of God. Archbishop Cranmer has been rightly criticized for unawareness and consequent deficiency at this point. The 1957 Memorandum of the Church of England Liturgical Commission on *Prayer Book Revision in the Church of England* states:

> It is to be expected, however, that four hundred years of biblical study will have taught the Church of England today to appreciate the positive guidance of Scripture more fully than was possible in the sixteenth century, when the reformers were only just disentangling themselves from their medieval heritage. To take an example, when Cranmer is emphasizing the need for the Church to do what the Lord did at the Last Supper, he frequently refers to the narrative of the Institution. On every occasion except one he fails to record that our Lord 'gave thanks' or 'blessed God'; and as a result of what can only be called this 'blind spot' the Church of England has inherited ever since a Consecration Prayer which, though in many ways a drastic revision of the pre-Reformation Canon, yet still retains its petitionary form and still lacks any eucharistic character.[86]

Indeed, this is a point in the ordering of the Lord's Supper at which common Free Church use is better than Anglican practice. For it is their custom explicitly and at length to offer thanks before administration; and according to the pattern of the institution to do it twice, first for the bread before it is distributed and later similarly for the wine.

At this point, when grace is said, first the bread and later the wine may be thought of as spread separately before the Lord upon the table. But they are not offered to God. Rather thanks are offered to God for His gift of them to us. Nor have they yet been given their sacramental significance. For the distinctive sacramental words, 'This is my body' etc, should not be said concerning the bread or the wine until after grace has been said and the administration manwards begun. If this scriptural pattern and dominical precedent were properly followed, then the Lord's Supper would correspond in principle to Christian baptism in which also the distinctive sacramental words are said, not to consecrate the water before it is administered but to declare to the recipient the

---

[85] *The Lambeth Conference, 1958*, part 2, p. 85.
[86] *Prayer Book Revision in the Church of England*, pp. 30-31.

significance of the administration itself. Such declaration manwards is the proper function of the sacramental words.

There is, therefore, need for the better understanding of true eucharist; and for its fuller expression in the ordering of the Lord's Supper, particularly in order to achieve the worthy consecration of the bread and wine and the appropriate ascription of praise to God before the sacrament itself is administered.

This Our Sacrifice

To glorify God, to give Him the worship which is His due, is the highest activity or 'chief end' of man. Such worship unquestionably involves offering or sacrifice to God, particularly self-oblation. This spirit of sacrificial service should find expression in the devotion to God of all our daily living. According to the teaching of the New Testament it is possible thus to offer to God in sacrifice oneself, one's faith, one's alms, one's good works, one's converts and, if occasion demand, one's martyrdom (see Rom. 12:1, Phil. 2:17, 4:18, Heb. 13:16, Rom. 15:16, 2 Tim. 4:6). As 'an holy priesthood' the redeemed community of God's people is called thus 'to offer up spiritual sacrifices, acceptable to God by Jesus Christ' (1 Pet. 2:5). But such offering to God is not something to be done by us with the consecrated elements in the Lord's Supper; and if the term 'eucharistic sacrifice' is used, as some appear to wish to use it, to describe a sacrifice offered only in the context of participating in the sacrament and involving the offering Godwards of the bread and wine, then such a use is completely unscriptural and foreign to the gospel, to the Thirty-Nine Articles and to the 1662 Anglican Prayer Book.

What some now explicitly teach is that, on the sacramental level, it is our baptism which unites us to Christ as the sin-offering and gives us acceptance in God's sight; and that the eucharist is the acceptable offering to God which our baptism thus enables us to offer. Participation in the eucharist is thus interpreted as an expression of the self-oblation which rightly follows reconciliation to God. But, according to the New Testament, the Lord's Supper is a sacrament of the gospel, 'a sacrament of our redemption by Christ's death'.[87] It commemorates the sin-offering offered once-for-all by Christ on the cross to make propitiation. Sinful men, such as we are, become fit to enter the sanctuary and offer worship only as we partake of the benefits of that sacrifice. The function of the blood then shed, as its merit is applied to us, is to make the service of the

---

[87] Article XXVIII of the Thirty-Nine Articles.

living God possible for us (see Heb. 9:13-14). The place and purpose of the Lord's Supper and of our participation in it are, therefore, continually to remind us of our dependence upon this one source of cleansing and to stir us afresh to appropriate its benefit, so that we may be consciously fit and free to render God acceptable worship and be moved to do so with fresh wonder and gratitude and thankful devotion. Consequently, in any proper scriptural and evangelical use of this sacrament our first 'sacrifice' should be, not to offer, but to take afresh with thanksgiving to God those tokens of atonement made and of cleansing and quickening freshly available.

In our ordering of the Lord's Supper it is, therefore, completely out of place, and a serious symbolical qualification in principle of the gospel of salvation by divine grace through faith only, to give significance to any preliminary offering to God of the bread and wine as the fruits and symbols of man's handiwork. Such action suggests that we are contributing to our own salvation. It reminds one of Cain's unacceptable offering. It is unmistakably Pelagian and a denial of the prior necessity of atoning sacrifice. For it suggests that salvation may be procured at the natural level by the addition to our efforts and gifts of what is brought into human life by the incarnation. Also, such action fails to recognize that in this sacrament the bread broken and the wine poured out speak of humanity under judgment because of sin. It is only beyond this necessary propitiation and through participation in its benefits that we can, by becoming partakers of Christ's resurrection, offer to God not a bloody atoning sacrifice but the glad devotion of our lives. Therefore, if the offering to God of our handiwork, as well as of ourselves, is to be symbolized, it should be done not with the bread and wine at all but by transferring the offertory to the post-communion part of the service and letting it include gifts in kind.

Yet the 1958 Lambeth Conference in its relevant Committee Report suggests as a desirable change: 'The Offertory, with which the people should be definitely associated, to be more closely connected with the Prayer of Consecration.'[88] One idea which is sometimes used to support this improper practice is a wrong deduction concerning our Lord's miraculous feeding of the multitude. The loaves which He used were not first deliberately offered to Jesus by the lad, as many suggest. Rather, when the utter inadequacy of the only available supplies had been fully recognized, our Lord surprised everybody by Himself taking the five barley loaves. This corresponds theologically to His assumption of our humanity. In order to work out man's redemption He condescended

---

[88] *The Lambeth Conference, 1958,* part 2, p. 81.

to take flesh and blood, and to let it be 'broken' and thus 'given for the life of the world'. But it would have been completely out of place for fallen and sinful man to think of offering his humanity to God to use to work redemption. On this issue the wording of the 1662 Prayer of Consecration is theologically sounder than the suggestion of the 1958 Lambeth bishops. For in it we speak to God of the bread and wine which we are to receive not as 'these our gifts', but as 'these thy creatures'. True participants in this sacrament of our redemption by Christ's death must come empty-handed to receive what God alone has provided.

Immediately following such reception is obviously the right point at which it is appropriate for us to give to God in responsive thanksgiving and thank-offering. So communion is rightly followed by self-oblation, the offering of ourselves, our souls and bodies, as a reasonable, holy and living sacrifice unto God. But such offering is ours not Christ's. We do not offer with Him; still less do we, or can we, offer His sacrifice. But through Him and following His example we offer ourselves. It is not we who here join Him in praying that His offering may be accepted by God. Rather it is His offering, once made and accepted for us, which makes ours acceptable. Indeed, we depend upon Him as our great High Priest to offer up us and our sacrifices – to 'bring us to God' (1 Pet. 3:18).

At this point of conscious and deliberate self-oblation it is appropriate for us to find in Christ's obedience unto death, His utter self-devotion to God's will, an example for us to follow. But according to the suggestion of the Lord Himself, we can express this readiness utterly to devote ourselves to God and particularly to share Christ's earthly suffering and reproach, not by offering the bread and wine as our oblation but by drinking His cup (see Mark 10:38-39). Also, however much we desire and determine thus to follow His steps, we cannot presume to associate our sacrifice with the one perfect sacrifice which availed to make atonement. On this point, Professor C.F.D. Moule (as previously quoted) has significantly declared: 'Each Christian act of obedience is indeed Christ's obedience in us; but not therefore identifiable with His own one-hundred-per-cent obedience in His own person.'[89]

The scriptural and evangelical principles already emphasized demand further that in the ordering of the sacrament not only should no offering Godwards be made by us with the consecrated elements, but also the prayer expressing our self-oblation should follow and not precede our reception of the bread and wine. Clear recognition of such

---

[89] Moule, *Sacrifice of Christ*, p. 40.

truth was well expressed in the Report entitled *The Fulness of Christ*. To quote:

> Both word and sacraments are primarily the means of God's gracious approach towards sinful men, and only on the basis of God's grace thus received can men make their response. (The Church of England's Order of Holy Communion admirably illustrates this Reformation principle by placing the Prayer of Oblation after the Communion of the people.) The Eucharist is the divinely instituted remembrance of Christ's sacrifice, and in it God gives and the Church receives the fruits of that sacrifice, the Body and Blood of Christ. In virtue of this, and only so, the Church is enabled to make that offering of praise, thanksgiving, and self-oblation which (apart from the alms) is the only sacrifice actually offered in the Eucharist. Only as united to Christ in His death and resurrection through receiving the Body and Blood of Christ is the Church able to offer itself acceptably to the Father.[90]

In an able article on this subject, which was published in *The Church Times* of 20 November 1959, John R.W. Stott wrote:

> Perhaps I do not understand the reasons why the Prayer of Oblation was placed after the Prayer of Consecration in the Interim Rite, or why this point has become the bone of contention in this debate. But it is on theological grounds that I would resist this transposition. It places the element of sacrifice in the wrong place. Our Anglican Reformers were clear that the Lord's Supper is primarily a sacrament not a sacrifice, and its movement primarily manward not Godward. To make the principal movement of the second gospel sacrament Godward is similar to the erroneous Baptist view of the first gospel sacrament. The Prayer Book view of both sacraments is that the congregation's chief function is not to offer anything to God (whether it be faith in the case of Baptism or worship in the case of Holy Communion) but to receive something from Him. Is it not the theology of grace which above all is being neglected in this proud self-confident age? We have nothing to offer to God on our own initiative. 'Nothing in my hand I bring; Simply to Thy cross I cling.' So we remember His 'one oblation of Himself once offered', and thankfully embrace its benefits by faith, feeding on Him in our hearts. But the offering of ourselves, our souls and bodies, our praise and thanksgiving is in response to His offering, rather than in association with it.

---

[90] *The Fulness of Christ: The Church's Growth into Catholicity* (London, 1950), p. 32.

Similarly, Professor C.F.D. Moule has declared himself on this point. To quote: 'For my own part, I feel, at present, the great importance of stressing the once-for-all uniqueness of Christ's sacrifice and the utterly dependent and derived character of ours. I am therefore inclined still to welcome the 1662 position of the Prayer of Oblation.'[91]

It is also of great importance to recognize that this responsive oblation or eucharistic sacrifice is rightly made not by the minister alone engaging in ritual acts with the consecrated elements, but by all the worshippers functioning together as the priesthood of the laity. In this connection there is value in the Prayer of Oblation like the General Thanksgiving being said by all together. It is wrong practice in this matter that has, in the course of church history, fostered two serious prevalent misunderstandings concerning priesthood in the Christian church. Discerning comment about this was made by the late Professor T.W. Manson, in one of his last contributions to scholarly understanding. Referring to developments in the church in the early centuries he wrote:

> We can already see two tendencies beginning to appear. In one case all believers are priests and what they offer in sacrifice is themselves: in the other the sacrifice is the Eucharist; and, in so far as the celebration of the Eucharist is or becomes the function of a particular person or group of persons in the local Church, the celebrant or celebrants will be the priest or priests of the community.[92]

So, he added, 'Along with the idea of the Eucharist as a sacrifice goes the idea that the minister of the Eucharist is the priest.' Later he pertinently commented:

> The fact is that there is here a parting of the ways: priesthood is on the way to be completely bound up with the right of a specialized group within the Church to offer the eucharistic sacrifice of bread and cup identified with the body and blood of Christ. The priesthood of all believers, on the other hand, is on the way to become a godly sentiment with little or no relevance to the day-to-day practice of the Church at worship.[93]

This means, therefore, that right ordering of the Lord's Supper in this matter of the proper offering of sacrifice by Christians is the way to undermine wrong ideas which are widespread in the church of a select sacrificing priesthood who offer the eucharist or the Mass. It is also

---

[91] Moule, *Sacrifice of Christ*, p. 57.
[92] T.W. Manson, *Ministry and Priesthood: Christ's and Ours* (London, 1958), p. 66.
[93] Ibid., p. 68.

the way to promote not only a renewed appreciation, but also a regular active corporate expression, of the priesthood of the laity.

Finally, it is of direct practical relevance to this theme that the New Testament indicates no ritual or ceremony to be used by Christians to express liturgically their self-oblation. There are ritual and symbol to remind us of Christ's one sacrifice long ago finished, and to help our appreciation and appropriation of its present benefits. But the responsive giving to God for His service both of ourselves and of our substance is something to be done not symbolically but substantially. It would be good to transfer to this point after the Communion, at which the Prayer of Oblation is said, the offertory; and to accompany our self-oblation with the giving of alms and of gifts in money or in kind for the worship, witness and work of the church of Christ in the world. The danger of some tendencies, described by some as 'the Liturgical movement', is lest the offering to God of a weekly or even daily liturgy take the place of, or at least take priority over, the offering to God of the obedience of our daily lives. Yet the latter is the true and the best eucharistic sacrifice.

Realizing Christ's Presence

In their day the Reformers sought to gainsay and to eradicate from Christian worship, two radical errors of doctrine and practice concerning the Lord's Supper. The first of these was the supposed objective presence of Christ's actual Body and Blood in or under the consecrated elements, together with the consequent desire to direct worship toward them. The second was the offering of these consecrated elements by the priest as a sacrifice to God upon the altar.

In principle these two errors are still very much with us; and have become more widely believed and practised within the Church of England during the last one hundred years than was the case for three hundred years after the Reformation. Their reappearance has been the direct result of the Tractarian movement. Indeed, these two ideas have been publicly reaffirmed by Dr A.M. Ramsey, when Archbishop of York, as the twin doctrines of the Tractarian movement which, he said, had been responsible for 'the revived Eucharistic faith' of the Church of England.

Before we seek to indicate the unscriptural character of these ideas by expounding positively over against them what the New Testament teaches, let us restate, in relation to the situation in which we now find ourselves, what these wrong ideas are. The first idea is the supposition of an objective 'change' in the elements consequent upon the utterance of the words of institution used in the Prayer of Consecration, and prior to and wholly independent of any subsequent or necessary administration to the congregation of worshippers in whose presence this happens. Such a 'change' in the elements makes it possible, and indeed proper, for worship to be directed towards them as the place where Christ is now specially present. Such a 'change' in them also makes it desirable for them to be reserved to perpetuate such a real 'presence' of Christ in the sanctuary. So, for instance, W. Norman Pittenger has written: 'The direction of devotion either privately or in regulated worship, to the person of Christ, present in his risen humanity through these instruments, is right and proper.'[94]

The second idea is, as we have already adequately recognized, the suggestion of an intended offering Godwards of the consecrated elements as the primary movement and purpose of the sacrament, to be done before administration to the congregation. And indeed, so significant in itself is this offering, that to be present when it is done with appropriate intention, yet without communicating, is a proper form of participation in Christian worship.

The best way to answer such unscriptural ideas is to grasp, and to concentrate on expressing positively both in teaching and practice, the simple scriptural truth which will either prevent their intrusion or undermine their influence. Such truth is in essence adequately stated by saying that, as first instituted, the Lord's Supper was an administration manwards by the Lord Himself. This means that the sole and whole movement with the elements is manwards not Godwards; and the Lord is to be acknowledged as present by the Spirit, not in the elements but in the action done with them, as its originating Author; and in the words spoken about them, as Himself the explicit announcer of their sacramental significance. For it ceases to be possible to hold and to practise the prevalent wrong ideas about the Lord's Supper, as soon as one realizes that the sacrament is a dynamic movement not a static object; and that the ordained movement is explicitly and exclusively directed manwards and not Godwards. What is wrong, and what has given rise to much abuse and misuse of the so-called 'consecrated elements', is the improper separation of the utterance of the decisive words of institution from the administration of which, in their original context, they formed an integral and an inseparable part.

One may illustrate and enforce the relevant truth by reference to baptism. If the water which is to be used to baptize is previously consecrated this action is no part of the sacrament. Nor ought such

---

[94] Pittenger, *The Christian Sacrifice*, p. 159.

water to become a focus of worship as a sphere of the localized presence of the regenerating Spirit. Rather the sacrament of baptism involves a dynamic movement. It only exists as the water is administered; that is, as the appointed deed is done and the significant words said to accompany and to explain it. This means that the sacrament cannot be 'reserved'. Its essential character also makes undeniably plain that its movement is wholly manwards.

Similarly, in the other sacrament of the gospel, Christ's special presence, His promised and active movement towards us in grace, is not associated with static and lifeless material elements which are supposed to be 'changed' by consecration; but rather with the address to us of a movement of administration accompanied by significant words which indicate its sacramental meaning, and thus confront the recipients with the present opportunity to have dealings with the Lord and to appropriate by faith His proffered blessing. According to this principle, if the sacrament is administered in a sick room with 'reserved' elements brought from a local church, what actually makes the elements sacramental to such a recipient (as would similarly be true of the water in a private baptism) is the words of administration said in his hearing and not the words of 'consecration' previously uttered in church.

In expression of this governing principle P.T. Forsyth wrote:

> In so far as our action is symbolical, it is symbolical of Christ's Act, not of His essence. But it is symbolical in the ancient sense of the word symbol. It does not simply point to the thing signified, nor suggest it, but conveys it, has it within it, brings it with it, gives it, does something, is really sacramental. We do not enact a small 'mystery' or tableau of Christ's sacrifice; but Christ the Redeemer, in His Church's Act gives Himself and His saving Act to us anew (to us, not to God); and we gives ourselves anew to Him in responsive faith.[95]

> The exact point is that *such symbolism did not lie in the elements but in the action*, the entire action – word and deed. (To fail to realise this is the defect of the patristic, the Chalcedonian mind. It is the lame foot of Anglicanism – be it said with respect – and it endangers the whole evangelical element so deep within it.)[96]

Again, comparison with other sacramental actions may be helpful. For both in baptism and in the laying on of hands the special presence or

---

[95] P.T. Forsyth, *The Church and the Sacraments* (second edition, London, 1947), p. 233.
[96] Ibid., p. 234.

coming of Christ, and the special activity of the Spirit, are to be associated with the administration of the rite to the candidates. Similarly, in the Holy Communion service the whole interest of the participants should be not in the coming of Christ to material elements over against us, but in His coming to us in and through their administration. Such interest should rightly make us concerned with worthy reception and no longer occupied with doing reverence, even after reception, to the detached consecrated elements.

All this implies that once the sacramental movement has been begun by repetition of our Lord's own deeds and words of institution, it cannot rightly be interrupted in the middle or turned in some other direction. The significant words, as in baptism, are themselves words of administration. No one can properly use them without speaking them to intended recipients, and without completing the sacramental action in an administration manwards not in presentation Godwards. Nor is reservation of the sacrament either possible or necessary. The sick can be given Holy Communion quickly without reservation of consecrated elements, just as the dying may be baptized quickly without specially consecrated water. For what makes the elements sacramental, whether in baptism or in Holy Communion, is the words and action of the movement of administration. So if occasion demanded such brevity, it would be possible to give communion to the sick by beginning where the rubric in the 1662 Prayer Book instructs the minister to begin, 'if the consecrated bread or wine be all spent before all have communicated'.

Such a scriptural understanding of the true character and intended function of the sacrament can but make one painfully conscious that it is improper and seriously misleading to associate a special presence or coming of Christ with the static material elements, once the words of institution have been said over them. This wrong idea has been widely propagated in the Church of England in modern times. It expresses what many in the Anglican Communion now believe and in relation to which they wish to order their practice in worship. For instance, Archbishop Michael Ramsey has defined the Tractarian doctrine of the real presence as 'the teaching ... that after the consecration of the elements there are indeed present not carnally but spiritually, the Body and Blood of the Lord, and that he, present in the sacrament alike in his deity and his humanity, is rightly to be adored.' This doctrine, he said, links

the Blessed Sacrament with the Incarnation itself. The Bread from heaven is none other than the Word-made-Flesh. Before ever we receive the gift as the food of our souls, we are lifted out of ourselves in adoration of the mystery of the Incarnation, of which the gift is already the present, effectual sign.[97]

But such a use of the consecrated elements as a local focus towards which to direct adoration of the incarnate Christ, is a wholly improper use of the sacrament of the gospel; and, what is worse, it involves a grievous caricature of true incarnation. For a person makes his living presence and his active goodwill known in deeds and words. We read of the incarnate Son of God that He went about doing good, and that men wondered at His gracious words. Therefore, for Christ to be conceived of as virtually confined within the consecrated elements, unable to move or speak and needing to be carried, is worthy of the same ridicule as the Old Testament prophets directed against idols.

It is wrong to think of either the bread or the wine when it is consecrated as if it were the Lord Himself, or the sphere of His special incarnate or human presence. For the bread and the wine are made to represent Christ's body and blood, not as they are now in His glorified humanity but as they were in death 'in the days of his flesh'. According to Christ's own institution of the sacrament they ought to be significantly kept apart, and received separately, that they may thus forcibly speak to us of His earthly flesh and blood divided in death. Bishop H.C.G. Moule wisely wrote:

> The sacramental 'Body and Blood of Christ' are not a sort of equivalent expression for the Lord Jesus Himself. They cannot be the equivalent; they are not enough to be so. 'Christ Himself' includes not only the Body and Blood, but the Human Soul and Spirit as He is Son of Man, and the Godhead as He is Son of God. The Roman Church boldly says that the Elements in the Eucharist do contain this 'whole Christ'; Body, Blood, Soul, Godhead. But this is indeed to be wise above what is written, wise above what He spoke. All He said was, 'This is my Body which is given', 'This is my Blood which is shed'.[98]

Our actual participation of Christ is after a heavenly and spiritual manner; not directly through the elements and by the mouth, but through God's word and Spirit, in the heart and by faith. In the days of His flesh when, for instance, He instituted the sacrament in the upper room, Christ Himself was physically present in flesh and blood. But in the administration of the Lord's Supper now there is no 'presence' of the actual localized humanity kind granted to believers. Rather is

---

[97] Ramsey, 'He Took', p. 17.
[98] Moule, *Pledges of His Love*, pp. 50-51.

it through faith and by the Spirit that we realize His presence as God, the Son of God, and appropriate benefits which He can make ours only through and because of His incarnation and His earthly human death and resurrection. So faith counts its values in terms of Jesus sinless, crucified, risen, glorified. The believer eats His flesh and drinks His blood. But the actual experience of benefit which we enjoy, including fellowship with the Father and the Son, is made ours by the Spirit and not by any objective presence of the glorified human nature of the God-Man Christ. 'It is the spirit that quickeneth; the flesh profiteth nothing' (John 6:63).

Indeed, instead of imagining that Christ is physically present in the lifeless material elements, it is important that faith should recognize Him as the Initiator of the movement of the sacrament as a whole; as the Lord who, so to speak, spreads the table and presides at it and gives to us as His guests. For instance, what startled the two disciples at Emmaus and awakened them to the identity of their visitor, was the fact that when they thought He was a guest at their table He treated them as guests at His table. For 'he took bread, and blessed it, and brake, and gave to them. And their eyes were opened, and they knew him.' He was thus 'known of them', His identity was recognized and His presence realized, not in the bread but in 'the breaking of the bread' (Luke 24:30-31, 35, compare John 21:12-14). So their eating and drinking became to them the occasion of realized fellowship with the risen Lord.

Such realization of present fellowship with the living Saviour was sealed on several of Christ's resurrection appearances by their eating and drinking with Him. These experiences were the promised complement of what happened before His death at the Last Supper. For after the familiar deeds and words of institution, Jesus had added: 'I will not drink henceforth of this fruit of the vine, until that day when I drink it new with you in my father's kingdom' (Matt. 26:29). So the repeated meal in the presence of the risen Lord, with Him sharing with them in eating and drinking, became the occasion of rejoicing in triumph gained, in His presence restored and in God's kingdom established. Similarly, as we now eat and drink at His table, we can and should not only consciously appropriate the benefits of His passion, but also rejoice in realized fellowship by the Spirit with the risen, living and reigning Lord. It is as our Melchizedek, 'the priest of God Most High', that He brings forth for us 'bread and wine' (see Gen. 14:18 RSV).

The experience of Christ's realized presence which the sacrament thus makes possible becomes ours, not through contemplation of the static elements but by our active personal response to a dynamic movement addressed to us. We may find an illustration, admittedly inadequate and unworthy, but able to suggest a relevant idea, in the possibility of a telephone conversation with a friend far away. When the friend rings us up and we find ourselves in living contact, we can for a few minutes enjoy his virtual presence. We can converse with him as if he were here or we were there. But this experience can be enjoyed only in active intercourse, as he speaks to us and we speak to him. The opportunity would be wasted if we gazed in silent wonder at the telephone receiver or did reverence before such a marvellous instrument of human intercourse. Rather must the opportunity be used in the proper way by personal reception and response, if the offered 'presence' and fellowship are to be fully experienced and enjoyed.

In ways like this, but far more wonderfully and with no make-believe, when I attend an administration of the Lord's Supper, and see and hear the sacramental movement begun, and realize that it is personally and imperatively addressed to me and to all there present with me, and that it demands corresponding reception and response; then it is right to believe that in this movement Christ Himself is present and active and offering afresh to give to me, through His death for me, His indwelling presence by the Spirit and the outworked experience of all the benefits of His passion. In such a moment of privilege and opportunity, if I am to enjoy Him and experience His blessing, I must answer His approach, first by reception and then by responsive self-oblation. To speak of answering a telephone call is indeed an illustration utterly inadequate and unworthy. For this movement is like the approach of the bridegroom to the bride. Its proper consummation is like the giving and the receiving of the ring in marriage. Indeed, it is like the crowning intercourse of love itself. So first, I give Him answer by receiving Him; and then I give Him myself because I have first received Him. So do I go on my way knowing afresh that He is mine and that I am His, and conscious that He abides in me and I in Him.

Scriptural Administration

In our actual use of the sacrament of the Lord's Supper in our churches, what is of chief importance is that the ordering of the service should be fully biblical and truly evangelical. What we do on such an occasion ought to be determined in detail by the scriptural witness – without improper omission, perversion or addition. We should seek to preserve scriptural fulness and simplicity. Also, what we do ought worthily to express the gospel of salvation by God's grace through Christ and His death; and our participation in its benefits apart from works or sacrifices on our part, through faith alone.

Taking these standards as our criteria, let us now seek first to appreciate the outstanding merit of the form of service that as Anglicans we have inherited in the Book of Common Prayer in order that, entering more consciously into its full significance and intention, we may use it more worthily and completely. Then let us seek, in the second place, to discern and to be willing to desire ways of possible improvement – details in connection with which practice and use could and ought to be made, first, more fully biblical, and consequently more truly evangelical.

In contrast to the Roman Mass and indeed, as we have seen, in contrast also to the content and order of the 1549 Prayer Book service, the form which Archbishop Cranmer produced in 1552 and which still obtains in the 1662 Prayer Book, which is the one in current authorized use, is one which is in character deliberately and explicitly true to the Bible and the gospel in certain significant ways. This has been fully admitted by all reasonable scholars, no matter what their own personal conviction and preference. For instance, in *The Shape of the Liturgy* Gregory Dix wrote:

> Compared with the clumsy and formless rites which were evolved abroad, that of 1552 is the masterpiece of an artist. Cranmer gave it a noble form as a superb piece of literature which no one could say of its companions: but he did more. As a piece of liturgical craftsmanship it is in the first rank, once its intention is understood. It is not a disordered attempt at a catholic rite, but the only effective attempt ever made to give liturgical expression to the doctrine of 'justification by faith alone'.[99]

Similarly the Committee Report of the Church of India, Pakistan, Burma and Ceylon on *Principles of Prayer Book Revision* declares:

> Cranmer's rearrangement in 1552 of the elements of the 1549 Canon is frequently described as a dislocation; this is an incorrect designation, since the new arrangement follows a logical order. It reveals a clear intention of adjusting the structure of the liturgy to the conception of the Lord's Supper which finds expression in the exhortation addressed to communicants in the order of Communion of 1548, in which the memorial aspect alone is mentioned. The act of Communion follows immediately upon the concluding command of the Institution Narrative 'Do this in remembrance of me', and the

---

[99] Gregory Dix, *The Shape of the Liturgy* (London, 1945), p. 672.

new Words of Administration, from which all reference to the Body and Blood is omitted, identify obedience to this command with the reception of the Sacrament.

The medieval climax of the Adoration of the Elevated Host was thus effectively replaced by making the act of Communion the devotional climax of the rite.

The identification of the making of remembrance with the act of Communion necessarily involved the abandonment of any oblation of the holy gifts 'as the memorial which Thy Son hath willed us to make'; and the combination of the remaining paragraphs of the 1549 Canon, in which offering is made of the sacrifice of praise and thanksgiving and 'of ourselves our souls and bodies', in a prayer for use after Communion was further designed to eliminate any possibility of interpreting the sacrifice in the Eucharist as propitiatory. The transposition of the prayer to its now familiar place implied that even the Church's self-offering in thanksgiving and entire devotion was only appropriate after it had been united in Holy Communion with its Lord. At the same time the 1549 Thanksgiving was left as an alternative to the Prayer of Oblation, so that, at the discretion of the celebrant, all reference to sacrifice could be omitted.[100]

Bishop Stephen Neill has also expressed his understanding of the deliberate intention of Archbishop Cranmer in his construction of the 1552 form of service. He says:

Cranmer saw that Christ's words of institution ... (words of distribution some have called them) were immediately followed by reception on the part of the disciples. This was the pattern he now determined to follow. Consecration and communion were to become a single act, separated in time by a brief moment, but not separable in thought or understanding.

Bishop Neill then adds this discerning and decisive comment: 'The moment this principle is grasped an immense number of difficulties in Eucharistic theology simply vanish.'[101] For instance, let us add at once that simple loyalty to this principle makes both reservation and Godward offering of the consecrated elements alike impossible. Whereas on the other hand, so Gustaf Aulén forcibly protests, 'This significance of the Lord's Supper as communion becomes imperilled, when Christ's own sacrifice in reality is set aside in favour of an emphasis on an offering of Christ which the church is supposed to make.'[102]

---

[100] *Principles of Prayer Book Revision*, pp. 34f.

[101] Stephen Neill, *Anglicanism* (London, 1958), p. 73.

[102] Aulén, *Eucharist and Sacrifice*, p. 202.

Since, however, no production of finite man is perfect, and since there's always room for improvement and also ever recurring need for fresh reformation according to the word of God, let us seek now to discern ways in which what we have inherited needs to be changed for the better; either because the way in which we have come to use it is unworthy, or because it is in itself deficient, or may even tend at certain points to hinder if not to harm rather than to help, the full spiritual experience by God's people of the blessings this sacrament was instituted to aid us to enjoy.

In introduction of such considerations, which may be unwelcome to some, let us quote some very apt and apposite words of Professor J.E.L. Oulton. He wrote:

> No doubt it is disconcerting for those who have been brought up in a certain liturgical tradition to be asked to consider afresh whether they must modify opinions perhaps unconsciously entertained through the use of a rite which does not adequately express some points of importance that may be deduced from the Gospel accounts of the Last Supper. Readiness to do so will largely depend on whether or no they accept the position, which the writer of these pages accepts, that the members of the Church must always be prepared to correct their views in accordance with such fresh light as a further study of the Holy Scriptures may reveal.[103]

'For example', continued Professor Oulton,

> a recent work on liturgiology speaks of 'those modern theorists who are fond of repeating that the so-called words of institution at the Last Supper are really words of administration'. On this, more than one observation may be made. To many – to all, we should hope – Christians the Gospel accounts of the Last Supper are ancient records of a peculiarly sacred character. It is not clear, therefore, why those whose aim it is to go back to these ancient records should be described as 'modern'. Again, in spite of many differences in the various accounts of the Supper, the order of actions of the Lord at its most solemn moment – namely, the institution of the Sacrament – stands out plainly. Therefore, it is again not clear why those who point out a simple fact – that it was when distributing or administering the bread and the cup that the Lord spoke certain words – should be styled 'theorists'.[104]

---

[103] Oulton, *Holy Communion and Holy Spirit*, pp. 191-192.
[104] Ibid., p. 192, quoting Dix, *Shape of the Liturgy*, p. 137.

Professor Oulton followed this up by explicitly indicating the point in Anglican usage at which he felt reform to be particularly necessary. To quote:

> When a prayer of consecration ... leads the congregation to suppose that the elements are consecrated apart from their use as the means of conveying a spiritual gift to the communicants, something much more is at stake than a liturgical tradition, however valuable or even sacred that may be.[105]

He further supported this protest by indicating in a footnote that J. Armitage Robinson said of the Western tradition that 'it fails to do justice to the conditioning command which limits the effectual character of the Sacrament to its prescribed use as food and drink.'[106] In what ways, then, let us ask, may desirable improvement be achieved? What changes would make our inherited familiar Church of England order of service more scriptural? We venture to suggest three.

The first has been already indicated in the earlier section on 'True Eucharist'; so we need only summarize here. Cranmer's form of service is deficient in thanksgiving. Blessing God the Giver is the proper way to consecrate material things for men's use. So new extended thanksgivings are desirable, first for the bread and later for the wine, similar to those regularly offered in some Free Church forms of service. Also, these thanksgivings should be regarded as the consecration of the bread and of the wine for their use; without any introduction at this point of the decisive words which indicate their sacramental significance.

In the second place, our Lord's declaratory words, 'This is my body given for you', 'This is my blood shed for many', should be removed from the introductory consecration and in accordance with the pattern of our Lord's institution, made an essential and simultaneous part of the actual administration. For what makes the elements used sacramental, whether in baptism or Holy Communion, are the words and action together of the movement of administration. To keep them separate stands condemned as a wrong putting asunder by man of what the Lord Himself joined together. The truth or principle which we here need to appreciate is that the sacrament exists only when and while the administration is taking place. It cannot, therefore, be reserved or half-done beforehand to the elements for administration to recipients later.

---

[105] Ibid., pp. 192-193.

[106] J. Armitage Robinson, *Giving and Receiving: Six Plain Sermons on the Holy Eucharist* (London, 1928), p. 82.

In the third place, in order fully to follow the pattern of our Lord's institution, and to preserve the vivid witness to His death which we thus dramatically remember, the bread and the wine ought deliberately to be kept apart and administered separately, first the bread to all and later the cup to all. This again is a use already common in many non-Anglican congregations; and so by becoming ourselves more scriptural in practice we should make fellowship with others at the Lord's table more easy to realize.

Such proper scriptural practice of administering the separated elements singly makes the association of the localized presence of the glorified humanity of Christ in or under either of them unthinkable. For the present living Lord cannot be thus divided. 'This bread' and 'this cup' speak of His death. Also, such awareness of the true character and meaning of the sacrament which our Lord ordained makes intinction (or the administration of both kinds together by the dipping of the bread into the wine first) theologically undesirable; and it makes administration in one kind only completely improper. Yet in February 1960 two thousand priests of the Church of England, who desire to practise 'the Reservation of the Blessed Sacrament', endorsed the following declaration: 'Although the chalice is not to be denied to the people in the public celebration, Christ is received whole and entire in either kind. It therefore suffices that (according to the ancient usage of the Church) consecrated bread alone be reserved and administered.' Such ideas and practices are neither biblical nor evangelical. To those who desire them the very presence in the sacrament of two separate elements is at times an embarrassment. One positive way in which to protest against them and to prevent them is to insist, on explicit grounds, that administration of both elements and administration separately are essential to a proper Christian celebration of the Lord's Supper.

There are other matters of great practical importance concerning the administration of this sacrament, in which there are room and urgent need for a fuller obedience to the teaching and the principles of God's written word. Let us indicate some of them.

First, since some one person present in any congregation must take the lead in administering the Lord's Supper, the question still needs to be faced – By whom may the Holy Communion be administered? The proper Christian answer is surely, in principle, by any member whom the body of believers may entrust with this ministry. There is no doctrinal necessity with Holy Communion, any more than there is with baptism, that one class of special ministers alone may administer it. Also, while it is, on the one hand, important that as a corporate activity of the local church its administration should be carefully ordered and entrusted only to responsible elders, yet there is, on the other hand, great practical need for an increase in the number of those who are thus allowed to do it. Why for the lack of a bishop or presbyter should congregations be deprived of the Lord's Supper, when they have in their midst mature and godly members who could if given the opportunity worthily fulfil the necessary ministry? Why should such Christians be allowed as lay readers to lead public worship and to preach the word in the congregation, but not to administer the Lord's Supper? Would it not increase in any congregation the awareness of equality and brotherhood and common unworthiness if different senior members, duly authorized or ordained as elders, administered the sacrament in turn? Also, it is time that by practice as well as by words we found ways to confess our conviction that there is in the New Testament no indication that proper administration can be performed only by someone who has been admitted to a special sacerdotal order of ministry.

Secondly, if Christian brethren who belong to the various denominational churches are to enjoy, as they ought, fellowship together in Christ at His table, we need a more Christian and a more constructive approach to the practice of intercommunion. The Lord's people ought to be welcome at the Lord's table in every congregation where the sacrament is administered. Qualification to partake ought to be determined not by one's attachment to a particular denomination, but directly by one's personal relation to Christ our Lord; that is, by evidence of personal baptism into Christ and by the present readiness personally to renew the baptismal confession of Christ in active repentance, faith and obedience.

Thirdly, the manner of the actual administration of the sacrament is obviously important. It does matter profoundly how we do it and to what spiritual values we give priority. For instance, it ought not to be detached from full ministry of God's word (see, for example, Acts 20:7, 11). So in the context of the one service, as a rubric of the 1662 Prayer Book enjoins, a sermon should be preached. Observance of this practice is particularly relevant to the occasions when large numbers attend Communion, as on Easter Day. They surely ought to hear the word preached before the sacrament is administered.

Fourthly, we ought not to suggest in our churches by a so-called sanctuary at the east end, and by an absurd distance between the holy table and the prospective communicants, that this sacrament is essentially the exclusive preserve of a special ministry. The Anglican Prayer Book is explicitly concerned by its plainly worded rubrics to make the Lord's Supper a corporate act in which a number share. Also, the rubrics enjoin not that there should be an awkward going up to a distant table in order to communicate, but that the table should at the Communion time be brought into the midst of the people 'in the body of the church', and that before the Communion proper is begun (that is, after the Prayer for the Church Militant) the congregation should already be conveniently placed for the reception of the sacrament, without further movement on their part. Such practice, if properly observed, would make every worshipper aware that he is directly at or around the Lord's table throughout the whole service.

With the holy table during the service still at the far end of the church, the north side position of the minister looks, to many, one-sided, particularly when the paten and the cup have to be removed to one end for the Prayer of Consecration. It is desirable that we should remember that the north side position was originally prescribed for a table brought into the midst of the congregation, with the worshippers all round it, and with no priority given to the east end or the so-called sanctuary. For the Lord's true sanctuary is His people. He has promised His presence in our midst, and this in relation to people not to detached material elements. We ought, therefore, to make visible in the service our belief in Christ's personal drawing near to assure us afresh of His grace and salvation by doing what Archbishop Cranmer intended. 'Part of the trouble is', so writes Bishop Stephen Neill,

> that hardly anyone now living has ever seen the Communion celebrated as Cranmer intended it to be celebrated. He had utterly repudiated the idea that the Communion is a form of individual and personal devotion, it is something that is done by priest and people together, according to the commandment of their crucified and risen Lord, and in the assurance of His presence with them. To this end he had ordered that the Communion table was to be brought into the body of the church. Churches in those days were not cluttered up with pews; clearly it was Cranmer's idea that the faithful would come and stand around the Table. This alone explains the otherwise mysterious complaint of the Cornish rebels that the Communion had been turned into 'a Christmas game'. There was indeed a startling contrast between Mass, in which the priest at the far end of the chancel recited almost inaudibly unintelligible words, and this new form, in which every word could be heard, every gesture seen, and in which the worshipper felt that he himself was an actor.[107]

---

[107] Neill, *Anglicanism*, p. 74.

Helped by Archbishop Laud, and by the keeping of the Communion table always at the east end of the church, the Tractarian movement and its followers have in modern times made their mark upon much current Anglican usage by forcing upon our churches, contrary to the rubrics of the Prayer Book, positions and practices in the celebration of this sacrament which visibly express their unscriptural doctrines. In answer to this it is high time that all true biblical Anglicans, acting together, did something distinctive to express our evangelical convictions; and that we stopped making excuses about the layout of our churches not permitting us to bring the table into the midst of the congregation. Where there is a will, there is a way. Before, therefore, we lose our biblical and evangelical heritage, or see it revised beyond recognition and acceptability, it is time we ourselves rediscovered in practice the true use and full value of our order for the administration of the Lord's Supper, by doing it as Cranmer and the 1662 Prayer Book intended it to be done. 1962 is an anniversary year in which this might well be decisively begun, not by a few 'odd' congregations, but by the common consent and simultaneous corporate action of a large number. It would be good to have a special '1662 Prayer Book Sunday' and to administer the Holy Communion accordingly. It is surely not disobedience or revolt to do what the existing rubrics order.

Such words as these obviously are primarily an appeal by an Anglican to his fellow Anglicans of similar biblical and evangelical conviction, first to seek more fully to value and use our rich Prayer Book heritage, and second, to aim together in a properly ordered way to move closer to the scriptural pattern in our administration of the Lord's Supper; and consequently to move at the same time closer to other Reformed churches and to many non-Anglican Christian brethren both in practice and in fully realized fellowship at the Lord's table; where together we may with fresh reason render 'true eucharist' and offer 'this our sacrifice' to the one Lord who died to save us all. May God so grant, according to His will.

SELECT BIBLIOGRAPHY OF THE WRITINGS OF ALAN STIBBS

1934-37
[co-compiler], *Search the Scriptures: The IVF Bible Study Course* (London: Inter-Varsity Fellowship, 1934-37; second edition 1947), edited by G.T. Manley

1938
'Evil and the Will of God', *Inter-Varsity Magazine* 10.3 (Easter Term 1938)

1939
[co-compiler], *United Bible Study: A Course of Nine Studies for Bible Study Circles* (London: Inter-Varsity Fellowship, 1939), edited by H.E. Guillebaud

1940
Propaganda: False and True (London: Inter-Varsity Fellowship, 1940)
'The Bible as Revelation: The Spiritual Issue', *Churchman* 54.4 (October – December 1940)

1941
'The Sermon on the Mount', *Inter-Varsity Magazine* 14.1 (Michaelmas Term 1941)

1942
'What Do We Mean by Original Sin?', *Inter-Varsity Magazine* 15.1 (Michaelmas Term 1942)

1945

'Shadow or Substance? The Real Choice Before the Church', *Churchman* 59.1 (January – March 1945)

'Confirmation in Relation to Holy Baptism', *Churchman* 59.2 (April – June 1945)

'The Authority of Scripture', *Inter-Varsity Magazine* (Summer Term 1945)

'Christ Crucified and Risen', *Inter-Varsity Magazine* (Michaelmas Term 1945)

1946

'Bible Study' in *In Training: A Guide to the Preparation of the Missionary*, (London: Inter-Varsity Fellowship, 1946), edited by A.T. Houghton.

1947

The Meaning of the Word 'Blood' in Scripture (London: Tyndale Press, 1947; second edition 1954)

'The Place of Theology', *Churchman* 61.1 (March 1947)

'Gideon's Prayers', *Oak Leaf* no.2 (Spring Term 1947)

[assistant editor], *The New Bible Handbook* (London: Inter-Varsity Fellowship, 1947), edited by G.T. Manley

1948

The Church, Universal and Local: Being Mainly a Survey of Bible Teaching, with Some Application to the Present Day (London: Church Book Room Press, 1948)

The Apostolic Pattern: Missionary Principles of the New Testament (London: Bible Churchmen's Missionary Society, 1948), Silver Jubilee Booklets no.12

'The Priesthood of the Laity' in *Evangelicals Affirm* (London: Church Book Room Press, 1948)

'The Place of Sacraments', *Churchman* 62.1 (March 1948)

'Taking the Church Seriously', *Christian Graduate* 1.3 (September 1948)

1949

'The Christian Education of Children: What Scripture Says', *Christian Graduate* 2.2 (June 1949)

'The Ministry of the Word', *Oak Leaf* no.9 (Summer Term 1949)

'The Revival of Biblical Theology', *Christian Graduate* 2.3 (September 1949)

1950

Understanding God's Word (London: Inter-Varsity Fellowship, 1950; second edition, revised by David and Clare Wenham, 1976)

'New Testament Teaching Concerning the Church', *Inter-Varsity Magazine* (Summer Term 1950)

'The Christian and the World: A Survey of Scriptural Teaching', *Christian Graduate* 3.3 (September 1950)

1951

'The Millennium', *Christian Graduate* 4.1 (March 1951)

1952

'Biblical Revelation', *Christian Graduate* 5.2 (June 1952)

'The Infallibility of the Word of God', *Inter-Varsity* (Summer Term 1952)

'Justification by Faith: The Reinstatement of the Doctrine Today', *Evangelical Quarterly* 24 (July 1952); republished in 1958 by the Fellowship of Evangelical Churchmen, and again in David Peterson (ed.), *Where Wrath and Mercy Meet: Proclaiming the Atonement Today* (Carlisle: Paternoster, 2001)

'Expository Preaching', *Christian Graduate* 5.3 (September 1952)

'Expository Preaching', *Oak Leaf* no.16 (1952)

1953

[assistant editor], *The New Bible Commentary*, edited by Francis Davidson (London: Inter-Varsity Fellowship, 1953; second edition 1954)

'Jesus Crowned and Enthroned', *Christian Graduate* 6.2 (June 1953)

'The Bible and the Pulpit', *Churchman* 67.4 (December 1953)

1954

The Finished Work of Christ (London: Tyndale Press, 1954)

'The Christian Use of Sunday', *Inter-Varsity* (Autumn Term 1954)

1955

Obeying God's Word (London: Inter-Varsity Fellowship, 1955), reprinted as *Obeying God's Word: The Call to True Discipleship* (Leicester: IVP, 1996)

'The New Standing', *Crusade* 1.2 (July 1955); reprinted as *The New Status* (London: Church Pastoral Aid Society, 1955), Fellowship Paper no.192

1956

'How Do You Interpret Hebrews vi. 4-6?', *Inter-Varsity* (Spring Term 1956)

'Miracles as Signs', *Christian Graduate* 9.1 (March 1956)

'Effective Witness', *Crusade* 2.9 (September 1956)

'Modern Christological Trends', *Tyndale House Bulletin* 1 (1956)

'Herbert William Hinde 1877-1955: An Appreciation', *Oak Leaf* no.20 (1956)

1957

God Became Man: Some Considerations of the Questions How? And Why? (London: Tyndale Press, 1957)

The Word of Faith Which We Preach (London: Westminster Chapel, 1957), Campbell Morgan Memorial Lecture no.9

'For Two or Three', *Christian Graduate* 10.3 (September 1957)

'Oak Hill College till 1945', *Oak Leaf* no.21 (1957)

1958

The Lord's Supper (London: Church Pastoral Aid Society, 1958), Fellowship Paper no.215

'The Witness of Scripture to its Inspiration', in Carl F.H. Henry (ed.), *Revelation and the Bible: Contemporary Evangelical Thought* (Grand Rapids: Baker, 1958; reprinted London: Tyndale Press, 1959)

'Meeting a Child's Spiritual Needs: What Scripture Says', *Christian Graduate* 11.4 (December 1958)

1959

God's Church: A Study in the Biblical Doctrine of the People of God (London: Inter-Varsity Fellowship, 1959; reprinted 1968)

The First Epistle General of Peter: A Commentary (London: Tyndale Press 1959; reprinted 1962, 1966, 1977 and 1983)

'Biblical Interpretation – Literal or Figurative?', *Inter-Varsity* (Summer Term 1959)

'The Nativity Narratives', *Crusade* 5.12 (December 1959)

[editor], *D.E. Hoste: The Insight of a Seer* (London: China Inland Mission, 1959)

1960

Expounding God's Word: Some Principles and Methods (London: Inter-Varsity Fellowship, 1960)

Christian Ministry (London: Church Pastoral Aid Society, 1960)

The Ministry of God's Word (London: Church Pastoral Aid Society, 1960)
Understanding the Sacraments (London: Church Pastoral Aid Society, 1960)
Baptism into Christ (London: Church Pastoral Aid Society, 1960)
The Lord's Supper (London: Church Pastoral Aid Society, 1960)

1961
Sacrament, Sacrifice and Eucharist: The Meaning, Function and Use of the Lord's Supper (London: Tyndale Press, 1961)
'With All Your Mind', *Christian Graduate* 14.3 (September 1961)

1962
The Epistles for the Sundays and Principal Holy Days of the Church's Year (London: Hodder & Stoughton, 1962)
'Is This Your Life?', *Inter-Varsity* (Summer Term 1962)
'"Half Christian" and "Post-Christian" Perils', *Christian Graduate* 15.3 (September 1962)
'Assurance', *Oak Leaf* no.26 (1962)

1963
Why I Value the North Side Position (London: Church Pastoral Aid Society, 1963), Fellowship Paper no.238 [with Alec Motyer and John Stott]
'Worldliness, Holy or Unholy', *Christian Graduate* 16.4 (December 1963)

1964
God's Friend: Studies in the Life of Abraham (London: Inter-Varsity Fellowship, 1964)

1965
The Gospel We Proclaim (London: Church Pastoral Aid Society, 1965)
'The Unity of All in Each Place' in J.I. Packer (ed.), *All in Each Place: Towards Reunion in England* (Abingdon: Marcham Manor Press, 1965)
'Great Texts Reconsidered', *Christian Graduate* 18.1 (March 1965)
'The Church of God: Invisible and Visible', *Churchman* 79.3 (September 1965)

1966
'In Defence of the Sermon or Why Preaching?', *Christian Graduate* 19.3 (September 1966)
'Putting the Gift of Tongues in Its Place', *Churchman* 80.4 (Winter 1966)

1967

The Spirit Within You: The Church's Neglected Possession (London: Hodder & Stoughton, 1967; reprinted 1972 and 1980), Christian Foundations Series no.18 [with J.I. Packer]

[as editor], *Search the Scriptures: A Systematic Bible Study Course* (completely revised, London: Inter-Varsity Press, 1967; sixth edition 2003)

1968

Christian Upbringing (London: Church Book Room Press, 1968) [with Raymond Johnston]

'Some Bible Teaching About Mission' in *Mission in the Modern World: The Islington Conference Papers 1968* (London: Patmos Press, 1968)

'Enjoying Life Together', *Inter-Varsity* (Summer Term 1968)

1970

So Great Salvation: The Meaning and Message of the Letter to the Hebrews (Exeter: Paternoster, 1970)

[as consulting editor], *The New Bible Commentary* (new edition, London: IVP, 1970), edited by Donald Guthrie and Alec Motyer

'Family Life: Biblical Principles', *Churchman* 84.3 (Autumn 1970)

'Family Life: In Britain Today', *Churchman* 84.4 (Winter 1970)

'Family Life: A Primary Sphere of Christian Establishment and Expansion', *Churchman* 84.4 (Winter 1970)

Family Life Today (Abingdon: Marcham Manor Press, 1970)

1973

God's Law for Man's Life: Studies in the Ten Commandments (London: Fellowship of Evangelical Churchmen, 1973)

Other Books of Interest
from
Christian Focus Publications

Evangelical Concerns:

*Rediscovering the Christian mind on issues
facing the Church today*

Melvin Tinker

We are sometimes left with the feeling that evangelicals stand in the shadows of a collapsing culture with nothing but two alternatives open to us: either to retreat into a ghetto or sell out on fundamental issues of truth. Here, Melvin Tinker suggests a 'Third Way' - to develop a fully orbed biblical approach to science and socio-political issues - and so to regain the Christian mind.

"The intelligence, breadth of learning, and readability offer important and timely lessons."

Paul Helm, Regent College, Vancouver

"Christians need to think deeply, and biblically about the issues facing society today. Melvin Tinker offers us a refreshing and insightful way into many such issues. You may not agree with all he says, but whoever reads the collection will be compelled to reflect more carefully and thoughtfully on how Christians should respond."

E. David Cook, Director, Whitefield Institute, Oxford,
also BBC Radio 4's "The Moral Maze"

If you lap up Francis Schaeffer, Os Guiness and David Wells, you will enjoy this – and find yourself agreeing with most of it.

Jonathan Stephen, Evangelicals Now

Melvin Tinker is Vicar of St John's Newland, Chairman of Yorkshire Gospel Partnership, Co-director of Northern Training Course and is a leading member of the Anglican group 'REFORM'. He is a popular author on culture and faith He is Married to Heather and they have 3 grown up sons.

ISBN 978-1-85792-675-0

CROSS WORDS:

The Biblical Doctrine of the Atonement

Paul Wells

The post-modern society is so focussed on the internal life of the individual that it makes the significance of the cross a difficult concept to grasp. Even Christians are trying to find alternative ways of explaining it - some have abandoned the concept of atonement entirely.

Jesus, though, is far more than a victim. When God receives and approves the condemned Jesus he transcends the world of oppressor and victim to create a new humanity, capable of new kinds of relationships. Atonement speaks of a transition from brokenness, alienation and the death of love to a place of restoration, healing, and wholeness. A place that holds out hope for deepening friendships and mutual confidence - the exact same things the post-modern mind is lacking, and is looking for.

'Paul Wells faces head-on the modern (and not-so-modern) challenges to a Biblical viewpoint on the atonement. He evaluates knowledgeably and fairly the most significant denials on such crucial issues as the wrath of God, penal substitution, imputation and propitiation.... It will be an important aid for those who wish to preach effectively the Gospel'

Douglas Kelly, , Reformed Theological Seminary,
Charlotte, North Carolina

'This is a satisfying book about the atonement, written by a man of God who lives in the biblical text, and yet is in close touch with the real world and today's church. Who can fail to profit from a book like this?'

Stuart Olyott, The Evangelical Movement of Wales

'Paul is emerging as one of the premier evangelical theologians of our day. Cross Words is at once accessible and erudite.'

William Edgar,
Westminster Theological Seminary, Philadelphia, Pennsylvania

Paul Wells is Professor of Systematic Theology at Facult' Libre Theologie Reformee in Aix-en-Provence, France. He has been editor of La Revue réformée, a leading evangelical journal in French, since 1981. He is married to Alison who teaches adult English. Together they are involved in church planting in Gardanne, a mining town between Aix and Marseilles, where there is no other Protestant church.

ISBN 978-1-84550-118-1

Christian Focus Publications
publishes books for all ages

Our mission statement –

STAYING FAITHFUL
In dependence upon God we seek to help make His infallible Word, the Bible, relevant. Our aim is to ensure that the Lord Jesus Christ is presented as the only hope to obtain forgiveness of sin, live a useful life and look forward to heaven with Him.

REACHING OUT
Christ's last command requires us to reach out to our world with His gospel. We seek to help fulfil that by publishing books that point people towards Jesus and help them develop a Christ-like maturity. We aim to equip all levels of readers for life, work, ministry and mission.

Books in our adult range are published in three imprints.

Christian Focus contains popular works including biographies, commentaries, basic doctrine and Christian living. Our children's books are also published in this imprint.

Mentor focuses on books written at a level suitable for Bible College and seminary students, pastors, and other serious readers. The imprint includes commentaries, doctrinal studies, examination of current issues and church history.

Christian Heritage contains classic writings from the past.

Christian Focus Publications Ltd
Geanies House, Fearn,
Ross-shire, IV20 1TW, Scotland, United Kingdom
info@christianfocus.com

Our titles are available from quality bookstores and
www.christianfocus.com